941 BAR

BARRO(
THE ANGL(
851640 0

GW01475144

CHESTER COLLEGE LIBRARY

Author ....

Title ....

Class No. .... Acc. No. ....

This book is to be returned on or before the last date stamped below

15 DEC 1986

12 JAN 1996
30 JAN 1996
CANCELLED

17 APR 1991

-8 JAN 1997

-8 JUN 1992

30 JAN 1992
CANCELLED

-2 MAY 1992

11 DEC 1992

THE ANGLO–NORMAN ERA
IN SCOTTISH HISTORY

THE
ANGLO-NORMAN ERA
IN SCOTTISH HISTORY

THE FORD LECTURES
DELIVERED IN THE UNIVERSITY OF
OXFORD
IN HILARY TERM 1977

BY

G. W. S. BARROW, F.B.A.,

*Sir William Fraser Professor of Scottish History
and Palaeography in the University of Edinburgh,
formerly Professor of Scottish History in
the University of St. Andrews*

CLARENDON PRESS · OXFORD
1980

Oxford University Press, Walton Street, Oxford OX2 6DP

OXFORD LONDON GLASGOW
NEW YORK TORONTO MELBOURNE WELLINGTON
KUALA LUMPUR SINGAPORE JAKARTA HONG KONG TOKYO
DELHI BOMBAY CALCUTTA MADRAS KARACHI
NAIROBI DAR ES SALAAM CAPE TOWN

*Published in the United States
by Oxford University Press, New York*

© *G. W. S. Barrow 1980*

All rights reserved. No part of this publication may be reproduced, stored in a retrieval system, or transmitted, in any form or by any means, electronic, mechanical, photocopying, recording, or otherwise, without the prior permission of Oxford University Press

British Library Cataloguing in Publication Data

Barrow, Geoffrey Wallis Steuart
   The Anglo-Norman era in Scottish history. –
(Ford lectures).
   1. Scotland – History – 1057–1603
   I. Title II. Series
941.102   DA779   79–40841
ISBN 0–19–822473–7

*Printed and bound in Great Britain by
Morrison & Gibb Ltd, London and Edinburgh*

PREFACE

WHEN I came to school in Oxford in the autumn of 1937, forty years before these lectures were delivered, someone gifted with second sight might have made two truthful predictions which I would not have been ready to believe, namely that I would find it difficult, indeed almost impossible, to gain admission to the university of Oxford, and that I would one day be invited to give the Ford Lectures. The fulfilment of the happier, though less credible, of these hypothetical predictions I owe to the kindness of Lord Blake and his fellow-electors to Ford's Lectureship. I thank them most sincerely for the opportunity thus given me to put my thoughts on the Scottish feudal age into some kind of order. It is a delight, but a somewhat daunting delight, to be admitted to such a goodly fellowship of historians. From a long list I would single out four names in particular: Maitland (descendant of one of the families discussed in the following pages), to a knowledge of most of whose work I came absurdly late; Powicke, who of all the English medievalists of this century seems to me to have exhibited most satisfyingly what the President of St. John's has called 'the power of intense realisation of remote situations'; Stenton, from whose writings—especially his own Ford Lectures—I first learned the esoteric joys of charter scholarship and the essential connection between documents and topography; and Galbraith, most fruitfully unpredictable of teachers, whose incredulous exclamation, uttered when I first came to Oxford to work for a higher degree, still makes my ears burn for very shame: 'What! You want to do research in medieval Scottish history and you've never heard of Lawrie's *Charters*! That's a *pretty bad show*!' Several generations of historians and would-be historians have learned much of what they know of their craft from these four masters; in my case, the debt seems to grow with every new reading and re-reading of their work. To follow in the footsteps of these and other great scholars is both an uplifting and a humbling experience.

There remain other debts to be gladly acknowledged. Failing to gain entry to Oxford through the front door of academic merit, I squeezed in through the side door of national prejudice, having excited the sympathy of that admirable Scotsman and Oxonian, the late R. B. McCallum. His readiness, as Vice-Gerent, to admit me to a college at that time deeply suspicious of post-graduate studies was one of those indefensible and agreeable anomalies which used to be characteristic of an Oxford which has already grown surprisingly remote. If 'Uncle Mac' (as he was affectionately known) was the necessary cause of my being able to embark on research, the efficient cause was without question Kathleen Major. When no one else in the university proved willing to take responsibility for an unknown, stravaiging Scot, Kathleen Major, despite her many other commitments, undertook the task of supervision which her sense of duty precluded from becoming a sinecure. No one venturing upon advanced study in the field of medieval ecclesiastical history could have wished for a more conscientious, knowledgeable, or inspiring supervisor. Among the scholars whom I first met in those days, my friend and colleague Professor Donald Watt, for whom ecclesiastical history, especially of medieval Scotland, has remained a leading interest, has very kindly read these lectures in typescript, and in their final form they have benefited greatly from his suggestions for correction and improvement. For permission to publish the documents in Appendix A I am indebted to the Trustees of the National Library of Scotland and the Master and Fellows of Balliol College, Oxford. Finally, I must thank the university of St. Andrews for granting me leave of absence in 1979, part of which has been spent preparing these lectures for publication.

St. Andrews, 1979

CONTENTS

List of Maps	page viii
List of Abbreviations	ix
I. A Land for Younger Sons	1
II. The Pattern of Settlement	30
III. The Colonists: (i) The great lords and their families	61
IV. The Colonists: (ii) Dependants and adventurers	91
V. Early Scottish Feudalism	118
VI. The Other Side of the Coin	145
Appendix A	169
Appendix B	172
Appendix C	199
Index	205

LIST OF MAPS

1. Secular divisions of southern Scotland before 1200
2. Feudal settlement in south-west Scotland before 1200
3. Settlement place-names: places of parochial status
4. Settlement place-names: places of less than parochial status
5. Settlement place-names: 'manorial' and 'ecclesiastical' names
6. Upper and Middle Wards of Clydesdale, twelfth century
7. Flemish settlement in the mid-west before 1214
8. Ayrshire: places named in feudal charters before 1214
9. Ayrshire: distribution of known vassals and lord's demesne before 1214
10. Annandale: settlement names before 1214

Errata
Map 3 has been printed on p. 54
Map 4 has been printed on p. 55
Map 5 has been printed on p. 53

ABBREVIATIONS

As far as practicable, abbreviations have been made to conform to the *List of Abbreviated Titles of the Printed Sources of Scottish History to 1560* published as a supplement to the *Scottish Historical Review* for October 1963. With a few exceptions, the criteria adopted for that *List* have been followed for abbreviations of titles which do not appear on the *List*. It has not been considered necessary to list in full well-established abbreviations for the publications of the Record Commissions and the Public Record Office, e.g. *Cal.Chart.* for the *Calendar of Charter Rolls preserved in the Public Record Office*, 6 vols., 1903–27; *Book of Fees* for *Liber feodorum. The book of fees commonly called* Testa de Nevill, *reformed from the earliest mss. by the Deputy Keeper of the Records*, 2 vols. in 3, 1920–31, etc.

Aberdeen-Banff Coll.	*Collections for a History of the Shires of Aberdeen and Banff*, Spalding Club, 1843
Aberdeen–Banff Illustrations	*Illustrations of the Topography and Antiquities of the Shires of Aberdeen and Banff*, Spalding Club, 1847–69
Aberdeen Reg.	*Registrum Episcopatus Aberdonensis*, Spalding and Maitland Clubs, 1845
Anderson, *Diplomata*	*Selectus Diplomatum et Numismatum Scotiae Thesaurus* (Half Title: *Diplomata Scotiae*). Ed. J. Anderson, Edinburgh, 1739
Anderson, *Early Sources*	*Early Sources of Scottish History 500 to 1286.* Ed. A. O. Anderson, Edinburgh, 1922
Anderson, *Oliphants*	J. Anderson, *The Oliphants in Scotland*, Edinburgh, 1879
Anderson, *Scottish Annals*	*Scottish Annals from English Chroniclers 500 to 1286.* Ed. A. O. Anderson, London, 1908
Arbroath Liber	*Liber S. Thome de Aberbrothoc*, Bannatyne Club, 1848–56

APS	*The Acts of the Parliaments of Scotland.* Edd. T. Thomson and C. Innes, Edinburgh, 1814–75
Ayr–Galloway Coll.	*Archeological and Historical Collections relating to Ayrshire and Galloway, 1878–99* (volumes for 1878–84 bear the title . . . *relating to the Counties of Ayr and Wigton*)
Ayrshire Coll.	*Collections of the Ayrshire Archeological and Natural History Society,* 1947
Balmerino Liber	*Liber Sancte Marie de Balmorinach,* Abbotsford Club, 1841
Bamff Chrs.	*Bamff Charters 1232–1703.* Ed. J. H. Ramsay, Oxford, 1915
Barbour, *Bruce*	J. Barbour, *The Bruce.* Ed. W. M. Mackenzie, London, 1909
Barrow, *Kingdom*	G. W. S. Barrow, *The Kingdom of the Scots,* 1973
Barrow, *Bruce*	G. W. S. Barrow, *Robert Bruce and the Community of the Realm of Scotland,* 2nd edn., Edinburgh, 1976
Beauly Chrs.	*The Charters of the Priory of Beauly.* Ed. E. C. Batten, Grampian Club, 1877
Becket Materials	*Materials for the History of Thomas Becket, Archbishop of Canterbury, Canonized by Pope Alexander III, A.D. 1173.* Edd. J. C. Robertson and J. B. Sheppard, Rolls Ser., 7 vols., 1875–85
Black, *Surnames*	G. F. Black, *The Surnames of Scotland: their origin, meaning and history,* New York, 1946
Bouquet, *Recueil*	M. Bouquet, *Recueil des historiens des Gaules et de la France,* new edn. Ed. L. Delisle, 24 vols., Paris, 1869–1904
Brechin Reg.	*Registrum Episcopatus Brechinensis,* Bannatyne Club, 1856
Brinkburn Chartulary	*The Chartulary of Brinkburn Priory.* Ed. W. Page, Surtees Soc., 1893
Bruton Cartulary	Bruton section of *Two Cartularies of the Augustinian Priory of Bruton and the Cluniac Priory of Montacute in the County*

List of Abbreviations xi

	of Somerset. Edd. H. C. Maxwell Lyte and others, Somerset Record Soc., 1894
Cal.Docs.France	Calendar of Documents Preserved in France, Illustrative of the History of Great Britain and Ireland. Ed. J. H. Round. i (all published), 1899
Calverley Charters	Calverley Charters Presented to the British Museum by Sir W. C. Trevelyan, Bt. Edd. W. P. Baildon and S. Margerison, Thoresby Soc., 1904
Cambuskenneth Reg.	Registrum Monasterii S. Marie de Cambuskenneth. Ed. W. Fraser, Grampian Club, 1872
CDS	Calendar of Documents relating to Scotland. Ed. J. Bain, Edinburgh, 1881–8
Cheshire Domesday	The Domesday Survey of Cheshire. Ed. J. Tait, Chetham Soc. (NS), 1916
Chron. Bower	Joannis de Fordun Scotichronicon cum Supplementis et Continuatione, Walteri Boweri. Ed. W. Goodall, Edinburgh, 1759
Chron. Fantosme	Chronicle of the War between the English and the Scots in 1173 and 1174, by Jordan Fantosme, Spiritual Chancellor of the Diocese of Winchester. Ed. F. Michel, Surtees Soc., 1840
Chron. Fordun	Johannis de Fordun, Chronica Gentis Scotorum. Ed. W. F. Skene, Edinburgh, 1871–2
Chron. Guisborough	The Chronicle of Walter of Guisborough previously edited as the Chronicle of Walter of Hemingford or Hemingburgh. Ed. H. Rothwell, Royal Historical Soc., Camden Ser., lxxxix, 1957
Chron. Holyrood	A Scottish Chronicle known as the Chronicle of Holyrood. Ed. M. O. Anderson, SHS, 1938
Chron. Howden	Chronica Magistri Rogeri de Houedene. Ed. W. Stubbs, Rolls Ser., 4 vols., 1868–71

Chron. Lanercost	*Chronicon de Lanercost*, Maitland Club, 1839
Chron. Melrose	*The Chronicle of Melrose* (Facsimile Edition). Edd. A. O. Anderson and others, London, 1936
Chron. Stephen	*Chronicles of the Reigns of Stephen, Henry II, and Richard I*. Ed. R. Howlett, Rolls Ser., 4 vols., 1884–9
Clay and Greenway, *Early Yorkshire Families*	C. T. Clay and D. Greenway, *Early Yorkshire Families*. Yorks. Arch. Soc., 1973
Cockersand Chartulary	*The Chartulary of Cockersand Abbey of the Premonstratensian Order*. Ed. W. Farrer, Chetham Soc. (New Ser.), 7 parts, 1898–1909
Coldstream Chartulary	*Chartulary of the Cistercian Priory of Coldstream*, Grampian Club, 1879
Comp. Pge.	*Complete Peerage of England, Scotland, Ireland, Great Britain and United Kingdom, etc.* By G. E. C[okayne]. New edn., revised and much enlarged, by V. Gibbs and others, 13 vols. in 14, 1910–59
Coupar Angus Chrs.	*Charters of the Abbey of Coupar Angus*. Ed. D. E. Easson, SHS, 1947
Coupar Angus Rental	*Rental Book of the Cistercian Abbey of Cupar Angus*. Ed. C. Rogers, Grampian Club, 1879–80
Cowan, *Parishes*	I. B. Cowan, *The Parishes of Medieval Scotland*, SRS, 1967
Cowan (Easson), *Religious Houses*	Ian B. Cowan and David E. Easson, *Medieval Religious Houses, Scotland, with an Appendix on the Houses in the Isle of Man*. 2nd edn., revised and enlarged, of D. E. Easson, *Medieval Religious Houses, Scotland* (1957). Ed. I. B. Cowan, 1976
Crossraguel Chrs.	*Charters of the Abbey of Crossraguel* (Archaeological and Historical Collections relating to Ayr and Galloway, 1886)

Cuninghame topographized	Cuninghame, topographized by Timothy Pont, A.M., 1604–1608, with continuation and illustrative notices by the late James Dobie of Crummock. Ed. J. S. Dobie, Glasgow, 1876
CWAAS Trans.	Cumberland and Westmorland Antiquarian and Archaeological Society, Transactions (Record Series cited by individual title)
Delisle–Berger, *Recueil*	Recueil des actes de Henri II concernant les provinces françaises etc. Ed. L. Delisle, rev. E. Berger. 4 vols., 1909–27
Dowden, *Bishops*	J. Dowden, The Bishops of Scotland, Glasgow, 1912
Dryburgh Liber	Liber S. Marie de Dryburgh, Bannatyne Club, 1847
Dugdale, *Mon. Angl.*	W. Dugdale, Monasticon Anglicanum, 3 vols., 1655–73
Dugdale, *Mon. Angl.* (New)	W. Dugdale, Monasticon Anglicanum. A new edition by J. Caley, H. Ellis, and B. Bandinel. 6 vols. in 8, 1817–30, repr. 6 vols., 1846
Dumfriesshire Trans.	Transactions of the Dumfriesshire and Galloway Natural History and Antiquarian Society, 1862–
Dunbar, *Scot. Kings*	A. H. Dunbar, Scottish Kings: A Revised Chronology of Scottish History 1005–1625, 2nd edn., Edinburgh, 1906
Dunfermline Reg.	Registrum de Dunfermelyn, Bannatyne Club, 1842
Dunkeld Rentale	Rentale Dunkeldense, SHS, 1915
Ekwall, *Concise Dictionary*	E. Ekwall, The Concise Oxford Dictionary of English Place-Names, 3rd edn., Oxford, 1947
EP-NS	English Place-Name Society, 1924– (volumes cited by editor's name and county)
Exch. Rolls	The Exchequer Rolls of Scotland. Edd. J. Stuart and others, Edinburgh, 1878–1908
EYC	Early Yorkshire Charters, being a collection

of documents anterior to the thirteenth century made from the public records, monastic chartularies, Roger Dodsworth's manuscripts, and other available sources. Yorkshire Archaeological Soc., Record Ser., Extra Ser. Vols. i–iii ed. W. Farrer, 1914–16. Vols. iv–xii, ed. C. T. Clay, 1935–65; with an index to vols. i–iii prepared by C. T. and E. M. Clay, 1942

Family of Rose — *A Genealogical Deduction of the Family of Rose of Kilravock*, Spalding Club, 1848

Family of Seton — *A History of the Family of Seton during Eight Centuries*. Ed. G. Seton, Edinburgh, 1896

Farrer, *HKF* — W. Farrer, *Honors and Knights' Fees: an attempt to identify the component parts of certain honors etc.*, 3 vols., London and Manchester, 1923–5

Fife Court Bk. — *The Sheriff Court Book of Fife 1515–22*. Ed. W. C. Dickinson, SHS, 1928

Foedera — *Foedera, Conventiones, Litterae et Cuiuscunque Generis Acta Publica*. Ed. T. Rymer, Record Commission edition, London, 1816–69

Fraser, *Annandale* — W. Fraser, *The Annandale Family Book*, 1894

Fraser, *Buccleuch* — W. Fraser, *The Scotts of Buccleuch*, 1878

Fraser, *Carlaverock* — W. Fraser, *The Book of Carlaverock*, 1873

Fraser, *Colquhoun* — W. Fraser, *The Chiefs of Colquhoun and their Country*, 1869

Fraser, *Colquhoun Cartulary* — W. Fraser, *Cartulary of Colquhoun of Colquhoun and Luss*, 1873

Fraser, *Douglas* — W. Fraser, *The Douglas Book*, 1885

Fraser Facsimiles — *Facsimiles of Scottish Charters and Letters prepared by Sir William Fraser*, Edinburgh, 1903

Fraser, *Grandtully* — W. Fraser, *The Red Book of Grandtully*, 1868

Fraser, *Grant* — W. Fraser, *The Chiefs of Grant*, 1883

List of Abbreviations

Fraser, *Haddington*	W. Fraser, *Memorials of the Earls of Haddington*, 1889
Fraser, *Keir*	W. Fraser, *The Stirlings of Keir*, 1858
Fraser, *Lennox*	W. Fraser, *The Lennox*, 1874
Fraser, *Melville*	W. Fraser, *The Melvilles Earls of Melville and the Leslies Earls of Leven*, 1890
Fraser, *Menteith*	W. Fraser, *The Red Book of Menteith*, 1880
Fraser Papers	*Papers from the Collection of Sir William Fraser*, SHS, 1924
Fraser, *Pollok*	W. Fraser, *Memoirs of the Maxwells of Pollok*, 1863
Fraser, *Pollok Cartulary*	W. Fraser, *The Cartulary of Pollok-Maxwell*, 1875
Fraser, *Southesk*	W. Fraser, *History of the Carnegies, Earls of Southesk, and of their Kindred*, 1867
Fraser, *Wemyss*	W. Fraser *Memorials of the Family of Wemyss of Wemyss*, 1888
Furness Coucher Bk.	*The Coucher Book of Furness Abbey*. Edd. J. C. Atkinson and J. Brownbill, Chetham Soc. (NS), 2 vols. in 6 parts, 1886–1919
Gesta Henrici II	*Gesta regis Henrici secundi Benedicti abbatis. The chronicle of the reigns of Henry II and Richard I, A.D. 1169–1192, known commonly under the name of Benedict of Peterborough.* Ed. W. Stubbs, Rolls Ser., 2 vols., 1867
Glasgow Reg.	*Registrum Episcopatus Glasguensis*, Bannatyne and Maitland Clubs, 1843
Glasgow St. Mary Liber	*Liber Collegii Nostre Domine: Registrum Ecclesie B. V. Marie et S. Anne infra Muros Civitatis Glasguensis 1549*, Maitland Club, 1846
Glastonbury Chartulary	*The Great Chartulary of Glastonbury*. Ed. A. Watkin, Somerset Record Soc., 3 vols., 1947–56
Greenway, *Mowbray Charters*	*Charters of the Honour of Mowbray, 1107–1191.* Ed. D. E. Greenway, 1972
Guisborough Cartularium	*Cartularium prioratus de Gyseburne, Ebor.*

	dioeceseos, ordinis S. Augustini, fundati A.D. MCXIX. Ed. W. Brown, Surtees Soc., 2 vols., 1889–94
Hailes, *Annals*	Sir David Dalrymple, Lord Hailes, *Annals of Scotland from the Accession of Malcolm III to the Accession of the House of Stewart*, 3rd edn., Edinburgh, 1819
Hedley, *Northumberland Families*	W. P. Hedley, *Northumberland Families*, Soc. of Antiquaries of Newcastle-upon-Tyne, 1968–
Henry of Huntingdon, *Historia*	*Henrici archidiaconi Huntendunensis historia Anglorum. The History of the English, by Henry, Archdeacon of Huntingdon, from A.D. 55 to A.D. 1154.* Ed. T. Arnold, Rolls Ser., 1879
Highland Papers	*Highland Papers*, Ed. J. R. N. Macphail, SHS, 1914–34
Hist. MSS Comm.	Royal Commission on Historical Manuscripts. 1st to 9th Reports cited by number; others normally by name of owner or collection
Holm Cultram Reg.	*The Register and Records of Holm Cultram.* Edd. F. Grainger and W. G. Collingwood, *CWAAS* Record Ser., 1929
Holt, *Northerners*	J. C. Holt, *The Northerners*, 1961
Holyrood Liber	*Liber Cartarum Sancte Crucis*, Bannatyne Club, 1840
Inchaffray Chrs.	*Charters, Bulls and other Documents relating to the Abbey of Inchaffray.* Ed. J. Dowden and others, SHS, 1908
Inchaffray Liber	*Liber Insule Missarum*, Bannatyne Club, 1847
Inchcolm Chrs.	*Charters of the Abbey of Inchcolm.* Edd. D. E. Easson and A. Macdonald, SHS, 1938
Innes Review	*The Innes Review*, 1950–
Instrumenta Publica	*Instrumenta Publica sive Processus super Fidelitatibus et Homagiis Scotorum Domino Regi Angliae Factis 1291–96*, Bannatyne Club, 1834

Jurid. Rev.	*Juridical Review*, 1889–
Kelso Liber	*Liber S. Marie de Calchou*, Bannatyne Club, 1846
Kendale Records	*Records Relating to the Barony of Kendale* (compiled by W. Farrer). Ed. J. F. Curwen, *CWAAS* Record Ser., 3 vols., 1923–6
Kinloss Records	*Records of the Monastery of Kinloss*. Ed. J. Stuart, Edinburgh, 1872
Kirkstall Coucher Bk.	*The Coucher Book of the Cistercian Abbey of Kirkstall, in the West Riding of the County of York*. Edd. W. T. Lancaster and W. P. Baildon, Thoresby Soc., 1904
Laing Chrs.	*Calendar of the Laing Charters 854–1837*. Ed. J. Anderson, Edinburgh, 1899
Laing, *Seals*, i	H. Laing, *Descriptive Catalogue of Impressions from Ancient Scottish Seals*, Bannatyne and Maitland Clubs, 1850
Laing, *Seals*, ii	H. Laing, *Supplemental Descriptive Catalogue of Ancient Scottish Seals*, Edinburgh, 1866
Lamont Papers	*An Inventory of Lamont Papers*, SRS, 1914
Lancashire Fines	*Final Concords of the County of Lancaster . . . preserved in the Public Record Office*, London. Ed. W. Farrer, Lancashire and Cheshire Record Soc., 4 parts, 1899–1910
Lancashire Inquests	*Lancashire Inquests, Extents and Feudal Aids*. Ed. W. Farrer, Lancashire and Cheshire Record Soc., 3 parts, 1903–15
Lancaster, *Bridlington Abstracts*	*Abstracts of the Charters and Other Documents contained in the Chartulary of the Priory of Bridlington in the East Riding of the County of York*. Ed. W. T. Lancaster, Leeds, 1912
Lawrie, *Annals*	*Annals of the Reigns of Malcolm and William, Kings of Scotland*. Ed. A. C. Lawrie, Glasgow, 1910
Lawrie, *Charters*	*Early Scottish Charters prior to 1153*. Ed. A. C. Lawrie, Glasgow, 1905

List of Abbreviations

Lennox Cartularium	*Cartularium Comitatus de Levenax*, Maitland Club, 1833
Le Prévost, *Mémoires . . . de l'Eure*	A. Le Prévost, *Mémoires et notes pour servir à l'histoire du département de l'Eure*. Edd. L. Delisle and L. Passy, 3 vols., Évreux, 1862–9
Lewes Chartulary	*The Chartulary of the Priory of St. Pancras of Lewes*. Ed. L. F. Salzman, Sussex Record Soc., 2 parts, 1933–5
Lindores Chartulary	*Chartulary of the Abbey of Lindores*, Ed. J. Dowden, SHS, 1903
Lindores Liber	*Liber Sancte Marie de Lundoris*, Abbotsford Club, 1841
Loyd, *Origins*	L. C. Loyd, *The Origins of some Anglo-Norman Families*. Edd. C. T. Clay and D. C. Douglas, Harleian Soc., 1951
Macfarlane, *Geographical Collections*	*Geographical Collections relating to Scotland*, made by Walter Macfarlane. Edd. A. Mitchell and J. T. Clark, SHS, 3 vols., 1906–8
Macphail, *Pluscardyn*	S. R. Macphail, *History of the Religious House of Pluscardyn*, Edinburgh, 1881
May Records	*Records of the Priory of the Isle of May*. Ed. J. Stuart, Edinburgh, 1868
Melrose Liber	*Liber Sancte Marie de Melros*, Bannatyne Club, 1837
Memoranda de Parliamento	*Records of the Parliament holden at Westminster on the twenty-eighth day of February, in the thirty-third year of the Reign of King Edward the First, A.D. 1305*. Ed. F. W. Maitland, Rolls Ser., 1893
Midlothian Chrs.	*Charters of the Hospital of Soltre, of Trinity College, Edinburgh, and other Collegiate Churches in Midlothian*, Bannatyne Club, 1861
Moncreiffs	*The Moncreiffs and the Moncreiffes*. Edd. F. Moncreiff and W. Moncreiffe, Edinburgh, 1929
Monkbretton Chartularies	*Abstracts of the Chartularies of the Priory*

List of Abbreviations

	of Monkbretton. Ed. J. W. Walker, Yorkshire Archaeological Soc., Record Ser., 1924
Montacute Cartulary	Montacute section of *Two Cartularies of the Augustinian Priory of Bruton and the Cluniac Priory of Montacute in the County of Somerset*. Edd. H. C. Maxwell Lyte and others, Somerset Record Soc., 1894
Moray Reg.	*Registrum Episcopatus Moraviensis*, Bannatyne Club, 1837
Morton Reg.	*Registrum Honoris de Morton*, Bannatyne Club, 1853
Munro Writs	*Calendar of Writs of Munro of Foulis 1299–1823*. Ed. C. T. McInnes, SRS, 1940
Myln, *Vitae*	A. Myln, *Vitae Dunkeldensis Ecclesiae Episcoporum*, Bannatyne Club, 1831
Nat. MSS Scot.	*Facsimiles of the National Manuscripts of Scotland*, London, 1867–71
Newbattle Reg.	*Registrum S. Marie de Neubotle*, Bannatyne Club, 1849
Newminster Chartularium	*Chartularium abbathiae de novo monasterio, ordinis Cisterciensis, fundatae anno MCXXXVII*. Ed. J. T. Fowler, Surtees Soc., 1878
Nicolaisen, *Scottish Place-Names*	W. F. H. Nicolaisen, *Scottish Place-Names: Their Study and Significance*, 1976
Nisbet, *Heraldry*	A. Nisbet, *A System of Heraldry*, new edn., Edinburgh, 1816
North Berwick Carte	*Carte Monialium de Northberwic*, Bannatyne Club, 1847
Northumberland Assize Rolls	*Three Early Assize rolls for the County of Northumberland, saec. XIII*. Ed. W. Page, Surtees Soc., 1891
Northumberland County History	*A History of Northumberland*. Issued under the direction of the Northumberland County History Committee. 15 vols., Newcastle-upon-Tyne, 1893–1940
Old Edinburgh Bk.	*The Book of the Old Edinburgh Club*, 1908–

OPS	Origines Parochiales Scotiae, Bannatyne Club, 1851–5
Orpen	G. H. Orpen, Ireland under the Normans, 4 vols., 1911–20
Paisley Reg.	Registrum Monasterii de Passelet, Maitland Club, 1832; New Club, 1877
Palgrave, Docs. Hist. Scot.	Documents and Records illustrating the History of Scotland. Ed. F. Palgrave, London, 1837
Panmure Reg.	Registrum de Panmure. Ed. J. Stuart, Edinburgh, 1874
Percy Chartulary	The Percy Chartulary. Ed. M. T. Martin, Surtees Soc., 1911
Perth Blackfriars	The Blackfriars of Perth. Ed. R. Milne, Edinburgh, 1893
Pitfirrane Writs	Inventory of Pitfirrane Writs 1230–1794. Ed. W. Angus, SRS, 1932
Pontefract Chartulary	The Chartulary of St. John of Pontefract. Ed. R. Holmes, Yorkshire Archaeological Soc., Record Ser., 2 vols., 1899–1902
PRS	Pipe Roll Society (1884–) (published Pipe Rolls cited by regnal year)
PSAS	Proceedings of the Society of Antiquaries of Scotland (1851–)
Raine, North Durham	Appendix to J. Raine, The History and Antiquities of North Durham, London, 1852
RAL	The Registrum Antiquissimum of the Cathedral Church of Lincoln. Edd. C. W. Foster and K. Major, Lincoln Record Soc., 12 vols., 1931–73
RBE	The Red Book of the Exchequer. Ed. H. Hall, Rolls Ser., 3 vols., 1896
RCAHMS	Royal Commission on the Ancient and Historical Monuments of Scotland, Inventories (by county)
Retours	Inquisitionum ad Capellam Domini Regis Retornatarum, quae in publicis archivis Scotiae adhuc servantur, Abbreviatio. Ed.

	T. Thomson, Record Comm., 1811–16
Rievaulx Cartularium	Cartularium abbathiae de Rievalle, ordinis Cisterciensis, fundatae anno MCXXXII. Ed. J. C. Atkinson, Surtees Soc., 1889
RMS	Registrum Magni Sigilli Regum Scotorum. Edd. J. M. Thomson and others, Edinburgh, 1882–1914
Robertson, *Index*	An *Index, drawn up about the year 1629, of many Records of Charters*. Ed. W. Robertson, Edinburgh, 1798
Rot.Litt.Claus.	Rotuli Litterarum Clausarum in Turri Londinensi asservati, 1204–27. Ed. T. D. Hardy, 2 vols., Record Comm., 1833–44
Rot. Scacc. Norm.	Magni Rotuli Scaccarii Normanniae sub regibus Angliae. Ed. T. Stapleton, Society of Antiquaries of London, 2 vols., 1840–4
Rot.Scot.	Rotuli Scotiae in Turri Londinensi et in Domo Capitulari Westmonasteriensi Asservati. Edd. D. Macpherson and others, 1814–19
RRAN	Regesta Regum Anglo-Normannorum. Edd. H. W. C. Davis, R. J. Whitwell, C. Johnson, H. A. Cronne, and R. H. C. Davis, 4 vols., Oxford, 1913–69
RRS	Regesta Regum Scottorum. Edd. G. W. S. Barrow and others, i (1153–65), 1960; ii (1165–1214), 1971
St. Andrews Liber	Liber Cartarum Prioratus Sancti Andree in Scotia, Bannatyne Club, 1841
St. Bees Reg.	The Register of the Priory of St. Bees. Ed. J. Wilson, Surtees Soc., 1915
Sallay Chartulary	The Chartulary of the Cistercian Abbey of St. Mary of Sallay in Craven. Ed. J. McNulty, Yorkshire Archaeological Soc., Record Ser., 2 vols., 1933–4
Sanders, *Baronies*	I. J. Sanders, *English Baronies: A Study of their Origin and Descent*. Oxford, 1960
Scalacronica	Scalacronica, by Sir Thomas Gray of

	Heton Knight, Maitland Club, 1836
Scone Liber	*Liber Ecclesie de Scon*, Bannatyne and Maitland Clubs, 1843
Scots Pge.	*The Scots Peerage*. Ed. Sir J. Balfour Paul, Edinburgh, 1904–14
SHR	*The Scottish Historical Review* (1903–28, 1947–)
SHS	Scottish History Society (1886–)
SHS *Misc.*	*The Miscellany of the Scottish History Society*, SHS, 1893–
Sibbald, *Fife*	R. Sibbald, *The History, Ancient and Modern, of the Sheriffdoms of Fife and Kinross*. Ed. L. Adamson, Cupar–Fife, 1803
Somerset Fines	Pedes finium, *commonly called Feet of Fines, the County of Somerset*. Ed. E. Green, Somerset Record Soc., 4 vols., 1892–1906
Somerset Pleas	*Somersetshire Pleas, Civil and Criminal, from the Rolls of the Itinerant Justices, close of 12th century–41 Henry III*. Ed. C. E. H. Chadwyck-Healey, Somerset Record Soc., 1897
Spalding Misc.	*Miscellany of the Spalding Club*, Spalding Club, 1841–52
SRS	Scottish Record Society
Stevenson, *Documents*	*Documents Illustrative of the History of Scotland 1286–1306*. Ed. J. Stevenson, Edinburgh, 1870
Stevenson, *Illustrations*	*Illustrations of Scottish History from the Twelfth to the Sixteenth Century*. Ed. J. Stevenson, Maitland Club, 1834
Stevenson and Wood, *Seals*	J. H. Stevenson and M. Wood, *Scottish Heraldic Seals*, Glasgow, 1940
Stogursey Charters	*Stogursey Charters. Charters and Other Documents Relating to the Property of the Alien Priory of Stogursey, Somerset, now belonging to Eton College*. Ed. T. D. Tremlett and N. Blakiston, Somerset Record Soc., 1949

Stones, *Relations*	*Anglo-Scottish Relations, 1174–1328: Some Select Documents.* Ed. E. L. G. Stones, 1965, repr. 1970
Theiner, *Monumenta*	*Vetera Monumenta Hibernorum et Scotorum Historiam Illustrantia.* Ed. A. Theiner, Rome, 1864
VCH	*Victoria History of the Counties of England*
Wardon Cartulary	*Cartulary of the Cistercian Abbey of Old Wardon.* Ed. G. H. Fowler, Bedfordshire Historical Record Soc., Manchester, 1931
Watson, *CPNS*	W. J. Watson, *The History of the Celtic Place-Names of Scotland*, Edinburgh, 1926
Watt, *Dictionary*	D. E. R. Watt, *A Biographical Dictionary of Scottish Graduates to A.D. 1410.* Oxford, 1977
Wetheral Reg.	*The Register of the Priory of Wetheral.* Ed. J. E. Prescott, *CWAAS* Record Ser., 1897
Whitby Cartularium	*Cartularium abbathiae de Whitby, ordinis S. Benedicti, fundatae anno MLXXVIII.* Ed. J. C. Atkinson, Surtees Soc., 2 vols., 1879–81
Wigtown Charter Chest	*Charter Chest of the Earldom of Wigtown*, SRS, 1910
Wigtownshire Chrs.	*Wigtownshire Charters.* Ed. R. C. Reid, SHS, 1960
Yester Writs	*Calendar of Writs preserved at Yester House 1166–1503.* Edd. C. C. H. Harvey and J. Macleod, SRS, 1930
Yorkshire Fines	*Feet of Fines for the County of York, 1218–72, 1327–77.* Edd. W. P. Baildon and J. Parker, Yorkshire Archaeological Soc., Record Ser., 5 vols., 1910–32
Yorkshire Inquisitions	*Yorkshire Inquisitions of the Reigns of Henry III and Edward I.* Ed. W. Brown, Yorkshire Archaeological Soc., Record Ser., 1892–1906

I

A Land for Younger Sons

As a title 'The Anglo-Norman Era in Scottish History' fulfils the requirements of the Ford Lectures in English history as long as it indicates a study of the relations between two countries or rather three countries—between, on the one hand, the country subject to influence, that is to say Scotland, and, on the other, the countries doing the influencing—England and France. That relationship is as much a part of English as of Scottish history. It is, moreover, entirely appropriate to discuss that relationship in a course of lectures delivered within the university of Oxford. From its earliest days Oxford attracted Scots as students and teachers, and their regrettable tendency, as perhaps the most prominent and articulate group among the Northerners, to engage in battle with the Irish, as perhaps the most conspicuous single group among the Southerners, may well have played an important part in the development of the proctorial system.[1] It was a Fifer, Master Peter of Ramsay, who succeeded Robert Grosseteste as lecturer to the Franciscan school in Oxford before returning to Scotland to become, in 1247, bishop of Aberdeen.[2] Another Fifer, the student Gilbert of Dunfermline, was not so lucky—but it was his homicide in 1248 at the hands of the townspeople of Oxford that prompted the university's first substantial royal charter of privileges.[3] It is from the now alas! faded pencil of another Scots undergraduate, William of Bernham, nephew of the bishop of St. Andrews and possibly son of the mayor of Berwick

---

[1] H. Rashdall, *The Universities of Europe in the Middle Ages*, 2nd edn., ed. F. M. Powicke and A. B. Emden (Oxford, 1936), iii. 49, 57–8.

[2] Watt, *Dictionary*, 460–1.

[3] H. E. Salter, *The Medieval Archives of the University of Oxford* (Oxford Historical Soc., 1920), 19 and n. 1; *Roberti Grosseteste Epistolae*, ed. H. R. Luard (Rolls Ser., 1861), 438.

upon Tweed, that we have the first examples in the British Isles of a university student's letters home.[4] They were not the last such letters to be mainly concerned with lack of money and complaints of the dilatoriness of his tutors;[5] nor was William the last Scots student to buy a copy of the best book then available on modern English history, in his case William of Malmesbury's *Gesta Regum Anglorum* and *Historia Novella*. By the side of Malmesbury's description of the Council of Windsor of 1072—at which the Church of all Britain was simply divided between Canterbury and York without any recognition of a special place for Scotland—William of Bernham wrote in the margin 'Salva Ecclesia Scoticana', 'Not applicable to the Scottish Church!'[6] He might be anticipating those many Scots students of the present day tempted into similar marginalia by the more outrageously tendentious or offensive statements about their country in the writings of Oxford's distinguished Regius Professor of Modern History.

Our earliest consumers' guide to the 'Best Buy' among Oxford colleges is to be found in the Chronicle of Melrose which, in a passage written about 1282, noted that John Balliol had endowed a house for students at Oxford where each scholar received eightpence a week. 'But there is another college there,' added the writer, apparently referring to the long-forgotten Burnell's Inn, 'better than that, where the scholars get twelvepence a week.'[7] At least three of the royal chancellors of Scotland in the thirteenth century were Oxford

---

[4] H. E. Salter, W. A. Pantin, and H. G. Richardson, *Formularies which bear on the History of Oxford, c. 1204–1420* [= *Oxford Formularies*] (Oxford Historical Soc., 1942), ii. 472–91, 'Letters of a Scottish Student', ed. N. R. Ker and W. A. Pantin. For the full Christian name of 'W. de Bernham', note that an unprinted charter of David Bernham bishop of St. Andrews (SRO B 65/1/1 [= 'Black Book' of St. Andrews], fo. 35) was witnessed by William 'de Berenham'. Sir Robert de Bernham, brother of Bishop David, was mayor of Berwick upon Tweed in 1249 (*APS* i. 413). A common ancestor may have been the William de Bernham appearing in a late-twelfth-century Berwick charter (*Melrose Liber*, no. 21).

[5] *Oxford Formularies*, ii. 478 ff., nos. 1, 3, 6, 10 (money worries), 2 (lecturers' promise to finish the course before the vacation).

[6] Ibid. 472.

[7] *Chron. Melrose*, 145. For the lost Burnell's Inn or London College see Rashdall, *Universities*, iii. 482–4. It may be noted that among the seals attached to the deed guaranteeing good behaviour after the riot of 1274 was that of 'P[eter] de Malros', suggesting that a student or master from Melrose was then in the university of Oxford (Salter, *Medieval Archives*, i. 32–3).

men,[8] and it is not surprising to find that King John of Scotland, whose mother the lady of Galloway, a great Scots noblewoman, had put her husband's intentions into effect by establishing Balliol College in the 1260s or '70s,[9] appointed as his first chancellor an Oxford don of many years' standing, Master Thomas of Hunsingore.[10] Master Thomas, a Yorkshireman to judge from his surname,[11] was evidently a retainer of the Balliol family, and his kinsmen seem to have been associated with Balliol College until well into the fourteenth century.[12] All this was part of an accepted academic intercourse between Scotland and Oxford which shrivelled and died in the later middle ages and, *pace* John Snell of Colmonell,[13] was only revived with some difficulty towards the end of last century. And this academic intercourse of the earlier middle ages in turn formed but a part of a much larger traffic between England and Scotland, and between northern France and Scotland, which it will be the aim of these lectures to illuminate.

Illumination has not been made easier by a curiously malign tradition of insularity among English and Scottish historians to which, of course, there have been honourable and distinguished exceptions in every generation. Two examples will suffice to make my point. Some of the worst instances of parochialism in Scottish historical scholarship are to be found in a number of articles contributed by its general editor to the

---

[8] Mr William Wishart, 1259–73, Mr William Fraser, *c.* 1273–9, Mr Thomas of Hunsingore, *c.* 1292.

[9] Frances de Paravicini, *Early History of Balliol College* (1891), 44–54, 60–4. The Lady Dervorguilla's statutes for the new college were issued in 1282 at Buittle near Dalbeattie, the caput of the lordship of Galloway (ibid., 64), while among the earliest endowments of the college was a payment of 120 head of Galloway cattle under the will of Alan 'son of the earl' (i.e. bastard son of Thomas of Galloway earl of Atholl, d. 1231), paid to Thomas MacCulloch by Roland Ascoloc in 1285 (ibid., 78; H. E. Salter, *Balliol Deeds* (Oxford Historical Soc., 1913), 329 and n. 2, 331, no. 601).

[10] Watt, *Dictionary*, 272

[11] Hunsingore is near Wetherby in the West Riding. In 1268–9 Eustace and Hugh de Balliol, about to go overseas, appointed Robert of Hunsingore as one of their attorneys (*CDS* i, nos. 2516, 2538).

[12] F. de Paravicini, *Early History of Balliol College*, 126–8, 138; A. B. Emden, *A Biographical Register of the University of Oxford to 1500*, ii, s.v. 'Hunsyngore'.

[13] W. I. Addison, *The Snell Exhibitions from the University of Glasgow to Balliol College, Oxford* (Glasgow, 1901). The requirement that those admitted to the university of Oxford should subscribe to the Thirty-Nine Articles, not lifted until 1854–6, was a major obstacle to the entry of Scots to the university.

Scots Peerage.[14] It became a favourite pastime of J. H. Round to trounce this parochialism. In his confident, aggressive fashion he did this in respect of the de Valognes family in a paper contributed to *The Ancestor* for October 1904, emphasizing the importance of material from the Binham Priory cartulary 'discovered' by J. A. C. Vincent in 1882.[15] At the very end of his article, Round printed by way of afterthought a revealing footnote: 'A Scottish publication, the *Registrum de Panmure* (1874), contains much information on the Scottish house of Valoignes and its heirs . . . The Binham Priory evidence is given.'[16] Clearly, the fact that Dr John Stuart's edition of the *Registrum de Panmure* (originally compiled in the early eighteenth century by Harry Maule of Kellie, titular earl of Panmure)[17] was only 'a Scottish publication' exonerated Round from the charge of not looking far enough afield before rushing into print with one of his accustomed diatribes.

The late and much loved Hugh Smith was anything but parochial in his approach to place-name problems, but it simply did not occur to him that Scottish evidence had any bearing on the early history of the West Riding of Yorkshire. The name of Farsley, a small place now swallowed up in the dense conurbation which has been allowed to sprawl between Leeds and Bradford, gave him much trouble. 'It is usually', he wrote, 'and correctly interpreted as "furze clearing", from OE *fyrs*.'[18] But he realized that *fyrs*, 'furze', if left to itself—even in the West Riding—would not produce the 'fars-' of Farsley, and in fact all the early recorded forms of the name

---

[14] *The Scots Peerage, founded on Wood's edition of Sir Robert Douglas's Peerage of Scotland*, ed. Sir James Balfour Paul (Edinburgh, 1904–14). See, e.g. Balfour Paul's contributions under the kings of Scotland, Comyn earl of Buchan and Home earl of Home.

[15] J. H. Round, 'Comyn and Valoignes', *Ancestor*, no. xi (1904), 129–35. See also the same writer's 'The Origin of the Comyns', ibid., no. x (1904), 104–19, for a general and not undeserved onslaught on Balfour Paul's scholarship. But Round himself could make mistakes, as when (art. cit. 105) he refers to a charter of *Alexander* (*recte* William) king of Scots of 1177, moreover without citing his reference or appreciating that the charter in question cannot be authentic.

[16] *Ancestor*, no. xi, 135, n. 2.

[17] *Panmure Reg.* i, pp. i–iii. Harry Maule and his son were influenced by Father Thomas Innes for whose invaluable labours among Scottish medieval archives in France see D. McRoberts, *Innes Review*, xxviii (1977), 69–82.

[18] A. H. Smith, *The Place-Names of the West Riding of Yorkshire* (EP-NS), iii (1961), 229–30.

known to him stuck stubbornly to 'Ferselee' leading naturally to Farsley. As long ago as 1910 F. W. Moorman had proposed to derive the name from OE *fersc*, 'fresh'.[19] Smith dismissed this, partly because of the complete absence, to his knowledge, of forms in 'fersh-' or 'fresh-'. He even fell back on the interesting alternative suggestion, as he called it, of Professor Löfvenberg, that 'the first element may be an unrecorded OE (Anglian) feminine substantive *fers (West Saxon *fiers), "heifer" '.[20] Now, it happens that in the reign of Alexander II of Scotland a prominent member, perhaps indeed the head, of the family surnamed from Farsley took service with the king of Scots,[21] and in that kingdom became the ancestor of two lines of Farsleys settled respectively in Perthshire and Fife. One line continued to hold Farsley in Yorkshire late enough to be forfeited twice by Edward I for being among his Scottish enemies.[22] In the record of these two branches of the Farsley family forms in 'fersh-' and 'fresh-' abound—certainly quite enough to support the etymology which the history of the name would indicate but which Smith rejected because he never thought of looking at the Scottish material.[23]

The starting-point of any evaluation of the Anglo-Norman Era in Scottish history must be the proposition that the medieval kingdom of Scotland consisted of an amalgam, still imperfectly understood, of elements which, for convenience, may be called pre-Celtic and Celtic, i.e. Pictish, Brittonic, and northern Irish; Anglo-Saxon; Scandinavian—especially Norwegian; and Frankish or French, French perhaps the better word provided we realize that it embraces Flemish and Breton strands as well as the more obvious ones from Normandy and elsewhere in northern France. It is essential to grasp that whereas, for our purposes, the Picts, Britons, Irish, Scandinavians, and French appeared on the scene only once, the Anglo-Saxons came twice.

[19] F. W. Moorman, *The Place-Names of the West Riding of Yorkshire* (1910), 70.
[20] Smith, *Place-Names of the West Riding*, iii, p. xiii.
[21] BL Add. Chr. 66570 (16 Apr. 1249), a grant of land in Crailshire to Sir Geoffrey 'de Ferseley' by Alexander II.
[22] *CDS* ii, no. 730 (Geoffrey 'de Friselay', 1296), nos. 1481, 1594 (Geoffrey 'de Freshelee', 'de Freshelegh', 1304).
[23] In addition to the forms given in the preceding notes, Scottish documents provide the following: Ferselay, Ferseleya, Forscley, Freschele, Fresele, Freslay, Fresley, Fresselei, Fushele. See below, Appendix B.

On the first occasion, in the sixth and seventh centuries, they came as conquerors, soldier colonists who if they did not settle *en masse* were nevertheless thick enough on the ground to anglicize in a true sense the districts of East Lothian, the Merse, lower Tweeddale, and Teviotdale, and to leave permanent Anglian traces in Mid and West Lothian, south Dumfriesshire, and even in mid Ayrshire, as is still evidenced by the place-names Maybole, Prestwick, and the River Cessnock—'Sasunnach'.[24] In the second place, some five to six centuries later, the English came as settlers certainly, as land takers, and perhaps here and there as expropriators. But they did not come to fill up an empty land nor to conquer and subjugate the existing native population. They came by invitation of the ruling dynasty and they acquired their new lands by formal infeftment and purchase and marriage. Moreover, they came in a period when the whole question of their 'Englishness' was in the melting pot as a result of the Norman Conquest of 1066. To contemporaries, it is true, most of them were *Anglici*, 'English', but many were still *Franci*, 'French'[25] and many even of those who would have thought of themselves as English bore names which pointed to recent ancestry or origins in Flanders, Picardy, or Normandy. Before 1066 there would not have been much doubt about what made an Englishman: his speech, his names, his customs and law, even his moustaches and his ale, marked him out. After about 1200 there was similarly little doubt, for if speech and customs no longer provided a test something which may fairly be called nationality was taking their place, together with unbroken experience over many generations of obedience to a king of England, *rex Anglorum* or *rex Anglie*. But between 1066 and 1200 there were real doubts and some confusion, and it would not be untrue to say that from the 1070s to the 1170s—when Henry II's chancery dropped the racial address from royal charters—the English

[24] Nicolaisen, *Scottish Place-Names*, 77, 133 (Maybole), 79 (Prestwick). The earliest recorded forms for the River Cessnock are in *Melrose Liber*, nos. 66, 67, 69, 71, 72, *72, 75 (12th and early 13th cent.), Saxenoc, Saxnoc(h), Saxnou, which seem to represent the early Middle Gaelic adjective saxanach, 'English'. Presumably Cumbric influence on the name cannot be ruled out.

[25] The Scottish royal chancery seems to have dropped the racial form of general address in charters (e.g. 'to French, English, and Scots') about the same period as its equivalent was dropped by the English chancery, in the third quarter of the twelfth century (*RRS* ii. 77).

were less confident about their own identity than in any period of their history before this present generation.

Of the various elements which made up the medieval Scottish kingdom it is this second phase of Anglo-Saxon settlement and the almost simultaneous and in any case inextricably intertwined continental or French settlement which I propose to examine in some detail. It may be said to have lasted for almost exactly two hundred years, from 1094 or 1097 (whichever date is preferred for the beginning of the reign of Edgar) to 1296 when, in the highly significant words of an unpublished contemporary chronicle, 'a general war between England and Scotland' broke out,[26] one of whose consequences was to make English settlement in Scotland, or for that matter Scots settlement in England, almost impossible for over three hundred years. During these two centuries the throne of Scotland was occupied by no more than seven sovereigns of only four different generations. All of them kept the doors of their kingdom open for foreign settlement, and in particular for settlement from England and northern France. Much of this settlement was at the unchronicled level of a new bourgeoisie and serviential class, some of it was highly specialized—a royal brewer with a Flemish name,[27] dynasties of royal cooks and bakers with Anglo-Norman names,[28] chaplains, scribes, and clerks in the *capella regis* with names such as Richard of St. Albans, Richard of Lincoln, William Malvoisin, William de Bois, Walter of St. Albans, and Gervase—such names speak for themselves.[29] But along with these merchants and craftsmen, servants and scriveners, the kings of Scots brought in or allowed to be brought in many men who were clearly destined from the beginning to be *domini*, 'lords', in their new country, or else the privileged, free, and honourable vassals of such lords. In this way Scotland became a land of opportunity for sons whose fathers had not yet died, for younger sons with no patrimony to inherit.

The phrase 'land of opportunity' may seem to need justification. Can the high road leading *into* Scotland ever have been

---

[26] BL MS Cotton Cleopatra D iii, fo. 49 (Chronicle of Hailes Abbey, Gloucestershire).
[27] For Walkelyn the king's brewer in twelfth-century Angus see *RRS* ii, no. 209.
[28] Ibid., nos. 174, 510, 563.
[29] Ibid., pp. 30–3.

a noble prospect? The younger son of Robert I de Brus was dissatisfied with Annandale because no wheaten bread could be got there—but this story comes from a late source of little historical authority,[30] and is made the more puzzling in that young Brus was given Hart and Harterness to make up the deficiency. However notable may be the merits of that unique corner of north-east England, it does not immediately spring to mind as a wheat-growing area. Beside the ill-authenticated complaint of a Bruce we may put the better-attested but perhaps not wholly spontaneous opinion of a Balliol. 'When I was king of Scotland,' the deposed John Balliol confided to his crony Anthony Bek and a few others, 'I was so disgusted by the malice, guile and treachery of the Scots that I never want to have anything to do with Scotland again', adding that he was sure the Scots were plotting to poison him.[31] Whether spontaneous or under duress, the opinion was surely a little ungrateful when one bears in mind that only four months after it was uttered several thousand Scotsmen fighting under Wallace at Falkirk laid down their lives for 'the eminent prince the lord John by God's grace illustrious king of Scotland'.[32]

More serious, perhaps, because less solicited, are the feelings expressed by a twelfth-century Breton princess and by Saint Louis as reported by Joinville. 'I would sooner be married to any of your vassals, even of humble rank,' wrote Constance, sister of Duke Conan of Brittany to King Louis VII of France about 1160, 'than become queen of Scotland.'[33] And Louis IX was hardly less outspoken when he urged his first-born son to love the people of his realm: 'For I would prefer', he said, 'that a Scot should come from Scotland and govern the people of France faithfully and well than that you should rule them with manifest injustice.'[34]

But the poor reputation from which Scotland apparently suffered in the mind of the French aristocracy is belied by the

[30] Dugdale, *Mon. Angl.* (New), vi, I. 267b.
[31] Stones, *Relations*, no. 27.
[32] This was King John's style as used by Murray and Wallace (ibid., no. 26) and by the Guardians of Scotland between 1298 and 1304 (e.g. *CDS* ii, Appendix II, no. 3, p. 535).
[33] Bouquet, *Recueil*, xvi. 23.
[34] *Jean sire de Joinville histoire de Saint Louis*, ed. N. de Wailly (Paris, 1874), 10-13, para. 21.

facts of immigration. At least from the second decade of the twelfth century, when David, the youngest son of King Malcolm and Queen Margaret, was given possession of Cumbria and the territory besouth Lammermuir which was soon to become the sheriffdoms of Berwick, Roxburgh, Selkirk, and Peebles, men and women of English, Anglo-Norman, and purely continental stock proved ready enough to take land and offices within the Scottish realm, and to settle there in as true a sense of the word 'settle' as could ever have been used of that restless and peripatetic nobility. In the second half of our two-century era it is possible to discern some variety of motive behind this settlement, some purpose ulterior to that of satisfying land-hunger, or merely being swept along in that extraordinary and as yet unexplained northern French explosion of the second half of the eleventh and first half of the twelfth centuries. For example, in 1278 the Cumbrian Alan of Pennington tried to establish his right to the estate of Giffen in Cunningham, a *feudum* (probably a knight's feu) dating from the twelfth century, partly in order to achieve a more rational rearrangement of a complex pattern of family lands, partly to strengthen his hand in manoeuvring for his son's marriage to a highly prized heiress and kinswoman Alice Muncaster.[35] The chief obstacle to Alan's plans was Alice's uncle Robert Muncaster, who grumbled that the marriage itself was a great enough matter without dragging in the estate of Giffen, and that in any case he was not bound to answer in an English court for any bargain he might have made anent lands in the kingdom of Scotland. At times it seems that deliberate advantage was taken of the fact that while the common law of both countries was substantially identical and interchangeable, jurisdictions were exclusive. Thus when a thirteenth-century Scots heiress named

---

[35] *CDS* ii, no. 133 (pp. 29–30). For the early ramifications of the family of Muncaster ('Mulcaster') or Pennington see *St. Bees Reg.*, 241n. and elsewhere, *passim*. What the English court record calls the 'manor' of Giffen is called a *feudum* in a charter of *c*. 1200 (*Dryburgh Liber*, no. 226, p. 165). This is in line with the use of *feudum* to refer to estates held by members of the knightly class, e.g. Pennersaughs (in Ecclefechan), Dumfriesshire (Fraser, *Annandale*, i. 3), Penneld in Kilbarchan, Renfrewshire, a *feudum* held for his service to his lord Walter I the Stewart by Henry de St. Martin (*Paisley Reg.*, 48–9), Kilellan or Houston, also Renfrewshire, the *feudum* of Hugh the knight son of Reginald (ibid., 372), and Hutton in Dryfesdale, Dumfriesshire, referred to as a knight's feu in the 1190s by Adam son of Gilbert (*Glasgow Reg.*, no. 78).

Euphemia, expecting to benefit when of age from her grandmother's generosity, unadvisedly entrusted her mother Isabel and English stepfather Simon Baard with the Scottish estate of 'Athelgalthethwyn' which she was due to inherit, the trustees defaulted on the bargain and retired to England.[36] Pursued at the Bedford Assizes in 1262, they pleaded that as the land in question lay in Scotland they were not bound to answer in an English court—having, in the meantime, as it was alleged, helped themselves to rents worth 540 marks. On the other hand, acquisition by inheritance, without any intention of settlement, might result quite honestly and lawfully in substantial profits. In the mid-1220s the Somerset freeholder Adam 'de Stawell'—his name from a hamlet 4 miles north-east of Bridgwater[37]—found himself rather unexpectedly the proprietor of a large estate in north Fife as heir to his elder brother Richard Revel, who had himself inherited from his uncle Henry. Within this estate, at Balmerino overlooking the Firth of Tay, the dowager queen of Scots, Ermengarde, was determined to found a Cistercian monastery in honour of Saint Edward the Confessor. In 1225 Adam of Stawell was bought out and reaped the windfall of 1,000 marks.[38]

Occasionally we see the chance piety of a pilgrim touching off a gift which might be the start of a long-term property interest reaching from one country to the other. Such was evidently the case with Michael Scot, grandfather of Sir Michael Scot of Balwearie, who about 1240 granted an annual rent of 20s from the estate of Rumgally near Cupar in Fife to the shrine of Saint Thomas the Martyr, a gift which may have been prompted by a personal visit to Canterbury.[39] The same explanation almost certainly underlies the gift by Sir John de Bosville, lord of Ardsley beside Barnsley, of a rent of 12d a year in Ardsley to Saint Andrew of Scotland. Sir John's gift was made about 1237, and sixty years later the land from which the rent was paid was meticulously confiscated by the sheriff of Yorkshire as being in the hands of King Edward's Scottish enemies.[40]

[36] *CDS* i, no. 2302. I have been unable to locate 'Athelgal(the)thwyn'.
[37] See below, p. 105.
[38] *Balmerino Liber*, nos. 4–6.
[39] G. W. S. Barrow (ed.), *The Scottish Tradition* (Edinburgh, 1974), 30–1.
[40] *St. Andrews Liber*, 293. The witnesses to John de Bosville's grant were all local

In at least one instance it might almost seem that an Anglo-Norman baron acquired property north of the Border in a spirit of antiquarian curiosity. Before 1296, the Northumbrian friend and kinsman of King John Balliol Hugh d'Eure *alias* Hugh of Iver *alias* Hugh Balliol, lord of Kirkley near Ponteland,[41] had come into possession of the estate of Kettins near Coupar Angus.[42] In the charter by which Hugh d'Eure granted the Cistercians of Coupar a permanent water supply from this estate he speaks of the spring called 'Braidwell' rising 'in the land of my *apthenagium* of Kettins'.[43] This is the earliest instance known to me of the antiquarian confusion, otherwise not found till John Fordoun's chronicle of the 1370s, between an *apdaine* ('appin'), i.e. the jurisdiction and territory of an *ab* or abbot in the old Celtic church, and a *thanagium*, i.e. a thanage or portion of royal demesne held and administered by a thane.[44] It looks as if Hugh d'Eure was quite happy to pose as 'abbot' or even 'thane' of Kettins, although he or his clerk had stumbled into the false etymology of the word which by Fordoun's time had become well established. In much the same way might we imagine a seventeenth-century English nobleman donning Highland dress at some great *timchioll* or hunting assembly in Badenoch or Mar, and wearing his plaid over the wrong shoulder.[45]

---

persons from the Barnsley district; for the date of the grant, see J. W. Walker, *Abstracts of the Chartularies of the Priory of Monk Bretton* (Yorks. Archaeological Soc., Record Ser., 1924), nos. 121, 138, 140, 141, 205, 211. On fo. 12 of the St. Andrews Priory cartulary is the note 'Memorandum that the 12d rent is to be received at the house of Randulph de Haya beside Monk Bretton by Randulph's own hand, because of his custody of John de Bosville's heir Amabilla, and afterwards from herself; which rent the same John granted to us' (*St. Andrews Liber*, 27). For the forfeiture of 1296 see *CDS* ii. 172 (West 'Erdeslawe').

[41] Hedley, *Northumberland Families*, i. 161a, 162, 184, 187. Hugh d'Eure was King John's first cousin and an executor of the will of the king's father (Paravicini, *Hist. of Balliol College*, 77, 79; *CDS* ii. no. 171). Sir Hugh d'Euer knight was a witness with Eustace de Balliol and others to a Final Concord of 1269 relating to Northumberland (Bodleian Library, MS Dodsworth 76, p. 48).

[42] *Coupar Angus Chrs.* i, no. 63.

[43] Ibid. Despite the editor's note on p. 137, the 'Abdenrie of Kettins' appears on the roll of lands holden of the archbishop of St. Andrews in 1630 (G. Martine, *Reliquiae Divi Andreae* (St. Andrews, 1797), 121).

[44] *Chron. Fordun*, i. 181.

[45] Cf. P. Hume Brown, *Early Travellers in Scotland* (Edinburgh, 1891), 120–1, for the custom whereby visitors were expected to don highland dress when hunting in the highlands.

If we go back to the earlier part of our two centuries there is little sign of any such subtleties or complexity of motive. Land and lordship were there in Scotland, if not quite for the taking then certainly for the asking. How much of the initiative came from the ruling dynasty, how much from a generation of adventurers and entrepreneurs whose appetite must surely have been keenly whetted by the massive land-seizure of 1066–86 in England, we have no means of telling. From Edgar onward the kings of Scotland wanted skilled foreign manpower, and from their point of view it must have been clear that the fewer ties the incomers had furth of Scotland the better. Abnormally, but notably in the case of Robert I de Brus, lord of Brix and Cleveland, who received Annandale in or before 1124,[46] the incoming settler was the senior member of his family and already well endowed. But at Robert de Brus's death in 1141 we observe that the main English estates passed to his elder son Adam de Brus, leaving the Scottish lands to the younger son Robert.[47] In general, the rule of England for the senior, Scotland for the junior line seems to have prevailed. It is precisely analogous to the practice already noted by Professor David Douglas[48] and critically discussed by Professor John Le Patourel[49]—namely that when a landowning Norman family acquired estates in England the Norman patrimony remained with or was left to the eldest son while the acquisitions north of the Channel went to the youngest or at any rate to younger sons. This practice often resulted in a reversal of ordinary expectations, for Norman fiefs tended to be small and chances of promotion through office-holding in Normandy remained relatively poor. Thus the younger son who ventured into England might soon outstrip his stay-at-home elder brother in breadth of acres, wealth of rentals, military power as expressed in castles and knight-service, and political influence wielded through office held in the royal household or in provincial

---

[46] Lawrie, *Charters*, no. 54 and p. 307, where, however, the statement that Robert de Brus was the son of a Norman who acquired many manors in Yorkshire is an error, since King David's follower and the Norman favoured by Henry I (who evidently gave him Cleveland) were one and the same man.

[47] Lawrie, *Charters*, 307; *Yorkshire Archaeological Journal*, xiii. 226–61.

[48] David C. Douglas, *William the Conqueror* (1964), 361.

[49] John Le Patourel, *The Norman Colonization of Britain* (Spoleto, 1969), 434–5; idem, *Normandy and England, 1066–1144* (The Stenton Lecture for 1970, University of Reading, 1971), 7–8; idem, *The Norman Empire* (Oxford, 1976), 183–4, 191–2.

government. This phenomenon, which might be called 'inverse expectation', reflects a colonializing period of legal development during which there was enough unity to give some protection and stability to property arrangements within families, but not yet so much uniformity that the rule by which the first-born son should take all would be applied throughout the territories involved.

The best-known Scots family to be founded in this period, the Stewarts, provide us with the most striking example of inverse expectation.[50] The pioneer of the family was Alan son of Flaald, hereditary seneschal of the bishops of Dol in eastern Brittany. Alan attached himself to Henry the youngest son of William the Conqueror, and benefited substantially, not to say spectacularly, after Henry had acquired the English throne, and especially after the fall of the house of Bellême in 1102. The rich heiress inevitably found for Alan was Avelina, daughter of Ernulf of Hesdin in Ponthieu, prominent in Domesday Book as a tenant-in-chief in ten counties, prominent in Reginald Lennard's study of *Rural England, 1066–1135* as an improving landlord.[51] Alan and Avelina had, it seems, three sons, Jordan, William, and Walter, while a brother of the last two named Simon may have been a son of Avelina by her second marriage. Jordan the first-born inherited the modest family patrimony in Brittany and his descendants never seem to have risen above knightly or minor baronial level.[52] William, the second son, inherited the larger share of the estates which Alan acquired north of the Channel and was ancestor of the great baronial house of FitzAlan, lords of Oswestry and eventually earls of Arundel.[53] Walter, evidently the third son, took service with David I of Scotland about 1136.[54] The king

---

[50] J. H. Round, *Studies in Peerage and Family History* (1901), 115–46; idem in *Genealogist* (NS), xviii (1902), 1–16. The article by Sir J. Balfour Paul and others on the Stewarts in *Scots Pge.*, i. 9–15 was one of the contributions criticized by Round, *Ancestor*, no. xi, 118–19, even although Balfour Paul and his colleagues had paid Round 'the compliment of adopting wholesale' Round's statements on Stewart origins. See also G. Washington, 'The origin of the Stewarts and the FitzAlans', *The Stewarts*, xii, no. 2 (1965), 143–6.
[51] R. V. Lennard, *Rural England, 1066–1135* (Oxford, 1959), 210–12.
[52] Round, *Studies in Peerage and Family History*, 126–8; idem (ed.), *Cal. Docs. France*, nos. 722, 1220, 1221.
[53] *Comp. Pge.* i. 239–41.
[54] Barrow, *Kingdom*, 338–9.

made him *dapifer*, steward, of his household, as an office to be held heritably by Walter's descendants.⁵⁵ King David, or perhaps his grandson King Malcolm IV, found a wife for Walter in Eschina de Londres (whose family will be discussed in Chapter IV), by whom Walter had an heir Alan whose own son and heir, a second Walter, adopted the more dignified title *senescallus* in place of *dapifer*.⁵⁶ This change of style was appropriate, for the holder of the office in his time became 'Stewart of Scotland' rather than merely steward of the king's household. The fifth Stewart of Scotland in succession to Walter I became king of Scots rather more than six hundred years ago. Knighthood and security for the eldest, Jordan, who took no risks. Wide lands and great lordships for William the second son, who may be said to have taken an appreciable risk. Even greater lordship, proportionately, and for his descendants a throne and a dynasty, for the third son Walter, who took the greatest risk of any. What of Simon, brother of William and Walter? With his usual brusque impatience J. H. Round proposed to dismiss him as 'merely a uterine or even a bastard brother'.⁵⁷ No doubt Round was all the readier to take this line because, as far as he knew, Simon appeared only in 'a Scottish publication', the *Registrum de Passelet*, the Maitland Club's edition of the cartulary of Paisley Abbey—even although the document in which he appears is a charter issued at Fotheringay in Northamptonshire, and shows the Stewart and his brother in the respectable company of Ailred of Rievaulx.⁵⁸ But in the unpublished cartulary of Castle Acre priory, Norfolk, a joint grant by Alan son of Flaald and his

---

⁵⁵ *RRS* i, no. 184.

⁵⁶ The change of title seems to have been connected with the attainment by Walter II son of Alan of his majority, c. 1219. In his earliest acts (*Paisley Reg.* 17–18; *Melrose Liber*, nos. 72, *72, 74) Walter II is styled *dapifer regis Scotie*, but in an act of 1219–20 (*Paisley Reg.* 1) he is styled *senescallus*. His father Alan normally had the style *dapifer*, although occasionally he appears as *senescallus*, e.g. in an unpublished charter for Malcolm grandson of Serlo of Edinburgh (SRO, J. M. Thomson's Notebooks 16, pp. 45–7, ex Polmaise Charter Chest), a lost charter to Alan of Thirlestane (*APS* vii. 138) and a grant to Christ Church, Canterbury (*The Stewarts*, ix, no. 3 (1953), 232). In a grant by Walter II for Canterbury of 7 July 1220 (ibid., 233) *senescalli* is perhaps a copyist's error for *senescallus*. The question of the minority of Walter II has been elucidated by William W. Scott, ibid. xiv, no. 1 (1972), 46–50.

⁵⁷ *Studies in Peerage and Family History*, 125, n. 3.

⁵⁸ *Paisley Reg.*, 2.

A Land for Younger Sons

wife Avelina de Hesdin of land belonging to Avelina's inheritance in Kempston, Sporle, and Newton is followed by a confirmation issued by Simon 'of Norfolk', who calls himself the son of Avelina and refers to a further grant by his brother William.[59] It would be wrong to suppose that Walter the Stewart was unaffected by the outlying Norfolk properties of his half-Breton, half-Pontevin family. His own Scottish charters were witnessed by his clerk Roger of Palgrave (in Norfolk)[60] and by Alexander de Hesdin.[61] There may even have been a link between the landholding family at Palgrave named Murdac, benefactors of Castle Acre,[62] and one Walter Murdac who turns up in the late twelfth century among the Stewart's circle of tenants and dependants, and was a benefactor of the Stewart's foundation at Paisley.[63]

Professor Le Patourel has warned us not to see any hard-and-fast rule in the custom of partition which reserved the continental patrimony for the eldest and left the possibly richer acquisitions north of the Channel to second or third sons.

---

[59] BL MS Harl. 2110, fo. 26. In his supplementary paper (*Genealogist*, NS xviii. 11–13), written after he had his attention drawn to the Castle Acre cartulary, Round believed that he had successfully demonstrated that Simon must have been the uterine brother of William and Walter sons of Alan, because in addition to being called their brother he was also called 'brother' by Margaret, daughter of Avelina de Hesdin's second husband Robert Fitz Walter by his first wife, Sybil de Chesney (de Quesnay). But Round did not allow for the possibility that there might have been two Simons, who used the surnames 'of Norfolk' and 'de Chesney' in order to be distinguished one from the other. The latter surname would have been very odd for a man who had no genealogical link with Sybil de Chesney; nor do we find one and the same Simon acknowledging fraternity simultaneously with the sons of Alan and the sons of Robert Fitz Walter by Sybil de Chesney.

[60] Raine, *North Durham*, no. 170.

[61] *Paisley Reg.*, 6 ('de Hesting'). Reginald 'de Asting' witnessed a charter of Walter I's son Alan (*Melrose Liber*, no. 67), and was perhaps the Reginald 'de Hedinge' who granted land at Aston Abbots (in Oswestry), Salop, to Haughmond Abbey (BL MS Add. 33354, fo. 8, a transcript of G.R.C. Davis, *Medieval Cartularies of Great Britain* (1958), no. 476).

[62] BL MS Harl. 2110, fo. 29 a twelfth-century charter of William Murdac, brother of Robert of Palgrave, granting property in Palgrave to Castle Acre priory. Among the small group of FitzAlan fees in Norfolk reported in reply to the enquiry of 1166 was one held by William of Palgrave (*RBE* i. 272).

[63] Walter Murdac was a twelfth-century benefactor of Paisley priory at Kirkurd (*Paisley Reg.*, 310, 412). He married Muriel, daughter and heir of an important tenant of Walter I and Alan, the first two Stewarts, named Peter son of Fulbert, *alias* Peter of Pollok, one of whose charters he witnessed (ibid., 98). With Muriel he acquired Rothes in Moray, which passed to their daughter Eve 'Morthach' (*Moray Reg.*, 458; see also ibid., nos. 106, 107, 111, 112; *Coupar Angus Chrs.* i, no. 12).

The greater Norman families [he says]⁶⁴ may already have been distinguishing between *propres* and *acquêts*, as in classical Norman custom . . . [but] it is difficult to be sure how general the practice was at this time [i.e. between 1066 and about 1100].

Where there was only one son to succeed there would clearly be no partition . . . There was nothing to prevent lands divided in one generation from coming together again: nothing to prevent a family based in one country from acquiring lands in the other—and in fact new cross-Channel estates, including some huge ones, were being created throughout the reign of Henry Beauclerk.

Mutatis mutandis, all Le Patourel's qualifications may be applied to families who held land in England or Normandy and subsequently acquired land in Scotland. But in contrast with England and Normandy, Scotland presented the man or the family who won land there with two peculiar features which must surely have worked in favour of partition. In the first place, there was the sheer distance and remoteness to be considered. There is nothing to suggest that the Scots kings, in creating generous fiefs for southern incomers, were willing to stock up their kingdom with absentee landlords. On the contrary, we may be sure that they expected value for money, as indeed we may see in the thirteenth century in their frequent requests to excuse the absence of their own feudatories from English courts and parliaments on the grounds that their services were needed at home.⁶⁵ Consequently, there must have been cases where greed, ambition, or family feeling were discouraged by the expense and inconvenience of trying to maintain an undivided patrimony in two or three countries. In 1251 a North Riding jury was asked whether Walter Bisset was seized of the manor of Ovington at the time of his death or whether his nephew Thomas had taken possession.⁶⁶ They replied that Walter had certainly been seized of the manor for many years before his death, but whether he was so seized at

---

⁶⁴ J. Le Patourel, *Normandy and England, 1066–1144,* 7, n. 10 and pp. 7–8
⁶⁵ e.g. *CDS* i, nos. 970 (1227), 2089 (1257), 2212, 2224 (1260), 2306 (1262), 2440 (1267), 2520 (1269); ii, nos. 40 (1275), 215, 219 (1282), and others. The same work lists numerous safe-conducts issued by the English chancery on behalf of barons and others holding land in England to allow them unmolested passage to Scotland.
⁶⁶ Ibid. i, no. 1836=*Cal. Inqu.* i, no. 251. The full story, with interesting details, is given in *Yorkshire Inquisitions* (Yorks. Arch. Soc. Record Ser.), i (1892), 26–7.

his death they could not say, 'for they know not the day of his death, nor can they know it. He died far away, in Scotland, in a certain island called Arran. Some say he died on Tuesday *before* Michaelmas, others that he died the Tuesday *after*, at Vespers; the truth is not yet known.'

It seems probable that only the richest and most powerful among the Anglo-Scottish aristocracy would be at pains to preserve the unity of an estate stretching perhaps from Wessex or the English Midlands to the Firth of Clyde. In 1200 Lachlan, *alias* Roland, son of Uhtred lord of Galloway,[67] remembered, or was reminded by his lawyers, that his wife Helen de Morville, heir of her father Richard and of her grandmother Beatrice de Beauchamp, was entitled to four knights' fees respectively at Bozeat, Northants, Whissendine and Whitwell in Rutland, Offord in Huntingdonshire and Houghton Conquest beside Bedford[68]—the 5 hides at Houghton having been originally acquired by Hugh de Beauchamp, Beatrice's grandfather, probably not long before 1086.[69] Roland of Galloway was ready to offer 500 marks to have the verdicts of four county juries, each of twelve good men and true, to vindicate his wife's claim. Whether or not he was successful we do not know, for he died almost in the act of making his bid. It is doubtful if there were many in the lower strata of feudal society who could afford to indulge such a long memory.

Secondly, and in the long run more importantly, there was the question of lordship and allegiance. For most of the century and a half between 1066 and 1204, any Norman taking lands in England knew that, whether or not he was a tenant-in-chief, his ultimate liege lord was the duke of the Normans; and for much of this period the equivalent was true for Manceaux and Bretons, for Angevins and Aquitanians. It seems probable that this consideration would also have held good for any Norman taking land in Scotland between 1097 and about 1135—namely, that while his new venture would obviously involve swearing allegiance to some new lord, perhaps the king of Scots, perhaps only a scion of the royal house such as David of Scotland

[67] Roland's alternative and probably 'true' name, Lo(c)hlan or Lachlan, appears in *Holyrood Charters*, no. 24 and *Cal. Charter R*. iii. 91. For later equations of Roland with Lachlan, see Barrow, *Kingdom*, 381, n. 2.
[68] *CDS* i, no. 294.
[69] *VCH, Bedford*, i. 200; iii. 290–1.

before his accession, or David's son Henry, it would not mean exchanging one lordship for another which was politically distinct, still less simultaneously accepting two incompatible lordships. The conflict of loyalty, in other words, for such a man would not have been more severe than that experienced by many feudatories of the post-Conquest generation, pondering, for example, whether their liege lord was Robert of Bellême or Robert Curthose or Henry Beauclerk. And it may be that even in the generations after 1135, as long as peace prevailed between the kings of England and Scotland, the question of divided allegiance remained in abeyance. But there are signs of a change in attitude from about the middle of David I's reign, with the death of Henry I and the succession of Stephen, to whom King David was careful not to do homage. Thus while Robert de Brus the elder formally defied King David in 1138 and remained loyal to the king of England, his younger son Robert adhered to the Scots.[70] In the same period some of the prominent families on the Honour of Huntingdon, for example Olifards and Lindsays, took the Scottish side,[71] while others, such as Grimbalds and Foliots, stayed with the rival line of Senlis earls.[72] As a direct result, neither Grimbald nor Foliot has become famous as a Scottish surname, while Lindsay and Oliphant need no comment. More serious and widespread problems of loyalty were occasioned by the great revolt against Henry II in 1173-4, when for example the Northumbrian Odinel de Umfraville and the Cumbrian Robert de Vaux took the English king's side[73] while the Northumbrian Thomas de Muschamp and the Cumbrian Hugh II de Morville, lord of Westmorland, supported the king of Scots.[74] Similar difficulties arose in 1215-16,[75] but hardly at all thereafter for some eighty years.

[70] Lawrie, *Charters*, 307
[71] *RRS* i. 100-1.
[72] Ibid.
[73] *Chron. Fantosme*, 28, 74-80 *passim* (Odinel de Umfraville), 62-6.
[74] *RRS* ii, nos. 147, 148, 175; *Pipe Roll, 21 Henry II*, 172; W. P. Hedley, *Northumberland Families*, i. 37, where it is shown that Thomas de Muscamp lord of Wooler took his mother's surname rather than that of his father Stephen of Bulmer. In an earlier generation Reginald de Muscamps had been an adherent of David I (Lawrie, *Charters*, nos. 35, 50). For Hugh de Morville, see below p. 75.
[75] William de Stuteville and Robert de Vieuxpont lord of Westmorland

Nevertheless, as definitions grew sharper during the twelfth and thirteenth centuries, and the dividing line between jurisdictions was drawn more tightly, there must have come into play, however gradually, an incentive to keep English estates distinct from Scottish. The first Stewart, with his holding at Cound in Shropshire, his estate of North Stoke near Arundel,[76] and his few acres at Manhood between Selsey and Chichester, an out-of-the-way spot immortalized by Rudyard Kipling,[77] exemplified a pattern which was to be followed by innumerable younger sons who set off to seek their fortunes in the north, many of them in the service of those three notable younger sons, King David I, King William I, and David earl of Huntingdon. Numerous though we know them to have been, these younger sons are a poorly chronicled and elusive band. The structure of Anglo-Norman feudal society and the character of the record to which it gave rise have made their eclipse inevitable. The documents overwhelmingly, and even the chronicles largely, tell of the triumphal progress of a monstrous regiment of eldest sons, their younger brothers trailing far behind and their sisters scarcely within sight. By way of conclusion to this first lecture, I have selected five men whose careers fell, precisely or approximately, into the pattern laid down by Walter the Stewart: John de Vaux, Robert de Quincy, Philip de Valognes, Philip de Moubray, and Robert of Mold or (to use the form of his name naturalized in Scotland) Robert Mowat.

A handful of royal charters surviving from the second half of Malcolm IV's reign, and several from the first two decades of William I's, are witnessed by John de Vallibus, de Wals, de

---

remained loyal to King John, while Robert's brother Ivo de Vieuxpont lord of Alston adhered to the king of Scots, as did Eustace de Vesci lord of Alnwick. See Holt, *Northerners*, 67, 82–3. Scottish links were not necessarily a matter of politics for English nobles, but might be connected with pilgrimage; e.g. a charter issued by Saher de Quinci apparently at Leuchars near St Andrews was witnessed by William (Longespee) earl of Salisbury (pro-John), Robert Fitz Walter (anti-John), and Baldwin Wake of Lincolnshire (*Cambuskenneth Reg.*, no. 73, badly copied). Similarly, Roger of Huntingfield (anti-John) appears to witness ibid., no. 71, before 1207.

[76] BL MS Harl. 2188, fo. 123ᵛ.

[77] R. W. Eyton, *Antiquities of Shropshire* (12 vols., 1853–60), vi. 70; *The Stewarts*, x, no. 2 (1956), 163. Kipling's poem 'Eddi's Service', published in *Rewards and Fairies* (1910), refers to the chapel at Manhood End.

Vaux—Vaux or Vans, to modernize his sadly unspecific surname.[78] Even though one of these charters was dated at Eldbotle in Dirleton (East Lothian),[79] we cannot be sure that John de Vaux was the first of his family to be lord of Dirleton, though it seems likely enough. For his continental origin we should look at a group of mid-twelfth-century charters relating to the district of Rouen issued by the Empress Maud, her son Henry, and their supporter Baldwin de Redvers, charters which were witnessed by Hubert and Godard de Vaux.[80] Hubert was the family's distinctive Christian name, for their other names, unhelpfully, were John, Robert, and William. Hubert I de Vaux was evidently one of Henry of Anjou's strong-arm men, and about the time that Henry deprived Malcolm IV of Cumberland he established Hubert as feudal lord of Gilsland, hard against the new Scottish Border, for the service of two knights—and, evidently, the building and maintenance of Brampton Castle.[81] One must suppose that at this point John de Vaux, as presumably a younger brother of Hubert, saw his opportunity and offered his services to the young king of Scots. Certainly the two lines of de Vaux kept up their links across the Border. In the 1160s, Hubert's son Robert founded a house for Augustinian canons at Lanercost,[82] and in the early thirteenth century John II de Vaux of Gullane

---

[78] *RRS* i, nos. 205, 221, 222, 228, 230, 255; ii, nos. 44, 116, 179, 188, 204, 238. See Black, *Surnames*, s.v. VANS. Like Wingate (from Uviet, O. E. Wulfgeat), Vans is a handful of Scots surnames which, however hard it may be to believe, have been transformed through confusion between 'u' and 'n'.

[79] Appendix A. This charter was omitted through ignorance from *RRS* i, in which no. 194 is dated at Eldbottle. In the medieval period, Dirleton and Eldbottle seem to have been included within Gullane parish, though there was a church of St. Nicholas on Fidra (Eldbottle Island), served by white canons of Dryburgh in the reign of Alexander II (*Dryburgh Liber*, nos. 23, 25, 26). Gullane was already called a serjeantry (*la sergaunterie*) in the time of William de Vaux, 12th cent., Raine, *North Durham*, no. 172.

[80] *Cal. Docs. France*, no. 1276; *BRAN* iii, nos. 71, 72, 112, 116a, 580, 665, 711, 748, 824–5, 836, 909. See also nos. 130, 587, 666, 795. Note that Roger 'de Hoto' witnessed a charter of the Empress Maud at Rouen (ibid., no. 607) while Robert and Reginald 'de Hotoft' ('de Hotot') witnessed charters of William de Vaux and his son John (II), Raine, *North Durham*, nos. 173–4. The name may refer to Hautot l'Auvray near Yvetot (dép. Seine-Maritime). Moreover, charters of William de Vaux were witnessed by a chaplain, bearing the de Vaux name of Godard, unfamiliar in Scotland (ibid., nos. 172–3).

[81] *VCH, Cumberland*, i. 310, 319 and facsimile intended to face p. 306 but, in the copy I have used, facing p. 320.

[82] Ibid. ii. 152.

and Dirleton endowed this house with land at Fenton and Kingston between Dirleton and North Berwick.[83] The late A. G. Little saw in a group of Haddington-centred stories in the Lanercost Chronicle evidence to support the notion of a basically Franciscan authorship for this chronicle first mooted by Joseph Stevenson;[84] but one of these stories relates to Fenton,[85] and since this estate belonged to Lanercost by gift of the de Vaux, it might be argued that not only this but other East Lothian passages derive from the Lanercost reshaping of a Franciscan narrative. A further link between the two branches of the family may be seen in 1213, when this same John II de Vaux, as the son of William de Vaux of Dirleton, was one of the fourteen noble hostages demanded by King John as security for the good behaviour of the king of Scots.[86] While in England John de Vaux was put in the custody of his cousin Robert de Vaux.[87] The fine castle of Dirleton,[88] which may have been the second successor to what William de Vaux in William the Lion's reign was already calling the 'old castle of Eldbottle',[89] proved a thorn in the flesh of Edward I's army in 1298 as it advanced to Falkirk.[90] Let us not be surprised at the thought of one branch of a Norman family defending the West March of England against the Scots while another branch defended the East March of Scotland against the English. It is an endearing characteristic of the English to adopt all the outsiders of their past history, and towards the Normans

[83] Mackenzie Walcott, 'A breviate of the cartulary of the priory church of Saint Mary Magdalene, Lanercost', *Transactions of the Royal Society of Literature*, 2nd ser. viii (1866), 453, 471, land of 'Kingiston' in Scotland and one furlong (*cultura*) in Fenton. The Hubert de Vaux who witnessed a charter of William de Vaux regarding Gullane (Raine, *North Durham*, no. 172) was presumably the Hubert son of John (I) de Vaux who witnessed two early charters for Lanercost (*Trans. Roy. Soc. Lit.*, 2nd ser. viii. 456, iii. 4, 5, and index).
[84] A. G. Little, *Franciscan Papers, Lists, and Documents* (Manchester, 1943), 45, n. 1, 48.
[85] *Chron. Lanercost*, 85.
[86] *Rot. Litt. Claus.* i. 137.
[87] For the chequered career of Robert de Vaux in King John's reign see Holt, *Northerners* (refs. in index).
[88] J. S. Richardson, *Dirleton Castle* (HMSO, 1950), refers to a single period of de Vaux castle building, but allows that a thirteenth-century stone castle superseded one of earth and timber. This account of the de Vaux begins with William, in William I's reign, omitting John I.
[89] *Dryburgh Liber*, no. 104.
[90] *Chron. Guisbrough*, 324-5.

in particular they are strangely possessive. For their part, the Normans had their own brand of possessiveness, not at all sentimental; what they wanted to possess was wealth and power, and they do not seem to have been unduly upset if that led to some curious contradictions. Consequently, we must learn to grow accustomed to the coexistence, within a single Anglo-Norman family whose interests lay astride the Border, of affection and suspicion, love and hatred. In the 1170s William of Lancaster, whose brother-in-law was the constable of Scotland, King William the Lion's right-hand man, speaks quite casually in a charter of land at Borrowdale, beside the great way running from Kendal to Penrith, of the 'pleshey', that is the pleached or interwoven hedge, which had to be built across Shap Summit 'on account of the Scots'.[91]

Robert de Quincy of Long Buckby in Northamptonshire is a less shadowy personage than John de Vaux.[92] A younger son of Saher I de Quincy, he belonged to a seigneurial family named from Cuinchy near Béthune in French Flanders.[93] The first Quincys probably came to England in the train of Gunfrid de Chocques, one of the many Flemings who came with or in the wake of the Conqueror.[94] More than a century later we find de Quincys acquiring by marriage the lordship of Henin-Liétard, near Douai, and acting as benefactors of the abbey there.[95] North of the Channel more adventurous de Quincys settled first of all in Northamptonshire, where Saher I married Maud de Senlis, stepdaughter of King David of Scotland who was one of the greatest landowners in that county.[96] Before the end of Malcolm IV's reign his son Robert de Quincy appears in Scotland in the king's service.[97] His earliest lands, like John de Vaux's, were in East Lothian, centred upon Tranent, but very soon a native heiress had been found for him in Orabilis

---

[91] *Hist. MSS Comm. 10th Rep.*, pt. 4, 323.

[92] The best guide to the family of de Quinci (de Quincy) is provided by the unpublished work of Grant G. Simpson, 'An Anglo-Scottish Baron of the thirteenth century. The acts of Roger de Quincy earl of Winchester and Constable of Scotland' (Edinburgh University Ph.D. thesis, 1965). See also Farrer, *HKF* i. 32–3; *Comp. Pge.* xii, pt. II, 745–54; Loyd, *Origins*, 84.

[93] Loyd, *Origins*, 84.

[94] Farrer, *HKF* i. 29 ff.

[95] J. Becquet, *L'Abbaye de Hénin-Liétard* (Paris, 1955), especially nos. 27, 40.

[96] G. G. Simpson, 'An Anglo-Scottish Baron', 9–10.

[97] *RRS* i. 283, n. 1.

daughter of Nes son of William, lord of Leuchars and Lathrisk and many other lands in Fife and Strathearn.[98] Since Nes had at least two sons, Constantine and Patrick,[99] there must be a suspicion that the succession to Nes's property had been forcibly diverted to Robert at the time of his marriage. The son of Robert and Orabilis, Saher de Quincy, whom King John made earl of Winchester in 1207,[100] was one of the richest and most powerful barons of Scotland, and long after the death in 1264, without sons, of Saher's son Roger de Quincy, earl of Winchester and constable of Scotland, the solidarity of the baronies built up by Robert de Quincy was still reflected in the succession arrangements among Earl Roger's heirs or those who benefited from their forfeiture.[101] A generation or two spent by the de Quincys in England did not prevent Robert importing fellow-Flemings into Scotland —Philip de Vermelles,[102] Robert de Béthune (whence 'Beaton'),[103] Roger de Orchies, Robert de Carvin, Hugh de Lens, and Alan de Courrières.[104]

Philip de Valognes was the third son in the mid-twelfth-century generation of a family from western Normandy which had been settled in England, especially in East Anglia and Essex, since soon after the Conquest.[105] It seems that Philip 'went to Scotland' at the start of William the Lion's reign, and was soon provided with land, first of all at Ringwood near Hawick[106] and later at Benvie and Panmure in Angus.[107] At

[98] G. G. Simpson, 'An Anglo-Scottish Baron', 12.
[99] *St. Andrews Liber*, 291. Nevertheless, Orabilis is explicitly called Nes's heir (ibid. 254, 290), so her brothers may have been of illegitimate birth.
[100] *Comp. Pge.* xii, pt. ii, 749.
[101] G. G. Simpson, 'An Anglo-Scottish Baron', 48–70.
[102] *Newbattle Reg.*, nos. 64, 125; Barrow, *Kingdom*, 329.
[103] *St. Andrews Liber*, 354.
[104] SRO GD 241/254, an unpublished knight-service charter, *c.* 1170, given by Robert de Quinci to Paganus (Pain) 'de Hedleia', witnessed by Roger 'de Orgis', Robert 'de Carvent' and Hugh 'de Lens', these being twelfth-century forms for, respectively, Orchies (dép. Nord), Carvin and Lens (dép. Pas de Calais); *SHR* xxx (1951), 43–5, an agreement of 1170 witnessed by (among others) Pain 'de Heleia' and Alan 'de Cureres' and his son, Cureres being a form for Courrières (dép. Pas de Calais); see Barrow, *Kingdom*, 319.
[105] *Panmure Reg.* ii. 86 ff.; *RRAN* i, nos. 93, 129, 235, 242, 258, 346; J. H. Round, 'Comyn and Valoignes', *Ancestor*, no. xi (1904), 129–35, esp. the table on p. 133.
[106] *Melrose Liber*, no. 150 (1165 X 72), a charter endorsed 'not to be shown without advice'.
[107] *RRS* ii, no. 405.

Ringwood he was successor to Uhtred son of Osulf, and since Uhtred had at least two sons, Thomas and Ralph,[108] there is once again a suspicion that Philip de Valognes either supplanted Uhtred or was put in over him by that royal *vis et voluntas* familiarized by the late J. E. A. Jolliffe.[109] At different periods during King William's long reign, Philip de Valognes enjoyed the office of chamberlain,[110] in which he seems to have alternated with Walter de Berkeley (Berkley) until the closing years of the twelfth century. The family to which Philip belonged was far too powerful and widely ramified for them to lose sight of even a third son who had migrated to Scotland. The Valognes pedigree is studded with some of the greatest names in Anglo-Norman history—de Varenne, du Hommet, de Mandeville earl of Essex, Robert FitzWalter, and others. When the heiress of the Honour of Valognes died in 1233, leaving no children by either of her marriages, three Scottish ladies, the daughters of Philip's son William, successfully claimed their equal shares in the English lands, chiefly in Essex.[111] The eldest of the three, Lora, had already brought the chamberlainship of Scotland to her husband Henry Balliol;[112] their son Alexander, lord of Cavers by Hawick and also an extensive landowner in England, might also be regarded as the personification of that Scots nobility castigated by Joseph Stevenson for putting their English estates before their Scottish patriotism.[113] And yet, as the Scots surname Vallance clearly demonstrates, a family whose loyalties waver in the main stem may become firmly established in its younger offshoots.[114]

We remain on the commanding heights of the Anglo-French aristocracy in considering the case of Philip de Moubray, who to judge from charter witness lists and other evidence had become one of the king's closest companions and councillors in the last decade of William the Lion's reign.[115] Philip was a

---

[108] *Melrose Liber*, nos. 9, 149.
[109] J. E. A. Jolliffe, *Angevin Kingship* (2nd edn., 1963), esp. pp. 50–86.
[110] *RRS* ii. 33.
[111] *Ancestor*, no. xi, 133–4.
[112] J. A. C. Vincent, *Genealogist* (NS), vi. 1–7; J. Greenstreet, in *Notes and Queries*, 6th ser., v (1882), 142–3.
[113] Stevenson, *Documents*, i, pp. lii–liii.
[114] Black, *Surnames*, s.v. VALLANCE.
[115] *RRS* ii, nos. 393–524 *passim* (references in index). Philip was constable of Edinburgh 1211 × 15 (*Dunfermline Reg.*, no. 189).

younger brother of William de Moubray, one of the 'Northerners' among the Magna Carta baronage.[116] They were great-grandsons of one of Henry I's henchmen, Nigel, from St. Martin-d'Aubigny in western Normandy, a principal figure in what might be called without exaggeration the 'second Norman conquest', at least of northern England. The preservation of the name Moubray is a striking instance of that passionate, surprisingly un-Scandinavian Norman love of surnames and belief that Honour and surname went together —something which the Normans most emphatically bequeathed to Scotland. In the rebellion of 1173–4 Philip de Moubray's grandfather Roger had ostentatiously attached himself to King William of Scotland's forces,[117] and although neither Roger himself nor his son Nigel seems to have acquired land in Scotland it is hardly surprising that the king of Scots should have shown favour to Philip by giving him in marriage Galiena, daughter and coheir of Waltheof son of Cospatric, native lord of Moncreiffe south of Perth and also of Dalmeny and Inverkeithing, at the south and north ends respectively of the crucially important Queensferry across the Forth.[118] In his new position, Philip de Moubray became patron of one ancient Scottish family, Dundas of that ilk, and may be said to have been in the founding of another, Moncreiffe of that ilk,[119] if as seems possible that family may be traced to one of Philip's knightly vassals.[120]

[116] *Comp. Pge.* ix. 373–6; Holt, *Northerners*, 10, 16, and elsewhere *passim*.

[117] *Chron. Fantosme*, 44, 60–2, 68. For Roger's almost equally ostentatious flight after King William's capture at Alnwick, ibid. 84, where Fantosme explains that Roger, not being a vassal of the king of Scots and therefore a traitor to King Henry, could not risk being taken along with King William and his own vassals. See also Greenway, *Mowbray Charters*, pp. xxix–xxxi.

[118] *Dunfermline Reg.*, nos. 165, 166, 211; *Scots Pge.* iii. 244–5. For Galiena as heiress of Moncreiffe, see *Moncreiffs*, ii, Appendix, no. I.

[119] Dundas was granted to Elias son of Uhtred, ancestor of the family of Dundas of that ilk, by Waltheof son of Cospatric, in the later twelfth century (*APS* i. 92). For a later Elias of Dundas in the entourage of Philip de Moubray's sons Roger and Nigel, see *Inchcolm Charters*, no. 17.

[120] The earliest recorded member of the Moncreiffe family was David, to whom Patrick of 'Nagtun' surrendered land *c.* 1227–30 (*Moncreiffs*, ii, Appendix, no. II). 'Nagtun' may be identified with Nawton, 3 miles east of Helmsley in the North Riding of Yorkshire, in the territory of the Honour of Mowbray (Greenway, *Mowbray Charters*, 263–4). It is noteworthy that the first known tenant of Kinmonth in Moncreiffe under Philip and Galiena de Moubray was a Hugh son of William, who has the same name as an earlier person found in a Moubray context witnessing

Like the Valognes, the Moubrays were too distinguished and well connected to allow their links to be severed with their rich relations in Yorkshire. Philip's son Nigel was one of the young Scottish hostages of 1213, and placed in the custody of William de Moubray.[121] Indeed, the Scottish branch of the family and its dependants still held land in Moubray territory, e.g. at Islebeck and Dalton near Thirsk, as late as 1296.[122] It would not be unjust to say that the Scots Moubrays played an ambiguous role in the first war of independence, identifying themselves closely with John Balliol and only making their peace with Robert Bruce tardily and reluctantly. Their position is neatly illustrated by the conduct of a later Sir Philip de Moubray who, though a Scot, commanded Stirling Castle for Edward II in 1313 but was of course compelled to yield it to King Robert after Bannockburn. His successor, Roger de Moubray, duly set his seal to the Declaration of Arbroath, the Scots barons' letter to the pope in 1320,[123] but almost immediately afterwards he and several other Moubrays were implicated in the de Soules conspiracy against the king.[124] The family incurred considerable forfeiture, surviving in later centuries in a comparatively modest way as barons of Barnbougle, in West Lothian.[125]

For my last example, Robert de Monte Alto, Robert Mowat, I shall move to a less exalted but probably more typical

---

a charter of 1163 × 69 relating to land adjoining Nawton (*EYC* i. 139-40, no. 164).

The origin of the knightly family of Moncreiffe of that ilk (who emerge clearly only in the 1240s in the person of Sir Matthew of Moncreiffe, for whom see *Moncreiffs*, ii, Appendix, nos. III-VIII) is unknown, but, on the male side at least, their use of scriptural personal names argues against native origin, and their evidently close connection with the Moubrays suggests immigration from the Honour of Mowbray.

[121] *Rot. Litt. Claus.* i. 137. The Scottish Moubrays' continuing links with the English stem are emphasized by the fact that Sir Oliver 'de Bu(s)ci' was the *socius* of Philip de Moubray in Scotland (*Arbroath Liber*, no. 119), for the de Buscy family was prominent among the tenants of the Honour of Mowbray in England (Greenway, *Mowbray Charters*, *passim*, references in index under Oliver, Ralph, and Robert de Buscy, twelfth century).

[122] *CDS* ii. 172 (para. 6); Greenway, *Mowbray Charters*, nos. 63, 353-4. John, son and heir of Gilbert of Islebeck tenant of Roger de Moubray in 1296, was then in the service of Archibald bishop of Moray; this was presumably the John of Islebeck who served as a juror in 1303 (*Yorkshire Inquisitions*, iii. 176).

[123] J. Fergusson, *The Declaration of Arbroath* (Edinburgh, 1970), 4-5.

[124] Barrow, *Bruce*, 429-30.

[125] *Scots Pge.* ii. 145; vi. 415; Nisbet, *Heraldry*, ii, Appendix, 21-2.

milieu than the Valognes and Moubray families. Robert was evidently a younger son in an early-thirteenth-century generation of the family which had held the hereditary stewardship of the earldom of Chester for over a hundred years.[126] Their surname was taken from Mold in Flintshire, where a French name, *le mont haut*, 'the high (castle) hill', had characteristically been given to the fortification built at Bistre by Hugh Fitz-Norman or his brother Ralph in the early days of the Conquest.[127] David of Scotland earl of Huntingdon married Maud daughter of Hugh of Cyfeiliog earl of Chester in August 1190.[128] The first members of the Mowat family to appear in Scotland seem to have been a certain Alexander of Mold or Mowat, described as chaplain to Ralph bishop of Brechin[129] (who had himself been chaplain to King William in the 1180s and '90s),[130] and a William of Mold who likewise appears in Bishop Ralph's company, about 1201.[131] At this period the hereditary seneschal of Chester was Ralph (II) de Mowat, who died about 1208,[132] being succeeded briefly by his brother Robert (II), who was in turn succeeded by his son Roger (I) before 1211.[133] At some date between 1212 and *c.* 1225–6 another Robert de Mowat—presumably a kinsman in a younger branch of the family—appears in the entourage of William Comyn earl of Buchan.[134] From then until the 1250s

[126] *The Domesday Survey of Chester*, ed. J. Tait (Chetham Soc., NS lxxv, 1916), 50–1, 241; Farrer, *HKF* ii, pp. vi and 110–2.
[127] Tait, *Domesday Survey of Chester*, 51.
[128] *Chron. Melrose*, 47; *Comp. Pge.* vi. 647.
[129] *Arbroath Liber*, nos. 185; see also nos. 174, 179–80, 182–4, 194. Alexander, who in *Coupar Angus Chrs.*, no. 10 is styled Alexander parson 'de Mualt' (this last doubtless merely a surname, not a reference to his benefice), was also clerk or chaplain to Bishop Hugh, 1214–18 (*Arbroath Liber*, nos. 78, 175, 186, 190, 195).
[130] *RRS* ii. 32.
[131] *Coupar Angus Chrs.*, no. 10; see also *Arbroath Liber*, no. 228 (1219) relating to the Forfar area.
[132] Farrer, *HKF* ii, pp. vi, 111.
[133] Ibid.; but note that G. Barraclough states that Roger I had succeeded to the stewardship by May 1204, citing *Cheshire Sheaf*, no. 7804 (*A Medieval Miscellany for Doris Mary Stenton*, ed. P. M. Barnes and C. F. Slade (P.R.Soc., NS xxxvi, 1960), 39).
[134] *Cambuskenneth Reg.*, p. xxx, n. 1, 'R. of Mwhantis'; *St. Andrews Liber*, 250–3; *Arbroath Liber*, no. 130; SRO RH 1/2/32, GD 101/2. I have been helped here by A. Young, 'The political role of the Comyns in Scotland and England in the thirteenth century' (Newcastle upon Tyne University Ph.D. thesis, 1974, unpublished), 113–14. The Scottish Robert de Mowat may perhaps have been a younger brother of Roger I steward of Chester. He is less likely to have been a son

he and his brother Michael were increasingly prominent in the affairs of eastern Scotland north of Tay, often associated with one or other chief of the powerful Comyn family, but also holding important crown offices such as sheriffdoms or even, at least jointly, the justiciarship of Scotia.[135] In England, there was some link between the family of Mowat and the Lincolnshire family of Orby of Dalby, who provided three justiciars of Chester in the thirteenth century;[136] and it is worth noting that in the 1220s and '30s two prominent servants of Andrew Murray bishop of Moray were Simon of Orby and Simon of Gunby—a village where the Orbys held property.[137]

The five men whose careers I have briefly sketched were all younger sons whose immediate origins lay in England but whose background, more or less remotely, was continental. Beyond that, however, they had little in common. The precise circumstances in which each made his decision to seek his fortune in Scotland are hidden from us. Not one of them, as far as we know, with the doubtful exception of Robert de Quincy, was connected territorially or tenurially with the Scottish Crown, nor had any of them close family ties with Anglo-Continental adventurers who had already established themselves north of the Border. The clue to their careers and success is surely to be found on the one hand in a monarchy gradually transforming Scotland into a feudal kingdom and in need of men with a particular background and possessing particular skills and experience, and, on the other hand, in the existence of a remarkable social mobility among the military and governing class of northern France and that part of it which had spilled over into England. It would not be hard to find parallels for

---

of Roger, brother of Ralph II de Mowat, for that Roger seems to have had only a daughter named Leuca (Farrer, *HKF* ii. 271–2).

[135] A. Young, 'Political role of the Comyns', 114; Barrow, *Kingdom*, 137 (this source, drawn to my attention by Professor D. E. R. Watt, was known to the eighteenth-century antiquary Alexander Nisbet: Nisbet, *Heraldry*, ii, Appendix 123).

[136] Farrer, *HKF* ii. 99–100, 271–2. Farrer draws attention to Roger II de Mowat's being on Henry III's Gascon expedition of 1244 with David de Mowat, whom he calls ancestor of the Mohauts of Blair in Scotland (ibid. 112), but he gives no reference for this last statement.

[137] *Moray Reg.*, nos. 59, 64, 65, 79, 80, 87; Farrer, *HKF* ii. 100. A later Simon of Orby is mentioned by Farrer in his account of Newton Solney, Derbyshire, ibid. 42.

John de Vaux, Robert de Quincy, Philip de Valognes, Philip de Moubray, and Robert Mowat. But their story will serve well enough to show that whatever might be written by English chroniclers or thought by French kings and princesses, the younger sons of north-west Europe in the twelfth and thirteenth centuries could indeed find in Scotland a land of opportunity and a career open to the talents.

II

The Pattern of Settlement

OVER much of Scotland, especially south of the Forth–Clyde line, the Anglo-Norman era was characterized by large-scale colonization of the land. Surviving record shows incomers from the south in almost every parish of southern Scotland except in Galloway and Carrick, while north of the Forth there was fairly intensive settlement in Fife, Gowrie, Angus, and Mearns, the Aberdeenshire districts of Garioch and Formartine and across most of the lowland country between the Spey and the Beauly River—the region known in later times as 'The Laich of Moray'. In the extreme south-west of Scotland, and in the Highlands proper, Anglo-Norman settlement had in general made little headway even as late as the death of Alexander III in 1286, but there were notable exceptions in some of the long valleys of Perthshire, e.g. Strathearn, Strath Tay, and Strathardle, in the central highland district of Badenoch, and in the eastern parts of the earldom of Ross and of that south-east extremity of the earldom of Caithness already known as Sutherland and recognized before the close of the thirteenth century as an earldom in its own right. Even in Carrick and Galloway there had been Anglo-Norman incursion, beginning about 1160, which was intended to be permanent. But here—and in parts of the Highlands—the impression left by admittedly scanty record strikingly resembles the chequered and wavering progress familiar to historians of the Anglo-Norman conquest of Wales[1] and Ireland[2]—rapid gains and rashly deep penetration of hostile territory being followed by reverses, setbacks,

---

[1] J. E. Lloyd, *The History of Wales from the Earliest Times to the Edwardian Conquest* (2 vols., 4th edn., 1948), ii, chapters XI–XIII; J. G. Edwards, 'The Normans and the Welsh March', *Proc. Brit. Acad.* xlii (1956), 155–77, esp. p. 164; see also *Glamorgan County History*, iii (1971), 23–4, 33–9.

[2] A. J. Otway-Ruthven, *A History of Medieval Ireland* (1968), esp. chapters II and III.

and withdrawal, in turn succeeded by a slower and more prudent advance and consolidation or by more or less permanent abandonment of areas which had once seemed attractive to settlement. Thus, as a consequence of Malcolm IV's subjugation of Galloway in 1160, Hugh de Morville the younger, son of Hugh de Morville the elder who died, as constable of the king of Scots and founder of Dryburgh Abbey, in 1162, was put in possession of Borgue,[3] between Kirkcudbright and Gatehouse of Fleet, but evidently abandoned this estate after the anti-foreign revolt of Uhtred and Gilbert of Galloway in 1174, when, as Roger of Howden tells us, the Gallovidians slew or expelled the officials placed over them by the Scottish Crown, killed many Frenchmen and Englishmen, and destroyed those castles—no doubt of the motte and bailey type—which the incomers had had time to erect in that stubbornly separatist province.[4]

Again, Thomas de Colville—another of our younger sons, of the Yorkshire–Lincolnshire family which held the lordship of Drax and of Castle Bytham[5]—took part in the second attempt at feudalizing Galloway, serving as constable of Dumfries castle about 1190[6] and acquiring land on the borders of King's Kyle and Carrick, well inside the intensely Gaelic-speaking area of the south-west, an investment which seems to have earned him the name of Thomas 'the Scot'.[7] He granted

---

[3] *Dryburgh Liber*, no. 68. It is suggested here (contrary to what has been assumed hitherto, e.g. Lawrie, *Charters*, 421; P. H. McKerlie, *History of the Lands and their Owners in Galloway* (Paisley, 1906), i. 121–2; R. C. Reid, *Wigtownshire Charters* (SHS, 1960), pp. xvi–xvii; *RRS* i. 13, n. 2) that this Dryburgh charter was issued by Hugh II de Morville, lord of Westmorland, one of the murderers of Archbishop Thomas Becket. Hugh, who is not styled constable, makes his grant to Dryburgh for the soul of his father, i.e. (if this suggestion is correct) Hugh the constable, founder of Dryburgh. Hugh the constable and his son witnessed an act of Malcolm IV of 1153 X 62 (*RRS* i, no. 125, where the note should be disregarded). The names of father (already dead) and son appear in a charter for St. Peter's Hospital, York, given by Thorphin of Allerston (*CWAAS Trans.*, NS xi (1911), 311), while Hugh the younger confirmed to Byland Abbey land at Asby in Westmorland which it had held in his father's time (ibid. ix, 1909, 253–4).

[4] *Chron. Howden*, ii. 63; *Gesta Henrici II*, i. 67–8.

[5] Documents relating to William de Colville as lord of Castle Bytham, witnessed by, i.a., Thomas de Colville (*c*. 1226), are in *RAL* iii, nos. 1019–20. For the Colvilles at Drax see *Chron. Stephen*, i. 94; Henry of Huntingdon. *Historia Anglorum* (ed. T. Arnold, Rolls ser., 1879), 291; *EYC* vi. 168–70.

[6] *St. Bees Reg.*, no. 60.

[7] *Melrose Liber*, nos. 192, 193; *Chron. Melrose*, 54.

a big hill-farm at Dalmellington to the Cistercians of Vaudey,[8] but by 1223 the Lincolnshire monks were forced to transfer this estate to Melrose abbey because it was, they said, 'useless and dangerous to them, both on account of the absence of law and order, and by reason of the insidious attacks of a barbarous people'.[9] Five years later, precisely such an attack was launched against the motte castle which had been built at Abertarff, at the southern end of Loch Ness, by the Berwickshire baron Thomas of Thirlestane[10]—perhaps not a Norman himself, but ancestor of the Scoto-Norman family of Maltalent or Maitland.[11] Thomas was slain and his castle razed. But these and other episodes were no more than setbacks, and did not mean a serious reversal of the long-term process of normanization. The Colvilles might vanish from the Doon valley but that did not prevent the earldom of Carrick passing into the hands of the Anglo-Norman family of Bruce by 1272; Abertarff might be sacked, but the Anglo-Norman family of Bisset still retained the neighbouring district of Stratherrick,[12] and from them it passed, still more permanently, to the Anglo-Norman family of Fraser.

It is natural to ask how far the existing, native population was displaced or dispossessed by Anglo-Norman settlement in those parts of the country where this was obviously intensive, e.g. in Lothian and the Merse, Teviotdale, Tweeddale, and Scottish Cumbria. Natural though the question must be, it is not at all easy to answer. We need to bring together all the relevant evidence, scattered as it is among charters and

---

[8] *Melrose Liber*, nos. 192, 193 ('Almelidun'=Dalmellington, through assimilation of 'de' before the name; 'Keresban'=Carsphairn). Note that it was from Castle Bytham that Henry III issued a writ (1221) commanding the justiciar of Ireland to allow the monks of Vaudey dwelling at 'Kar' (=Carsphairn) in Galloway to buy victuals in Ireland (*CDS* i, no. 795).

[9] *Melrose Liber*, no. 195.

[10] *Chron. Bower*, ii. 57, bk. IX, cap. xlvii (where for *quendam latronem* read *quendam baronem*). See *Moray Reg.*, no. 28 (1225). The royal archives in 1282 contained a charter of Abertarff, a charter of Thomas of Thirlestane, and a quitclaim by Richard Mautaland of the land of Abertarff (*APS* i. 110).

[11] *Scots Pge.* v. 276–8. Cf. *Dryburgh Liber*, nos. 123, 126 for Richard Maitland as successor to Thomas of Thirlestane.

[12] The royal archives in 1282 contained a charter of Walter Bisset of 'Strathark'k', to be identified as Stratherrick (*APS* i. 110); cf. *Beauly Chrs.* 33–7. For the name see also *Moray Reg.*, p. 31, where for the printed 'Stratharedoch' read (as corrected from the MS) 'Stratharchoch' (1236).

chronicles, in surviving and obsolete place-names, in remains or traces still to be seen on the ground of motte castles, village sites, parish kirks, and dependent chapels, and we shall be constantly aware that this evidence is variable in quality and will never seem sufficient in quantity. As we follow the sequence of maps which form the core of this chapter, we may bear in mind one or two general considerations. In the first place, it will hardly need arguing that the incomers were not settling an empty land. To this day there survives across southern Scotland from the Firth of Clyde to the North Sea a conspicuous stratum of Brittonic or Cumbric place-names, e.g. Paisley, Renfrew, Glasgow, Lanark, Peebles, and Melrose, which can scarcely have been formed anywhere later than the early eleventh century and which on the east side of the country at least, e.g. in names such as Tranent or Aberlady, must go back to the seventh century or earlier.[13] Overlying this stratum here and there, especially in the eastern seaboard, is that thinner layer of oldest Anglian names (seventh–eighth century?), e.g. Auldhame, Tynninghame, Whittingeham, Oldhamstocks, Kimmerghame, Birgham, and Yetholm.[14] The preservation of all these names, many of them belonging to important centres, proves continuity of settlement among a relatively stable population. A second consideration concerns the distribution of races and languages. We need not doubt that at the start of the twelfth century south-eastern Scotland—Scottish Northumbria—was thoroughly English in speech and broadly English or Anglo-Scandinavian in culture, even though the basic population was probably something of a mixture of old Brittonic, Votadinian stock, and an Anglian strain which had had many generations to work its way down from the dominant warrior families of the earliest Germanic settlement. Between the mid-tenth century and the end of the eleventh a certain Scottish, that is to say Gaelic-speaking, element had been intruded into this Anglo-Brittonic mixture, perhaps amounting to no more than a modest scoticizing of the landholding class. The resulting amalgam seems to be nicely symbolized in the

---

[13] Watson, *CPNS* 358, 360, 459–60; Nicolaisen, *Scottish Place-Names*, 164, 168. No doubt all the names mentioned (along with many others) go back to the seventh century or earlier.

[14] For the earliest Anglian stratum see Nicolaisen, op. cit. 20–3, 68–83.

personal names of a late-twelfth-century freeholder of Coldinghamshire, Liulf son of Elgi, and his five sons: Cospatric (Brittonic), Gamal (Scandinavian), Macbeth (Scots), Reginald (Anglo-Norman), and Eggard (Old English).[15]

On the west side of southern Scotland the mixture was even more pronounced. The great fascination which English Cumbria has always had for place-name scholars lies in the fact that as soon as adequate record becomes available one may see the melting pot in action with its ingredients still in the molten state.[16] Exactly the same is true of Scottish Cumbria, of which an anonymous clerk of St. Mungo's church at Glasgow remarked about 1120: 'in the long period which has elapsed since Saint Mungo's death different tribes belonging to different races have poured in from all the airts and settled this deserted region. Racially distinct and differing in speech and ways of life, they have found it hard to live peaceably together and have practised heathenism rather than holding to the Christian faith.'[17] As late as c. 1200 a panel of men appointed to perambulate the marches of Stobo west of Peebles epitomizes the Cumbrian melting pot.[18] The list begins with Sir Adam son of Gilbert and Sir Milo Cornet (we could hardly ask for names more redolent of the continental incomers), continues with Sir Adam son of Edulf, head of a native family which had not been submerged, and then among some twenty-eight other names includes John Ker the hunter at Swinehope, Gillemihhel Queschutbrit[19] at Traquair, Mihhyn 'Brunberd' at 'Corrukes', Cospatric 'Romefare' (pilgrim to Rome), Gilmor 'Hund' at Dawyck, Coso(s)uold son of Murin at Oliver Castle, Dodin of Broughton, and Matthew, James, and John sons of Cosmungho the priest of Eddleston. At first glance it is the polyglot quality of the list which strikes us, but on closer inspection the feature which seems even more interesting in what is after all a Latin docu-

---

[15] Raine, *North Durham*, no. 388.
[16] A. M. Armstrong, A. Mawer, F. M. Stenton, and Bruce Dickins, *The Place-Names of Cumberland* (EP-NS, 3 vols., 1950–2), esp. pt. 3, Introduction.
[17] Lawrie, *Charters*, p. 45.
[18] *Glasgow Reg.*, no. 104.
[19] Queschutbrit for Cumbric *gwas*, 'vassal' or 'servant', hence 'devotee', with Cuthbert; cp. the contemporary East Fife name Gillequdberit, a Q-Celtic equivalent (*North Berwick Carte*, no. 4).

ment is the markedly English flavour of the qualifying elements, 'Brunberd', 'Romefare', 'Hund', an English element among the saints mentioned (Cuthbert, Oswald), and the use of Middle English *swire*, 'neck' in the document's account of the marches newly perambulated.[20] This unmistakable English ascendancy in a context of four vernaculars—Cumbric, Gaelic, English, and French—is closely in line with what we find generally in twelfth- and thirteenth-century charters,[21] and warns us to be on our guard when so many of the personal names in our record obviously belong to either a French or Flemish-speaking milieu.

It is with these continental personal names that our sequence of illustrations begins. The first (Table 1(a)) shows us some thirty names either of continental (chiefly Germanic) origin, or else drawn from the Scriptures and therefore not normal in this form to the native usage even of southern Scotland. All are known to have been used in the formation of names of permanent settlements before *c.* 1250. Admittedly, we have no *terminus post quem* for these settlements, but most are unlikely to have arisen before 1100 and many can be shown to belong to the century from *c.* 1150 to 1250. One name on the list is Milo or Miles, for that very same Milo Cornet whom we have just seen perambulating the marches of Stobo evidently bequeathed his name to the estate of Myles in Tranent, where he was the tenant of Robert and Saher de Quincy.[22] Myles and Clarabad, the name of another farm, this time in Berwickshire,[23] are

[20] 'Whiteshopessuirles', 'Glemubsuirles', no longer identifiable, but presumably referring to two of the pronounced cols between hills on the south-west boundary of Stobo parish.

[21] See Appendix C.

[22] Milo Cornet witnessed a twelfth-century charter of Robert de Quinci (*St. Andrews Liber*, 354), an early thirteenth-century charter of Saher de Quinci *Dunfermline Reg.*, no. 155) and an agreement of 1222 between Holyrood Abbey and Roger de Quinci (*Holyrood Liber*, no. 62). The link with Myles is provided by an unpublished charter of Simon Korneth son of John Korneth dealing with the land of 'Mylis' (SRO AD 1/7).

[23] Earlier forms for Clarabad in Hutton, Berwickshire, are Clarobald, 1465, Claribald, 1518, Clarebald, 1542, Clariebauld, 1705 (*Hist. MSS Comm., Report on Various Collections*, v (1909), Mordaunt Hay, Duns Castle, 65–7). A thirteenth-century tack by Clarembald 'de Esseby' (i.e. of Castle Ashby, Northants, evidently a dependant of the Olifards), of a fishery at Fishwick in the same parish, 1½ miles from Clarabad, is in Raine, *North Durham*, no. 158. See Farrer, *HKF* ii. 334 and *EYC* vii (Honour of Skipton), 112–13.

Table 1 Colonization: the formation of place-names

(a) Continental and scriptural personal names used to form place-names before c. 1250

Personal name	Place-name
AGNES [DE BRUS]	Annieston, Lan[arkshire]
BEREWALD	Borrowstoun (Bo'ness), W[est] Lo[thian]
BODRIC	Botherickfield, Renf[rewshire]
CLAREMBALD	Clarabad, Berw[ickshire]
	Clermiston, M[id] Lo[thian]
[ROBERT] CROC	Crookston, Renf.
DODIN	Duddingston (2), M.Lo., W.Lo.
FOLCARD	Folkerton, Lan.
GOCELYN	'Gocelyneston', M.Lo.
HERVEY	'Rula Herevei' (Abbotrule), Roxb[urghshire]
	Harviestoun, Clackmannanshire (?)
HUGH	Houston or Houstoun (3), E[ast] Lo[thian], Renf., W.Lo.
JOHN	Crawford John, Lan.
	Johnstone, Dumf[riesshire]
LAMBIN	Lamington, Lan.
LEVING	Livingston, W.Lo.
LOCCARD	Lockerbie, Dumf.
MALGER	Mangerton, Roxb. (?)
[GEOFFREY DE] MELVILLE	Melville, M.Lo.
MILES (MILO)	Myles, E.Lo.
MORICE	Morriston, Berw.
NEIL (NIGEL)	Neilston, Renf.
PAGAN (PAIN)	Penston, E.Lo.
PETER (PIERS)	Pearsby, Dumf.
	Perceton, Ayr[shire]
PHILIP	Philpstoun, W.Lo.
PHILIP D'EU	Philpingston, W.Lo.
RALPH (RAOUL)	Ralston, Renf.
RICHARD	'Ricardestun', Perthshire
	Riccarton (3), Ayr., Roxb., W.Lo.
ROBERT	'Roberdesbi', Dumf.
	Roberton (2), Lan., Roxb.
SIMON (SIMUND)	Symington (2), Ayr., Lan.
SIBBALD	Sibbaldbie, Dumf.

Personal name	Place-name
STEPHEN (STEVEN)	Stevenson, E.Lo.
	Stevenston, Ayr.
TANCARD (THANCARD)	Thankerton (2), Lan.
WEREMUND	Warmanbie, Dumf.
WICE (WIZO)	Wiston, Lan.
	Wyseby, Dumf. (?)
WILLIAM	'Willambi', Dumf.

(b) Continental personal names not known to have been used to form place-names, but associated with holders of names in (a)

ARKENBALD (= ARCHIBALD)
ASA (ACE, AZO)
BALDWIN
FRETHEBALD
FRETHESKIN (FRESEKIN, FRESKIN)
RACE (RAZO)
THEOBALD
WARNEBALD (WERENBALD)

remarkable as instances of settlements simply taking the founder's personal name without the addition of any generic term for homestead or farm. In the large majority of cases, we see that this generic term was Middle English *tūn(e)*, which has of course survived into present-day Scots (*toun*). Vernacular French forms are emphasized in such names as Penston, the toun of Paganus de Hanle, who was obviously called 'Pain' in ordinary usage;[24] Pearsby and Perceton, the '-by' and '-tūn' of Piers rather than Peter;[25] Ralstoun, the toun of Raoul rather than Radulf;[26] and Anniestoun, the toun of Anneis or Agnes de Brus, exceptional in being named after a woman.[27]

[24] Land in Tranent was granted to Pain, *c.* 1170 (SRO GD 241/254; see above, p. 23, n. 104). This grant, forming a knight's feu, appears as Paynistona in 1381 (*RMS* i, no. 638) and Paynstoune in 1466 (ibid. ii, no. 884); now Penston.
[25] Pearsby (in Thundergarth), Dumfriesshire, is Peirsbie in 1608 (*Retours, Dumfries*, no. 53). Perceton, Ayrshire, is Peristone, early fourteenth century (*RMS* i, no. 39).
[26] Raulyston, 1346 (*Paisley Reg.*, 10); cf. Barrow, *Kingdom*, 341.
[27] *Kelso Liber*, no. 275 (1180 × 1193), a charter which refers to Thankerton in the Upper Ward of Lanarkshire as a knight's feu.

Short work has been made of a continental name of some complexity in West Lothian Philpingston, the toun of Philippe d'Eu (Philippe d'Eustune = Philpdewston = Philpingston,[28]) and in Renfrewshire we may note the Flemish name Boderic, perhaps a rare variant of Baldric, still preserved in Botherickfield in Houston,[29] itself the toun of Hugh, a follower of Baldwin the Fleming, King Malcolm IV's sheriff of Lanark.[30]

Table 1 (b) shows us a few continental names which are not known to have given rise to place-names but which belong to the same milieu as those which did, and incidentally help to emphasize the Flemish character of continental immigration. The second table (p. 39) reminds us that internal colonization was going on in this period, and that strongly proprietary place-names could be just as appropriate for native landowners, such as Liulf at Lyleston or Maccus at Maxton, as for incomers from the south. Ketil(l) of Kettlestoun (before 1153[31]) is probably to be placed among native 'colonizers' but the name might just possibly have belonged to an incomer.

Map 1 shows the pre-existing secular divisions or districts of a large part of southern Scotland. As we may see in the following map (2), these were the divisions into which the feudal settlement was fitted. This may be demonstrated relatively simply for south-western Scotland, but a comparable map for the south-east would be very much more complex. The contrast may have something to tell us about the difference in social organization between Lothian on the one hand and Scottish Cumbria on the other.[32]

On the next three maps (3, 4, and 5) are plotted on the map of southern Scotland the place-names derived from, or at least affected by, Anglo-Norman settlement. It is surely significant of the lasting consequences which this settlement had for the human landscape of Scotland that so many of these names still

[28] A. MacDonald, *The Place-Names of West Lothian* (1941), 32.
[29] Barrow, *Kingdom*, 329.
[30] Ibid.; *OPS* i. 83.
[31] MacDonald, *Place-Names of West Lothian*, 59.
[32] It would, e.g. be worth investigating whether nucleated villages, tending to encroach upon and subdivide an earlier 'shire' organization, had been established widely in the south east, but had made little or no progress in the south west. A fairly high proportion of what appear to be nucleated village settlements in the south east have Old English names, e.g. Whittingehame, Tynninghame, Stenton, and Oldhamstocks.

The Pattern of Settlement

Table 2 Insular personal names (i.e. Anglo-Saxon, Scandinavian, and Celtic) used to form place-names certainly or probably in the period *c.* 1100–*c.* 1250

Personal name	Place-name
ARNKELL	Arkleston, Renf.
BALDRED	Balderston, W.Lo.
COLBAIN	Covington, Lan.
CORMAC	Cormiston, Lan.
EDULF	Eddleston, Peeblesshire
GILLEMURE	'Gillemurestun', Peeblesshire
	Gilmerton (3), E.Lo., Fife, M.Lo. (also (2), Dumf., Perthshire?)
GIRIG	Greigston, Fife
ISLEIFR (EILAF)	Elliston, Roxb.
	Illieston, W.Lo.
KETILL	Kettleston, W.Lo.
LIULF	Lyleston, Berw.
MACCUS	Maxton, Roxb.
	Maxwell, Roxb.
MAELCARF	Makerston, Roxb.
MUREDACH	Murdieston (Murdostoun), Lan.
ORM	Ormiston (2), E.Lo., Fife
SVEINN (SWAIN, SWEIN)	Swanston, M.Lo.
THOR	Thurston, E.Lo.

survive and that a considerable proportion apply to places of parochial status. Map 3 shows the places which had attained to this status by the thirteenth century.[33] In general, exotic settlers found most scope for creating parishes which perpetuated their own names in three areas, Lothian proper, the Upper Ward of Clydesdale, and Cunningham and Strathgryfe. In the two western areas the explanation may be relative depopulation, or simply the concentration of large blocks of royal demesne only loosely and extensively exploited and therefore susceptible of much more intensive settlement. In the case of Lothian the opportunity was probably provided not by the emptiness or poverty of the country but by its very prosperity and the consequent need for new parishes which were formed

[33] My authority for assigning parochial status has been Cowan, *Parishes*.

by subdividing larger old-established ones. In this area the most remarkable name is Melville, a small parish south of Edinburgh formed in the mid-twelfth century by Geoffrey de Melville (who came to Scotland, perhaps directly, before the death of David I) and given the name of the Norman village from which he took his surname.[34] This transplantation of a place-name from Normandy to Scotland seems to be unique, though there are of course parallels elsewhere, e.g. Montgomery in Wales.[35] A different kind of name-formation is represented by Duddingston in Midlothian, Wiston in Lanarkshire, and Houston in Renfrewshire. In these cases the parish churches are known to have had older names, respectively Treverlen, Abercarf (both Brittonic), and Kilpeter (Gaelic), which survived well into the medieval period.[36] The inference is that in each place the newcomer, though quite prepared to benefit from being granted the territory of the parish with its rights of lordship, felt it necessary to establish a distinctive settlement on a fresh site. It was this new settlement which bore his name and eventually became identified with the parish as a whole. This conclusion has important implications when we try to understand the meaning of a place-name formed by adding '-tūn' or '-by' to a personal name in the genitive case.[37]

The following map (4) contains essentially the same information but shows only places of less than parochial status. The large majority either still are today or were until fairly recent times independent farms or agricultural estates, in general occupying attractive sites on fertile land. A few, such as Lockerbie in Dumfriesshire or Borrowstoun (Bo'ness) in West Lothian, have developed into very large villages or small

[34] Lawrie, *Charters*, no. 186 ('de Mailuil').
[35] Named after Montgommery (Saint-Germain-de, Ste-Foy-de) in Calvados, arr. Lisieux; cf. M. Gelling, W. F. H. Nicolaisen, and M. Richards, *The Names of Towns and Cities in Britain* (1970), 137; Loyd, *Origins*, 68. The Scots family of Montgomery, dependants of the Stewarts, may have derived their surname from Montgomery in Wales (Barrow, *Kingdom*, 344).
[36] *Book of the Old Edinburgh Club*, xxx (1959), 1-9 (Treverlen/Duddingston); Lawrie, *Charters*, p. 46 and Barrow, *Kingdom*, 290, n. 55 (Abercarf/Wiston); ibid. 345-6 and G. Crawfurd, *History of the Shire of Renfrew* (1710), 71 (Kilpeter/Houston).
[37] For example, whatever may have been true of the earliest period of English or Anglo-Scandinavian place-name formation, settlement names formed in the twelfth century with a personal name plus *tūn* (or *by*) do not imply a wholly new unit of settlement.

towns; a large number, especially in the central industrial belt, have been swallowed up by the vast conurbations of modern times. Of the places shown on the map, only 'Roberdesbi' and 'Willambi' in Annandale have actually been deserted or have decayed to vanishing point. 'Folcardeston' in Lanarkshire, though almost a lost site, is in fact still represented on the large-scale maps by the name Mill of Folkerton. Folcard, the presumed founder (whence the Scots surname Flockhart), appears in the mid-twelfth century as witness to a tack issued by John abbot of Kelso.[38] Clarabad near Berwick has already been mentioned, named after Clarembald of Ashby (Castle Ashby in Northamptonshire), a follower of the Olifards.[39] Along with Clarabad we should take Myles near Penston (East Lothian), named after Milo Cornet. An odd-sounding name is Sorrowlessfield between Earlston and St. Boswells, called after a certain William Sorrowless, evidently a dependant of the Lindsays.[40] Relatively speaking there are fewer names of this type in the south-east, and we may infer that feudal settlers in that corner of Scotland could more easily be fitted into existing settlements whose older names were retained.[41]

The next kind of settlement name to be considered (Map 5) is much more familiar in England (especially south of Westmorland and the River Wear) than in Scotland, Cumberland, or Northumberland. Such names were formed by adding the lord's family surname as a separate qualifying element after some old-established name. Usually the qualifier does not appear

[38] Henry abbot of Kelso (1208–18) granted a feu charter of Folcariston to Richard son of Solph' (read Folch'?), as his father and ancestors held it (*Kelso Liber*, no. 106). Fulcard witnessed an earlier tack of neighbouring land in Lesmahagow parish by Abbot John (1160–80), ibid., no. 115.

[39] See above, p. 35, n. 23. Clarabad was probably named after the Clarembald of Ashby there mentioned, but the place might possibly have been named after Clarebald who witnessed a charter of Earl Henry, David I's son, at Huntingdon, 1139 × 1141, and who may have been an ancestor of the later Clarembald (*RRS* i, no. 21).

[40] *Melrose Liber*, no. 12 (reading corrected from the original charter in SRO). For the place-name, see ibid., no. 104.

[41] There does not seem to be any serious danger of distorting the evidence in the fact that, for practical reasons, only the country south of Forth has been mapped and discussed in this chapter. Attention, however, should be drawn to a handful of settlement-names of the same type as those dealt with in the text which seem to have been formed north of Forth before *c*. 1200; e.g. Wormistone in Crail, Fife (*RRS* ii, no. 196), the lost Ricardeston in Rhynd, Perthshire (*St. Andrews Liber*, 396–7), and possibly Harvieston near Dollar, Clackmannanshire.

in record until a generation or two after the time of the first settler,[42] but popular usage may well have been ahead of the clerks and lawyers here, and in any case the qualifier can hardly be later than some date when the family thus commemorated was either still in possession or at least very well remembered. At one period this form of name, which is surely French, not English, in structure, was by no means uncommon in Scotland, even north of the Forth,[43] but for some unknown reason the fashion died out in the sixteenth century, leaving only a vestigial handful of names as evidence of a once general practice—e.g. Cranstoun Riddel,[44] Keith Marischal,[45] Calder Clere.[46] Cranstoun belonged to Hugh Ridel of Abbotsley in Huntingdonshire, who belonged to a family of uncertain origin although formally the name is identical with that commemorated at Azay-le-Rideau south of Tours. Keith Marischal is from Hervey, first of the Keiths, marischal to Malcolm IV and William the Lion.[47] Calder Clere, now called Mid Calder, is from Ralph de Clere of a well-known Yorkshire-

[42] See, e.g. Ekwall, *Concise Dictionary*, under Ashby de la Zouche, Boughton Malherbe, Boughton Monchelsea, Coombe Bissett, Hurstpierpont, Seaton Delaval, Seavington Denis. The total of such 'manorial' names in midland and southern England is of course very large.

[43] See, e.g. *Dunfermline Reg.*, nos. 86, 87, 177, 178 (rubric), for such forms as Beeth Waldef and Beeth Fleming; but note that in the text of no. 178 the latter name appears as Flemisse (and Fleminges) Beeth, which is the Middle English form characteristic of post-medieval Scottish estate names, for which see, e.g. Sibbald, *Fife*, 454 (under Beath parish). *Fife Court Bk.* 396–7, 400 shows that proprietorial suffixes could survive as late as 1517, e.g. Lindiffren-Barclay, Leuchars-Monipenny and Cleish-Meldrum.

For Cumberland, see *Place-Names of Cumberland*, iii, p. xxxiv, 'Manorial additions are exceedingly rare in Cumberland, the only surviving example of the type being Newton Reigny', but the editors point out that names of this kind had once been commoner in the county.

[44] In Cranston, Midlothian; see *Retours, Edinburgh, passim*. For the connection between the Ridel family and Abbotsley, see Appendix A.

[45] In Humbie, E. Lothian; 'Keth Hervei', twelfth–thirteenth centuries (*Kelso Liber*, nos. 425, 460), 'Keithe Marescalli', 1324 (*RMS* i, App. I, no. 47).

[46] i.e. Mid Calder, Midlothian. The earlier form survived into the seventeenth century (*Retours, Edinburgh, passim*). A Middle English form is, however, to be seen from the outset in Chalmerlayn-newton, Chamberlain Newton, i.e. Newton in Hawick, apparently the 'Neutun' granted as a knight's feu to Walter of Berkeley the chamberlain by William I (*RRS* ii, no. 171, where the place is wrongly identified).

[47] *RRS* i. 35; ii. 38. The 'Hervei' referred to was the royal marischal Hervey of Keith, ancestor of the Keiths eventually earls marischal. The last of eight witnesses to a charter of Henry of Anjou duke of Normandy and Aquitaine, given at Leicester in June 1153, was Herveus the marischal (*RRAN* iii, no. 104).

The Pattern of Settlement 43

Norman family.[48] Another obsolete name is Yetholm-Neym, now Town Yetholm,[49] from the continental family called 'le Nain', 'dwarf', whence Neym or Neame, a family endowed with land not only at Yetholm but also at Broughton near Biggar and at Inverugie (St. Fergus) on the coast of Buchan.[50] Perhaps the most interesting name is Gifford, acclimatized to look like a typical Lothian Anglian vernacular name, although originally it must have been Giffards' Yester or Yester Giffard.[51] The owner here was Hugh Giffard or 'Jiffard', a dependant of the great family of de Varenne, and the place-name would be comparable with Longueville-la-Gifart in Seine Maritime, the parish from which the family of Giffard came to Britain.[52] On the same map there are a few names to show colonization by religious houses with an Anglo-Norman background: Canonbie from Jedburgh,[53] Canongate from Holyrood,[54] Monkland in Lanarkshire from the Cistercians of Newbattle,[55] two Monktons, one in Ayrshire from the Cluniacs of Paisley,[56] the other in Midlothian from the Benedictines of Dunfermline[57] (the English character of these names is noteworthy) and the self-explanatory Temple on an upland site south of Edinburgh, which seems formerly to have borne the Brittonic name Plent(r)idoc, containing Welsh *blaen*, 'upland'.[58]

The remaining five maps are designed to show twelfth-century settlement in detail in three areas of south-west Scotland, Clydesdale, Ayrshire and Annandale. In the first (Map 6), we have a general view of the Middle and Upper Wards of

[48] Clay and Greenway, *Early Yorkshire Families*, 20–1. See below, pp. 109–11.
[49] *CDS* iii, no. 345 and pp. 322, 374; *RMS* i. 528, n. 1.
[50] *OPS* i. 201, 428.
[51] For the history of the estate in the possession of the Giffard family till the end of the fourteenth century, see *Yester Writs, passim* between nos. 1 and 43.
[52] Loyd, *Origins*, 45.
[53] Lydel canonicorum, *c*. 1275, *SHS Misc.* v (1933), 95; Canenby, 1290, Stevenson, *Docs.* i. 129.
[54] Vicus canonicorum, 1426–7, *Holyrood Liber*, p. 230, le Canongate, 1530, ibid., 257.
[55] Le Munkland, 1323, *Newbattle Reg.*, no. 204.
[56] Munkton, 1361, *Paisley Reg.*, 67.
[57] Munctune, 1163, *Dunfermline Reg.*, p. 152.
[58] *TRHistS*, 5th ser., xxviii (1978), 112, n. 65. For the earliest recorded form of the name see *Glasgow Reg.* i, no. 41, where the letters as printed might stand for Plentridoc. A thirteenth-century form preserved in *St. Andrews Liber*, 344, is Baltrudoc. The second element is obscure.

Clydesdale. Two black squares, Cadzow and Lanark, stand for ancient sites of Cumbrian royalty preserved as royal centres throughout much or all of our period. The black circles are the known sites of twelfth-century foreign settlement, much of it carried out by Flemings. These are some of the classic knight-service baronies of Scottish feudalism, remarkably artificial and cut-and-dried even compared with English feudal creations.[59] Under the Crown, with its castle at Lanark to whose ward many of these fiefs contributed equal quotas of service,[60] and the seat of a royal sheriff at least since Malcolm the Maiden's time,[61] there were three first-class lordships, Biggar held by a Flemish dynasty without a surname,[62] Carnwath held by the Somervilles[63] and Bothwell held from about 1150 by the Olifards.[64] Beneath these great lordships were some dozen or more baronies of lesser rank, each no doubt with its motte castle and each held for knight service.[65] The next map (7) brings out the intensity of Flemish settlement, and demonstrates that often enough it was settlers who had no surname who have left their personal names at the localities where they established their castle, hall or chief seat. This map shows that the Flemings in particular were ready to acquire land promiscuously, holding one estate as a fief from the Crown (Lambin at

[59] In the Upper Ward of Clydesdale there seems to have been a general correspondence between the laird's estate, the knight's feu and the parish. The sums recorded in the fourteenth-century Exchequer Rolls as due in respect of castle ward at Lanark are highly standardized (*Exch. R.* i. 582; G. Neilson, 'Tenure by knight service in Scotland', *Juridical Review*, xi (1899), 71–86, 173–86). The knight's feu seems to have been regarded as the tenurial norm in district, if we may judge from the wording of Anneis de Brus's charter granting the church of Thankerton 'as the monks of Kelso most freely hold and possess any church in any knight's feu within the realm of Scotland' (*Kelso Liber*, no. 275).
[60] *Exch. Rolls*, i. 582. The 'castleries' (*castellariae*) of Ayr, Lanark and Rutherglen are mentioned in a royal charter of 1221, *Foedera*, i. I 165.
[61] *RRS* i, nos. 108, 198.
[62] *OPS* i. 134.
[63] Ibid., 127 (and see below, p. 107).
[64] *OPS* i. 55; Barrow, *Kingdom*, 288–9.
[65] In the Upper Ward of Lanarkshire undoubted mottes survive as follows (probable corresponding knights' feus given in parentheses): Abington (Crawford John), Biggar (Biggar), Carnwath (Carnwath), Crawford (Crawford Lindsay), Douglas (Douglas), Easterton Burn (Lamington), Hyndford (unknown), The Lee (The Lee), Moat (Roberton) and Wolfclyde (Coulter). There is evidence for probable or possible motte sites at Covington (Covington), Bower of Wandel (Hartside) and Wiston (Wiston). See C. Tabraham, 'Norman Settlement in Upper Clydesdale', *Dumfriesshire Trans.*, 3rd ser., liii (1977–8), 114–28.

Lamington),[66] another from a religious house in feu-ferme (Lambin Asa at Draffan),[67] yet another as a rear-fief from a great feudatory (James son of Lambin Asa at Loudoun).[68] If, as may be the case, the Olifards were themselves of Flemish origin,[69] then at Thankerton by Bothwell we find one Fleming, Thancard, holding of another,[70] while in Upper Clydesdale

[66] *OPS* i. 173-4. Lambin Asa received the lands of Draffan and 'Dardarach' (in Lesmahagow) in feuferme from Arnold abbot of Kelso 1147 × 60 (*Kelso Liber*, no. 102). Lambin Asa may be identified as the man after whom Lamington is named, and his brother Robert was the eponymous laird of Roberton. Three successors of Robert, William, his son Henry and Henry's son Robert, held Ardoch in Lesmahagow of Kelso Abbey (*Kelso Liber*, no. 190); see also *RRS* i, no. 317. Lambin Asa was succeeded by James son of Lambin, otherwise known as James of Draffan (below, p. 129, n. 65) or James of Loudoun, and afterwards by James's son 'A.' (*Kelso Liber*, no. 103). Although ignored by *Scots Pge.* in its article on Campbell earl of Loudoun, which mentions only a daughter as James's heir, 'A. son of James' was presumably the Adam of Loudoun who witnessed a charter of Alan son of Roland (Marquess of Bute, Dumfries House, Loudoun Chrs., no. 4). It is not clear whether a contemporary (Sir) Andrew of Loudoun (ibid. and no. 3) was Adam's brother or son.
[67] *Kelso Liber*, no. 102.
[68] Marquess of Bute, Dumfries House, Loudoun charters, no. 1; Stevenson, *Illustrations*, 15, no. VIII. In the earlier charter the donee is called James son of Lambin, in the later James 'of Loudoun'. For his third name, James 'of Draffan', cf. Fraser, *Lennox*, ii, no. 1, *Kelso Liber*, nos. 104, 114, 115, 284, 349.
[69] The form of the name seems similar to several names originating, or at least favoured, in north-east France and north-west Belgium in the eleventh-thirteenth centuries. The Olifard presence in Northamptonshire may be associated with the Flemish following of Gunfrid and Sigar 'de Cioches' (i.e. Chocques, *anglicé* Chokes) for which see Farrer, *HKF* i. 20 ff. The first of the name recorded in England, Roger Olifard, witnessed an early charter given to St. Andrews Priory, Northampton by its founder Earl Simon I de Senlis (*Mon. Angl.* v. 190b), but if the unsurnamed Walter who held Lilford, Northants, of the Countess Judith in 1086 was an Olifard (Walter was a characteristic Olifard name at a later period), the Olifards would antedate Earl Simon in the Honour of Huntingdon, and might have settled in England soon after the Conquest (Farrer, *HKF* ii. 354).
[70] A solemn privilege of Pope Honorius III (date unknown: *Paisley Reg.* 412) shows that Paisley acquired land at Motherwell from Thomas Thancard, whose son Frethebald witnessed a charter probably dating × 1195 (ibid., 98, reading 'Frethebaldo filio Thome Tancardi'; cf. *RRS* ii, no. 310 for lower date-limit). The location of Thomas Thancard's estate in Motherwell is further shown by *Kelso Liber*, no. 183, describing land at Ross in Cadzow, at the foot of the River Avon, as 'opposite to the land of Thomas Thancard (across) the Clyde'. It may therefore be accepted as reasonably certain that Thankerton, in Bothwell parish but adjoining Motherwell, was called after Thomas's father, who had been given Auchterheadmuir, only a few miles distant, by Malcolm IV (*RRS* i, no. 304). In the eighteenth century the family of Roberton of Earnock preserved an original free marriage charter given by Thomas son of Thankard to his sister Beatrice and her husband John Logan of 'one ploughgate of land' (Nisbet, *Heraldry*, ii, Appendix, 140, unfortunately not locating the estate).

apparently the same man held of the Crown direct.[71] The ubiquity of the Loccards (Lockharts) is remarkable: Simon Locard at The Lee and at Symington;[72] Stephen Loccard at Stevenston;[73] and probably one or other of them at Lockerbie.[74]

The next two maps (8 and 9) give similar information for Ayrshire, showing first of all the places known to have formed feudal tenements, or parts of feudal tenements, before c. 1250. In this sheriffdom only one royal centre was retained, Ayr, with its castle built as late as 1197.[75] Irvine and Dundonald were mediatized early, the first to de Morville, the second to the Stewart.[76] We may note the striking contrast between 'feudalized' Cunningham and Kyle and 'unfeudalized' Carrick. The second Ayrshire map (Map 9) locates, by emphasizing, the demesne estates of the great lords and the tenements of their vassals, normally knights' fees. In Carrick we can see only one or two fiefs in the extreme north, including Greenan belonging before 1199 to Roger de Scalebroc, i.e. of Skelbrooke, between Pontefract and Doncaster.[77] Skelbrooke had been a member of the Honour of Lacy of Pontefract since the Conquest, belonging to a family named from Campeaux in Calvados and afterwards to a family called Butler.[78] No link between

[71] *OPS* i. 143–4.
[72] *OPS* i. 121, 145.
[73] Marquess of Bute, Dumfries House, Loudoun charters, no. 4: Alan son of Roland confirms to Hugh Crawford the third part of 'Steventun' sold to Hugh by Margaret daughter of Adam Loccard.
[74] The name Lockerbie does not seem to be recorded before 1198 (*CDS* i, no. 2666, 'Locardebi') when it was disputed between William de Brus lord of Annandale and Adam Carlyle. It may be significant that Simon Locard witnessed William I's charter of Annandale to Robert de Brus at Lochmaben (*RRS* ii, no. 80, 1165 × 72). A later Annandale charter (*CDS* i, no. 606, 1194 × 1214) was witnessed by Malcolm Loccard, Simon's son and heir, who also witnessed charters of Alan the Stewart and his son Walter (Fraser, *Lennox*, ii, nos. 1 and 2, 1177 × 1204; *Kelso Liber*, no. 253) and an act of 1229 (ibid., no. 186); see also ibid., no. 333.
[75] *Chron. Melrose*, 49.
[76] Irvine ('Strathirewin in Galwegia') was evidently still royal demesne at the date of Lawrie, *Charters*, nos. 84, 85, the former of which was witnessed by Hugh de Morville. Thereafter no royal association with Irvine is recorded, and it may be safely reckoned to have been in Morville hands by the date of the founding of Kilwinning Abbey (1162 × 90). The castle is referred to in 1184 (*Chron. Howden*, ii, 285). For Dundonald, see Barrow, *Kingdom*, 347.
[77] *Melrose Liber*, nos. 31, 34.
[78] W. E. Wightman, *The Lacy Family in England and Normandy* (1966), 35, 39; W. Paley Baildon, 'Notes on the early Saville pedigree and the Butlers of Skel-

The Pattern of Settlement 47

Duncan of Carrick and either of these families can be traced, nor with the Lacys before 1204, when Hugh de Lacy of the Hereford branch of the family ousted John de Courcy from Ulster,[79] where Duncan was busy acquiring land. The late-twelfth-century appearance in south Ayrshire of the two Yorkshire knights, Thomas de Colville and Roger of Skelbrooke, is for the present impossible to account for.[80]

Our last map (10) takes us to Annandale, the lordship of which had been granted to Robert I de Brus by David I about 1124, long before there was a sheriffdom of Dumfries. On this map are plotted the settlements recorded before 1214 which contain the names of Anglo-Continental immigrants. In this part of Scotland there is a uniquely high proportion of place-names using Scandinavian elements—especially 'by', 'thwait', 'keld', and 'beck'—familiar in English Cumbria and the northern Danelaw. This Scandinavian intrusion is obviously related to settlement in English Cumbria and quite distinct from what we find in the Western and Northern Isles and the far north of mainland Scotland.[81] It is to be noted therefore that our Anglo-Continental settlement names conform to what was clearly a living Scandinavian tradition, so that while we have Johnstone ($<$*Jones tūn*) in the north of Annandale,[82] further south among the thwaites and becks we have Sibbaldbie, Lockerbie, Pearsby, Warmanbie and two lost settlements, 'Roberdesbi' and 'Willambi'.[83] It would probably be safe enough to add to the list such surviving names as

---

brook and Kirk Sandal', *Yorks. Archaeological Journal*, xxix, 68–89. A William 'de Scalebroc' is recorded in Henry III's reign (ibid. v. 309), but no link between him and Roger (whose heirs were two daughters) can be established.

[79] A. J. Otway-Ruthven, *History of Medieval Ireland*, 75, 80.

[80] An interesting link between Alan son of Roland of Galloway and the de Lacy lords of Pontefract, involving the de Lacy estates of Kippax and Scholes not far north of Skelbrooke, has been demonstrated by K. J. Stringer, 'A new wife for Alan of Galloway', *Dumfriesshire Trans.*, 3rd ser., xlix (1972), 49–55. But Roger of Skelbrooke was associated in Scotland not with Alan of Galloway but with his rival and kinsman Duncan of Carrick.

[81] Nicolaisen, *Scottish Place-Names*, chapter 6 and especially pp. 111–12.

[82] Fraser, *Annandale*, i. 3 (no. 3), 'Jonistune'; *CDS* i, no. 705 ('Joneston').

[83] 'Roberdesbi' occurs in a late-twelfth-century charter and must have been close to the Kirtle Water, Dumfriesshire (Raine, *North Durham*, no. 167).'Willambi', in the *feudum* of Pennersaughs (in Middlebie, Dumfriesshire), occurs in an early-thirteenth-century charter (Fraser, *Annandale*, i. 2–3 and facsimile facing p. xii).

Gillesbie, Gimmenbie, Wyseby and Rickerby,[84] but I have not found them in early record. There is a slightly Flemish flavour about the personal names, e.g. Sibbald, Loccard, and Weremund, which need not surprise us when we bear in mind that there was appreciable Flemish immigration into Cleveland in the first half of the twelfth century; for it was from Cleveland rather than from Normandy that the Brus lords of Annandale seem to have brought many of their knights and feudal dependants to Scotland.[85]

What conclusions might we reasonably draw from the evidence reviewed in this chapter? It appears that the Anglo-Norman feudal settlement of southern Scotland consisted of more than simply the acquisition of feudal lordship, whether by confiscation, forfeiture, marriage, or inheritance, of more than the building of castles and the assembling of landed estates to form permanent infeftments. It was, certainly, a great 'landtaking' in the barbaric tradition of north-west Europe, but it also involved in detail the creation of new agricultural colonies of a strongly proprietary character. The leading men in this process can be judged, from their personal names or from more specific evidence, to have come from Norman England or from the continent. But the linguistic usage by which the names of their settlements have become embedded in the Scottish landscape was already, in the twelfth and thirteenth centuries, a Middle-English or Anglo-Scandinavian usage. The Annandale evidence seems to rule out the notion that the incomers brought their own English-speaking peasantry with them *en masse*. We are left with one of two inferences: either English speech had gained ground more rapidly among the Anglo-

---

[84] NG refs. NY 181854, NY 165915, NY 166784, NY 243725. Rickerby should be compared with the Riccartons of Roxburghshire, Ayrshire, West Lothian, and (lost) Perthshire. Wyseby should be compared with Whisby Graffoe in Lincolnshire, which Ekwall (*Concise Dictionary*) derives from the Old Norse personal name Hvit. Since Whisby seems to have been colonized between 1066 and 1086 under Baldwin the Fleming it might be worth considering whether we have another instance of the Flemish personal name Wizo or Wice, as at Wiston, Lanarkshire, and Wiston, Pembrokeshire. Wyseby in Annandale may also incorporate a Flemish name (for Whisby see *The Lincolnshire Domesday and the Lindsey Survey*, ed. C. W. Foster, T. Longley, and F. M. Stenton (Lincoln Record Society, 1924), 196).
[85] Below, pp. 111–12.

Norman feudal class than has usually been supposed, or else, and this seems to me rather more probable, English was making rapid progress during our period among the indigenous population of large areas of southern Scotland, though it had not yet become dominant in southern Annandale, still strongly Scandinavian, and had made no headway as yet in such a strongly Celtic-speaking district as Carrick. It may also have been the case that as the incoming feudalists embarked upon a more intensive exploitation of the soil an internal migration was encouraged which brought into hitherto Celtic-speaking districts like Upper Tweeddale, Clydesdale, and northern Ayrshire men and women of English-speaking stock from Lothian, Northumberland, or even further south. Yet at the same time we must put firmly from our minds the belief that the earlier Celtic-speaking population was driven out; and although at the higher levels it lost much, it was not wholly expropriated. The charters, land perambulations and other documents which show us English advancing rapidly in what must have been the usage of ordinary folk[86] also show us plenty of settlement names, both of main centres and of small hamlets and farms, of either Brittonic or Gaelic type, or a hybrid of the two.[87] At many old churches, e.g. Paisley, Kilwinning, Kilmarnock, Glasgow, and Lesmahagow, the cult of native saints not only survived but positively flourished.[88] For almost the whole of our period, the names of natural features, especially stream names mostly containing the element 'pol', remain overwhelmingly Celtic in character everywhere west of the Tweed–Clyde watershed, with considerable Celtic survival in areas to the east of it.[89] Above all, the larger land divisions of southern Scotland, originating in some earlier period, remained

---

[86] See Appendix C.

[87] For the spread of Middle English, see Appendix C below. As for Celtic names, main centres include Annan, Dumfries, Irvine, Lanark, Glasgow, Renfrew, Paisley. Among many which might be given, a few examples of hamlet and farm names are Aberlosk, Trailtrow (Dumf.), Troquhain (Ayr), Pollok, 'Talahret' (*tal y rhyd*, 'ford end'?) (Renf.) all Brittonic; Affleck, Ardoch, Auchtyfardle, 'Dardarach', Dillars (Lan.), Gaelic; while Lesmahagow and Drumclog appear to be hybrid.

[88] Evidence of continuing cults may be found as follows: Paisley, *OPS* i. 68, 73; Kilwinning, *Chron. Howden*, ii. 285, *Cuninghame topographized*, 254–6; Kilmarnock, Watson, *CPNS* 187; Lesmahagow, ibid. 196–7 and *OPS* i. 110.

[89] See generally Watson, *CPNS*, chaps. V–VII.

in force and the new royal sheriffdoms and feudal lordships were to a surprising extent adapted to fit them. The pattern of settlement, in other words, reveals a fairly thorough-going mixture. We have the impression of a country far from depopulated, but settled loosely and extensively enough for newcomers to enter by royal favour and practise a more intensive exploitation of resources. Militarily speaking, these new settlers were secure from internal revolt and, for a century and a half, from external enemies. However much many of them may have thought themselves as French or Flemish or Breton, the general culture of the society which they dominated was unmistakably English.

The Pattern of Settlement

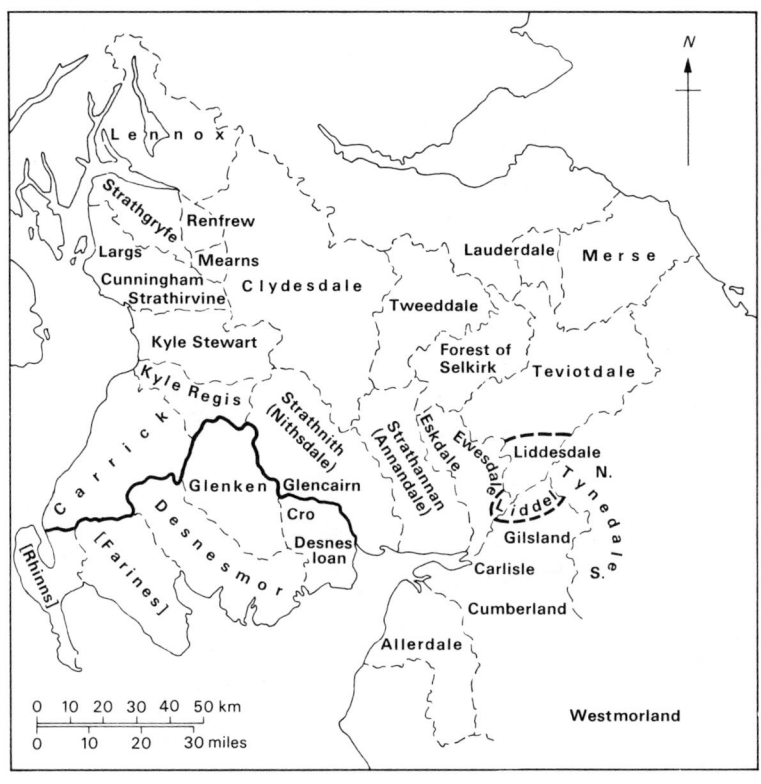

Map 1. Secular divisions of southern Scotland before 1200

Map 2. Feudal settlement in south-west Scotland before 1200

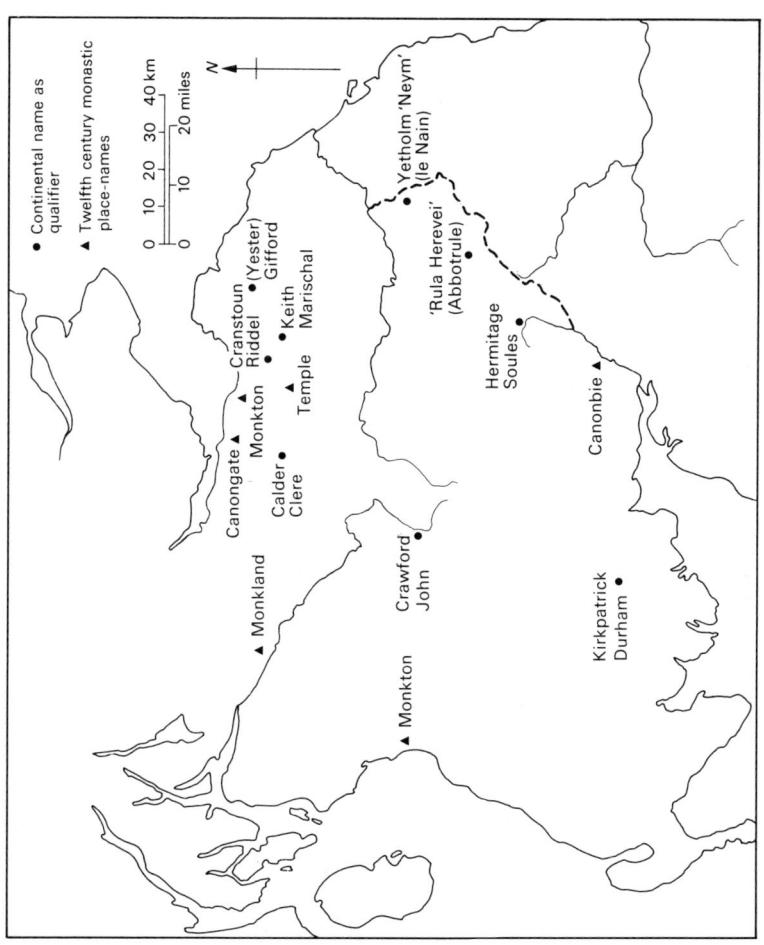

Map 3. Settlement place-names: places of parochial status

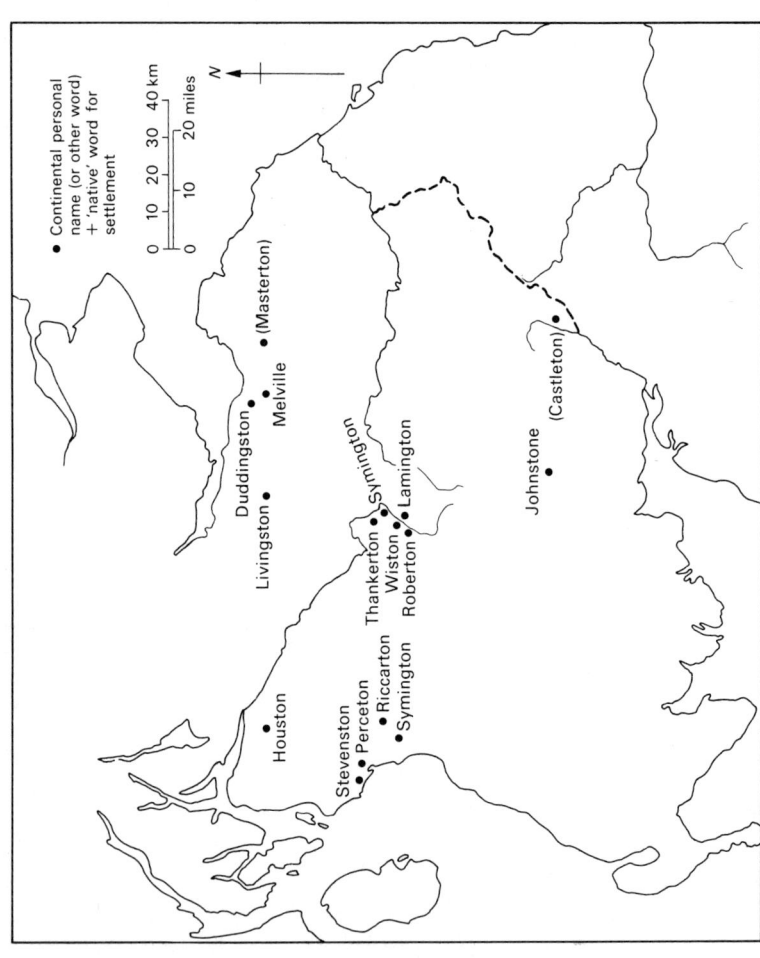

Map 4. Settlement place-names: places of less than parochial status

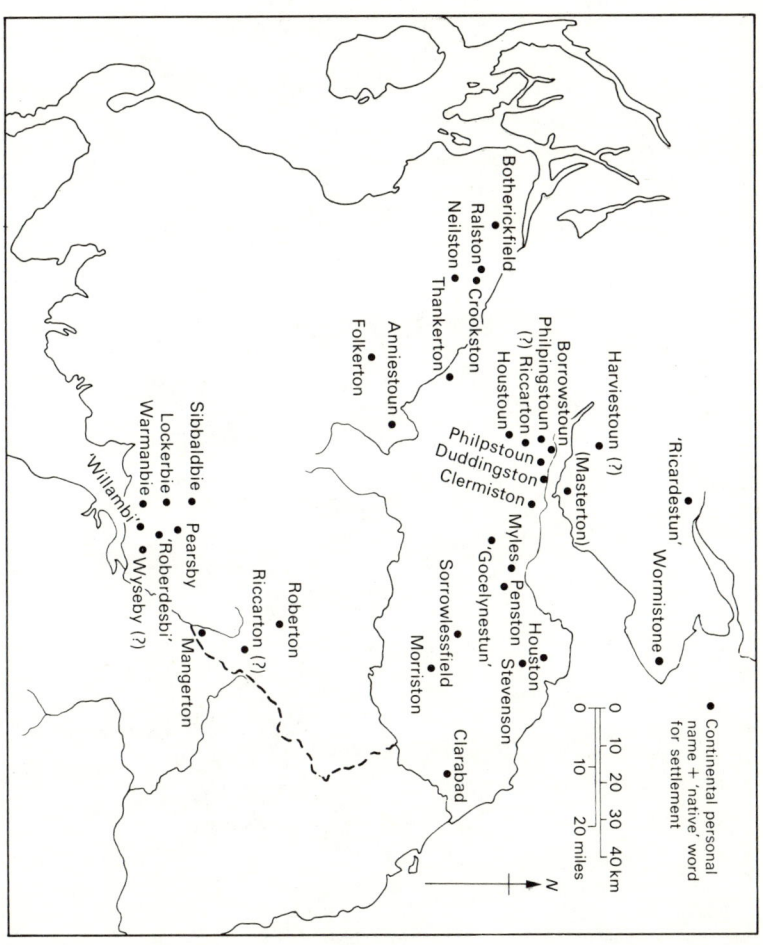

Map 5. Settlement place-names: 'manorial' and 'ecclesiastical' names

Map 6. Upper and Middle Wards of Clydesdale, twelfth century

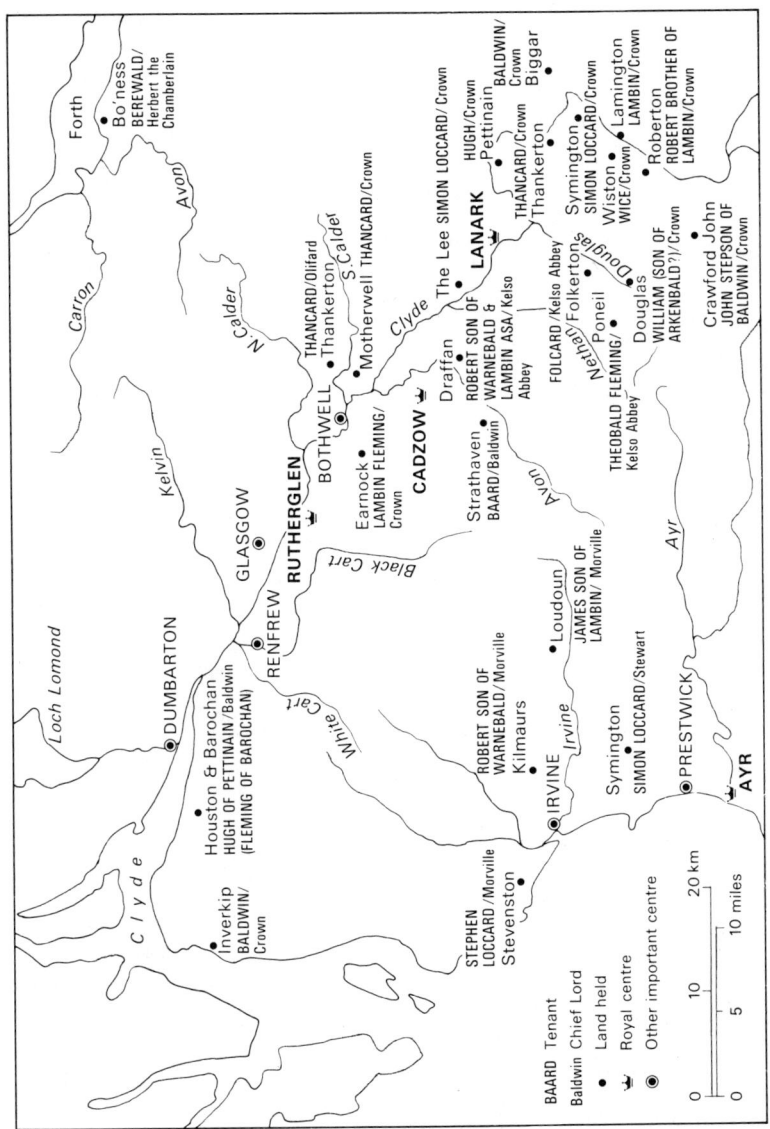

Map 7. Flemish settlement in the mid-west before 1214

Map 8. Ayrshire: places named in feudal charters before 1214

The Pattern of Settlement

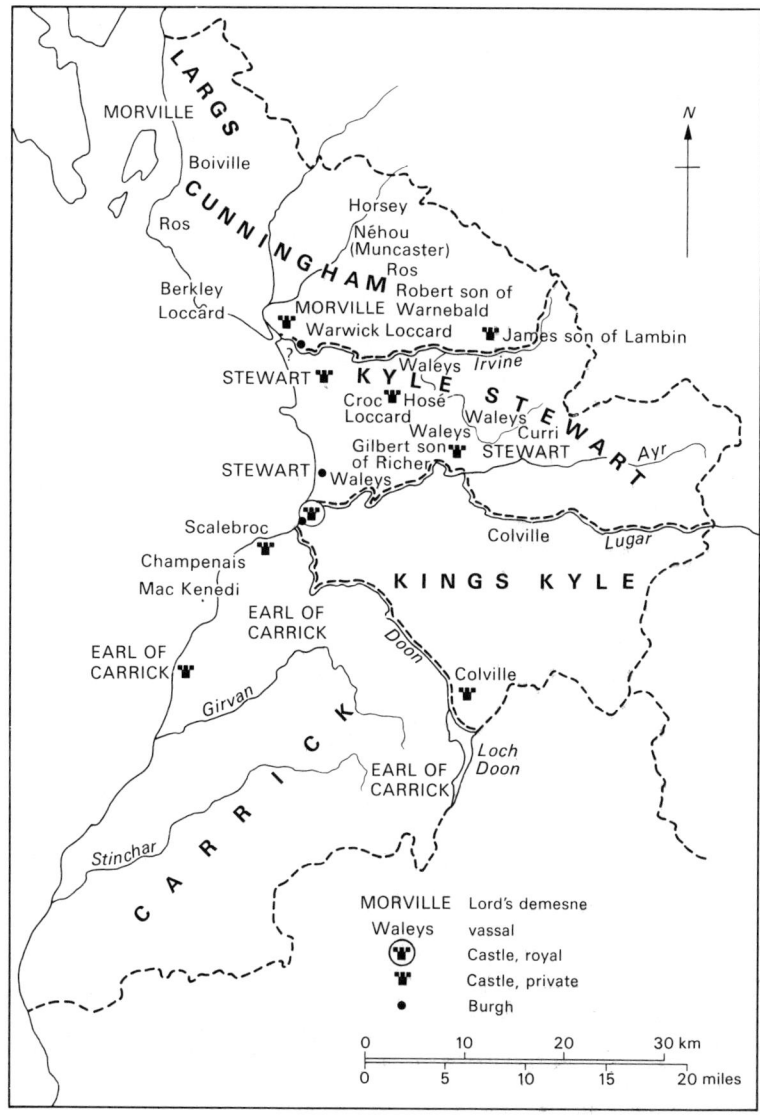

Map 9. Ayrshire: distribution of known vassals and lord's demesne before 1214

Map 10. Annandale: settlement names before 1214

III

The Colonists: (i) The great lords and their families

DELEGATION is the essence of feudalism. Boldly, and with a remarkably comprehensive vision, David I followed the lead given by his elder brothers Edgar and Alexander I and transformed the kingdom of the Scots into a feudal state by delegating royal authority, power, and wealth both territorially and institutionally. His descendants maintained, consolidated, and extended the feudal state by further acts of delegation. This long-drawn-out process provided Scottish society with a new aristocracy which nevertheless did not supersede the old, as in England after 1066 a new foreign aristocracy had superseded the old Anglo-Scandinavian aristocracy. Instead, it had to be fitted in beside the old, although it was based so closely on grants of royal demesne that throughout the south except for Galloway, and in Fife, Gowrie, Angus, Mearns, and Moray, whatever there had been of native nobility must in practice have been elbowed to one side or simply replaced.

Everyone knows that in England William the Conqueror did not concern himself with trifles, but on the contrary established a powerful feudal aristocracy consisting of surprisingly few individuals and families, hardly more than two hundred all told. It was otherwise in Scotland, where normanizing kings had to proceed in more gradual and piecemeal fashion. David I's infeftments of Ernulf at Swinton (Berwickshire),[1] Walter of Ryedale at Lilliesleaf and Whitton (Roxburghshire),[2] and of Alexander de St. Martin at Athelstaneford (East Lothian)[3]—single knights' fees comprising at most two

[1] Lawrie, *Charters*, nos. 100, 101, the former a joint infeftment by David I and his son Henry.
[2] Ibid., no. 222 (better text, *RRS* i, no. 42).
[3] Lawrie, *Charters*, no. 186.

village-sized estates—are probably not untypical examples of Scottish tenancies-in-chief. Nevertheless, it is clear that King David was prepared to feudalize on a large scale, using the older divisions of royal demesne to create great permanent lordships, e.g. Annandale, Lauderdale, Cunningham, and the first Stewart's great quadruple lordship of Renfrew, Mearns, Strathgryfe, and North Kyle.[4] It scarcely needs to be said that the new aristocracy was an aristocracy of royal service, for that would surely be a truism for our period. What is remarkable is that while some of the greatest lordships went to men who were given office in the king's household on an hereditary basis—seneschal, constable, butler, and perhaps panetar—others were given to men who merely seem to have enjoyed the king's favour, men who could be trusted to maintain adequate contingents of knight service, build defensible castles, and enforce law and peaceable behaviour among the inhabitants of their allotted fiefs. In the first group we find Walter Fitz Alan and his heirs, the hereditary Seneschals or stewards (STEWART), Hugh de Morville and his heirs, hereditary Constables, Ranulf de Soules, ancestor of a line of royal Butlers (*pincerne*, later *buticularii*), and, at least by a somewhat analogous process, Richard Cumin (COMYN), who acquired his lands in Tynedale and southern Scotland in virtue of being the nephew of King David's chancellor William Cumin,[5] though this was an office which could hardly become hereditary. In the second group are to be numbered Walter and William of Lindsey (LINDSAY), Robert de Brus (BRUCE), William de Somerville, Robert Avenel, Geoffrey of Conisbrough and the Fleming Freskin, ancestor of the family of *de Moravia* (MURRAY).

Occasionally, a great lordship might be created for social reasons, as for example the dower estate provided for Ada de Varenne, who married King David's son Henry earl of Northumberland in 1139.[6] Comparable lordships were created for Margaret of Scotland, widowed when Conan duke of Brittany died in 1171,[7] and Joan of England on her marriage to

---

[4] G. W. S. Barrow, 'The pattern of lordship and feudal settlement in Cumbria', *Journal of Medieval History*, i (1975), 117–38, especially pp. 130–2.
[5] J. H. Round, 'The origin of the Comyns', *Ancestor*, no. x (1904), 104–19.
[6] *RRS* i. 6; *Symeonis monachi opera omnia* (ed. T. Arnold, Rolls ser., 1882–5), ii. 200 (Continuation of Symeon by John of Hexham).
[7] *APS* i. 116.

Alexander II in 1221,[8] the first consisting of 100 librates of land *and* (perhaps we should read '*or*') twenty knights' fees mostly made up from estates in West Lothian, the second assessed at 1,000 librates of land comprising the Roxburghshire estates of Jedburgh, Hassendean, and St. Boswells together with the two Fife royal centres of Kinghorn and Crail, provided the queen dowager could be persuaded to surrender them.[9] When royal ladies were married furth of Scotland in the thirteenth century their tochers (marriage portions) tended to take the form of cash, as in the case of the 6,000-mark dowry contemplated for Margaret of Scotland, Alexander II's sister, in 1219, when a marriage contract was negotiated but never completed between that princess and Theobald count of Champagne and Brie.[10] Another instance of a socially-motivated lordship was the extensive complex of estates granted by William the Lion in the 1170s to his younger brother David, afterwards earl of Huntingdon. The grant put Earl David in possession of Morton beside Edinburgh, Lindores in Fife, Dundee and Newtyle in Angus, Longforgan in Perthshire, and the entire district of the Garioch in Aberdeenshire.[11] At a rather later period, David must have received from the king a large estate in Mearns (the parish of St. Cyrus) and some undefined interest in the old episcopal centre of Brechin.[12] On a lesser scale, though still substantial, was the lordship provided for the eldest and most favoured of King William's bastard sons, Robert of London, whose mother evidently belonged to the family of *de Londres* or *de Londoniis*. Robert's fiefs were mostly in Fife and

---

[8] *Foedera*, i. I. 165.
[9] Ibid. It is not known whether Queen Ermengarde was persuaded to surrender these estates.
[10] D. W. Hunter-Marshall, 'A proposed marriage alliance between Scotland and Champagne', *Scottish Notes and Queries*, 3rd ser., vii (1929), 207–9. An account, by Guillaume de Joinville archbishop of Rheims (1219–26), of the marriage negotiations is contained in BL MS Add. 30666, fos. 94^r–95^r. See also *CDS* i, no. 727. This episode deserves to be better known than it is.
[11] *Lindores Chartulary*, no. 1.
[12] Earl David's possession of 'Eglesgirg' (St. Cyrus) is shown by *St. Andrews Liber*, 238 (evidently later than the date of *RRS* ii, no. 352). For the earl's connections with Brechin, from which one of his bastard sons named Henry took his surname in his father's lifetime, see *Brechin Reg.*, nos. 3, 4, showing that Henry of Brechin's son William held lordship at Brechin, almost certainly including the castle; *Lindores Chartulary*, nos. 60, 61, an annual rent granted to Lindores Abbey by Henry of Brechin payable at Brechin.

Strathmore, but they included Cadzow, the royal centre in Clydesdale afterwards called Hamilton, and lands from his mother's family at St. Boswells.[13]

The setting up of all these great lordships profoundly affected, indeed may be said to have determined, the feudal landscape of Scotland. It is hard to find any common factor in the Crown's choice of one individual or family rather than another in dispensing the large-scale patronage which the lordships implied. Nevertheless, we may reasonably assume a common background of Anglo-Norman feudalism for the incoming great lords, and it is also safe to assume a relatively standardized pattern of social and military organization within the great lordships which they set up. Their holders, even in twelfth-century Scotland, are too numerous for us to examine in general, and at the same time no selection can be put forward as typical. Nevertheless, we may choose a small group of lordships which taken together should provide a representative impression. The rest of this chapter will examine in detail three of the greatest lordships of twelfth-century and thirteenth-century Scotland, two created by David I and the third an old pre-feudal lordship which successfully adjusted itself to the feudal age and was actually expanded in the process. These lordships are the Stewarts', the Constables', and the earldom of Fife.

When Robert, seventh hereditary Stewart of Scotland, came to the throne in 1371 he and his family already held land and lordships which placed them on a footing not far short of equality with the Crown itself, and effectively paved the way for what Professor Ranald Nicholson has called 'the stewart-ization of the Scottish nobility'.[14] The nucleus of this Stewart empire, already substantial at its inception, was formed in the lifetime of Robert's direct male ancestor Walter son of Alan, who came to Scotland about 1136 and served as *dapifer* or steward successively to David I, Malcolm IV, and William I.[15]

[13] For Robert of London's lands see *Spalding Misc.* v. 243; *Inchcolm Chrs.*, no. 7; *RRS* ii, no. 463; *Dunfermline Reg.*, nos. 167, 168 (Fife); *Arbroath Liber*, no. 61 (Strathmore); *Glasgow Reg.*, no. 49 (Cadzow), no. 165 (unjust occupation of the bishopric lands of Stobo during the episcopate of his cousin Floris of Holland); *Dryburgh Liber*, no. 60 (St. Boswells).
[14] Ranald Nicholson, *Scotland: The Later Middle Ages* (Edinburgh, 1974), 204; cf. ibid., 187, 232–3.
[15] Barrow, *Kingdom*, 337–9.

The Colonists: (i) The great lords and their families 65

Walter acquired directly from the Crown the Berwickshire estates of Birkenside and Legerwood on the left bank of the Leader Water, Hassendean near Hawick (later surrendered),[16] Stenton and Innerwick in East Lothian, Renfrew and Mearns with their dependencies, Strathgryfe—i.e. the western and largely upland part of later Renfrewshire—and the northern part of Kyle, the middle division of what had become by *c.* 1200 the sheriffdom of Ayr. No doubt his wife also was found for him by the king: Eschina, variously known as 'de Londres' or 'of Mow',[17] styles which point to her being the granddaughter and heir of Uhtred son of Liulf, native lord of Mow in Roxburghshire,[18] her father being a member of the de Londres or London family. The service stipulated for Kyle is unknown, but the burden laid upon the remaining estates, a mere five knights' service, can hardly be seen as anything other than beneficially light.

The Stewart lordship brought under the control of a single family lands in English-speaking north Northumbria and along the mixed Cumbric- and Gaelic-speaking southern shores of the Firth of Clyde. These widely-separated territories were thus opened up for colonization by a single cohort of settlers from England, the Welsh Marches, and the continent. Among about a hundred vassals, tenants, and other dependants, of the first three Stewarts to be found in record of the period *c.* 1160 to 1241 are men bearing the names 'de Hesdin',[19] presumably related to Walter's Ponthevin mother, and 'of Palgrave', recalling his parents' Norfolk possessions.[20] A large and

---

[16] *Paisley Reg.*, 255 (=*RRS* ii, no. 219), inferring from 'quamdiu in manu sua fuit' that Hassendean did not remain in Walter I's possession.

[17] *Kelso Liber*, nos. 146, 147, 148; *Melrose Liber*, i. 259.

[18] *Kelso Liber*, no. 176. Uhtred son of Liulf seems to have had a son named Adam and a brother named Liulf who had a son William (*St. Bees Reg.*, 550-1; *Kelso Liber*, no. 170), so that when Malcolm IV in 1161 granted Mow (in marriage?) to Walter I son of Alan (*RRS* i, no. 183) he may have been overriding the rights of male heirs, for which practice see above, pp. 23-4. In the case of Mow, the problem is complicated by our ignorance of the identity of Eschina of London's second husband Henry, by whom she evidently had daughters Cecily and Maud who were her heirs in Mow. Was he, perhaps, Henry son of Anselm, *alias* Henry of Carmunnock (*Paisley Reg.*, 105) and son of the Anselm 'de Wichetune' or 'of Mow' noticed below, n. 20?

[19] Barrow, *Kingdom*, 355, 357-8; and see above, p. 15, n. 61.

[20] Barrow, *Kingdom*, 356. Note also that documents relating to the Stewart lordship of Mow were witnessed by William and Richard of Swaffham (*Kelso Liber*, nos. 146, 153, 155, 170). Swaffham in Norfolk is near Sporle and Palgrave

66   *The Colonists: (i) The great lords and their families*

conspicuous group of individuals and families obviously came to Scotland from Shropshire and its borderland, for example the Hosés of Albright Hussy,[21] the important but mysterious Robert 'of Montgomery',[22] Robert Hunald from Marchamley,[23] Stephen of Kinnerley,[24] a family from Great or Little Ness,[25] possibly the 'de Costentin' or Constantine family, from Eaton Constantine,[26] and the widely-ramified family of Wallace (*Walensis*), beginning with Richard Wallace, holder of a garrison-serjeant's fee in Shropshire under William II FitzAlan in 1166.[27] Richard was probably endowed by Walter the Stewart with the lands south of Kilmarnock on which he founded *Ricardes-tūn, Riccarton.[28] Before 1241 we find mention of some seven Wallaces in a Stewart context, Adam, Alan, Henry, two Richards, a Stephen, and a William.[29] William Wallace of Elderslie, the champion of Scotland, was surely a descendant of Richard Wallace or of one of his kin.[30] Lest we be tempted to see the great Wallace out of context, let us remember that in the period from 1296 to 1306 men known to have fought for Wallace, the Guardians, and Robert Bruce

---

where the FitzAlans held land (above, p. 15). A landowner in Mow by *c.* 1175–89 was Anselm 'de Wichetune' or Anxel 'de Hwitheton' (*Melrose Liber*, nos. 116, 134, 135, 137) who may perhaps be identified with Anselm 'de Hwichintona', witness to a confirmation (X 1147) for the FitzAlan abbey of Haughmond of Bradford Mill in High Ercall, Salop, by William Peverel of Dover (*Collectanea topographica et genealogica*, v (1838), 175).

[21] Barrow, *Kingdom*, 349–50.
[22] Ibid., 344.
[23] Ibid., 352.
[24] Ibid., 358. Stephen of Kinnerley (presumably independently of the Stewarts) acquired the lands of Drumsleed and Pittengardner (in Fordoun), Kincardineshire (*Arbroath Liber*, nos. 242, 245).
[25] Barrow, *Kingdom*, 352–3.
[26] Ibid., 351.
[27] Ibid., 349.
[28] Ibid., 350.
[29] Ibid., 356, 359, 361.
[30] The descent of William Wallace cannot be proved from surviving documents, but his family's connection with Elderslie (*Paisley Reg.*, 151, 370; Macfarlane's *Geographical Collections*, ii, 202) in the heart of the Stewart lordship, coupled with the use of the personal name William by earlier Wallaces who were vassals of the Stewarts (e.g. *Melrose Liber*, no. 64, 1207 X 1211), makes it all but certain that Wallace belonged to the family brought to Scotland from Shropshire in the train of Walter I son of Alan. For the suggestion that these Wallaces may have been identical with the family called 'of Ness' (Great or Little Ness, Salop), see Barrow, *Kingdom*, 352–3.

The Colonists: (i) The great lords and their families

included Reginald Crawford, descendant of the Fleming John after whom Crawford John is named,[31] the laird of Wiston, descendant of Wice the Fleming who founded that barony,[32] Simon Lockhart, descendant of an earlier Simon Lockhart who founded Symington in Kyle as the neighbouring fief to Riccarton,[33] Robert Baird of Strathaven, descendant of the Baards, perhaps also Flemish in origin, who had come from Cleveland to settle the Avon valley in the twelfth century,[34] Alexander Folkard, descendant of the twelfth-century Folcard who had founded the settlement of Folkerton,[35] and John of Montgomery, laird of Eaglesham, doubtless the descendant of the twelfth-century Robert de Montgomery.[36]

Along with the laymen and women there had come, typically enough, the religious colonists. Walter the Stewart, like his master King Malcolm, venerated Saint James the Great. In 1163 he founded, first at Renfrew but shortly afterwards at Paisley, a house of Cluniac monks drawn from the Shropshire priory of Much Wenlock.[37] They brought with them to the valley of the Cart the West Mercian dedication of Saint Milburga, but, significantly, precedence was given to the dedication to Saint James, while in some ways even more significantly it proved impracticable to leave out the local dedication of the church of Paisley to Saint Mirinus or Mirren, and eventually it was Saint Mirren who won the day. Wenlock Priory itself was given some property at Renfrew, but that was quickly exchanged for land which Walter the Stewart held, no doubt of his brother, at Manhood near Chichester. Although Manhood was hardly less remote from Shropshire than Renfrew, Wenlock managed to hold on to this estate till 1536.[38]

The Stewart lordship was slow to shed its possessions on the

[31] *OPS* i. 161–2; Barrow, *Bruce*, 448. By this date Crawford John had passed into the hands of the Murrays of Petty (BL MS Add. 28024, fo. 180).
[32] Barrow, *Bruce*, 450, 452 (Walter of Wiston and Austin Murray). The previous laird, Sir Henry of Wiston, kt., for whom see *Kelso Liber*, no. 339, had died by 1293 (*Rot. Scot.*, i. 15).
[33] Barrow, *Bruce*, 448.
[34] Ibid., 160; see below, p. 111 and n. 121 and Appendix B.
[35] Above, p. 41; Barrow, *Bruce*, 450 (where the estates should be located in Lanarkshire, not Lennox; cf. *Kelso Liber*, nos. 188, 191 (1315–16), 192 (1294); *TRHistS*, 5th ser. xxviii, 118 and n.).
[36] *CDS* ii, no. 1183; cf. Barrow, *Kingdom*, 344.
[37] Cowan (Easson), *Religious Houses*, 64–5.
[38] Barrow, *Kingdom*, 338.

east side of the country, but its distinctive development during the thirteenth century was to form a bridge from the south-west lowlands into the west highlands and even into northern Ireland. We know so little about the distribution of power in eleventh-century Scotland that we cannot tell how far this westward movement of successive Stewarts was following an older pattern of behaviour. No doubt throughout history the Firth of Clyde has imposed its own unity upon the peoples who have settled its shores and its islands of Arran, Bute, and the Cumbraes. The first of the Stewarts to acquire Bute seems to have been Alan, Walter I's son and heir, around 1200,[39] about the time that his daughter Avelina—named after her great-grandmother Avelina de Hesdin—was married to Duncan of Carrick, apparently without the king's consent.[40] In the time of Alan's grandson Alexander of Dundonald (1241–83) the Stewarts had gained an ascendancy over Cowal, the hilly district facing Bute on the north, and had become patrons of its chief native family, the Lamonts.[41] In the 1260s, Alexander's younger brother Walter, already earl of Menteith, obtained from Dugald MacSween a large part of Knapdale and lands in Cowal,[42] and may have ousted the Bissets from Arran.[43] It is surely significant of this *Drang nach Westen* by the Stewarts that Earl Walter, who lies buried with his wife in the priory of Inchmahome,[44] had a contemporary Gaelic by-

[39] *Paisley Reg.*, 15 (grant of the church of 'Kengaif', i.e. Kingarth, in the isle of Bute, with the parish of the whole island, by Alan the Stewart, 1198 X 1204).

[40] *Chron. Howden*, iv. 145. The grant of Kingarth may have been due partly to Alan's desire to appease the king's wrath.

[41] See *Paisley Reg.*, 132–9 for charters by members of the Lamont family, descendants of a certain Farquhar, granting to Paisley abbey churches and lands at Kilmorie in Glassary and Kilfinan and Kilmun in Cowal. They were witnessed by the Stewarts and/or members of the Stewart entourage, and the charter by Malcolm Lamont (ibid. 138–9) bore James the Stewart's seal. Lauman son of Malcolm son of Farquhar and his second cousin Angus (son of Duncan) son of Farquhar are referred to in the abortive scheme for west-highland sheriffdoms of 1293 (*APS* i. 447). For the Stewart as lord of Bute and Cowal in 1296 see *Rot. Scot.* i. 31b.

[42] NLS MS Adv. 29.4.2, vol. vii, p. 27.

[43] Walter Bisset died on Arran in 1251 (above, p. 16), after which no hint of Bisset lordship appears before 1298 when Thomas Bisset came over from Ireland to vindicate his claim to Arran (*Chron. Guisbrough*, 329). Circa 1275, Adam parson of Arran witnessed a charter of Walter Stewart earl of Menteith (NLS MS Adv. 34.6.24, p. 377).

[44] John A. Stewart, *Inchmahome and the Lake of Menteith* (privately printed, The Stewart Society, 1933), 83–5.

The Colonists: (i) The great lords and their families   69

name, *ballach* or 'freckled'.[45] The dominant position which the Stewarts had reached by the end of the thirteenth century in the Firth of Clyde and south Argyll was recognized in the abortive measures for reorganizing highland administration agreed upon in King John Balliol's first parliament of 1293.[46] According to these proposals, James the Stewart was to be sheriff of a new sheriffdom comprising Kintyre, lower Cowal, Arran and Bute. At that time private castles in Stewart hands west of the Clyde included Rothesay on Bute,[47] Brodick on Arran,[48] Dunoon,[49] possibly the 'impregnable castle' (as Bower has it) of Eilean Dearg in Loch Riddon,[50] and an unidentified castle of 'Glasrog', perhaps Glassary north of Knapdale.[51] If to this we add that James the Stewart married a sister of the earl of Ulster and obtained an estate near Coleraine,[52] and that he and his brother John and their uncle Walter of Menteith were parties to the Turnberry Band of 1286[53] made with the earl of Ulster and Thomas de Clare, an actual and speculative settler in North Munster,[54] we can appreciate that in the last decades of the thirteenth century the Stewarts were among the most powerful of West Highland chiefs, disposing of a sizeable fleet of galleys and commanding the loyalty of a large number of Gaelic-speaking tenants and

---

[45] *Chron. Fordun*, i. 298 (Walter 'Bullok'); Theiner, *Monumenta*, no. 237 (Walter 'Bulloc').
[46] *APS* i. 447.
[47] Taking 'a certain steward' in Hakon Hakon's son's Saga (Anderson, *Early Sources*, ii. 476) to refer to Walter II son of Alan. See also Stewart Cruden, *The Scottish Castle* (Edinburgh, 1960), 29–35.
[48] Barbour, *Bruce*, 66–9; Barrow, *Kingdom*, 373; *OPS* ii, pt. I, 251. This assumes that John Hastings, to whom Arran had come only in 1306, would not have had time to build 'a stith castell of stane' at Brodick; nor is it likely to have been the work of Edmund Hastings, who had acquired or claimed the capital lordship of the earldom of Menteith ('Enchimeholmok'=Inchmahome) between 1296 and 1301 (*Ancestor*, no. viii (1904), 101).
[49] *OPS* ii. I. 64. John constable of Dunoon witnessed with Walter II son of Alan a charter of Lauman son of Malcolm (*Paisley Reg.*, 132–3).
[50] *Chron. Bower*, i. 46.
[51] Stevenson, *Documents*, no. 445 (ii. 191). It seems probable that despite the tenure of Glassary by Mr Ralph of Dundee and his heirs (*Highland Papers*, ii. 117, 221 ff.) the name 'Glasrog' in this letter does represent Glassary, known to have had a castle by 1374 (*Highland Papers*, ii. 149), but that does not determine the location of the castle.
[52] Stevenson, *Documents*, no. 401 (ii. 111–12).
[53] Ibid., no. 12 (i. 22–3).
[54] Orpen, *Ireland*, iv. 66, 69–75.

dependants.⁵⁵ The well-nigh monopolistic power which the Campbells wielded in the southern West Highlands from the later fifteenth to the eighteenth century was derived in part from their successful exploitation of the decline of the Macdougall lords of Lorne and the Macdonald lords of Islay; but in large measure it was also due to the fact that the Campbells of Lorne fell heir to the complex of lordships built up by the Stewarts between 1200 and *c.* 1370, and that in turn was based upon the Clyde lordship created for the first of the Stewarts by David I and Malcolm IV.

As far as families are concerned, the fate of the de Morvilles could hardly stand in sharper contrast to that of the Stewarts. In modern Scotland the name de Morville means nothing. The main stem of the family had failed in the male line by 1196, and even of the baronial dynasties which succeeded to most of the de Morville inheritance the lords of Galloway, the de Quincys, and the Balliols all suffered extinction, biologically or politically, in the thirteenth and earlier fourteenth centuries. Yet in some respects the de Morvilles and their early Scottish lordship take us further than the Stewarts into the heart of the Anglo-Continental web in whose toils the kingdom of Scotland was entangled. In the manner in which the de Morvilles gained lands, marriages, and high office the Norman network is revealed at its highest level of effectiveness.

The commune of Morville in the canton of Bricquebec is about four km south of Valognes, about 25 km south of Cherbourg.⁵⁶ The family, evidently of knightly rank, which was proprietorial enough to take a surname from the village belonged to the same class of minor but substantial gentry or petty nobility as the Bruces, who took their surname from the commune of Brix only 12 km north-west of Morville.⁵⁷ In Normandy and England, the de Morvilles looked for patronage to the lords of Vernon and their kinsmen the de Reviers (Redvers), extensive landowners in Wessex, and from 1141 earls of Devon. It is indeed in Devon, Dorset, and Somerset that we find most evidence of the earliest Morville colonization

---

⁵⁵ For James the Stewart's men of Rothesay, Bute, and Cowal, with their galleys and sea-power, see *Rot. Scot.*, i. 31b.

⁵⁶ Loyd, *Origins*, 49–50, 70.

⁵⁷ Barrow, *Kingdom*, 322.

of lands in England. Reviers, however, is not in the Cotentin but lies between Bayeux and Caen, in a district from which originated Ivo Taillebois, steward of William Rufus, and a number of dependants of Ivo's associate Hugh de Beauchamp, already by 1086 the greatest landowner in Bedfordshire under the king.[58] Whether through the Redvers connection, or by some other route, Hugh de Morville, probably another of our younger sons, allied himself to the Beauchamps of Bedford by marrying Beatrice, daughter of Hugh de Beauchamp's younger son Robert, and heiress of Houghton Conquest.[59] Almost as soon as David of Scotland gained the Honour of Huntingdon about 1114 Hugh de Morville occurs as a witness to David's writs and charters,[60] and for a fleeting moment William de Morville, a landowner in Dorset and probably Hugh's elder brother, also appears at David of Scotland's court.[61] Hugh evidently committed himself decisively to a lifetime of service to the Scottish king. He was made King David's constable by about 1150, and although he held a number of fees of the Honour of Huntingdon, including Bozeat in Northamptonshire, it was in Scotland that he obtained land and lordships which placed him in the very first rank of the Anglo-Norman nobility.[62] These comprised Lauderdale together with detached estates at Saltoun, Nenthorn and Newton Don, at Dryburgh on the Tweed opposite Old Melrose, and probably also at Heriot.[63]

[58] *VCH, Bedford*, i. 201.
[59] It seems probable that Beatrice was daughter of Robert younger son of Hugh de Beauchamp, and thus sister of Miles and Pain de Beauchamp; *VCH, Bedford*, ii. 9–10; *Wardon Cartulary*, 331.
[60] *RRS* i, nos. 2, 3; see Lawrie, *Charters*, nos. 32, 35, 50.
[61] Ibid., no. 54. It is not certain that this William, appearing *c.* 1124, is to be identified with the William de Morville who witnessed charters for Montebourg Abbey given by Baldwin (de Redvers) earl of Exeter, 1142 X 1155 (*Cal. Docs. France*, nos. 879, 880) and himself granted the chapel of Bradpole, Dorset, to Montebourg (ibid., no. 885), but it seems probable. It further seems probable that the father of William and Hugh I de Morville was the Richard de Morville who witnessed charters by Richard de Redvers for Montebourg and the church of St. Mary in the castle of Néhou in the early twelfth century (*Rot. Scacc. Norm.* ii, p. cclxxii). It is possible that the unidentified Richard son of Baldwin killed by the Scots in 1168 along with Ralph Malchael, a de Morville dependant, was a member of the Redvers family (*Chron. Holyrood*, 150–1; *CWAAS Trans.*, NS ix (1909), 254).
[62] Barrow, *Kingdom*, 281; *Journal of Med. Hist.* i. 130–2. For Bozeat see *VCH, Northants*, iv. 3.
[63] *Dryburgh Liber*, *passim*; G. G. Simpson. 'An Anglo-Scottish Baron', p. 262, citing *Exch. Rolls.* i. 33 and *Newbattle Reg.*, no. 59.

72   The Colonists: (i) The great lords and their families

In the west of Scotland Hugh de Morville was given the whole of Cunningham, the northernmost third of Ayrshire.⁶⁴ Later in the twelfth century Hugh's son Richard was able to add Eddleston north of Peebles to these vast estates.⁶⁵ Lauderdale, with a castle at Lauder, was held, it seems, for six knights' service; Cunningham possibly for two, with a castle at Irvine.⁶⁶

English west-country documents give a few tantalizing glimpses of Morville connections with families such as Le Breton or Bret (whence Sampford Brett in Somerset)⁶⁷ and Engaine, the last a link which may explain or be explained by the marriage of a certain Simon de Morville to Ada Engaine, heiress of Burgh by Sands in Cumberland.⁶⁸ The de Morvilles were obviously on the march in the twelfth century, and their most important English acquisition seems to have come about as the direct result of the civil war of Stephen's time, when the king of Scots took possession of English Cumbria, lost by his

⁶⁴ No charter of Cunningham survives, but Hugh's lordship may be deduced from the distribution of the first Stewart's lordships created c. 1136–53, i.e. Renfrew, Mearns, and Strathgryfe immediately north of Cunningham and North Kyle immediately to the south. It is unlikely that the Crown retained Cunningham as late as 1162, or that if it had there would be no trace of royal lordship later than c. 1124–30, the date of Lawrie, *Charters*, nos. 84, 85. On the other hand, it must be noted that one of the earliest recorded Cunningham charters, Robert son of Wernebald's gift of Kilmaurs church to Kelso abbey (*Kelso Liber*, no. 283) is not known to have been confirmed by Hugh de Morville, though the confirmation of Robert's son was itself confirmed by Hugh's son Richard, X 1174 (ibid., nos. 284, 285).
⁶⁵ *Glasgow Reg.*, nos. 44, 45.
⁶⁶ *CDS* ii. 215 (one-third of half Lauder and Lauderdale for one knight's service), ii. 216 (one-third of half Irvine for one-third of a knight's service). This refers to 1296, but in 1316–20 Cunningham was granted to Robert Stewart for three knights' service (*RMS* i, no. 54), so that two knights may represent the service for Irvine alone.
⁶⁷ *The Times Literary Supplement* for 12 June 1969, p. 641, prints a photograph of an original charter shown that year at the Historical MSS Commission exhibition held at the National Portrait Gallery in London. The charter records a grant by Reginald Fitz Urse to his brother Robert and was witnessed by, i.a., Hugh II de Morville, Richard le Bret (Brito), and William (or Gilbert?) Engaine. (I owe this reference to Dr William Urry.) See also *Hist. MSS Comm. 9th Rep.* i. 353b for Somerset charters by Reginald and Robert Fitz Urse witnessed by members of the Le Bret and de Reigny families.
⁶⁸ See previous note and also *Wetherhal Reg.*, 186–8 nn., 193 n.; *CWAAS Trans.* NS ix, Table facing p. 241. For the de Reigny family holding in both Somerset and Cumberland, see Farrer, *HKF* i. 132–3 (where incidentally a Somerset charter is noted, confirming a de Reigny grant to Plympton priory, witnessed by Robert 'of Cumberland').

The Colonists: (i) The great lords and their families 73

father in 1092. King David, it seems, granted to Hugh de Morville the lordship of Westmorland proper—that is, Westmorland north of Shap Fell and the Howgill Fells, with its centre at Appleby on the upper Eden.[69] The lordship must have been left in Hugh's hands when Henry II wrested the northern counties from the Scots in 1157, unless indeed it had already passed to Hugh's son and namesake Hugh, whom we have already noticed as temporary owner of Borgue in Galloway.[70] On the evidence at present available it does not seem possible to be sure whether Hugh was older or younger than his brother Richard; my guess, but it is hardly more than a guess, is that Hugh was the eldest. What is certain is that he rose fast in the service of Henry II, acting as a royal justice and being entrusted with the castle of Knaresborough—whose territory he held at farm under the Crown.[71] Meanwhile, his brother Richard, who succeeded to the office of constable and to most of the Scottish lands in 1162, had also gained a large-scale estate in north-west England by his marriage to Avicia, daughter of William I of Lancaster, lord of Kentdale or South Westmorland and a landowner partly of native Anglo-Scandinavian stock.[72] Other Morvilles of this generation included Maud, who has bequeathed her name to Maulds Meaburn near Appleby and who married William de Vieuxpont.[73] It was through Maud that the Vieuxponts and after-

[69] *The Scottish Genealogist*, xxv (1978), 102–3.
[70] Above, p. 31, n. 3.
[71] W. Farrer, 'On the tenure of Westmorland temp. Henry II and the date of creation of the baronies of Appleby and Kendal', *CWAAS Trans.* (NS) vii, 100–7. Hugh de Morville seems to have received the Honour of Knaresborough by 1158 (*Pipe Roll 4 Henry II*, 148; compare entries under Yorkshire for subsequent years).
[72] F. Ragg in *CWAAS Trans.* (NS) ix. 237–8; G. H. L. Washington, ibid. lxii. 95–100.
[73] *CWAAS Trans.* (NS) xi. 307–8; *Kelso Liber*, no. 319. Despite the careful work of R. C. Reid, 'De Veteripont', *Dumfriesshire Trans.*, 3rd ser., xxxiii (1956), 91–105, the history of the earliest generations of the Vieuxponts in Scotland and northern England is not firmly established. For instance (1) the source noted in *RRS* ii, no. 84, comment, might suggest that William de Vieuxpont, husband of Maud de Morville, was the son of an earlier William de Vieuxpont to whom King Malcolm IV gave Hardingstone, Northants; (2) Emma de St. Hilaire, mother of three sons all called William de Vieuxpont (Reid, art. cit. 98–9), seems not to have been the only wife of her husband William de Vieuxpont. It may be suggested that Maud de Morville and Emma de St. Hilaire were wives of the same husband, and that he had died several years before 1203 (*Kelso Liber*, no. 143).

wards the Cliffords obtained the lordship of Westmorland.[74] There were also the significantly Scottish-named Malcolm de Morville, a younger brother, who was accidentally killed by Adulf de St. Martin while hunting,[75] and another sister, Ada de Morville, who married Roger Bertram lord of Mitford.[76] Just possibly Simon, founder of the Cumberland branch of the family which held the Solway barony of Burgh by Sands, was another brother. On balance, however, the evidence would point to Simon's being the first cousin rather than the brother of Hugh, Richard, Maud, Malcolm, and Ada.

It is due to the fact that Hugh de Morville the younger was one of the murderers, indeed the senior murderer, of Archbishop Thomas Becket[77] that we have some intimate biographical details of a kind which are sadly rare for members of the Anglo-Scottish baronage in the twelfth century. Much the most interesting of these details is the story told by William of Canterbury about Hugh's mother, Beatrice de Beauchamp.[78] According to William, who discreetly does not give the lady her name, she fell passionately in love with a young man called Lithulf. When he spurned her advances, she tricked him into drawing his sword in her husband's presence and then cried out 'Hughe de Morville, yare, yare, yare; Lithulf hath his swerd ydrawen', whereupon for his treason Lithulf was put to death by boiling. As Dr A. L. Poole pointed out,[79] a tale originally told to illustrate the fickleness of womankind in general and the iniquity of the de Morvilles in particular holds its chief interest for us in its demonstration that English speech was quite normal not merely in a 'knightly household', as Dr Poole thought, but in fact in a substantial baronial family. If the tale was founded on fact and the incident took place in Scotland or northern England, the Englishness of the cultural background might be easier to accept. Were it not for this piece of scandalous gossip, Beatrice de Beauchamp would be known to history as a devout and pious lady who shared fully

---

[74] *CWAAS Trans.* (NS) xi, Table facing p. 320.
[75] *Dryburgh Liber*, no. 94.
[76] Ibid., no. 92; Hedley, *Northumberland Families*, i. 27–8.
[77] *Becket Materials*, ii. 9.
[78] Ibid. i. 128.
[79] A. L. Poole, *From Domesday Book to Magna Carta* (Oxford, 1951), 252–3.

in her husband's foundation of a Premonstratensian abbey at Dryburgh[80] in which, having become a member of the order of White Canons, he died in 1162. The man who served as steward of Beatrice's English estates—incidentally, he had the Morville personal name of Herbert—owned some land at Goldington, just east of Bedford, and at the end of his life entered Wardon Abbey, the full sister house of Melrose, as a lay brother.[81] Whether Beatrice lived long enough to witness the popular disgrace of her son for Becket's murder we do not know. Hugh the younger also fell from Henry II's favour, but not because of the crime. Characteristically, he was forfeited only after he seemed in King Henry's eyes to have taken the Scottish side in the great revolt of 1173–4, when his defence of Appleby and Brough under Stainmore proved inadequate.[82] Even so, his lordship of Westmorland, or most of it, passed to his sister Maud, and with her to the family which took its surname from Vieuxpont-en-Auge in Calvados and was fully as Anglo-Scottish, in terms of lands and loyalties, as the de Morvilles.[83] We may note in passing that in the case of both these families there was partition of estates, despite the rule clearly enunciated by Glanvill, that if the deceased ancestor were a knight 'then, according to the law of the realm of England, the eldest son succeeds to his father in everything'.[84] The Morville estates in Scotland passed with the constableship to Richard de Morville, while Westmorland went first to Hugh, who died without heirs, and then (at least in part) to their sister Maud.[85] The fees on the Honour of Huntingdon, partly inherited from the elder Hugh de Morville, partly from Beatrice de Beauchamp, were successfully claimed by Richard de

---

[80] *Dryburgh Liber*, nos. 14, 15, 93, 143.
[81] *Wardon Cartulary*, no. 163.
[82] *CWAAS Trans.* (NS) vii. 103–4. Since Hugh was deprived of Knaresborough and Aldborough early in 1173 it would seem that Henry II's suspicions of his loyalty had already been aroused.
[83] R. C. Reid, *Dumfriesshire Trans.*, 3rd ser., xxxiii. 91 ff., especially 97–105. The order of birth of the sons of William de Vieuxpont husband of Maud de Morville has not been satisfactorily determined; see Holt, *Northerners*, 67, n. 7.
[84] Glanvill, *Tractatus de Legibus et Consuetudinibus Angliae*, ed. G. D. H. Hall (1965), 75.
[85] *CWAAS Trans.* (NS) vii. 100–3; ix. 253–4 (where Hugh is wrongly identified by the editor); xi. 314–15 (where the error is rectified). The land held by Maud de Morville was perhaps no more than a part of the lordship.

Morville and his daughter Helen.[86] The lordship of Westmorland, whether or not derived from Maud de Morville, passed to her son Robert de Vieuxpont, noted for his staunch loyalty to King John;[87] the Vieuxpont land in Scotland, made up of knights' fees in Berwickshire and Lothian, passed to another son William;[88] while the Pennine manor of Alston in South Tynedale, enjoying a somewhat ambivalent situation between England and Scotland, formed the share of a third son, Ivo.[89] Whether the motive for this partition was to avert difficulties posed by dual loyalty, or simply to deal more generously than usual with younger sons or daughters, the process was clearly made easier by the fact that some lands lay in the realm of England and some in Scotland.

The fortunes of the de Morville family suffered remarkably little from the younger Hugh's involvement in Becket's martyrdom. The Scottish line of the family, however, is linked to the murder by some evidence which, though slight, is curious and worth at least a brief mention. The Reverend Timothy Pont, minister of Dunnet in Caithness, laboured assiduously on the topography of Scotland at the turn of the sixteenth and seventeenth centuries. One of his most ambitious achievements was a detailed survey of Cunningham.[90] The survey contains a lengthy passage on the abbey of Kilwinning, north of Irvine, of which a great deal more survived in Pont's time than in ours, including the abbey's cartulary, which Pont was evidently able to consult.[91] This is what Pont wrote about the beginnings of the abbey:

> It wes foundit by a noble Englich man named Sir Richard Morwell, fugitive from his auen countrey for the slaughter of Thomas Beckett Archbischope of Canterburrey (being one of them) in the Rainge of K.

---

[86] *CDS* i, no. 294 ('Hocton' being Houghton Conquest, inherited from Beatrice de Beauchamp); Farrer, *HKF* ii. 356–60.

[87] *CWAAS Trans.* (NS) ix. 257–9; *Wetherhal Reg.*, p. 394; Holt, *Northerners*, 67 and n. 7, 220–1. Maud de Morville's lands in Westmorland seem to have been, in part at least, inherited by her son Ivo (*CWAAS Trans.* (NS) xi. 316–19).

[88] *Dumfriesshire Trans.*, 3rd ser., xxxiii. 97–103. For the suggestion that William de Vieuxpont who inherited the Scottish estates was son of William de Vieuxpont by a different marriage (viz. to Emma de St. Hilaire) from that which produced Robert and Ivo (viz. to Maud de Morville), see above, p. 73, n. 73.

[89] *RRS* ii, no. 468.

[90] *Cuninghame topographized* (see List of Abbreviations).

[91] Ibid., 254–5.

The Colonists: (i) The great lords and their families 77

Henry 2d of England, quho flying to Scotland wes be the then Scotts king welcomed, and honoured with the office of grate Constable of Scotland, as also inriched with the Lordeschips of Cuninghame, Largis and Lauderdaill, quhosse posterity for divers generations possessed the said office and lands. Now the forsaid Richard, being, as vald seime, tuoched with compu(n)ctione for the savety of hes soul (according to the custome of thesse tymes) did found this Abbey of Killvinnin in testimoney of hes repentance.[92]

It is impossible to guess from what source Pont derived this quaint mixture of fact and falsehood. There is no question of *Richard* de Morville's being implicated in Becket's murder, but it is not improbable that he should have been moved by it to found a religious house. When we recall that King William the Lion founded Arbroath Abbey in honour of Saint Thomas as early as 1178, and that both Arbroath and Kilwinning were houses for Tironensian monks, the former certainly and the latter probably colonized from Kelso, the connection between Kilwinning and Thomas Becket suggested by Pont seems to be at least plausible.[93] Among Pont's brief and tantalizing extracts from the lost cartulary of Kilwinning is the note of a grant towards the building of the abbey by Dorothea de Morville—said to be Richard's daughter—and her husband, Philip de Horsey, a grant confirmed by their son Walter, by Jocelin bishop of Glasgow (therefore not later than 1199) and by a pope Honorius in his second year, which can only refer to Honorius III between July 1217 and July 1218.[94]

Unknown to Pont, William FitzStephen, alone among the biographers of Becket, preserved the detail that the clerk Hugh who accompanied and assisted the four knights Bret, FitzUrse, Morville, and Tracy, was called Mauclerc (*malus clericus*) only as a nickname, and that his real name was Hugh de Horsea.[95] Also surely unknown to Pont, the Devonshire squire and antiquary of James I's time, Sir William Pole of Colcombe and Shute, whose collections were not published until the end of the eighteenth century, says that Leigh Powlet in Bampton Hundred was held in Henry II's reign by Philip de Horsey and

[92] Ibid., 254.
[93] The choice of the Tironensian order for Kilwinning seems particularly significant in view of the de Morville links with the Premonstratensians at Dryburgh and the Cistercians at Byland.
[94] *Cuninghame topographized*, 255. The reported confirmation by King Alexander 'the 3rd' was probably by Alexander II.
[95] *Becket Materials*, iii. 142.

Thomas de Horsey:[96] while Hutchins, whose *History of Dorset* was first published in 1774, fifty years before Pont's notes on Cunningham were printed (and then only in a private edition of twenty-five pages),[97] says that the first known lord of Clifton Maubank south-west of Sherborne was Philip de Horsey, whose son Walter occurs in the time of Henry II.[98] Finally, John Batten's work on South Somerset, including a paper on the Horsey family published in 1897, cites documents mentioning Philip de Horsey which date from the late twelfth century or from early in John's reign.[99]

The evidence for a twelfth-century Philip de Horsey, probably with a son named Walter, may therefore be taken as reasonably firm. Horsey itself, held at different times of Walter of Douai, Fulk Painell, and William Briwerr and rated at a knight's fee, is about 2 miles north of Bridgwater.[100] That the family taking its name from this Somerset hamlet and holding land in that county and in Devon and Dorset should have been associated with the de Morvilles is in no way improbable. One line of the Morvilles represented by Herbert de Morville in the period 1204–20 held land at Portbury near Bristol and a junior branch at Bradpole near Bridport.[101] A Somerset setting for no fewer than three out of Becket's four assassins is strikingly provided by an original charter which has enjoyed some recent publicity,[102] by which Reginald FitzUrse granted to his half-brother Robert a moiety of the manor of Williton near Watchet, the list of ten witnesses being headed by Hugh de Morville and Richard *Brito* or Bret. Even Robert FitzUrse, the grantee of this charter, must have had some slight connection with Scotland, for he is found witnessing an act of King William

---

[96] *Collections towards a Description of the County of Devon by Sir William Pole of Colcombe and Shute, knt.*, ed. Sir J. W. de la Pole, Bt., of Shute (1791), 210.

[97] *Cuninghame topographized*, p. xi.

[98] J. Hutchins, *History of Dorset* (1774), ii. 458–9.

[99] John Batten, 'The Horsey Family', Somerset Archaeological and Natural History Soc., *Proceedings*, xliii (1897), 84–5. See also T. D. Tremlett and N. Blakiston, *Stogursey Charters* (1949), no. 26, a charter of Philip de Columbers witnessed by, i.a., Philip 'de Horsi'.

[100] J. Batten, art. cit., 84–93.

[101] Loyd, *Origins*, 70.

[102] Above, n. 67, the charter being given by one of the four knights, Reginald Fitz Urse, and witnessed by two others, Hugh II de Morville and Richard le Bret (Brito).

The Colonists: (i) The great lords and their families 79

belonging to the earlier years of his reign.[103] It would not be surprising to find Philip de Horsey helping to endow Kilwinning Abbey if the murderers' clerical accomplice Hugh de Horsea had been a younger brother. There remains the difficulty that if Philip's wife Dorothea (otherwise unknown to record) had really been Richard de Morville's daughter, she or her son ought to have shared in the family inheritance on the death without issue in 1196 of her putative brother William de Morville, whereas in fact all the lands and the constableship went to William's sister Helen, and thus to her husband's descendants, lords of Galloway. Perhaps Dorothea was the daughter of another member of the de Morville family.

I have compiled a list of about 150 men and women who were in some way associated with the de Morville lordship in Scotland from the time of Hugh the elder to the death of Alan of Galloway in 1234. A good many names on the list are nothing but names, and others were either of merely local importance or connected with the de Morvilles only incidentally. But those which remain illustrate clearly enough from how wide a range of territories and through what a variety of channels the vassals of one of the greatest feudal lordships of Scotland might be assembled. There are, first, the families of obviously Norman origin, some attributable to a Morville or Beauchamp source, others to the alliance between Morville and Lancaster, others again without any evident connections. The Haigs of Bemersyde took their surname from the district of La Hague, the extreme north-west corner of the Cotentin peninsula.[104] The family which held the fee of Giffen in Cunningham was surnamed 'de Néhou' from a parish near Morville which formed the *caput* of the Honour of Vernon.[105]

---

[103] *RRS* ii, no. 45 (1166 X 71); cf. *Hist. MSS Comm. 9th Rep.* i. 353b for a charter of Robert Fitz Urse in favour of St. Andrew of Stogursey.
[104] Loyd, *Origins*, 49–50.
[105] Ibid., 70; *Rot. Scacc. Norm.* ii, pp. cclxxii, cclxxv, for Néhou as the caput of the Honour of Vernon. For members of the family in England, see *Cal. Docs. France*, no. 885 (William de Néhou and his brother Richard, apparently incumbent of Bradpole chapel, Dorset). For their association wtih the de Morville family and its successors in Scotland, see Marquess of Bute, Dumfries House, Loudoun charters, no. 1 (William de Néhou with Richard de Morville); SRO RH 6/12 and Stevenson, *Illustrations*, p. 15 (Richard de Néhou with William de Morville); Anderson, *Diplomata*, pl. LXXXI and Loudoun charters, no. 4 (Alexander de Néhou with, respectively, Roland son of Uhtred and his son Alan). From *Dryburgh*

80   *The Colonists: (i) The great lords and their families*

Beauchamps in person figure among witnesses to Morville or successor charters for Westmorland and Cunningham[106] and the Beauchamps almost certainly account for the establishment in Scotland of the Sinclairs of Herdmanston (East Lothian), from whom all the Scots Sinclairs claim descent.[107] Saint-Clair-sur-l'Elle is only a little way south of the Beauchamp between Carentan and Bayeux whence the Bedfordshire Beauchamps originated.[108] Another Beauchamp link may be seen in the knightly family of de Ros or Ross, characterized by their use of the first name Godfrey, and settled in Cuningham at Stewarton and Ardneil opposite the Cumbraes.[109] Their Norman origin is probably to be sought at Rots, between Bayeux and Caen, among a group of parishes from which several Beauchamp dependants are known to have come to England.[110] In the same area is Biéville-sur-Orne, whose church was granted to St. Stephen's, Caen, by Ranulf le Meschin, vicomte of Bayeux and first Norman lord of Carlisle.[111]

Liber, nos. 226, 227, it may be seen that William de Néhou, who held Giffen, and his wife Syrit, had sons Richard and Alexander, and that Alexander's eventual heir at Giffen was Walter of Mulcaster. The late *Dryburgh Cartulary* has rendered the name 'Neu' (which is how it appears in Loudoun charters, no. 4) and (nos. 228, 229), 'Neuch' and 'Neuhan'.

[106] *CWAAS Trans.* (NS) ix. 253–4; xi. 315 (Reginald de Beauchamp); ibid. 310 (Robert de Beauchamp); ibid. xvii. 229 and NLS MS 42676, charters by Alan son of Roland witnessed by Roger de Beauchamp.

[107] For the Sinclairs in England see Farrer, *HKF* iii, *passim* and especially pp. 287–91; Loyd, *Origins*, 88–9. The Beauchamps of Bedford apparently took their name from Beauchamp in Vouilly (canton Isigny, dép. Calvados), only a few miles north of Saint-Clair-sur-l'Elle. The earliest recorded Sinclair associated with the de Morvilles was Alan de Sancto Claro, witness to a charter (1162 X 67) by Hugh II de Morville (*CWAAS Trans.* (NS) ix. 253–4). In Scotland Morville charters were witnessed by and given to Henry, and after him Alan, de Sancto Claro as follows:

(1) Henry Sinclair: Loudoun charters, no. 1; *Glasgow Reg.*, nos. 45, 46; SRO RH 6/12; Stevenson, *Illustrations*, p. 15; Anderson, *Diplomata*, pl. LXXVa and b; NLS MS Adv. 34.1.9 (II), pp. 244–5;

(2) Alan Sinclair: Anderson, *Diplomata*, pl. LXXXI; Stevenson, *Illustrations*, p. 15; *Glasgow Reg.*, no. 173. The *Scots Pge.* gives no convincing evidence to support its view that the Sinclairs of Herdmanston and of Roslin had different continental origins (vi. 564; vii. 577 ff.).

[108] Saint-Clair-sur-l'Elle, arr. Saint-Lô, dép. Manche; Beauchamp, cant. Isigny, arr. Bayeux, dép. Calvados.

[109] *Cuninghame topographized*, 98, 357.

[110] *VCH, Bedford*, i. 201.

[111] Delisle–Berger, *Recueil* i. 277.

The Colonists: (i) The great lords and their families 81

Biéville, formerly Boiavilla or Boeville,[112] may safely be regarded as the home parish of the Boivilles of Levington (i.e. Kirklinton), Cumberland.[113] The first of the family to be established in this territory, which became the barony of Levington, was Richer de Boiville, who seems to have had a younger son Gilbert who acquired a considerable position in Scotland.[114] Another branch of the family, or else a distinct family also taking its surname from Biéville, is to be found in documents relating to Coupland, a lordship given to Ranulf le Meschin's younger brother William. These Coupland Boivilles are sometimes found in association with West Cumberland families associated with the de Morvilles or their successors, and indeed intermarried with the presumably junior de Morville family which survived in thirteenth-century Cumbria.[115] It therefore does not seem improbable that the ancient Cunningham family of Boyle (⟨de Boiville⟩) of Kelburn, who first appear in the late thirteenth century,[116] and who obtained the title of earl of Glasgow from Queen Anne in 1703,[117] were an offshoot of the Cumbrian Boivilles who migrated from the Bessin in the first half of the twelfth century.

The Maitland family first emerges towards the end of the twelfth century, and if an ancestor of the Scottish branch is to be sought he may perhaps be found in the William Maltalent who witnessed a charter for Lanercost Priory, Cumberland,[118] issued by Hugh de Morville (son of Simon) lord of Burgh on

[112] Ibid., loc. cit. and p. 578.
[113] J. Wilson, *Ancestor*, no. 3, 80; *Wetheral Reg.*, 385.
[114] A Richer occurs along with Godard (de Boiville) among witnesses to William Meschin's charters for St. Bees (*St. Bees Reg.*, pp. 30, 35), and is probably the 'Richard' who witnessed Godard's own charter, ibid., no. 76. See also Appendix B, and (for Godard de Boiville) Clay and Greenway, *Early Yorkshire Families*, 6–7.
[115] *St. Bees Reg.*, 87, 106–7; *Ancestor*, no. 3, 82–4; *CDS* ii. 12, 37.
[116] The names of Robert de Boyville and Hugh del Blare of Ayrshire occur close together in the homage record of 1296 (ibid., p. 205) and the same two men served as jurors on an Ayrshire inquest held at Berwick, 28 Aug. 1296 (ibid., p. 216). Robert 'de Bouyll' witnessed a charter by Hugh Franciscus *alias* del Blare concerning Blair (in Dalry, Cunningham), NLS Adamton charters, no. 9, along with other Cunningham notables. Richard de Boyville of Ayrshire also did homage in 1296 (*CDS* ii. 210).
[117] *Scots Pge.* iv. 183 ff.
[118] *Trans. Roy. Soc. Literature*, 2nd ser., viii. 454 (ii. 13, see Index). William was the name given to the son and heir of Richard Maitland (*Scots Pge.* v. 278) and had been the name of at least one earlier member of the family in Scotland (*Kelso Liber*, nos. 186, 194, 233, 242, 365, 419, 456).

Sands (d. 1201). In the thirteenth century one of the Maitlands succeeded, by marriage with an heiress, to the important lordship of Thirlestane by Lauder, previously held by freeholders of native Northumbrian stock.[119] The family's origin is unknown, but the name, *mal talent*, 'evil genius', is typically Norman. An undoubted adventurer hitching his wagon to the Morville star (perhaps by way of the Honour of Lancaster) was Vivian des Moulineaux (Molyneux), a younger son of one of the twelfth-century lords of Sefton in south-west Lancashire.[120] Vivian des Moulineaux got land from the de Morvilles first of all at Oxton in Lauderdale and afterwards at Saltoun in East Lothian.[121]

As dependants of Morville or Beauchamp, families of Norman provenance are only to be expected. The number of Morville families whose surnames point to origin in England is rather more surprising. In contrast with the continental invasion of 1066, which has left record of hundreds, indeed thousands, of individuals known to us only by a single personal name, Robert, Walter, William, etc., the Anglo-Norman settlement of Scotland coincided with a new social fashion whereby families which had taken root in England, or whose roots had long been there, adopted more or less fixed surnames, often from the village or manor where the family held most of its property. Although many of these families may have had continental ancestry, as far as Scotland was concerned they would to all intents and purposes have been English. Their speech was doubtless English, their experience was limited to England, and they would have regarded themselves as English by race. Thanks to this twelfth-century use of surnames we can trace the movement of families to de Morville lands in Scotland

[119] Barrow, *Kingdom*, 297–8; *Scots Pge.* v. 278. This last account omits the attestation by Thomas Maitland of a charter by Philip de Valognes of 5 Aug. 1213 X 5 Nov. 1215 (*Panmure Reg.* ii. 125–6). A Gilbert 'de Maltalent' witnessed an earlier charter of Philip de Valognes, 1195 X 1205 (*ETC* vi, no. 54).

[120] *VCH, Lancaster*, iii. 67; *Cockersand Chartulary*, 488 n., 591; *Lancashire Inquests, Extents and Feudal Aids*, ed. W. Farrer (Lancashire and Cheshire Record Soc., xlviii, 1903), 12–15 (see especially p. 14, a charter of Richard de Molyneux for Simon de Molyneux witnessed by Vivian de Molyneux). Farrer (*VCH, Lancaster*, iii. 67, n. 7) believed that the place of origin was Moulineaux, dép. Seine-Maritime, but the name is not uncommon.

[121] *Soutra Reg.*, nos. 12, 32. Vivian occurs as a witness to a number of Morville or successor charters, e.g. *Glasgow Reg.*, no. 46, *Kelso Liber*, no. 246, *CDS* i, no. 265; cp. *Holyrood Liber*, no. 70.

from a wide area of north-west England. The Pennine villages of Hillbeck near Brough and Smardale near Kirkby Stephen provided two such families, obviously by way of the Morville lordship of Westmorland.[122] Farther south, another Pennine village, Clapham between Ingleton and Settle, in territory brought to Richard de Morville by his marriage with Avicia of Lancaster,[123] was the home of a family of 'de Clapham' one of whose branches eventually became naturalized north of the Forth through the patronage of an earl of Fife and persisted for many centuries as the Clephanes of Carslogie near Cupar.[124] The Lancaster connection seems also to have been responsible for the appearance in Scotland under Morville patronage of the much interrelated and probably largely native English families of Pennington and Muncaster from south-west Cumberland and of the Derwentwaters from farther north.[125] The Warwicks also, commemorated in two Cunningham place-names, may have come from Cumbria as part of this movement from north-western England.[126]

[122] *CWAAS Trans.* (NS) ix. 254 (Thomas of Hillbeck, 1154 X 1168, referred to in the past, ibid. xvii. 228); *APS* i. 92 (reading Helebec), *Melrose Liber*, no. 99 reading Hellebec for Hellehec: (William of Hillbeck, 1189 X 1196); William son of Hamo of Hillbeck witnessed a charter by Alan son of Roland, *CWAAS Trans.* (NS) xvii. 229. The homage of William of Hillbeck of Dumfriesshire was recorded in 1296, *CDS*, ii. 206). *Dryburgh Liber*, nos. 126–8 (Adam and Simon of Smardale, 12th–13th cents.).

[123] W. Farrer, *Lancashire Pipe Rolls and Early Charters* (1902), *CDS* i, no. 195; *Furness Coucher Book*, i. 201. Alan of Clapham appears in numerous de Morville and connected charters, e.g. BL MS Royal 11 B ix, fos. 102ᵛ–103ʳ; Anderson, *Diplomata*, pl. LXXXI; SRO RH 6/12; he was given land in Lauderdale by William de Morville (*APS* vii. 153, col. 2) and served as sheriff of Lauder in 1203 (*Kelso Liber*, no. 143).

[124] In 1296 Sir Mark de Clapham was a tenant in Fife of the bishop of St. Andrews (*CDS* ii. 205). For the Clephanes of Carslogie, see Nisbet, *Heraldry*, ii. 27; Sibbald, *Fife*, 394–5; NLS MS Adv. 34.6.24, p. 109.

[125] Members of the complicated family of Pennington *alias* Mulcaster (Muncaster) evidently succeeded to Giffen in Cunningham as heirs to the de Néhou family (*Dryburgh Liber*, no. 227; *CDS* ii. 29–30). Alan of Derwentwater witnessed a charter of Alan son of Roland (grandson of Richard de Morville) concerning land in Kirkcudbrightshire (SRO Register Ho. charters, no. 308); for his family, see *St. Bees Reg.*, p. 401n.

[126] Richard 'de Warewic' was a prominent witness to charters of William de Morville (*Glasgow Reg.*, no. 46) and his sister Helen (BL MS Royal 11 B ix, fos. 102ᵛ–103ʳ), while Thomas of Warwick witnessed a charter by Alan son of Elsi of land in Lauderdale (BL MSS Loans 29/255). No doubt it is their family name which is preserved in the Cunningham place-names Warrix and Warrickhill (in Dreghorn). According to Pont, presumably basing his statement on the lost Kilwinning abbey cartulary, Warrix was held by Philip de Horsey (*Cuninghame topographized*, 382). The well-known Cumberland family of Warwick usually, though not invariably, appear as 'de Warthewic' (from Warwick in Wetheral; see *Wetheral*

Walter son of Alan and Hugh de Morville the elder belonged to Anglo-Continental families and came to Scotland as colonists in the ordinary sense of the word, outsiders who rose from modest beginnings through the favour and in the service of the kings of Scotland. Their careers remind us of the early thirteenth-century Barnwell chronicler's comment that 'the more recent Scottish kings count themselves Frenchmen by race, manners and speech and retain only Frenchmen in their household',[127] or Jordan Fantosme's remark that William the Lion 'held only foreigners dear, and would never love his own people'.[128] Benefiting from generous infeftments of land and the delegation of a large measure of royal power, Walter the Stewart and Hugh the Constable established in southern Scotland seigneurial empires important in their own time and directly ancestral to some of the dominant baronial lordships of the later middle ages. It may seem strange to set beside them the earls of Fife, even by way of contrast. The earls were leaders of the native aristocracy both by blood and in the role they played within the Scots kingdom. In what sense, therefore, could they be called colonists? Were they not among the most prominent of King William's 'own people' whom he would never love? How could families such as the Fifes hope to prevail against the new men from the south who for something like a century enjoyed social and political ascendancy? And yet an examination of the fortunes of the Fifes may take us further towards an understanding of twelfth- and thirteenth-century Scotland than we are likely to achieve by keeping only Norman company.

The influence of the earls of Fife derived from a delegation of royal authority analogous to that which activated the feudal barons whom we have already been considering. Whether we call them mormaers or earls, the provincial governors of Scotland north of Forth clearly had their roots far back in Scottish history. King David I must have recognized the

---

Reg., references in index; Lanercost cartulary, *Trans. Roy. Soc. Literature*, 2nd ser., viii, references in index; *St. Bees Reg.*, 309, 377), so that identity with the Scottish family can only be suggested tentatively. The homage of Richard de Warwyk of Ayrshire was recorded in 1296 (*CDS* ii. 199).

[127] *Memoriale Fratris Walteri de Coventria* (ed. W. Stubbs, Rolls ser., 1872–3), ii. 206.
[128] *Chron. Fantosme*, lines 640–3.

analogy between their position and that of the newer lords when, about 1136, he granted the earldom of Fife to Earl Duncan I by royal charter. The Crown could thus feudalize an institution which it would not, or could not, abolish. The economic and social basis of the earls' power lay in a complex of estates between Forth and Tay, mainly in East Fife but with outlying possessions in East Lothian, at the southern end of the 'earls' ferry',[129] and in the shire of Culross between Clackmannan and Dunfermline.[130] It is a striking fact that much of what we know to have belonged to the earls by the second decade of the thirteenth century was in fact acquired by them, through royal favour or in some other way, from the time of Earl Duncan I onward. Balbirnie in Markinch was obtained by exchange with the Abernethy family;[131] Strathleven was given by William the Lion;[132] a circle of estates round the Howe of Fife by Malcolm IV, together with Strathbraan west of Dunkeld;[133] while the future barony of West Calder in Midlothian, was acquired from David I as a fief to be held for knight service.[134] The earls certainly possessed Cupar in the twelfth century, but the ambiguity of its status in later times as a royal burgh and capital of the sheriffdom of Fife raises the question of whether it too had been mediatized fairly recently when Earl Duncan II granted its church to St. Andrews Priory about 1170–80.[135] We cannot even be certain that it was the earls and not the king who built the original phase of the motte and bailey castle of Cupar, which evidently existed by *c.* 1170.[136]

[129] Barrow, *Kingdom*, 283; G. W. S. Barrow, 'The earls of Fife in the 12th century', *PSAS* lxxxvii (1952–3), 51–62, especially p. 56.

[130] SRO Register ho. supplementary charters, under date 1217 (confirmation by Robert I of a charter of Malcolm I earl of Fife). For the earls' lordship of Abercrombie (West Fife) and Cleish, see *Dunfermline Reg.*, nos. 144, 145.

[131] *RRS* ii, no. 14.

[132] Ibid., no. 472.

[133] Ibid. i, no. 90.

[134] Ibid. ii, no. 472. Note also that by ibid., no. 496 (1211?) Earl Malcolm I was recognized as nearest heir to the estate of Bangour, West Lothian.

[135] *St. Andrews Liber*, 241–2. Cupar was already a prosperous town when Earl Malcolm I gave his principal endowment to Culross Abbey, *c.* 1217 (above, n. 130). It was called a burgh in 1294 (Stevenson, *Documents*, i. 416), and burgesses of Cupar already appear in 1293 (*Highland Papers*, ii. 125–8). Its recognition as a 'king's burgh' (later 'royal burgh') seems to date from *c.* 1357 (G. Pryde, *The Burghs of Scotland*, ed. A. A. M. Duncan (Oxford, 1965), 21).

[136] Peter constable of Cupar witnessed charters of 1160 × 72 (*North Berwick Carte*, no. 3; *St. Andrews Liber*, 137).

86   *The Colonists: (i) The great lords and their families*

Thus, at the time when Duncan I succeeded to the earldom in the 1130s he may not have held more than a nucleus of property in East Fife and East Lothian.

Within fifty years, the Fifes were looking much further afield. In the last two or three decades of the twelfth century, the country south of the Moray Firth was being opened up to outside settlement, chiefly because King William's defeat of Donald MacWilliam in 1187 brought to the north a long period of peace. No doubt there were rewards to be had by those who had played a part in the king's campaigning. Earl Duncan II was granted by the bishop of Moray the extensive and mainly mountainous lands of Stratha'an (Strathavon), stretching from Ballindalloch on the Spey 27 miles southwestward to the summit of Beinn Macduibh.[137] Indeed, it is not impossible that the name of Beinn Macduibh, 'Macduff's Hill', dates from this infeftment, when the mountain which for so long was believed to be the highest in Scotland would have served as the earl's western boundary mark.[138] One of the earl's younger sons, David, likewise acquired a great north-country estate from the bishop of Moray, in his case the group of parishes about the middle River Deveron which became the lordship of Strathbogie.[139] The Fife empire was further augmented by Earl Duncan II's eldest son Malcolm. From the king he obtained Auchtermuchty in Fife and the reversion of Bangour in West Lothian.[140] From the earl of Strathearn, as the marriage portion of the earl's daughter, he acquired Glendevon and Fossoway.[141] The marriage seems to have brought Redgorton north of Perth into the possession of the Fife family, at least temporarily (for Earl Malcolm I died childless, and his wife's tocher reverted to Strathearn).[142] Finally we may note that the lordships of Strathord immediately north of Redgorton and of Kinnoull a few miles to the east were in the hands of the earls of Fife later in the thirteenth century.[143]

[137] *Moray Reg.*, nos. 16, 62.
[138] Watson, *CPNS*, 238.
[139] *Moray Reg.*, no. 35.
[140] *St. Andrews Liber*, 228–9.
[141] *PSAS* lxxxvii. 60–1.
[142] *Laing Chrs.*, no. 6; *Scone Liber*, no. 72; *Lindores Chartulary*, nos. 30–2.
[143] *Balmerino Liber*, no. 10; *CDS* ii, no. 1108 (for 'Kimile' read 'Kinule'). An

The Colonists: (i) The great lords and their families 87

In short, the Fifes, no less than the Stewarts and Morvilles, the Bruces, Cumins, Olifards, and the rest, were empire-builders in this period. They were internal colonists. If they, as magnates of the *ancien régime*, were to hold their own beside Anglo-Norman newcomers, they would have to adapt themselves to the conventions of military feudalism. They must obtain land with which to reward new followers with knights' fees, exotic dependants such as William 'of Holderness',[144] Miles de Raiville,[145] and William de Wyville,[146] or the unknown ancestor of Sir Gilbert the knight of Cleish, the traces of whose fortified home, evidently a motte, may possibly be discerned a little to the south-west of Cleish Castle.[147] Above all, the Fifes needed to form social alliances which would identify their dynasty with the new order. Earl Duncan II married a lady named Ela.[148] Although for the present her parentage remains uncertain, it seems likely that she was a daughter of Reginald de Varenne, ancestor of the Warennes of Wormegay, and brother of Ada de Varenne mother of the Scots kings Malcolm and William.[149] In Balfour of Denmilne's bad seventeenth-century text of King Malcolm's marriage grant to Earl Duncan II we should take the grantees to have been, not 'Earl Duncan and the heir born to his wife Ada my niece', but 'Earl Duncan and the heir born to his wife Ala, my mother's niece'.[150] The existence of such a relationship is suggested by at least three facts which would otherwise be puzzling. A writ of

---

unpublished charter of Earl Duncan III for Sir Nicholas Hay (Earl of Moray, Darnaway Castle, Gray of Kinfauns muniments, bdle 84, no. 2) refers to the earl's court of Kinnoull (*c.* 1286); another, of John son of Duncan of Inchyra (12 May 1283), was witnessed by Alexander son of the earl of Fife, parson of Kinnoull ('Kynule'; NLS MS Adv. 15.1.18, no. 45).

[144] *St. Andrews Liber*, 241, 243.
[145] Ibid. 241, 243, 244, 260; and note the name Milo among companions of Earl Duncan II of Fife when he visited Durham cathedral and was commemorated in the Liber Vitae (*Liber Vitae Ecclesiae Dunelmensis*, facsimile edn., Surtees Soc., 1923, fo. 36ᵛ).
[146] *St. Andrews Liber*, 260 (and elsewhere); *Dunfermline Reg.*, nos. 144, 213, 214; *Moray Reg.*, no. 50; *North Berwick Carte*, nos. 7, 10; *SHS Misc.*, iv. 311.
[147] SRO GD 254/1. I am grateful to Mr Michael Spens, owner of Cleish Castle, for showing me the probable site of this motte.
[148] *PSAS* lxxxvii. 53–4.
[149] For Reginald see *Comp. Pge.* xii, pt. I, 496, n. 'g'; *EYC* viii. 26–7.
[150] *RRS* i, no. 190. For Ala as a variant of Ela cf. *Comp. Pge.* xii, I. 497.

Earl Duncan II anent army service in Fife was witnessed by Reginald de Varenne.[151] A charter by Reginald's son William, granting land at Brighton in Sussex, was witnessed by the earl's second son Duncan.[152] And a family named 'de Varenne', using the first name Reginald, appear on the borders of Fife and Perthshire at the turn of the twelfth and thirteenth centuries.[153] An alliance with the Varennes would at once bring the Fifes into the charmed circle of the great Anglo-Norman nobility. In 1188 the earl bought the marriage of Roger de Merlay lord of Morpeth for his daughter Ada—note the Varenne personal name—at a price of 500 marks— apparently the first step in a modest piece of counter-colonization or investment in English lands.[154] Towards the close of the twelfth century a second step brought the earl and his son into Yorkshire. Sir Charles Clay has published a charter by which Earl Duncan granted land at Plompton in Spofforth, between Knaresborough and Harrogate, to Nigel of Plompton.[155] A sustained Fife involvement in this corner of the West Riding seems to be proved by the fact that Duncan II's son and heir Malcolm was attended at various dates by Silvester son of William of Sicklinghall and three other Yorkshiremen, William Fairfax and David and William of Ayton.[156] Moreover, Earl Malcolm granted a group of farms immediately south of Cupar in Fife to make up a knight's fee for Richard son of Andrew of Linton, almost certainly Linton

---

[151] *PSAS* xc. 74.

[152] *The Chartulary of the Priory of St. Pancras of Lewes*, ed. L. F. Salzman (Sussex Record Soc., xxxviii, 1932), 55, charter witnessed by Dunecan son of Dunecan, and dating X 1179 if given before the death of Reginald de Varenne. See ibid. 54, for a charter (*c.* 1164) of Countess Isabel, daughter of William III earl Warenne and his wife Ela of Ponthieu, witnessed by William de Bellencombre, who held land of the Countess Ada at Lethington, East Lothian (*RRS* ii, no. 459).

[153] Fraser, *Douglas*, iii. 349–50, no. 281; *PSAS* lx. 71–2; *Lindores Chartulary*, nos. 70–2.

[154] *CDS* i, no. 191; W. P. Hedley, *Northumberland Families*, i. 197.

[155] *EYC* xii. 74, no. 53. For the family of Plompton (Plumpton) see ibid. xi, *passim*, especially pp. 46–51, 56–7, 59, 64–5, 76, 85–6, 116.

[156] *SHS Misc.* iv. 309, 311; *Moray Reg.*, no. 50; *Dunfermline Reg.*, no. 144. Sicklinghall is 3 miles south of Plompton, 1 mile west of Wetherby. A William son of Robert of Sicklinghall witnessed a charter with Nigel of Plompton *c.* 1175 X 94 (*EYC* xi, no. 62). 'Aton' in the charters has the spelling of the Yorkshire place-names now called Ayton. For William Fairfax see *EYC* i, nos. 247, 291, 526.

in Spofforth, west of Wetherby.¹⁵⁷ Sir William de Wyville, who was grand enough to call himself one of the 'fellows' or 'colleagues' (*socii*) of the earl of Fife—presumably the fashionable euphemism for 'vassal' current in the earlier thirteenth century—seems to have belonged to a well-known Yorkshire family descended from Robert de 'Guidvilla' (Iville near Évreux) who flourished in the early twelfth century.¹⁵⁸

Finally, we should notice Earl Malcolm's own marriage, to Maud or Matilda, daughter of Earl Gilbert of Strathearn by his wife Maud d'Aubigny, daughter of William d'Aubigny 'the Breton', lord of Belvoir.¹⁵⁹ Here was yet another link with the greater nobility of Anglo-Norman England. The earls of Fife, themselves almost certainly of the same kin as the kings of Scotland, moved within a closely knit aristocratic group of Anglo-Normans intimately related to the Scottish royal house. The group is neatly illustrated by a charter given about 1180 to the royal foundation at Dunfermline.¹⁶⁰ The granter was the countess Ela of Fife, her gift the church of West Calder with half a ploughgate of land—part of her dower. The witnesses included a bishop and an abbot, Ela's husband the earl, two of his chaplains, three of his clerks, and his kinsman Adam of Ceres. The three remaining witnesses were Alexander de St. Martin, who was a prominent tenant and retainer of Ada de Varenne the king's mother, Maud de Senlis, mother in law of the earl of Strathearn, and her son William III d'Aubigny of Belvoir. Many years later, in 1213, when King John took into England as hostages for the good behaviour of King William some fourteen children of the great nobles of Scotland, it was this William d'Aubigny who was given charge of the son and heir of Earl Gilbert of Strathearn.¹⁶¹

Although the history of the earldom of Fife is still beset by many unsolved problems, the fact emerges clearly enough that a magnatial dynasty of native Scottish descent could adapt itself successfully not only to the customs and institutions of feudalism but also, on the social level, to the dominant French

---

¹⁵⁷ *SHR* viii. 222.
¹⁵⁸ *Dunfermline Reg.*, no. 214; Clay and Greenway, *Early Yorkshire Families*, 103–6.
¹⁵⁹ *PSAS* lxxxvii. 56–61.
¹⁶⁰ *Dunfermline Reg.*, no. 153.
¹⁶¹ *Rot. Litt. Claus.* i. 137.

aristocracy of the Angevin period. In this process of adaptation the Fifes became colonizers as avid as any of the foreign adventurers who flocked to Scotland to take advantage of royal favour. Here at least was one family of his own people upon whom King William's love was poured in abundance.

IV

The Colonists: (ii) Dependants and adventurers

FROM the standpoint of the constitution of medieval Scotland the importance of the great lordships is in no danger of being underestimated. In the twelfth century, the most formative period for the medieval kingdom, the achievement of David I and his two grandsons would hardly have been possible unless they had been able to use these lordships as a principal instrument in imposing a much enhanced royal authority. In the reception of a common feudal law, the great lordships, spread as they were across much of the country from the Cheviots to the Moray Firth, and in close touch with the Crown through the chief tenants' regular attendance at court, must have played a decisive part. Moreover, from the social point of view, the great lordships opened up widely separated territories to a comparatively standardized pattern of settlement, enabling members of a single family, for example from Shropshire or Northamptonshire, from Normandy or Flanders, to acquire fiefs and establish themselves as freeholders or knights simultaneously in several different parts of the country. Thus the spread of a common form of agrarian settlement went hand in hand with the general, if not quite universal, acceptance of a common law and a common set of ideas about lordship, vassalage, service, and tenure.

It is nevertheless arguable that the thoroughness of the feudalization of Scotland, and, still more, that the peculiar nature of medieval Scottish society, with its vigorous, strongly emphasized, long-preserved northern Middle English language and culture, coupled with a resilient political independence, owed much to the individuals and families of middling position or even of relatively small substance who had little or no prospect of founding lordships on the largest scale. Many of these individuals and families either were already attached to the great Anglo-Norman lords before they came to Scotland or attached themselves to one or other of the great lordships after they arrived. These may broadly be classed as dependants. But many more again seem to have remained independent of the great lords and to have entered into a direct relationship with the Crown, either as specialized royal servants—stewards, marischals, falconers, armourers, cooks, bakers, brewers, and the like—or as small-scale tenants-in-chief owing the service of a knight or a military sergeand. Men of this kind may be considered adventurers; and while the majority of them probably never rose above the level of the average freeholder a certain proportion could be classified among the *nobiles viri* or *gentilhommes*, to use expressions familiar in the thirteenth and fourteenth centuries.

The theme of these lectures is the 'Anglo-Norman Era' and this chapter will therefore concentrate on dependants and adventurers who came to Scotland as immigrants from the south. It is all the more necessary to stress at the outset that there seems to have been no bar to native Scots or Cumbrians or Northumbrians swelling the numbers of such dependants and adventurers. The line may only be drawn with difficulty between the man of native stock who received a knight's or sergeant's feu from the king or from one of the great lords, thus entering the ranks of what was in effect a new aristocracy, and the native landowner whose established position in his own part of the country was deliberately feudalized. The ancestor of the West Lothian family of Dundas of that ilk, Elias son of Uhtred, seems to have been paternally of native descent; but when the undoubtedly native lord of Dalmeny granted Dundas to him as half a knight's feu,[1] Elias's position was indistinguishable from that of any small-scale feudatory who had come from England or the Continent. On the other hand, the lairdly family of Lochore of that ilk, in West Fife—who in the thirteenth century were surely as 'feudal' as any of their neighbours—can be traced to the mid-twelfth century when they appear to have formed part of the native Scottish gentry

[1] *APS* i. 92.

The Colonists: (ii) Dependants and adventurers

of Fothrif.² And the position is complicated yet further when we reflect that at any time a 'native' aspirant to knighthood might win a feu from a 'foreign' lord—e.g. Edulf son of Uhtred taking 'Gillemurestun' (which was then renamed 'Edulfestun', Eddleston) from Richard de Morville,³ or conversely an incoming 'foreign' dependant might be given a knight's feu by a 'native' magnate, e.g. Richard son of Truite taking 'Lochkindelo' (New Abbey) from Uhtred son of Fergus of Galloway.⁴

Eschewing as best we can the rather fruitless complexities arising from too rigid an attempt to classify natives and outsiders, dependants and adventurers, let us try to keep our attention fixed on what may be called the broad middle band of Anglo-Continental settlers. It would surely be of interest to learn something of their immediate place of origin, of the permanence or intensity of their settlement in Scotland, of their relationships before they migrated and whether these were maintained or broken, and of the relationships they formed after settling in Scotland.

Much of the evidence to be offered in this chapter will relate to three main areas of origin, the Honour of Huntingdon, Somerset, and Yorkshire. But before the going becomes regional and relatively easy, I should like to illustrate the difficulties which beset an enquiry of this kind, where the source materials are so scattered and have survived so haphazardly. This is especially true once one looks south of the English Channel. I am conscious of lacking the expertise of a Lewis Loyd or a Charles Clay when it comes to extracting the right information from the sources available for the study of feudal Normandy and its neighbours. So often the search will seem promising, only to be brought up short with a tantalizing hint of the connection or identification which is being sought.

---

² See *St. Andrews Liber*, 128, for Constantine of Lochore in the time of Bishop Arnold of St. Andrews (1160–2). There are numerous references to the family in the thirteenth century, for which see *St. Andrews Liber*, *Dunfermline Reg.*, passim, *SHS Misc.* iv. 317, *Pitfirrane Writs.* nos. 1–4 and G. W. S. Barrow (ed.), *The Scottish Tradition* (1974), 39, 42.

³ *Glasgow Reg.*, no. 45. The surprisingly rapid and well-recorded change in the name of this estate from Penteiacob (Cumbric, 'head' (or 'end') of James's house') through Gillemureston to Edulfeston, now Eddleston, is documented ibid., nos. 1, 44, 45, 46, 111.

⁴ *CWAAS Trans.* (NS) xvii (1917), 218–19, with facsimile.

So often the only conclusions which can be drawn will be valid in the manner of an impressionist painting, convincing if one stands well back, but baffling if one peers at any part of the canvas in detail.

Charters of William II de Vieuxpont relating to Scotland were witnessed by William 'de Butemund'[5] and by Roger and William 'de la Lecqueraye'.[6] Bouttemont, in the commune of Ouilly-le-vicomte, is in the district of Auge in middle Normandy, some 25 km north-east of Vieuxpont-en-Auge, whence the Vieuxpont family is believed to have come to Britain.[7] Saint-Jean-de-la-Lecqueraye is a little further east, nearer to Pont-Audemer. One may surely proceed to the cautious conclusion that even after they reached Scotland the Vieuxponts were not quite unaccompanied by compatriots. So far, so good. It is harder to feel confident about a family which used the surname de Bosco, not simply because Dubois is to a Frenchman what Smith is to an Englishman, nor because Normandy is richly supplied with boscage, but rather because the particular clues in this case hardly do more than tantalize. Walter del Bois or de Bosco, whose son and heir was called Richard, held at the close of the twelfth century the now deserted village of Carruthers, in a heavily depopulated corner of Annandale.[8] He and others of his surname are found from the second half of the twelfth century onwards associated with the Bruces, lords of Annandale and Hartlepool.[9] The charters by which Walter gave land at Carruthers to Durham Cathedral Priory were witnessed by two men apparently from Yorkshire, Ralph of Wassand in the East Riding[10] and Robert 'of Lithum', probably Kirkleatham in the North Riding.[11]

---

[5] *Holyrood Liber*, no. 43, earlier in date than *Kelso Liber*, no. 142, both witnessed by William 'de Butemund'.

[6] *Kelso Liber*, nos. 139–41; *Holyrood Liber*, nos. 33, 41, 44; *Coldstream Chartulary*, no. 27 (Roger de la Lecqueraye). See *Cambuskenneth Reg.*, no. 73, for W. de la Lecqueraye; *Rot. Scacc. Norm.* i. 248 and ii. 329, for Richard and Robert de la Lecqueraye. Saint-Jean-de-la-Lecqueraye is in the canton of Saint-Georges-du-Vièvre, arr. Pont-Audemer.

[7] See *Sussex Archaeological Collections* (Sussex Archaeological Society), ii (1849), 77, where the authority for this attribution is stated to be Benjamin Thorpe.

[8] NG Ref. NY 253807 (now in Middlebie); Raine, *North Durham*, nos. 166, 167.

[9] *CDS* i, nos. 606–7, 700, 704, 707, 1682; Fraser, *Annandale*, i. 1–5 (mostly references to Richard del Bois); *Arbroath Liber*, i, no. 37.

[10] Raine, *North Durham*, nos. 166, 167. For the form 'Wausant' see *EYC* ii. 280.

[11] *EYC* ii. 65, 107–8.

They were also witnessed by William 'de Hispania'—an uncommon name—and his nephew Walter. Now, a family taking its surname from Epaignes (*Hispania*) near Cormeilles, in the *arrondissement* of Pont-Audemer, were among the twelfth-century English tenants of the counts of Brittany and earls of Richmond,[12] and William and Walter de Epaignes occur about the period of the Carruthers charters,[13] while, rather later, after 1204, a Walter de Epaignes was provost of Évreux for Philip Augustus.[14] The surname Epaignes therefore directs us to record of the Pont-Audemer district in the later twelfth century. There we find a Walter de Bosco-Bernardi, evidently the successor of a Richard de Bosco-Bernardi, granting to Longueville Priory land at Touville, 8 km west of Bosc-Bénard.[15] This Walter de Bosco's charter was witnessed by Robert de Cliponville, from a village of that name north of Rouen, a name which in fact seems to occur at only one place in Normandy. This uncommon name nevertheless brings us back to southern Scotland, for Robert de Cliponville witnessed a Roxburghshire charter of this period[16] in which figure a high proportion of men with continental surnames—Corbet, Le Nain, and an Enguerrand 'de Dunmar' who probably came either from Domart-en-Ponthieu, between Abbeville and Amiens, or from Domart-sur-la-Luce, south-east of Amiens.[17] We cannot, on the basis of such dubious evidence, pinpoint Bosc-Bénard as the

[12] *EYC* v. 230–1; *Cal. Inq. misc.* i, nos. 519, 520.
[13] *EYC* v. 230–1.
[14] Le Prévost, *Mémoires* . . . *de l'Eure*, ii. 44. This was perhaps the Walter de Hispania who became a monk at Notre-Dame-de-la-Trappe, Mortagne, in 1215 (*Cartulaire de l'abbaye de N.–D. de la Trappe*, ed. Comte de Charencey (1889), 3).
[15] *Chartes du prieuré de Longueville*, ed. P. Le Cacheux (Société de l'Histoire de Normandie, 1934), 89, no. 80.
[16] *Melrose Liber*, no. 137. Cliponville is in the canton of Fauville-en-Caux, dép. Seine-Maritime.
[17] A charter of Enguerrand 'de Dumard' granting his nephew Robert Duredent land at Faxton, Northants, *c*. 1175, was printed by Sir Frank Stenton, *The First Century of English Feudalism, 1066–1166* (2nd edn., Oxford, 1961), 276. The charter was witnessed by Robert 'de Chippenuill', who was surely identical with Robert de Cliponville. It refers to Walter de Balliol as the grantor's uncle. Stenton's note refers to an earlier charter, of Bernard de Balliol, granting Faxton to Gerold 'de Dumart' in exchange for land which Gerold and his father held 'beyond the sea' for four knights' service. From this it might appear probable that Enguerrand de Dunmar came to Scotland with the Balliols, who at an unrecorded period acquired the lordship of Cavers in Roxburghshire. This would point to Domart-en-Ponthieu being the place from which Enguerrand took his name, since it is only about 20 km from Bailleul-en-Vimeu.

Norman home of the Scottish family of Bois or Boece.[18] Yet the conjunction of these names, merely in record which has chanced to survive, is suggestive of social intercourse between Scotland and northern France at a level below that of the great lords.

We could find ourselves skating on even thinner ice if we considered the two notable families of Melville and Malherbe. Geoffrey de Melville (*Malevilla*), the first of his name in Scotland, appears quite unheralded and unprovenanced at the very end of David I's reign.[19] Geoffrey was a favourite personal name with several generations of Melvilles, so it is worth noting that Auguste LePrévost cites a charter of 1210—once again, it comes from the Pont-Audemer district—witnessed by a Geoffrey 'de Malevilla', who took his name from Malleville-sur-le-Bec.[20] Unlike Malleville or Melville, Malherbe was a very common name in Normandy and points to no particular locality. Even the comparatively well-attested family of this name holding land in Lincolnshire and Yorkshire has provided no more than a few tantalizing hints to suggest a link with the Scottish Malherbes.[21] Yet to assume coincidence at each contemporary occurrence of the name in Scots and English

---

[18] Black, *Surnames*, s.v. BOYCE.

[19] Lawrie, *Charters*, no. 186. For the name Geoffrey used by the early Melvilles in Scotland see Fraser, *Melvilles*, i. 3–7 (Geoffrey I and II); *Cambuskenneth Reg.*, no. 37, *St. Andrews Liber*, 381 (which seem to be evidence of a third Geoffrey). *Dunfermline Reg.*, no. 299, is presumably an inflated forgery based on ibid., no. 158. It is hard to place in its true context, either chronological or geographical, the somewhat primitive agreement anent 'Buna' (Boon in Legerwood, Berwickshire?) between Geoffrey 'de Malavilla' and Robert Hutlaga ('Outlaw') preserved among the Lundin charters (SRO GD 160, Box 47), witnessed by, among others, Adam son of Swain, Ralph Noble, Dodin (of Duddingston?), and Robert the goldsmith ('Gulden faber').

[20] Le Prévost, *Mémoires . . . de l'Eure*, i. 136; ii. 366–8.

[21] There are numerous undated charters of the Malherbe lords of Morham in *Newbattle Reg.*, many given by one (or more than one) John Malherbe. In Scotland, Maud Malherbe was wife to Geoffrey I de Melville and mother of Geoffrey II, but not, it seems, of Gregory de Melville, father of Richard and ancestor of the main Melville line. In Yorkshire a John Malherbe was husband of Maud daughter of the wealthy West Riding landowner Adam son of Swain (see above, n. 19) and a benefactor of Rievaulx Abbey (*Rievaulx Cartulary*, 62, no. 107). A witness to this Rievaulx charter was Doun Bardolf, and both he and a John Malherbe witnessed a charter of William brother of King Henry II given to the nunnery of Our Lady at Mortain (*Rot. Scacc. Norm.* ii, p. ccxv, n.p. 1154 X 64). For the Yorkshire-Lincolnshire Malherbes see *EYC* iii. 253–406 *passim* and especially pp. 305, 318, 327–9.

record would surely be unjustified. King Malcolm the Maiden was briefly at Les Andelys in 1159, attended by, among others, John Malherbe and William de Colville.[22] Both names point to Yorkshire–Lincolnshire families and also to Scottish families which intermarried.[23] Since the Colville parts of the equation were undoubtedly identical, the probability of an identity between the Malherbe parts of the equation seems at least provisionally acceptable. Even when a man appears in Scotland with a surname derived from an uncommon continental place-name it does not follow that we can always trace the connection between him and his patron. For instance, Saer 'de Tenes', who evidently came from the village of Thennes, south-east of Amiens,[24] is found in the entourage of the Countess Ada,[25] and served her youngest son Earl David as constable.[26] He may merely have been one of a number of Picard adventurers for whom there is some evidence in twelfth- and early thirteenth-century record.

One might speculate in this fashion almost indefinitely, but not very profitably. The picture of Anglo-Norman migration to Scotland is fortunately by no means wholly impressionistic. It comes into sharper focus as soon as we turn to three fairly well marked regions of England, the East Midlands, West Wessex—especially Somerset—and Yorkshire. It is of course a commonplace of Scottish history that the Honour of Huntingdon, with estates scattered across ten or eleven counties, though concentrated chiefly in the shires of Huntingdon,

[22] *RRS* i, no. 155.
[23] See Appendix B. *Newbattle Reg.*, nos. 99, 213, provide evidence of marriage between Ada de Colville and one of the Malherbes. For the Colvilles in Yorkshire and Lincolnshire see *EYC* xi. 303, 305; vi. 168–70; *RAL* iii. 345–8; *Chron. Stephen*, i. 94. The Colville–Percy connection found in Yorkshire was reproduced in Scotland at Heiton, Roxburghshire, where Philip de Colville was successor to Henry and Geoffrey de Percy (for whom see *EYC* xi. 3), and where Geoffrey and Alan de Percy were benefactors of Kelso and Whitby Abbeys (*Dryburgh Liber*, nos. 224, 225 (reading *fratris* for *patris*); Lawrie, *Charters*, nos. 251–4).
[24] Thennes is close to Boves, south-east of Amiens.
[25] *Laing Charters*, no. 2 (the name of the witness printed as '(torn) of Cenef' may be read in the original as Seih(er) de Tenes: Edinburgh University Library, Laing chrs. 67, Box 2). See also J. G. Wallace-James, *Deeds relating to East Lothian* (1899), no. 1.
[26] *Yester Writs*, no. 6. See also *CDS* i, no. 644, showing that Saher 'de Tenys' held land at Great Doddington, Northants.

98 The Colonists: (ii) Dependants and adventurers

Cambridge, Bedford, and Northampton, formed the main catchment area from which the stream of feudal entrepreneurs flowed into Scotland. As Graeme Ritchie put it in his fine book on *The Normans in Scotland*, 'Earl David's associates were in great part gentlemen adventurers . . . whose fathers and grandfathers appear in Domesday, mostly under Northamptonshire . . . Most [of David I's] followers came from his midland earldom. Loyalty to the Earl of Northampton and Huntingdon was their guiding star.'[27]

At first glance the truth of this proposition seems undeniable. The lordship of Huntingdon was held by the Scottish royal house and its offshoots almost continuously from 1114 to 1286. Occupying a fertile part of England which was likely to carry a surplus population, the Honour must surely have been the obvious recruiting ground for young men capable of taking on the knight's feus newly created by their lord north of the Border. At least this could be argued for David I's time or a little longer. If we take the period ending with Malcolm IV's death in 1165, we find that the following families, known to be holding land of the Honour of Huntingdon, had gained a foothold in Scotland: Morville of Bozeat and Whissendine;[28] Corbet of Draughton;[29] Soules of Great Doddington;[30] Olifard of Lilford and Sawtry;[31] Ridel of Abbotsley and Wittering;[32] and Lindsay of Molesworth.[33] To these might be added Engaine of Pytchley[34] and Bidun of Lavendon,[35] holding estates adjacent to some of the Honour's chief manors,

---

[27] R. L. G. Ritchie, *The Normans in Scotland* (Edinburgh, 1954), 157, 214.

[28] Farrer, *HKF* ii. 357–60; Lawrie, *Charters* and *RRS* i, *passim*.

[29] Farrer, *HKF* ii. 386–7; Lawrie, *Charters*, nos. 35, 46, 50, 74, 83, 94, 103; *RRS* i, nos. 6, 7, 131.

[30] *RRS* ii. 165; *Records of the Templars in England in the Twelfth Century*, ed. B. A. Lees (British Academy, 1935), 78; Barrow, *Kingdom*, 325.

[31] Farrer, HKF ii. 354–5; Barrow, *Kingdom*, 288–9.

[32] Farrer, *HKF* ii. 316–17; below, Appendix A.

[33] Farrer, *HKF* ii. 376–80; Lawrie, *Charters*, and *RRS* i and ii, *passim*, references in indices s.v. 'Lindsay'.

[34] Lawrie, *Charters*, 309, *RRS* ii. 164. *Dunfermline Reg.*, no. 164, is a grant to Dunfermline Abbey by William Engaine of the Somerset branch (above, p. 72) of saltpans at Burgh on Sands, Cumberland. I do not know what relationship there was, if any, between the Northamptonshire Engaines and those of Somerset and Cumberland. A William 'de Engene' and his brother Geoffrey witnessed a deed relating to Duddingston before 1219 (*Inchcolm Chrs.*, no. 11).

[35] *RRS* i. 28–9.

while Saher de Quincy (though not his younger brother Robert who settled in Scotland) had acquired Eynesbury in St. Neots by 1163.[36] Even in the later twelfth century, the Honour of Huntingdon did not cease to be a source of Scottish recruitment, providing (for example) de la Carneille of Great Stukeley, probable ancestor of Guthrie of that ilk,[37] 'de Fotheringay', ancestor of Fotheringham of Powrie (both in Angus),[38] and 'de Rameseia', ancestor of the Ramsays of Fife, Angus, and Perthshire.[39]

And yet, despite all this, the emphasis on Huntingdon may have been overdone. The longer I have studied the sources of this period the more I have come to feel that the twelfth and thirteenth centuries should be seen as a single phase of Scottish history whose unity is particularly marked in the matter of Anglo-Scottish relations. In the context of these two hundred years the Honour of Huntingdon no longer takes the dominant part in exporting Anglo-Norman feudalism to Scotland. Even where David I is concerned, there must be more than a suspicion that he drew his chief supporters—Brus, Morville, Soules, and Avenel—direct from Normandy, and that such connection as they had with the Honour of Huntingdon was the result, not the cause, of their association with the Scottish royal house. At the date of the Northamptonshire Survey of Henry I's time (after 1124) the Morville tenancy of Bozeat and the Soules tenancy of Doddington were both still in King David's hands,[40] while there is nothing to connect the early Bruces with the Honour of Huntingdon save for a grant to the Templars at Stretton in Rutland which might have been made as late as the mid-twelfth century.[41] Moreover, we cannot help noticing the large number of prominent families holding of the Honour of Huntingdon who did not choose to participate in the settlement of Scotland, e.g. Foliot, Grimbald, Senlis, Briouze, Keynes (de Cahagnes), and Broy.[42]

[36] Farrer, *HKF* ii. 370.
[37] Barrow, *Kingdom*, 334.
[38] *Lindores Chartulary*, no. 65; *Yester Writs*, no. 18; *CDS* ii. 200.
[39] Watt, *Dictionary*, 460–1, reviews much of the difficult evidence for the early Ramsays in Scotland.
[40] *VCH, Northants*, i. 376.
[41] Lees, *Templars*, 79.
[42] Farrer, *HKF* ii. 302–6, 327, 360–1; *RRS* i, nos. 7, 149, 180; *Wardon Cartulary*, *passim*, references in index s.v. 'Broi'.

The truth is that the kings of Scotland were extremely eclectic in their recruitment of suitable vassals, and the great feudatories of foreign origin hardly less so. How otherwise would the remote English West Country, where the Scots held no lordships, have proved such a rich source of supply for the feudal nobility and gentry of Scotland over several generations? At the outset of Stephen's reign, Robert lord of Bampton in North Devon ('Baentona'), whose honour, inherited from his father the Flemish Walter of Douai, consisted of many manors in Devon, Somerset and Dorset,[43] rebelled against the king and was banished with his knights and other military retainers.[44] The author of the *Gesta Stephani* says that 'they lived for a long time with the king of Scotland'.[45] When, according to the same writer, King David took his ill-fated decision to invade the north of England in 1138, he was spurred on to the invasion by the son of Robert of Bampton and his kinsmen, one of whom was evidently Ralph Lovel.[46] We do not know why Robert of Bampton sought help from what might seem an unexpected quarter, but it is worth pointing out that the Scottish connection would appear to go back long before the rebellion against King Stephen, for a senior witness to Earl David's foundation charter for Selkirk, afterwards Kelso, Abbey, dating to about 1120, four years before Earl David became king of Scots, was one Robert 'de Paintona',[47] for whom no other identification can plausibly be suggested. A few years later, a senior witness to David's principal charters for the abbeys of Dunfermline and Holyrood was Robert of Montacute (or Montagu),[48] suggesting once again a Somerset link with the Scottish court which is otherwise unrecorded. It may not be fanciful to envisage these west country lords travelling north to

[43] Sanders, *Baronies*, 5.
[44] *Gesta Stephani*, ed. K. R. Potter (1955), 18–20.
[45] Ibid., 20.
[46] Ibid., 36; Sanders, *Baronies*, 27–8.
[47] Lawrie, *Charters*, no. 35 (p. 28). Cp. the form for Bampton in *RRAN* iii. 103, 'Baentona'.
[48] Lawrie, *Charters*, nos. 74, 153 (1128 × 36). See *Comp. Pge.* ix. 75–6. Robert de Montagu was presumably a younger son of Drogo de Montagu recorded in Domesday (*VCH, Somerset*, i. 526a). Robert is not mentioned in the cartularies of either Bruton or Montacute priories, but a William son of Robert de Montagu appears in 1198 (*Somerset Fines*, 3). It may be noted that a gift to Bruton by Henry Lovel (for whom see below, n. 54) was made for the soul of the younger Drogo de Montagu (*Bruton Cartulary*, no. 83).

prospect the possibilities of future settlement not so much on their own behalf as on behalf of their followers and dependants.

Before the end of David I's reign, Thomas 'de Londres' (de Londoniis, Londoniarum, 'of London'), brother of Richard de Londres who in 1166 held knights' fees of William de Mohun in Somerset and Devon,[49] appears at the Scottish court.[50] Evidence from the next two reigns points to Thomas's having acquired the Roxburghshire lands of Lessudden or St. Boswells.[51] Thomas married a lady named Margaret who before 1161 had been the wife of Ralph Lovel,[52] a kinsman of Robert of Bampton who had kept Castle Cary in Somerset on Robert's behalf in 1138.[53] It was perhaps from Margaret that her son Henry Lovel inherited the Roxburghshire barony of Hawick;[54] and it may be that the Robert, after whom Roberton just west of Hawick was named, was Henry's younger brother Robert who was Henry's tenant for a knight's fee in Somerset in 1166.[55] For several generations the well-known Lovels and little-known Londons were prominent among the feudal nobility of the sheriffdom of Roxburgh.[56] Thomas of London, leaving no children, was succeeded by his nephew Robert who, though he had acquired with his wife Isabel the small English Honour of Visdelou, proved enough of a Scotsman to be forfeited in 1173–4.[57] It was evidently a kinswoman of Thomas and Robert

[49] *RBE* i. 225, 227, 253.
[50] Lawrie, *Charters*, nos. 90, 220 (see *RRS* i, nos. 132, 133, 174, 197).
[51] *Dryburgh Liber*, nos. 53–5, 58, 59. Note that in *Melrose Liber*, no. 88, Thomas of London was said to be the uncle of Robert of London, granter of the last of the Dryburgh charters just cited. Note also that William de Causi, described as parson of Lessudden in *Dryburgh Liber*, no. 62 (1174 × 80), witnessed two charters of Robert of London, one for his kinsman Walter of Berkeley (BL Loans 29/355) as 'William clerk de Chausi', and one for Melrose Abbey (*Melrose Liber*, no. 88).
[52] *Comp. Pge.* viii. 199–205; *RRS* ii, no. 62.
[53] Above, p. 100, n. 46.
[54] Margaret granted Outerside in Roberton to Jedburgh Abbey with consent of her son Henry Lovel (*RRS* ii, no. 62), and Henry granted land at Branxholm to St. Andrews (*St. Andrews Liber*, 60, 261). His son's charter of confirmation was witnessed by, i.a., Roger of 'Pittecumb'. Pitcombe lies between Castle Cary and Bruton, Somerset. See also *Exch. Rolls*, i. 28–9; *Rot. Scot.* i. 39a–b; *CDS* i, nos. 1684, 1685.
[55] *RBE* i. 234. Robert Lovel's holding at Wrington is mentioned in the *Liber Henrici de Soliaco abbatis Glaston*, ed. J. E. Jackson (Roxburghe Club, 1882), 92.
[56] This statement is based chiefly on the surviving charters of Teviotdale, especially those printed in *Dryburgh Liber*, *Kelso Liber*, and *Melrose Liber*.
[57] *Dryburgh Liber*, nos. 53, 54, 59; Farrer, *HKF* i. 55. Farrer pointed out that Robert of London either died or forfeited the Honour of Visdelou in 1173–4, but

who became William the Lion's mistress and mother of the most honoured and favoured of his bastards, Robert of London, of whose lordships in various parts of Scotland something has already been said.[58]

Three original charters of the Somerset Robert of London survive, two written or composed by his clerk Roger.[59] Although only one of these charters relates to Somerset, all three were witnessed by Somerset men, such as Maurice de Reigny, William of Forscote, Ralph Belet, and Walter son of Geoffrey.[60] By the most interesting of the three charters, Robert granted land at St. Boswells and at Plenmeller in Tynedale to his kinsman Walter of Berkeley, for a rent of two falcons, saving the king's service.[61] Walter of Berkeley and his brother Robert first appear in Scottish record at the end of Malcolm IV's reign.[62] It looks very much as though they took their surname from the manor of Berkley beside Frome,[63] and like the Lovels and Horseys belonged to the circle of families who looked for patronage to the lords of Bampton. Both the Berkeley brothers did well for themselves in Scotland. Walter was given the royal chamberlainship (to alternate with Philip de Valognes[64]) together with what became the baronies of Chamberlain Newton beside Hawick,[65] Inverkeilor on the Angus coast,[66]

---

he did not realize that Robert was a substantial feudatory in Scotland and must have incurred forfeiture because of his loyalty to William the Lion.

[58] Above, pp. 63–4 and n. 13. That there was a relationship between the London family and King William's bastard son Robert of London seems to be shown not merely by his choice of surname but also by *Dryburgh Liber*, no. 60, which is evidence of Robert's property in Lessudden (St. Boswells).

[59] *Melrose Liber*, no. 88 (with facsimile); BL Loans 29/355 (both written by Roger the clerk); T. D. Tremlett and H. N. Blakiston, *Stogursey Charters*, no. 27 (original in possession of Eton College, ECR 6/24). I have to thank Mr. Patrick Strong, Keeper of the College Library and Collections, Eton College, for kindly providing me with a photostat of this document.

[60] Farrer, *HKF* i. 132–4; *RBE* i. 243; J. Collinson, *History and Antiquities of the County of Somerset* (1791), iii. 349; *Stogursey Charters*, no. 27; *RBE* i. 44; ii. 497, for William and Ralph Belet.

[61] See Appendix B.

[62] *RRS* i. 283, n. 1.

[63] Barrow, *Kingdom*, 332–3.

[64] *RRS* ii. 33.

[65] Ibid., no. 171, where editorial suggestions as to the identity of 'Neutun' should be ignored. The true identity is indicated by the name 'Cha(m)birlayn-neutone', 'Chambirlayne–newtona' (etc.), for which see Fraser, *Douglas*, iii. 1–2 (no. 1), *RMS* i, no. 481 (and elsewhere).

[66] *RRS* ii. no. 185.

The Colonists: (ii) Dependants and adventurers 103

and Conveth (now Laurencekirk) in the Mearns.⁶⁷ Of his two daughters, Agatha gave her father's surname to her husband Humphrey son of Theobald de Addeville and their descendants, whence almost the whole tribe of Scottish Barclays;⁶⁸ her sister, whose name is not known, married Enguerrand de Balliol and transmitted to a line of Balliols the barony of Redcastle at Inverkeilor.⁶⁹ Robert of Berkeley married Cecily, native heiress of Maxton in Roxburghshire,⁷⁰ and their heir in turn was their daughter Alina, who brought Maxton to the de Normanvilles of Stamfordham in Northumberland, a family which, perhaps by no coincidence, was closely associated with the Balliols.⁷¹

At the start of the great revolt of 1173 an envoy from King William the Lion to Henry II was a certain Brother William Dolepene who, with or without the title *frater*, figures as a witness to a few charters belonging to the 1160s and '70s.⁷² He evidently took his surname from the little South Somerset village of Lopen,⁷³ part of which was held of the Lovels of Castle Cary by the preceptory of the Templars at Temple Combe.⁷⁴ Brother William of Lopen was either a knight of the Temple or (since one of his Scottish appearances concerned the knights of St. John at Torphichen) of the Hospital.⁷⁵ He was perhaps a younger brother of Henry of Lopen who with John Belet held a knight's fee in Somerset in 1166 under William de Mohun, the chief lord of Richard of London.⁷⁶ That the Lopens took root in Scotland is suggested by the fact that charters of David earl of Huntingdon, including Scottish charters, together with charters of John I bishop of Dunkeld, were witnessed by Gilbert 'Dolepain' ('de Holepen'),⁷⁷ and by

---

⁶⁷ Ibid., nos. 344, 345.
⁶⁸ Ibid.; Barrow, *Kingdom*, 333–4.
⁶⁹ *Arbroath Liber*, nos. 58, 293 (note that the former charter was witnessed by Thomas 'de Wadrithurt'; Vaudricourt is about 20 km west of Bailleul-en-Vimeu).
⁷⁰ *Melrose Liber*, nos. 90, 91.
⁷¹ Ibid., no. 92; *Northumberland County History*, xii. 305; *EYC* i. 457.
⁷² *Chron. Fantosme*, line 323; see also *RRS* ii, nos. 59, 60; *Kelso Liber*, no. 214; *St. Andrews Liber*, 319.
⁷³ J. Collinson, *History of Somerset*, iii. 122.
⁷⁴ Ibid.
⁷⁵ *St. Andrews Liber*, 319.
⁷⁶ *RBE* i. 227.
⁷⁷ *Lindores Chartulary*, nos. 4, 11; *Arbroath Liber*, no. 83; *Coupar Angus Chrs.*, no. 6; *Coupar Angus Rental*, i. 351 (no. 94).

the homage to Edward I in 1296 of a later Gilbert 'de Leppeine' of the sheriffdom of Lanark.[78]

Finally, among the Somerset families whose younger sons saw their chance in Scotland, we may note the Revels of Downhead in West Camel, Langport, and Curry Rivel, named after them.[79] Richard Revel the elder, who died in 1213 and could not be given Christian burial for two years because of Pope Innocent's interdict, seems to have been a comparatively 'new' man in Henry II's time.[80] In 1190 Richard I gave him Langport and Curry as a double knight's fee, as well as socage in Somerton.[81] His eldest son and heir was the younger Richard Revel who by his wife Mabel Hunsworth had an only child Sabina, who married Henry de l'Orty.[82] Both the elder and younger Richard Revel had had younger brothers, respectively Henry Revel and Adam 'of Stawell'.[83] Henry Revel found favour with William the Lion in the 1170s, when the king provided him with a wife from among the native aristocracy, Margaret daughter of Orm lord (strictly speaking, secularized abbot) of Abernethy on the Tay.[84] The tocher which Margaret brought to Henry Revel consisted of Coultra, Corbie (now Birkhill), Balmerino, and their outlying farms.[85] Just as Robert of London had unexpectedly succeeded to his uncle Thomas's Scottish estates so, between 1211 and c. 1215, Richard Revel junior unexpectedly succeeded to his uncle Henry's, presumably because Henry's son Alan had died before his father.[86]

Some ten years before the younger Richard Revel became a Fife laird he lodged a vigorous protest in the county court of

[78] *CDS* ii. 213; *Instrumenta Publica*, 167.
[79] *Somerset Fines*, 27, 57; *Bruton Cartulary*, no. 19b; *Muchelney Cartulary*, 63, 111; also nos. 28–32; *VCH, Somerset*, iii. 22, 51, 73.
[80] *Muchelney Cartulary*, nos. 31, 32; *VCH, Somerset*, iii. 73.
[81] *Cartae Antiquae, Rolls 11–20*, ed. J. Conway Davies (Pipe Roll Soc., 1960), nos. 513, 514.
[82] *Somerset Fines*, 57; *Comp. Pge.* x. 182; *Cal. Inqu. p.m.* i, no. 84; *Somerset Pleas*, nos. 602, 619.
[83] *St. Andrews Liber*, 271–2; *Balmerino Liber*, no. 1.
[84] *RRS* ii, nos. 147, 152; *St. Andrews Liber*, 271–2.
[85] *Balmerino Liber*, nos. 3, 7. The name Birkhill replaced Corbie in the seventeenth century (*Retours, Fife*, no. 1397). 'Balnedan' ('river farm') is represented by Ballindean; 'Balnedart' ('farm on the height') may be represented by Grange; 'Esterardint' or 'Ardin' seems to be represented by Ardie (Hill) in Balmerino, but it has been alternatively identified with Hayston in Leuchars, formerly Easter Airdit.
[86] Alan witnessed, with his father, *RRS* ii, no. 330 (1189 × 1194).

Somerset against one William Dennis (Dacus, 'the Dane') because Dennis had obtained a writ from the king's justices commanding the sheriff to recover for Dennis 60 marks damages from Richard Revel senior on account of a disseisin.[87] Young Richard Revel declared no fewer than three times that the sheriff ought not to execute the writ because he and his father and his brothers were 'native-born men and gentlemen (*gentiles de patria*) of that country [i.e. Somerset]', while Dennis was only an immigrant (*adventicius*). Despite the fierce argument which ensued the sheriff persisted in executing the writ, saying that though Dennis was undoubtedly a newcomer to Somerset he was surely as native-born and as much a gentleman of his own country as the Revels were of theirs. It is curious that Richard Revel should have pressed the argument of being a native son and local gentleman so vehemently when his uncle —soon to be followed by himself—was deeply committed as a settler in Scotland.

Richard the younger died between 1221 and 1225 and his English property passed, not without legal disputes, to his daughter and her husband Henry de l'Orty.[88] The Scottish lands, significantly, came to Richard's brother Adam of Stawell, to whom the king of England had granted Langford Budevile.[89] Perhaps Adam, like Henry Revel, would have become a naturalized Scot in course of time; but by 1225 the likelihood that he would remain a Somerset man was turned into a certainty by the decision of the dowager queen of Scots, Ermengarde, to buy an estate on which she could establish a religious house. Thus, for 1,000 marks, payable to Adam de Stawell at the New Temple in London, Balmerino was taken over, to form the endowment of an abbey of Cistercians drawn from Melrose.[90] As far as Scotland was concerned, that was the end of the Revels.

When I embarked on the detailed investigation required for these lectures I expected the Honour of Huntingdon to loom large in the formative years of Scottish feudalism. I have been

---

[87] *Curia Regis Rolls*, iii. 129–30.
[88] *Somerset Fines*, 57; *Cal. Inqu. p.m.* i, no. 84; *VCH, Somerset*, iii, 22.
[89] *Somerset Pleas*, no. 1288.
[90] *Balmerino Liber*, nos. 1, 4, 5.

surprised to find that it may not have been so important as was once believed. The undoubted importance of West Wessex, on the other hand, has proved a greater surprise. But by far the greatest surprise of all has been the discovery of how richly Yorkshire, or rather individuals and families originating in, settled in, or closely associated with Yorkshire, contributed to feudal plantation north of the Border. The whole process must have amounted to a considerable movement of population whose social significance might all too easily be underestimated. The labours of many antiquaries and historians of Yorkshire, and in particular the indexed publication in a single series of volumes under the editorship of William Farrer and Sir Charles Clay of several thousand *Early Yorkshire Charters*,[91] have made it possible to appreciate the peculiarities of Yorkshire society in the age of Norman and Angevin dominance. In Yorkshire, as in southern Scotland, Normans mingled with Bretons and Flemings in something like equal numbers. All three foreign contingents clearly had to reckon with a much more substantial survival of native Anglo-Scandinavian families in the ranks of freeholders and petty nobility than was experienced in most of southern and midland England. Early Yorkshire charters admittedly contain their quota of continental personal names, technical terms and phrases. But they are shot through with Middle English, and to a less extent Scandinavian, words and usages, and they demonstrate the stubborn persistence of numerous native personal names far into the thirteenth century. Knight-service and feudal incidents, castleries and castle-guard had no impact, or only the most gradual of impacts, upon distinctive social customs such as the division of the rent-paying year at Whitsun and Martinmas, the reckoning of productive land by ploughgates and oxgangs, the marking of focal points of ancient communities by technical terms such as 'Kir(k)by' (*kyrkja-by*) and Kir(k)ton, and the functioning of pre-feudal shires with their ministerial class of thegns and dregns.[92]

[91] *Early Yorkshire Charters*, i–iii, ed. W. Farrer; index, ed. C. T. and E. M. Clay; vols. iv–xii, ed. C. T. Clay (1914–65).
[92] This statement is based on study of many hundreds of documents and cannot be substantiated in a single footnote. Some points, however, are illustrated in J. E. A. Jolliffe's work on Northumbrian customs (*EHR* xli. 1–42) and in A. H.

The Colonists: (ii) Dependants and adventurers

All this has a familiar ring for the Scottish medievalist. At point after point he can draw fruitful comparisons with the evidence, sadly much less abundant, which he possesses for Scotland. It brings home the fact that from the social, if not from the political, standpoint, the Anglo-Continental migration from Yorkshire—into southern Scotland at least—was a redistribution of population from one part of Northumbria to another.

With regard to Yorkshire migration to Scotland in the twelfth and thirteenth centuries three facts stand out conspicuously. It began early and continued late. It involved some of the greatest families, e.g. Brus, Balliol, and Moubray, and many families of humble and obscure origin. Finally, it included individuals and families of native English and Anglo-Scandinavian stock along with those of continental origin, and presumed French speech. Since we have evidence for far more families and individual men and women than can possibly be mentioned in a single chapter, I shall comment in detail only on two well-known families of Norman origin, a few families which were either native Northumbrian or of mixed Northumbrian and Flemish stock, and a handful of individuals of varying significance, the occurrence of some of whom in Scottish record adds point to the impression of restlessness which the sources for this period suggest.

William de Somerville may fairly be placed among the adventurers. Evidently a younger son, he served the kings David I and Malcolm IV from *c.* 1124 to *c.* 1164.[93] His reward was two estates formed into knight-service baronies—Linton, south-east of the royal castle of Roxburgh, and Carnwath, east of the royal castle of Lanark, an upland fief at whose centre

---

Smith's on Yorkshire place-names (EP-NS, vols. 5, 14, 30–7); see also G. W. S. Barrow, 'Northern English Society in the 12th and 13th centuries', *Northern History*, iv (1969), 1–28.

[93] Lawrie, *Charters*, no. 54 and elsewhere, *passim* (references in index); *RRS* i, nos. 11, 12, 17, 25, 28, 35, 41; and nos. 114–241 *passim* (references in index). I know of no evidence to support Sir Archibald Lawrie's belief (Lawrie, *Charters*, 309) that there were two Williams, father and son, living in Scotland between 1124 and 1161. Consequently I also differ from William Farrer (*EYC* iii. 307) in my view of the sequence of Williams de Somerville in the twelfth century, believing that the individual whom Farrer calls William III was really William II.

there still stands a small motte in a good state of preservation.[94] The Somervilles belonged to that interesting stratum of Conquest families in England, substantial enough to hold important fees of several different major tenants-in-chief, or perhaps to hold, simultaneously, a tenancy-in-chief and important mesne tenancies.[95] The Somervilles held Wichnor of the Honour of Stafford,[96] Aston Somerville in Gloucestershire,[97] Stockton in Warwickshire,[98] and in Yorkshire a number of fees of the Honour of Lacy of Pontefract, especially Seacroft, Thorner, and Barnbow east of Leeds.[99]

William de Somerville and his descendants must have retained some landed interest in the West Riding. In 1158 an English exchequer clerk noting a debt of 20 marks owed by William wrote 'but he resides [*manet*] in Lothian in the land of the king of Scotland'.[100] His grandson William III de Somerville was present at Damietta in 1218, in the company of John de Lacy.[101] He was buried at Melrose in 1242[102] and his descendants, some of whom played a notable part in the wars of independence, continued to hold the lordship of Carnwath for many centuries.[103] In Yorkshire, however, William III was succeeded by Walter de Trembleye, to whom

[94] *Glasgow Reg.*, nos. 16, 52; *OPS* i. 127, 432.
[95] Compare the families of Kime and Burdet (Farrer, *HKF* ii. 118, 329–31; *RRS* i. 101).
[96] R. Hardy, *A History of the Parish of Tatenhill*, i (1907), 34 ff. (I have to thank Miss Ann Kettle for this reference.)
[97] R. Atkyns, *The Ancient and Present State of Glocestershire* (2nd edn., London, 1768), 119. No evidence is given for Somervilles at Aston before the reign of Henry III.
[98] W. Dugdale, *The Antiquities of Warwickshire* (2nd edn., revised, London, 1730), i. 340b–341a (Stockton in Knightlow hundred, said to have come to Walter de Somerville with his wife Cecily de Limesi).
[99] W. E. Wightman, *The Lacy Family in England and Normandy, 1066–1194* (1966), 39, 93, n. 4, 100.
[100] *Pipe Roll, 4 Henry II*, 146. Walter de Somerville, apparently the head of the Yorkshire branch of the family, is recorded as holding one knight's fee of Henry de Lacy in 1166 (*RBE* i. 423), and witnessed a charter of Malcolm IV for Harrold Priory, Bedfordshire, 1157–8 (*RRS* i, no. 139).
[101] *The Chartulary of the Priory of St. John of Pontefract*, ed. R. Holmes (Yorks. Arch. Record Soc., 1899–1902), i, no. 21.
[102] *Chron. Melrose*, 90.
[103] *Scots Pge.* viii. 2 ff. *The Memorie of the Somervilles by James 11th Lord Somerville*, ed. Sir Walter Scott (2 vols., 1815), and J. Somerville, *The Baronial House of Somerville* (privately printed, Glasgow, 1920) are almost worthless for the early history of the family.

the king of Scotland is known to have granted land in Kincardineshire before 1264.[104] Yorkshire antiquaries have failed to grasp that the William de Somerville who was dead by 1243 was the Scottish lord of Carnwath and Linton, while Scottish antiquaries have not perceived any connection between Somerville, a name still plentifully with us, and Trembleye, naturalized as Turnbull.[105] The link may confirm the suggestion that the Somervilles came from Sémerville (now Graveron-Sémerville), a little way north-west of Évreux.[106] That commune is separated only by an important Roman road from Le Tremblay-Omonville.[107]

Another Yorkshire family closely comparable with the Somervilles is that of Clere (de Clères), taking their name from the commune of Clères about 20 km north of Rouen.[108] Clères was part of the fief held by the powerful family of de Tosny, and the de Clères may actually be traced back before 1066 as tenants of the lords of Tosny.[109] In the Clere family the favoured men's Christian names were Roger and Ralph, names also much used by the Tosnys. Sir Charles Clay has traced the descent of the Yorkshire Cleres, holding at Brompton

[104] *Excerpta e Rotulis Finium*, i. 401; *EYC* iii. 306–7, 308–9; *Kirkstall Coucher Bk.*, 121–2; *Yorkshire Fines, 1218–72*, 128. See also *Exch. Rolls*, i. 13, where it is possible that the unidentified Dolany or Delany is a misrendering of Delathy, i.e. Dalladies, with which the Turnbulls were later associated. (For the form Delathy see PRO MS Itinerary of Edward I, s.d. 16 Aug. 1303).
[105] A. Jervise, *Memorials of Angus and the Mearns* (1861), 381–3; Black, *Surnames*, s.vv. 'TREMBLAY', 'TURNBULL'.
[106] *Scots Pge.* viii. 2.
[107] *Carte de France*, 1 : 100,000, Sheet I 7, 'Évreux'. Sémerville proper is 16 km north-west of Évreux. Le Prévost, *Mémoires . . . de l'Eure*, iii. 235–6, deals with this Sémerville without citing any early form corresponding to the surname Somerville. He does, however, cite the form Soumerville in dealing with Quatremarre (canton and arr. Louviers), whose demesne included Sémerville (ibid. iii. 1). Le Tremblay and La Tremblaie (etc.) are common place-names in Normandy, but the proximity of Le Tremblay (canton Neubourg) and Sémerville supports the identification proposed here. It was presumably from this Le Tremblay that Everard and Boschard 'de Tremblei', who witnessed two charters of Amaury count of Évreux given in the Holy Land in 1188, took their surname. One of these charters was also witnessed by the great Yorkshire landowner, Roger de Mowbray, evidently just before his death (Le Prévost, *Mémoires . . . de l'Eure*, i. 133; Greenway, *Mowbray Charters*, p. xxxii). There was, however, a substantial family surnamed du Tremblay in the Falaise district (L. Delisle, *Cartulaire normand* (1852), nos. 905, 918; Lechaudé d'Anisy, *Extrait des chartes et autres actes normands ou anglo-normands qui se trouvent dans les archives du Calvados* (2 vols., Caen, 1835), ii, 2–3, 302).
[108] Clay and Greenway, *Early Yorkshire Families*, 20.
[109] Ibid.

and Sinnington near Pickering, from Roger de Clere in the third decade of the twelfth century to Agatha daughter of a later Roger de Clere in the middle of the thirteenth.[110] The Cleres also held land in Sussex, a fact explained by the territorial connection between the families of Varenne lords of Lewes and Tosny.[111] Sir Charles did not pursue the trail of the Cleres north of the Border. A junior branch of the Yorkshire line, in the person of Ralph younger brother of Roger de Clere, not only established itself in Scotland under Malcolm IV— who was a Varenne on his mother's side and the great-nephew of a Tosny[112]—but actually acquired a position of much greater consequence in the northern kingdom than the senior line enjoyed in England. The fiefs, no doubt military, which were provided for Ralph de Clere in Scotland were Mid Calder, or Calder Clere, in Midlothian, the site of whose motte castle still remains,[113] and the almost adjacent parish of Cambusnethan in Lanarkshire.[114] Ralph de Clere was a benefactor of the abbeys of Paisley and Kelso.[115] By 1185 the English line had failed and Ralph de Clere succeeded his brother Roger II in the North Riding and Sussex estates.[116] From then until the middle of the thirteenth century a single Anglo-Scottish line of Cleres preserved their inheritance in both kingdoms, but it is to be noted that in 1244 Roger de Clere took his place as a leading baron of Scotland in an international agreement.[117] By the time two successive Clere heiresses had married English husbands the reliability of the barons of Calder Clere and Cambusnethan may have become

[110] Ibid., 21.
[111] Ibid. *The Chartulary of the Priory of St. Pancras of Lewes*, ed. L. F. Salzman (Sussex Record Soc., 1933–5), contains many references to members of the de Clère family, including charters issued by them (ii, 50–3).
[112] See the chart pedigree in Anderson, *Early Sources*, ii. 155.
[113] *Kelso Liber*, ii, nos. 348, 349; O.S. 7th ser., NT 075677 (not listed by G. G. Simpson and B. Webster, 'Charter evidence and the distribution of mottes in Scotland', *Château Gaillard*, v (Caen, 1970), 175–86).
[114] *Kelso Liber*, no. 272. Mid Calder and Cambusnethan may be called almost adjacent in terms of boundaries, but they are separated by the extensive parish of West Calder, and the site of the old church of Cambusnethan is some 20 miles west of Mid Calder village.
[115] See preceding notes, and also *Paisley Reg.*, 310, 412, record of the grant to Paisley Abbey by Ralph (I) de Clere of Garrion in Cambusnethan.
[116] Clay and Greenway, *Early Yorkshire Families*, 21.
[117] *CDS* i, no. 1655.

The Colonists: (ii) Dependants and adventurers

suspect in Scottish eyes. Robert I eventually granted Mid Calder and Cambusnethan to his loyal supporters James Douglas of Lothian and Robert Baird of Strathaven respectively.[118]

Robert Baird, whom King Edward I complimented with the title 'one of my worst enemies',[119] conveniently leads us from the Norman aristocracy of Yorkshire to families of humbler status and more obscure origin. Robert and his ancestors had held a fief at Strathaven in the Middle Ward of Lanarkshire since the late twelfth century.[120] The earliest known member of the family seems to have been a certain Durand Ba(a)rd of Loftus and Butterwick in Cleveland, who is found in the first half of the twelfth century as a dependant of the Brus lords of Cleveland.[121] We know that there was for a time a substantial Flemish settlement in Cleveland, and it may be that the Ba(a)rds were of Flemish origin. The earliest Bairds in Clydesdale held their land of the Fleming Waltheof son of Baldwin of Biggar,[122] and in view of the prominence of another Fleming, named Thancard, in the plantation of Clydesdale,[123] it is worth noting that Tancard was the name of a leading Flemish settler in Cleveland in Henry I's time, who seems to have sold up his lands there between 1115 and 1135, presumably to go in search of some other lands available for settlement.[124] A further clue to the link between the Bruces of

---

[118] *RMS* i, nos. 59, 79.
[119] *CDS* ii, no. 1147.
[120] *Kelso Liber*, nos. 181, 186.
[121] See Appendix B. *Abstracts of the Charters and Other Documents contained in the Chartulary of the Priory of Bridlington in the East Riding of the county of York*, ed. W. T. Lancaster (Leeds, 1912), 90–1, provides evidence of Durand (II?) Bard of Butterwick and his son William Bard. Between 1160 and 1175, Adam II de Brus confirmed a gift in Loftus by Richard Baard, while other charters of the same Adam were witnessed by Geoffrey Baard (*EYC* ii, nos. 656, 659, 661–3, 666). A charter of Durand (I) of Butterwick, c. 1120 X 35, whose son and heir was Geoffrey, refers to Roger Baarth as son of Durand's wife (ibid., no. 1071). The Richard Ba(a)rd who appears in Lanarkshire c. 1200 was perhaps the son of Geoffrey, son of Richard Baard, but their relationship to Durand Bard is not clear. The first Durand was a dependant of the Fossard family, but there were many links with the Brus family also. There is a discussion of the early generations of this family (without reference to the Scottish evidence or to the use of the surname Ba(a)rd) in Clay and Greenway, *Early Yorkshire Families*, 11–12, s.v. 'Butterwick'.
[122] *OPS* i. 103.
[123] Ibid. 143–4; *Paisley Reg.*, 310, 412; *RRS*, i, no. 304; Nisbet, *Heraldry*, ii, Appendix, 146.
[124] *EYC* ii, no. 859.

Cleveland and the Flemish colony in Clydesdale is provided by the fact that a lady named Agnes de Brus was in possession of the knight's feu of Thankerton, 'Thancard's toun', near Lanark about 1185.[125] Agnes's relationship to the Brus family is unknown, but an Agnes de Brus appears on the Yorkshire Pipe Roll for 1156,[126] and the name itself twice entered the Brus pedigree in the twelfth century with the marriages respectively of Robert I to Agnes Bainard of Burton Agnes[127] and of Adam II to Agnes daughter of the count of Aumâle.[128] As we have seen, the Scottish Agnes de Brus has left her name in Anniestoun near Thankerton.[129] Provisionally we may conclude that the Scottish Bairds were descended from a younger son of one of the Baards of Loftus, who may have been Flemish and were certainly tenants of the Bruces. Yet another link between Cleveland in this period and Flemish settlers in Scotland is provided by a family bearing the uncommon surname of Wyrfald or Wyrfalc. In Yorkshire they were benefactors of Whitby Abbey; in Scotland Roger Wyrfalc was associated with two prominent Flemish settlers, Hugh son of Waltheof (of Biggar) and Robert son of Werenbald, ancestor of the Cunninghams.[130] Surviving record allows us these few tantalizing hints which suggest that the Flemish settlement of Clydesdale in the 1150s and '60s was the second and permanent stage in a Flemish migration which had begun in Cleveland.

We seem to be considering much the same social milieu when we look at the two West Riding families of Ripley and Farsley (or Fressheley). The overlordship of Ripley on the Nidd north

---

[125] *Kelso Liber*, no. 275.
[126] *Pipe Roll, 2 Henry II*, 27.
[127] *EYC* ii. 12, 30–1.
[128] Ibid. 12.
[129] Above, p. 37.
[130] See Appendix B. For the Wirfalchs, Wirfalds, Wirfaucs, or Wirfauks in Yorkshire, see *EYC* ii, nos. 663, 665, 905, 906 (a grant of land in Hinderwell to Whitby Abbey by William Wirfauc with consent of his son William). In Yorkshire the Wirfaucs appear regularly in a Brus context. In *EYC* ii. 372 the William Wirfauk litigating *versus* Ingram de Monceaux may really have been the one who lived in the mid-thirteenth century, for Sir Ingram de Monceus appears in a Brus context in 1248 (*Lindores Chartulary*, no. 41) along with Sir Hugh de Beaumys, who also appears in a deed of 1242 referring to Roger Wyrfauk holding land in Laurencekirk, Mearns (*Arbroath Liber*, i, no. 272). See also *St. Andrews Liber*, 279–80, 285–7, 334–5.

of Harrogate was held in the twelfth century by a Breton family descended from Wihomarc steward of Alan earl of Richmond.[131] Under these doubtless absentee Breton lords, however, and actually resident at Ripley, was a family of native proprietors whose ancestry, remarkably, may be traced to a certain thegn named Archil living in the Conqueror's reign.[132] Enough documents survive, mostly in the muniments of the Ingilby family, to show the Ripleys steadily consolidating their hold on land in and around the village from which, in the closing decades of the twelfth century, they were beginning to adopt a permanent surname.[133] Yet there must have been some incentive for members of even so deep-rooted a family to look far beyond the borders of Yorkshire for new and quite possibly risky ventures. Before 1214 William of Ripley, of the fifth generation since the Northumbrian Archil, had been tempted to the north of Scotland by King William the Lion's grant of the estate of 'Dolaysmichel', that is Dallas, 7 miles south-east of Forres in Moray.[134] Dallas was to be held for the fourth part of a knight's service, exactly what had been performed by his father Richard and his uncle Bernard the clerk for their shares of the ancestral lands of Ripley.[135] Before the death of Alexander III the descendants of William of Ripley had become thoroughly naturalized as the knightly family of Dallas of that ilk.[136] Meanwhile, in Alexander II's reign, a younger brother of William of Ripley, Bernard, had ventured into another remote corner of Scotland. By marrying

---

[131] The chief sources for the early history of the Ripley family are *EYC* i. 403 ff. and x. 97–9; W. T. Lancaster, *The Early History of Ripley and of the Ingilby Family, with some account of the Roos Family of Ingmanthorpe* (privately printed, 1918), especially the documents in the Appendix.

[132] The descent worked out by Lancaster, op. cit., p. 5, is Archil (living 1066–86) →Waltheof of Studley→Uhtred (benefactor of Fountains Abbey)→Norman, who was the father of Adam, Bernard the clerk and Richard (see *EYC* i, no. 524).

[133] Lancaster, op. cit., Appendix, nos. 4, 6, 7, 8.

[134] SRO Reg. Ho. chrs. no. 58. The descent of the Dallases from a member of the Yorkshire family of Ripley is stated by J. Dallas, *The History of the Family of Dallas and their Connections and Descendants from the Twelfth Century* (posthumous; privately printed, Edinburgh, 1921), 22–4, but the author of this account was not able to make use of Lancaster's *History of Ripley* or *EYC*.

[135] Lancaster, op. cit., Appendix, no. 1.

[136] J. Dallas, *Family of Dallas*, gives the documentary references for members of the family from the mid-thirteenth century.

an heiress whom we know only by her Christian name of Margaret, he acquired 'Kirkanders' in Galloway, a village which, though long since lost, can be located between Gatehouse of Fleet and Kirkcudbright.[137]

There seems to be no way of telling whether the Farsley family was of continental or native ancestry. It may be significant that from the mid-twelfth century, when men of this designation first appear, to the fourteenth the family used continental personal names together with the biblical Simon and Philip.[138] Oddly enough for a Yorkshire family destined to produce an important offshoot in Scotland, the Farsleys of Farsley were much intermingled with their near neighbours, the Scots of Calverley, which was held of the Honour of Lacy.[139] The Farsleys appear in Scotland as suddenly and inexplicably as the Ripleys, towards the end of Alexander II's reign. What makes their case unusual is that the knight Sir Geoffrey of Farsley to whom King Alexander gave land near Crail in Fife seems to have been the head of his kin and not a younger son.[140] It is true that there was a stay-at-home Philip of Farsley in the 1250s and '60s,[141] but when the Scottish war broke out in 1296 the lands of Farsley were confiscated by the sheriff of Yorkshire because their owner, Geoffrey of Farsley, was a Scots rebel.[142] He would no doubt have made his peace after Balliol's surrender, but by 1301 he was again forfeited and got his lands back only after the general submission of 1304.[143] By this date at least two well-established lines of Farsleys had settled down permanently in Scotland, one in East Fife and the other in the area of Glenfarg near Bridge of Earn.[144] Like those Ripleys who had turned into Dallases, the 'Fressheleys' or 'Fusheles', for over fifty years lieges of the Scots Crown, had become thoroughly naturalized.

---

[137] *St. Bees Reg.*, no. 67.
[138] *EYC* vi, no. 69; *Pontefract Chartulary*, i, nos. 214–5; *Kirkstall Coucher Bk.*, nos. 16 (pp. 13–14), 359, note; *Calverley Charters*, ed. W. Paley Baildon and S. Margerison (Thoresby Soc., 1904), nos. 3, 5, 11, 12, 20, 27, 29, 142.
[139] *Calverley Charters*, passim.
[140] BL Add. chrs. 66570 (RRS, *Handlist of Acts of Alexander II*. no. 297).
[141] *Calverley Charters*, references in index.
[142] *CDS* ii. 172.
[143] Ibid., no. 1594.
[144] See Appendix B.

The Colonists: (ii) Dependants and adventurers

In the later nineteenth and earlier twentieth centuries a conspicuous Scottish migration directed itself towards the West Riding of Yorkshire. Whether the Scots in the thirteenth century recognized a movement in the reverse direction of comparable significance we have no means of telling. Had there then existed a Society of Yorkshiremen in Scotland, as for many generations there has been a Society of Yorkshiremen in London, then without doubt it need never have lacked for members. Yorkshire names occur in Scots record of this period over and over again, in many different parts of the country, in contexts expected and unexpected alike. Sir Roger of Skelbrooke held his fortified outpost of Greenan in Carrick in the 1190s.[145] Hugh 'Sans Manche', from the Honour of Richmond, perhaps a refugee after the suppression of the revolt of 1173–4, struck out on his own behalf in the lordship of Morton in Nithsdale, afterwards owned by the famous Randolph family.[146] Sir Alan Lascelles the elder, who was associated with the Scottish royal house from the 1150s[147] and fought valiantly at Alnwick in 1174 to save his royal master from the humiliation of capture, 'though he had not jousted for thirty years',[148] had a son Alan who became a prominent laird in north-east Fife.[149] As for another of Sir Alan's sons, Duncan Lascelles, we could hardly fix upon any man who more perfectly epitomized the Anglo-Norman-Scottish triangle. Against a Yorkshire background, he had a Norman surname, a Gaelic Christian name, no doubt in compliment to the earl of Fife, and he married a lady named Christian of Windsor who despite her surname was a native Northumbrian, daughter of Uhtred son of Halden lord of Catterlen in Cumberland and yet styled herself 'Christian de Windsor of Scotland'.[150]

---

[145] *Melrose Liber*, nos. 31, 32, 34; *North Berwick Carte*, no. 2.
[146] *Kelso Liber*, no. 404; see *RRS* ii. 241.
[147] Lawrie, *Charters*, no. 244.
[148] *Chron. Fantosme*, lines 1856–9.
[149] *St. Andrews Liber*, 260, shows that Alan de Lascelles, father of the Alan who granted this charter of 1200 X 1202, was married to Juliana de Somerville, perhaps a daughter of the William de Somerville who died *c.* 1164. It is not clear whether Juliana's husband was the veteran of 1174 or his son.
[150] W. P. Hedley, 'The sons of Halden lord of Catterlen', *CWAAS Trans.* (NS) lxiv (1964), 98–109, especially 105–7; Dean and Chapter, Carlisle, MS Transcript of the Cartulary of Lanercost Priory, p. 58, charter of Christian de Windsor 'of Scotland', A.D. 1202, granting two oxgangs in Paston (Northumberland) to Laner-

Christian brought her husband lands in Cumberland and Northumberland and also at Burnham in Buckinghamshire, a few miles from Windsor.[151] In 1209 King John led an army against the king of Scots and Duncan Lascelles was duly summoned to bring the knight-service due from his wife's estates.[152] He failed to appear, no doubt because he was serving in the king of Scots' army, and his lands were forfeited.[153] He recovered them, but because the lands were encumbered with Jewish debts he was evidently persuaded to sell them, along with the marriage of his daughter, to William Briwerr, an Exchequer official who notoriously exploited his friendship with King John by successful speculation in other men's property.[154]

Walter of Ryedale in the North Riding forsook the Honour of Bulmer to win the favour of David I and found the Scots family of Riddell.[155] Ranulf son of Walter of Lowthorpe in the East Riding became William the Lion's falconer and founded the long-lived dynasty of Halkerton in Mearns.[156] In 1296 the sheriff of Yorkshire could not be answerable for John son of Gilbert of Islebeck near Thirsk because he was in Scotland in the service of the bishop of Moray.[157] Simon de Cresseville of Attercliffe near Sheffield tried to defend Jedburgh Castle against Edward I in the autumn of 1298.[158] William Cosyn of Linthorpe near Middlesbrough nearly got into serious trouble at the end of Edward I's reign because he had remained in Scotland after the king had made a proclamation—otherwise

---

cost for the souls' weal of King William and his wife and children and of her own brother Walter. For this Walter see *RRS* ii, *passim*, references in index; *Trans. Roy. Soc. Literature*, 2nd ser., viii (1866), *Breviate of Lanercost Cartulary*, references in index.

[151] *Pipe Roll, 2 John*, 244, *13 John*, 143; *Memoranda Roll, 10 John*, 42. See also *Pipe Roll, 8 John*, 41, *11 John*, 193. Note that Duncan de Lascelles witnessed Lanercost charters of Robert son of Ralph de Vaux (*Trans. Roy. Soc. Lit.*, 2nd ser. viii, 451–2 and Index, 518).

[152] *Pipe Roll, 12 John*, 14.

[153] Ibid. For Duncan de Lascelles's land of Seggie (in Leuchars, Fife), see PRO S.C. 1/6/7; *St. Andrews Liber*, 340–1.

[154] *Pipe Roll, 13 John*, 143, 148.

[155] *RRS* i, no. 42; *EYC* i. 115 ff.

[156] *RRS* ii. 452–3.

[157] *CDS* ii. 172.

[158] Ibid.; Stevenson, *Documents*, no. 595; *Yorkshire Inquisitions*, iii, ed. W. Brown (Yorks Arch. Soc., 1902), 48; see also *TRHistS*, 5th ser. xxvii.

unknown, but apparently in 1298 or 1303—that all Englishmen must depart from Scotland.[159] Cosyn was ninety years old and pleaded bodily infirmity and fear of violence owing to the war. He must have passed his hundredth birthday when he died at Guisborough in 1311.[160] He had had the misfortune to survive into a world grimly different from what he had known in youth and prime, for during nearly all his long life there had scarcely been a hint of conflict between the two kingdoms.

Restlessness, curiosity, adventure, love; job hunger, land hunger, arranged marriages, and the squeezing out of younger sons from the family patrimony; particular loyalty or attachment to some powerful patron; refuge from defeat in war or simply from legal pursuit—no doubt all these acted as motives for the migration to Scotland of many men and women from England and northern France before the end of the thirteenth century. Although we cannot calculate the numbers of dependants involved, we may feel sure from the evidence available that the movement was large-scale in relation to the existing population. That the great lords and their followers and the host of lesser individuals exerted a profound and permanent influence on the law and custom of Scotland cannot be doubted. But over and above that I would argue strongly for the probability that Anglo-Norman settlement greatly reinforced the Middle English elements in Scots speech and culture, and had a decisive effect upon the texture of Scottish society as a whole.

---

[159] *Yorkshire Inquisitions*, ii, ed. W. Brown (1898), 1–2; *CDS* ii, no. 88; *Cal. Inqu. misc.* i, no. 1090. This inquisition (5 Edward I, no. 71) has been wrongly filed. It must belong to 5 Edward II, i.e. 29 Mar. 1312, when Robert Wodehouse was escheator, and it refers to Mr Richard de Havering taking an inquest on William Cosyn then staying in Scotland against the king's proclamation, i.e. between 2 Apr. 1299 and 19 Apr. 1305.
[160] Ibid.

V

Early Scottish Feudalism

THE 'Ordinance for the government of the land of Scotland' published in Edward I's parliament of September 1305 provided that 'the laws which King David [I] enacted, together with amendments and additions made by subsequent kings' should be read aloud before an assembly composed of the king's lieutenant and council in Scotland and *les bons gentz*, the substantial or responsible men of the country.[1] These laws, of which there was evidently some written statement, such as may be found in the so-called Berne Manuscript of the later thirteenth century,[2] consisted presumably of the 'assizes' of the various kings together with a register of the brieves or royal writs which initiated actions in the courts of justiciar or sheriff and of such lords as enjoyed seigneurial jurisdiction.[3] Although in the light of the developments which had taken place in England since 1272, Scots law and custom may have seemed somewhat too simple and old-fashioned in King Edward's eyes, it is not likely that he and his council contemplated wholesale reform or even revision in the new dominion. The 'Laws of David', as the common law of Scotland was known, were closely similar to the common law of England. Even though contemporaries drew a formal distinction, as in the Treaty of Birgham of 1290,[4] between the laws of England and the laws of Scotland, there is evidence which points to similarity as far as the substance of the law was concerned.

---

[1] Stones, *Relations*, 240, 250.
[2] *APS* i. 177–8; *An Introductory Survey of the Sources and Literature of Scots Law*, by various authors (Stair Soc., 1935).
[3] *The Register of Brieves, 1286–1386*, ed. T. M. Cooper (Stair Soc., 1946); H. McKechnie, *Judicial Process upon Brieves, 1219–1532* (University of Glasgow, David Murray Lecture, Glasgow, 1956).
[4] Stevenson, *Documents*, i. 165.

In 1285, for example, Melrose Abbey successfully claimed 'English law' (*lex anglicana*) for its tenants in Carrick, a conservative region where Celtic custom still persisted.[5] In 1296 Alexander MacDonald lord of Islay actually reminded King Edward in a letter that a procedural point of property law was identical in the laws of both Scotland and England.[6] In 1271 a Northumbrian heiress named Denise of Bitchfield (in Belsay) was abducted (or so she alleged) and carried across the Border to Jedburgh.[7] There she was able to put herself in the peace of the king of Scots. She then accused her supposed abductors in the king's court—presumably the court presided over by the Justiciar of Lothian, Hugh Barclay.[8] The judgement of that court acquitting the accused was at a later date so fully accepted by the justices and jury at the Northumberland Assizes that Denise was in mercy for a false accusation.[9] This curious episode is scarcely explicable unless a broad identity between Scots and English law was assumed. In 1297, one Henry 'the Scot' brought an action of novel disseisin against Laurence son of Henry Trynedyn in the court of the Justiciar of Ireland at Cork.[10] Laurence's first line of defence was to allege that the plaintiff was an Irishman, and therefore incompetent to bring a possessory action of English law. To this Henry replied that he was English (*anglicus*) and born in Scotland, and that he and all his predecessors had used English law. The jury supported him, declaring that Henry 'the Scot' and all his forebears originated in Scotland, were regarded as Scots, and were accustomed to use English law.[11]

The most influential treatise on Scots law in the middle ages was *Regiam Majestatem*, an adaptation to Scots use of the famous English treatise known by the name of Glanvill.[12] One of the largest pieces of adaptation was the incorporation of Romano-canonical material, now shown by Professor Peter Stein to have

[5] *Melrose Liber*, no. 316.
[6] PRO S.C. 1/18/147 (I have to thank Dr G. G. Simpson for bringing this document to my notice).
[7] *Northumberland Assize Rolls*, 369–72; *CDS* ii. 43–4.
[8] Barrow, *Kingdom*, 123, 138.
[9] *Northumberland Assize Rolls*, 371.
[10] *Calendar of the Justiciary Rolls of Ireland*, ed. J. Mills, i (1905), 158.
[11] Ibid.
[12] *Regiam Majestatem and Quoniam Attachiamenta*, ed. T. M. Cooper (Stair Soc., 1947).

been taken from the *Summa in titulos decretalium*, compiled by Gioffredo di Trano not long before his death in 1245.[13] Whether we take the view that the *Regiam* was produced during the reign of Alexander III (1249–86) or accept Professor Duncan's argument that the treatise cannot be earlier than 1318,[14] the inference of the treatise itself is that English feudal law of the late twelfth century, with Romano-canonical additions of sixty years later, was basically identical with the common law of Scotland prior to the reign of Robert I.

English common law of the period between Glanvill and Bracton was designed to serve the needs of a feudal society with a comparatively simple structure. Its guiding principle was tenure, the relationship of lord and vassal, of landlord and tenant. In the mind of feudal lawyers, the normal person— which is not the same thing as the average person or the person who, with others of his kind, constitutes the majority of the population—the normal person was beholden to a lord of whom he held land in which the lord had enfeoffed him, whether or not the tenant had inherited it from an antecessor. This normal person enjoyed seisin and could vindicate his freehold right, at least until a rival appeared prepared to vindicate a better right.

If we find an approximate identity between the common law of England, which was essentially feudal law, and the law current in the kingdom of Scotland, we expect to find also a closely comparable feudalism. The language of Scottish charters and other legal documents, and the ease with which Scots lawyers of a later age assimilated those early materials into a consciously feudal structure, go far to confirm our expectation. The sources are replete with such terms as *feudum* (Scots 'feu', English fee'), feu and heritage, *saisina* (Scots 'sasine', English 'seisin'), *servitium militis*, 'knight-service', *feudum militis*, 'knight's feu' or 'fee', default of service, and the technical verbs to infeft (*infeodare*), to hold (*tenere*) and to render, as of service (*reddere*).[15]

[13] P. Stein, 'The source of the Romano-canonical part of Regiam Maiestatem', *SHR* xlviii (1969), 107–23.
[14] A. A. M. Duncan, 'Regiam maiestatem: a reconsideration', *Juridical Review* (1961), 199–217.
[15] All these terms occur, most of them many times, in the major charter collections, including Lawrie, *Charters*, and *RRS* i and ii (see the subject index to the

The precise ranks held by free men were carefully stated: 'as freely as any of our earls . . . hold and possess their earldoms',[16] 'as freely as any of my barons holds',[17] 'as any knight may freely hold of a baron',[18] 'as any free man holds land of any earl or baron'[19]—these and similar phrases occur again and again. Towards the end of the twelfth century, Edward son of Peter, laird of Restalrig, used the word *baro*, 'baron', as a personal title (*baro regis Scottorum*, 'baron of the king of Scots').[20] Such self-consciousness seems to have been rare, but *miles*, 'knight', came into regular use in this way during the thirteenth century, not only for men of local importance such as Henry of Braid, sometime sheriff of Edinburgh,[21] but also for powerful magnates like John Comyn of Badenoch.[22] This use of *miles*, at once honorific and descriptive, was much favoured by the Church and especially by the papal chancery.[23]

There is little doubt that in the course of the thirteenth century the social and political significance of knighthood overtook its military significance. It would, however, be unwise to draw too sharp a distinction in Scotland between the two aspects of knighthood even as late as the fourteenth century. Certainly before *c.* 1240 the knight was characteristically the

---

last two volumes). For the concept of the knight's feu or fee, see above, Chapter I, p. 9, n. 35.
[16] *Lennox Cartularium*, no. 1.
[17] *RRS* i, no. 184; ii, no. 204 (compare ibid. i, no. 183, 'as any earl or baron in the realm of Scotland most freely holds').
[18] Fraser, *Lennox*, ii, no. 1; SRO GD 241/254.
[19] *SHS Misc.* iv. 318, no. 14; compare ibid. 316, no. 12, 'as any free man within the realm of Scotland may most freely give his land to his son', and Fraser, *Grant*, iii. 5 (no. 7), 'as much as any man can do in his own land'.
[20] Raine, *North Durham*, no. 170. More usual is the indirect reference to 'any baron of the whole realm of Scotland' as used, e.g. by Gilchrist MacNaughton of Argyll *c.* 1246 (*Inchaffray Chrs.*, no. 73).
[21] *Holyrood Liber*, no. 57.
[22] Raine, *North Durham*, no. 176; compare, for a man of equal or even greater rank, Eugenius (=Ewen) the knight, son of Duncan of Argyll, in SRO MS Reg. Magni Sigilli, xiv. 389. A man of still higher rank, Sir William Comyn, kt., earl of Buchan, witnessed under that style a charter of his son Richard Comyn II concerning Carraw, Northumberland, 1212 X 1233 (J. Hodgson, *History of Northumberland*, pt. II, iii. 397).
[23] e.g. Theiner, *Monumenta*, nos. 32, 102, 105 (Nicholas of Culenes, knight), 37 (D(uncan) of Perth, knight), 190 (William of Frendraught, knight). But in papal letters *nobilis vir* was more usual: e.g. ibid., nos. 142, 196, 237.

personal retainer, vassal and/or tenant of the king or some great lord, and we have no reason to doubt that his chief role was a military one. David I granted Swinton in Berwickshire in feu and heritage to his knight Ernulf,[24] although in fact Swinton belonged to Saint Cuthbert and the church of Durham. Here the king was providing a permanent endowment on the cheap for one of his mounted warriors. The proprietary manner in which a lord spoke of 'his' knights was in evidence for at least a century after David I's time. A charter for Jedburgh Abbey issued by Ranulf de Soules lord of Liddesdale in Malcolm IV's reign vividly conveys the atmosphere of one of the freshly created feudal lordships of Scotland.[25] It begins 'Ranulf de Soules, butler of the king of Scots, greets his heirs and all his friends and responsible men and all faithful people, future and present'. It goes on to narrate gifts of the churches of Great Doddington near Earls Barton and St. Martin of Liddesdale— that is, Castleton—together with land at Nisbet near Jedburgh. The witness list opens suitably with the names of seven ecclesiastical personages, including the bishop of Glasgow and the abbot of Kelso. Then follow the names of William de la Haye, Malger, and Elias, described as 'the knights of Ranulf de Soules', after whom come two other strangers, Richard 'of Barnack'[26] and Malger 'of Calceby',[27] and finally two local men, Hethna of Nisbet and Archil the grieve[28] of Nisbet. William de la Haye, the first of Ranulf's knights, was in fact his nephew, and took his surname from the village of La Haye-Bellefonds next door to Soulles, near Saint-Lô in the department of La Manche, in Normandy.[29]

Agreements made by the successive Stewarts, Alan and Walter II, with the abbeys of Kelso and Melrose anent sheep grazings on Lammermuir had to be confirmed by a group of the Stewarts' free tenants whom Alan merely called his 'men'

---

[24] Lawrie, *Charters*, nos. 100, 101.
[25] SRO, Crown Office Writs, no. 1.
[26] Berneche is close to the twelfth-century forms for Barnack cited in Ekwall, *Concise Dictionary*.
[27] Caluesb' is a form to be expected for Calceby, Lincolnshire, if the explanation in Ekwall, op. cit., is correct. Malger may have given his name to Mangerton in Castleton.
[28] Archil *prepositus*.
[29] Barrow, *Kingdom*, 325–6.

but whom Walter II called his 'knights'.³⁰ When Ralph II de Clere confirmed the church of Cambusnethan to Kelso he ended his charter thus: 'because I do not have my great seal with me at present, I have corroborated this writing with my secret seal, together with the seals of my knights and of Sir William Avenel.'³¹ The witnesses included Richard de Lanquetôt,³² Thomas of Worcester, and Roger de Clere the grantor's son, all of whom may reasonably be thought to have been the knights in question. A charter issued in 1245 by the baron William of Brechin, the son of one of Earl David of Huntingdon's bastards, was witnessed by nine named knights in respect of whom William used the possessive pronoun 'mine'.³³ The distinction between the retained, household knight and the lairdly, territorialized knight seems to be emphasized in the witness list of a charter issued about 1230 by David II de Lindsay lord of Crawford, surely at a session either of the justiciar's court or of a joint sheriff court.³⁴ The sheriffs of Ayr and Lanark head the list and among the names which follow are William of Hartside, Robert of Roberton and Walter of Congleton, all lords of knights' feus though not called knights. Against these names that of 'John de Hubeschaun my knight' stands out in sharp relief.³⁵ But it was certainly not unknown for a man to be styled by his rank as well as by his landed estate, although we have no way of telling why a freeholder who appears on numerous occasions simply as 'Walter of Congleton' can be dignified once or twice as 'Walter the knight of Congleton'.³⁶

Often enough, however, we find mention of knights who do not seem so clearly attached either to a lord or to an estate.

---

[30] *Kelso Liber*, nos. 248, 253; see also *Melrose Liber*, nos. 61, 62.

[31] *Kelso Liber*, no. 272.

[32] Ricardus de Langetoft, his surname representing the place now called Lanquetot, arr. Le Havre, dép. Seine-Maritime.

[33] *Lindores Chartulary*, no. 55, given at Lindores where William of Brechin had a castle (ibid., no. 62).

[34] *Newbattle Reg.*, no. 139.

[35] Ibid., p. 106. The only instance I have discovered of a surname similar to this is in *RAL* iv, no. 1283 (c. 1230–40), a deed witnessed by Alan Hubchun.

[36] *Trans. Roy. Soc. Lit.*, 2nd ser. viii, 471; *Dryburgh Liber*, nos. 285, 289; *Newbattle Reg.*, nos. 77, 78, 86, 90, 91, 103, 105, 106; *Holyrood Liber*, no. 64; contrasted with *Dryburgh Liber*, p. 33 and *Newbattle Reg.*, no. 100. Only if the last two documents cited could be shown to be later in date than the rest would the explanation lie in Walter's formal promotion to knighthood.

Gerard 'the knight' is conspicuous among the witnesses to the earliest charter of Dundas, partly because he comes so low down on the list and partly because everyone else listed seems to have a territorial or an official designation.[37] But he may not have been landless, for Henry de Bohun earl of Hereford gave Illieston in Kirkliston to an otherwise unknown Gerald, perhaps identical.[38] What mattered to the charter scribe was Gerard's knightliness. The same may be said of Sir Sybald 'the knight of Mearns' who was witness to an early thirteenth-century charter from Kincardineshire, though doubtless he belonged to the family of Sibbald of Kair.[39] Some subtle gradations within the general rank of knighthood are suggested by documents coming from the milieu of the earls of Carrick and Strathearn. One of Earl Duncan of Carrick's charters was witnessed by 'Sir John the knight, the earl's son', others simply by 'Hector and Alan the knights', while the earl's elder son Neil calls Hector 'my knight'.[40] Between 1189 and 1196 Earl Duncan confirmed to Melrose Abbey a grant which, as the charter has it, 'I and Roger of Skelbrooke my knight have made',[41] and lest there should be any doubt of the relationship between Roger as immediate lord and the earl as chief lord, the charter concludes with the phrase 'as any earl, or any patron of a feu (*feoudi advocatus*) may freely grant and confirm to a conventual church'.[42]

The earl of Strathearn's entourage reveals a similar state of affairs. Many of Earl Gilbert's charters (1171–1223) were witnessed by the officials and local gentry of the earldom whose names prove how little Strathearn had been touched by Anglo-Norman settlement.[43] But a handful of exotic names appear, and some are associated with knighthood. Thus, we hear of Sir Roger de Louvetôt (Loutit in Scots),[44] normally among

[37] *APS* i. 92.
[38] Fraser, *Facsimiles*, no. 27.
[39] *St. Andrews Liber*, 286; J. Crabb Watt, *The Mearns of Old* (Edinburgh and Glasgow, 1914), 191, 359.
[40] *North Berwick Carte*, nos. 1, 13, 15.
[41] *Melrose Liber*, no. 32 (p. 25).
[42] Ibid., p. 26.
[43] Most of Earl Gilbert's surviving charters are printed in *Inchaffray Charters*, *passim*, from no. 2 to no. 45.
[44] Ibid., nos. 56, 57; *Lindores Chartulary*, nos. 24, 44. Strathearn charters of the earlier thirteenth century were witnessed by Roger and William de Louvetot.

senior witnesses and once described as 'my knight' by Earl Gilbert's son Fergus.[45] Earl Gilbert's own charters were witnessed by Gilbert 'the knight', and the fact that once or twice he is called the earl's 'fellow' or 'companion' (*socius*) suggests membership of the earl's household.[46] Both Earl Gilbert and his son Earl Robert were attended by their knight Richard son of Lugan (Luguen),[47] whose status as a gentleman retainer is occasionally indicated by the possessive pronoun but whose infeftment in a landed estate is also shown by his style 'Richard the knight of Kinbuck'[48] and by the fact that he was duly succeeded by Sir Joachim the knight of Kinbuck.[49] The exotic quality of this knightly family in the context of Strathearn is shown by their choice of personal names, Richard, his brother Geoffrey, and their sister Ysenda or Iseult, who became Earl Gilbert's second wife after Maud d'Aubigny died.[50]

The contemporary earl of Fife's charters likewise discriminate between Adam 'the knight of Ceres', who was probably the earl's kinsman, endowed with a substantial fief,[51] William 'of Holderness', described merely as the earl's knight,[52] and the yet humbler Milo de Raiville, the earl's 'man'.[53] We see in all these instances the heads of native comital dynasties attracting to themselves small retinues of trained cavalry soldiers who in

---

They were presumably kinsmen (sons, or son and grandson?) of Nigel de Louvetot who held Dalpatrick (in Crieff) by 1200 (*Inchaffray Chrs.*, p. lxxxiii and nos. 9, 27, 55. Nigel was evidently a cadet of the Anglo-Norman family which took its name from Louvetot, canton Caudebec, arr. Yvetot, dép. Seine-Maritime. A Nigel de Louvetot, descendant of Nigel, younger son of Richard de Louvetot, lord of Worksop and Hallam (d. 1171), died in 1219. The Louvetot migration into Strathearn may be accounted for by the fact that Earl Gilbert's mother-in-law, Maud de Senlis, married Richard de Louvetot as her second husband. See Clay and Greenway, *Early Yorkshire Families*, 53–6 (where the Scottish evidence is not mentioned); *PSAS* lxxxvii, 56–7; Loyd, *Origins*, 55–6.

[45] *Lindores Chartulary*, no. 26.
[46] *Inchaffray Chrs.*, nos. 4, 12, 14.
[47] Ibid., nos. 30, 31, 55, 56, 58.
[48] Ibid., no. 27; *Cambuskenneth Reg.*, no. 68.
[49] *Inchaffray Chrs.*, nos. 74, 76, 87, 95.
[50] Ibid., no. 46.
[51] *St. Andrews Liber*, 244, 247 (see also ibid. 264, 265; *Dunfermline Reg.*, no. 153; *North Berwick Carte*, no. 3).
[52] *St. Andrews Liber*, 241, 243.
[53] Ibid. 241, 243, 244, 260.

districts still markedly Celtic in character were obviously a comparative rarity as late as the thirteenth century. Whenever we find one or two Anglo-Continental or non-Scottish personal names in the entourage of a native earl, we may infer the beginnings of such a retinue, whether or not the description 'knight' is actually stated. For example, Earl Henry of Atholl was attended by Alexander 'the knight',[54] and the milieu of the earls of Lennox, still strongly Gaelic in the 1220s and 1230s, was nevertheless marked by the appearance of such figures as Alan and Simon Croc, Roger son of Glai, Simon son of Bertolf and his son Simon,[55] an indication that Earl Maoldomhnaich was recruiting, evidently from the Stewart's circle of vassals, knights of a type which could not yet be provided locally.

Secular landowners' charters from the thirteenth century have survived plentifully enough for us to see the groups of knights, landed or otherwise, attendant upon the greater magnates in the 1190s or early 1200s evolve easily into the groups of gentry, freeholders, esquires, bachelors, and knights by rank who still gathered around the rich and powerful lords in the middle and later decades of the thirteenth century. No doubt the social dignity and economic security of the knight increased during that century, but, even so, men of knightly rank continued to attach themselves to the great lords and to form the élite of their retinue or meinie. An unbroken line in the development of social custom links the bonds of manrent, i.e. contracts of homage, of fifteenth- and sixteenth-century Scotland[56] to the possibly less formal yet none the less effectual affinities by which younger men in the lower strata of nobility placed themselves under the patronage of an earl or one of the greater barons in the days of William the Lion and his son.

---

[54] *Dunfermline Reg.*, no. 148; perhaps the Alexander 'de Setona' who witnessed Earl Henry's charter, *St. Andrews Liber*, 246; see also *Coupar Angus Chrs.*, no. 22.

[55] Fraser, *Lennox*, ii. 3; *Hist. MSS Comm. 7th Rep.*, App., 704; *Lennox Cartularium*, 14, 27, 96; *Paisley Reg.*, 158–9, 171. Some of these retainers seem to have been sons of men who appear in the entourage of the Stewarts (see Barrow, *Kingdom*, 355, 357, 359 for Robert Croc, Glai, and Alan and Simon Croc as Stewart followers. Glai may be a Breton name).

[56] I have benefited here from reading the unpublished Glasgow University Ph.D. thesis (1974) by Jennifer M. Brown, 'Bonds of Manrent in Scotland before 1603'.

The normal expectation of a knight was to be infeft by his lord in an estate which could form a knight's feu. As a generalization, it would not distort the truth to say that the foundations of the lairds' class in Scotland which was to play so crucial a part in the politics and religion of the country from the reign of James V to the end of the eighteenth century were laid in the twelfth and thirteenth centuries through the creation of knights' feus or fees by the king, the earls and other great nobles. The process was gradual, and though it went ahead faster in some parts of the country than in others, it was nevertheless steady, save for Galloway, the north-west highlands and the isles.

The gradualness was not only a matter of geography; it might arise from a shortage of resources. Towards the end of his reign, David I granted Athelstaneford and other lands near Haddington to Alexander de Saint-Martin, who had evidently come to Scotland in the suite of Ada de Varenne when she married King David's son Henry in 1139. Saint-Martin is the name of a hamlet beside Bellencombre in Upper Normandy, the *caput* of the Norman fief of the de Varenne family.[57] The king's infeftment of Alexander de St. Martin fell short of what could properly be regarded as a full knight's feu. 'It is my will', the king says, 'that Alexander and his heirs shall hold of me and of my heirs in feu and heritage by the service of half a knight; and I shall pay him ten merks of silver a year from my chamber until I am able to make up for him the full feu of one knight.'[58] At some point within the next twenty years Ada de Varenne herself, by now in complete control of the shires of Haddington and Crail as her dower, fulfilled King David's intention by adding substantially to Alexander de St. Martin's holdings in both districts. Alexander was now to hold this much enlarged estate for one knight's service, and as if to mark his new status would enjoy sake, soke, toll, team and infangen-

[57] Loyd, *Origins*, 111–12, *EYC* viii. 81 (commune and canton Bellencombre, dép. Seine-Maritime); *EYC* viii, nos. 23, 92; for the St. Martins as dependants of the Varenne family, see ibid. 78 and 132; *Lewes Chartulary*, i. 146–7, 150. Although none apparently was named Alexander, the personal name Ralph, occurring among the Varenne dependants, is also found in Scotland in the person of Ralph de St. Martin, parson of Bolton, East Lothian, son of a Gilbert de St. Martin (*Holyrood Liber*, 27; *May Records*, nos. 33, 34).
[58] Lawrie, *Charters*, no. 186.

thief.⁵⁹ In the 1160s or '70s Robert de Quincy similarly created an incomplete knight's feu out of the lands of 'Aldenestun' (Adniston) and 'Ulkelestun' for his dependant Pain 'de Helleia' or 'Hanle'.⁶⁰ Pain was infeft immediately in 7 librates (land worth £7 per annum) and his lord undertook to provide three more 'from the first increase which God may give me of 20 librates', as his charter puts it. Firmly established in the lands which then took his name, Painston or Penston, Pain was to hold his feu 'as freely and honourably as any knight holds land of any baron in the realm of the king of Scotland'.

Of the creation of knights' feus by the twelfth-century kings I have little more to say. That aspect of early Scottish feudalism has been dealt with at some length,⁶¹ and the publication in Lawrie's *Early Scottish Charters* and the first two volumes of the *Regesta Regum Scottorum* of a series of infeftments for knight-service makes the study of feudalization by the Crown comparatively straightforward. What should be emphasized is that 1214, the year of William the Lion's death, was in no sense a terminal point in what was a long-drawn-out process. Mr Scoular and Dr Simpson, who compiled the provisional *Handlists* of the surviving written acts of the reigns of Alexander II, Alexander III and John, list some 21 charters of military infeftment for the first (to which at least one more should be added) and nine for the other two.⁶² If these totals seem slender, it is nevertheless significant that they show knights' feus being created in widely separated regions of the Scottish kingdom— Nithsdale, Argyll, lowland Stirlingshire and Clackmannan, the border of Clydesdale and Lennox, the Perthshire Highlands, the Braes of Angus, Banffshire and Moray. By the beginning of the thirteenth century much of southern Scotland had already been distributed in knights' feus. The scope for fresh creations

---

⁵⁹ *Laing Charters*, no. 2.

⁶⁰ SRO GD 241/254; above, p. 23, n. 104.

⁶¹ In addition to chapters 10 and 12 of Barrow, *Kingdom*, and the literature there cited, see now A. A. M. Duncan, *Scotland: the Making of the Kingdom* (1975), chapter 15.

⁶² J. Scoular, *Handlist of the Acts of Alexander II* (RRS 1959), nos. 24, 29, 42, 75, 76, 86, 95, 96, 158, 160, 163, 170, 175, 202, 221, 245, 255, 285, 286, 337, 342, to which add NLS MS Adv. 34.3.25, pp. 217–8. G. G. Simpson, *Handlist of the Acts of Alexander III*, etc. (RRS 1960), nos. 13, 41, 55, 125, 127, 165, 207, 210, 364. Besides these the Handlists contain numerous royal confirmations of private infeftments certainly or probably for military service.

was consequently restricted to the relatively unfeudalized earldoms and to remoter parts of the kingdom.

Rather less attention, at least in print, has been paid to the way in which the great nobles, including the native earls, imitated the example of the Crown and set about forming knights' feus on their own estates. The position of the Maitlands of Thirlestane, for example, was secured when William de Morville the Constable, son of Richard and nephew of Hugh the murderer, infeft Alan son of Elsi, Richard Maitland's father-in-law, for one knight's service in the lands of Thirlestane which his father Elsi son of Winter had previously held for the older Northumbrian rent, perhaps a thanage rent, of 3 merks a year.[63] The same William found enough land at Carfrae, at the upper end of Lauderdale, to make a knight's feu for Henry de St. Clair (Sinclair) to whom William's father Richard had already granted Herdmanston in East Lothian as half a knight's feu.[64] Appropriately enough, the Carfrae charter was witnessed by four, perhaps five, men who held knights' feus in the de Morville lordship, Godfrey de Ros of Stewarton and Stephen son of Richard (from Cunningham),[65] Alan of Thirlestane in Lauderdale, Peter Haig of Bemersyde, and Edulf son of Uhtred, of 'Edulfestun', Eddleston near Peebles. A surprising absentee among the witnesses at what was surely a session of the honorial court was the Fleming James son of Lambin Asa, otherwise 'James of Draffan', to whom Richard de Morville had granted Loudoun in Cunningham for one knight's service.[66]

What the Morvilles could do in the twelfth century the earls of Fife could imitate in the opening decades of the thirteenth. A lucky chance has preserved the texts of a small series of charters of infeftment issued by the son of Earl Duncan II, Malcolm, who was earl from 1204 to 1228. These charters are remarkably standardized, using the formula 'for one knight's

[63] Barrow, *Kingdom*, 297.
[64] NLS MS Adv. 34.1.9 (II), pp. 244–5; Anderson, *Diplomata*, pl. LXXVb.
[65] They are respectively first and third witnesses (after the granter's wife) to William de Morville's confirmation of Loudoun to James, son of Lambin (Stevenson, *Illustrations*, 15, no. VIII); they also witnessed together the charters of Richard and William de Morville concerning Eddleston (*Glasgow Reg.*, nos. 44, 45). For Godfrey's place in Cunningham see *Cuninghame topographized*, 97–8.
[66] Marquess of Bute, Dumfries House, Loudoun charters, no. 1.

(or half a knight's) service, as freely as any knight holds his feu (or land) of any earl or baron in the realm of Scotland'. On these terms, Richard of Linton—evidently known as Richard 'the Englishman' or Inglis—got the west part of Tarvit parish, which came to be known as Inglistarvit.[67] (Somewhat curiously, the estate and particularly the stout tower house of Inglistarvit have been known as Scotstarvit since 1611, when they were acquired by Sir John Scot, author of *The Staggering State of Scottish Statesmen*.)[68] Alexander son of William of Blair got Teasses, Hall Teasses, and Bandirran south of Ceres;[69] Nes son of Nes of Ramsay got part of Forthar in Markinch;[70] while it is probable that the ancestor of David of Carslogie (west of Cupar) received that estate together with Uthrogle, for in the 1280s Earl Duncan III granted these lands to John de Clephane, first of the Clephanes of Carslogie, 'as David of Carslogie and his predecessors held it for knight service' of Earl Duncan's predecessors.[71] This all took place in the heart of the earldom, in East Fife; but further afield, in his barony of Earls Calder or West Calder in Midlothian, the same Earl Malcolm granted part of Livingston and 'Hiredmanston' (now Hermand) to Archibald son of William of Douglas in succession to a vassal from the shire of Cupar, William of Kilmaron, who had held the land on identical terms.[72]

The impetus of royal feudalization may possibly have slackened by the 1230s or '40s, but the century from *c.* 1160 to *c.* 1260 was a busy period for the formation of military fiefs by the nobility. From David I's time the Crown would expect its tenants-in-chief to create numerous dependant tenancies. The

---

[67] *SHR* viii (1911), 222. Evidently ancestor of the family of Inglis, clearly recorded as lairds of 'Ynglistarwet' by *c.* 1315 (Fraser, *Wemyss*, ii. 9, no. 5), Richard *Anglicus* witnessed, with Earl Malcolm and his entourage, *North Berwick Carte*, no. 10, and also, as Richard *Anglus*, Earl Malcolm's charter for Ness of Ramsay (below, n. 70).

[68] *RMS 1609-20*, no. 588; *RCAHM, Fife, Kinross and Clackmannan* (1933), 50-2.

[69] *SHS Misc.* iv. 311, no. 7.

[70] NLS MS Adv. 34.6.24, p. 409.

[71] NLS MS Adv. 34.6.24, p. 109, a grant of 'Cleslogie' (Carslogie) and 'Erithirrogewale' (Uthrogle) as David de Cleslogie or his predecessors held; to be preferred to the version given in Sibbald, *Fife*, 394–5, where David de Cleslogie has become David 'de Clephan', father of John.

[72] *Morton Reg.* i, App., no. 1.

creation of fractional knights' feus in areas as far apart as mid Aberdeenshire, Strathmore, Lennox, Fife, Lothian, Annandale, and Cunningham argues for the general acceptance of military tenure and its obligations. As far as the richer men were concerned, these obligations could be met by personal service in the host as well as by financial contributions. The poorer tenants would pay their share of the king's *auxilia* or aids in proportion to the size of their holdings. There was nothing to stop these men aspiring to knighthood, but presumably until their fortunes improved, perhaps with a grant from the king or a great noble, perhaps with a lucky marriage, they could support a knight's way of life only by placing their service on hire, perhaps borrowing the money to buy horses and arms. In any case, the practice of fractionalizing the knight's feu must have resulted from an assumption by the Crown that the *plenarium feudum unius militis* was the standard unit on which aids and service were assessed.

There is evidence for a measure of systematization in feudal tenures and in the relationship between the feudal lord and his vassals of knightly or lesser free rank. Thus, when Reginald de Varenne exchanged 'Coventre' (now Coven Trees) in Forgandenny, held in chief of the Crown, for Wester Dron, to be held of Laurence lord of Abernethy, Reginald's charter stipulated that Laurence must meet the king's forinsec service due from Coventre, but that he, Reginald, would perform the quantum of knight-service laid upon Coventre.[73] In 1232, Alexander II made a compendious grant to Gillandres MacLeod, an heir of the 'lay abbots' of Brechin, whereby he was confirmed in possession of Navar and other lands for one knight's service. Certain food and money rents were reserved to the clergy and abbot of Brechin, and the king's charter concludes: 'We also grant to Gillandres and the heirs whom he shall have by his wife Forveḷeth, daughter of Brice the *judex*, the lands of Cardean and Braikie by their rightful marches, within the aforesaid service of one knight.'[74] In 1237 land near Dumfries previously given to the Yorkshire tenant-in-chief Thomas de Aunay (Alnou, Annou, etc.[75]) for one quarter-knight's service was

---

[73] Fraser, *Douglas*, iii. 349–50, no. 281.
[74] *Brechin Reg.* i, no. 2 (with facsimile).
[75] See Appendix B.

transferred to Melrose Abbey.[76] The Cistercians were to pay the aids appropriate to a quarter-knight's feu but were not to perform the strictly military service. In 1240 the king infeft Gillespie MacGilchrist in the five pennylands of Fincharn for half a knight's service in the host but a whole knight's service in aid.[77] In 1247 he gave the thanage of Inverlunan in Angus to Anselm of Camelon, to be held partly as a half-knight's feu, partly for a money rent of which a certain sum was set aside as dower for the late thane's widow.[78] Similar arrangements may be seen in the next reign. At its start, for example, Roger de Moubray converted Moncreiffe and Balgonie into a military feu for the tenant, Matthew of Moncreiffe.[79] Matthew was relieved of the 'ancient ferme' and would in future be liable for one-twentieth knight's service in addition to the king's forinsec service. The Angus knight Henry of Nevay surrendered to the king an estate consisting of Nevay near Glamis and Lour near Forfar.[80] Henry was allowed to keep Nevay but Lour was granted to Hugh lord of Abernethy who was to perform the proportion of a knight's service due from that estate. Malcolm Murray, himself a knight, granted to his younger son William Murray first of Tullibardine Lhanbride near Elgin for a pair of white gloves or one penny at Whitsun, a rent which was to satisfy the donor for all the service due to him. Nevertheless, William was to perform half a knight's service for the feu in addition to the ordinary forinsec service.[81]

Arrangements of this sort would hardly have been made unless there had existed an established system of knights' feus and knight service due to the Crown, with its incidents, including aid. Early Scottish feudalism, far from appearing undeveloped or only half formed, seems remarkably cut and dried, almost a copybook version of the feudalism of north-west Europe. This quality is nicely exemplified in a charter by which Walter Olifard the younger, about 1208, granted the hill farm named Colzie, between Abernethy and Strathmiglo, to

[76] *Melrose Liber*, nos. 205–7 (see also BL Loans 29/255, no. 4, briefly calendared, *HMC 13th Rep.*, pt. II, 1).
[77] *Highland Papers*, ii. 121–3 (facsimile, p. 227).
[78] Fraser, *Carnegies*, ii. 478, no. 26.
[79] *Moncreiffs*, ii, App., no. V.
[80] Fraser, *Carnegies*, ii. 479, no. 27.
[81] *Moray Reg.* 461, App., 'Carte originales', no. 7.

Alan grandson of Cospatric of Swinton.⁸² It was not a knight's feu, and Alan, who is described simply as Walter's man or vassal (*aliquis hominum meorum*), paid only a money rent. But his incorporation as a freeholder within a self-conscious and articulate feudal system is emphasized by the fact that Alan was to hold in feu and heritage and that his rent of two merks would satisfy all the service due to the lord save for his aids, namely for his ransom from imprisonment if that fate befell him, the knighting of his first-born son and the marriage of his first-born daughter.⁸³

The whole question of infeftment by the subject-superior, as the typical tenant-in-chief was later known in Scotland, deserves fuller and more detailed study than can be devoted to it in a single chapter. Care might be taken to emphasize that knight-service was a royal prerogative. Thus, when Robert II de Brus, who died in 1191, confirmed a whole feu in Dryfesdale to Hugh son of Ingebald, as his father had held it, the knight-service was explicitly assigned to the king's army, while the tenant undertook to render to his lord the forinsec service of two touns or *ville*—although that also must ultimately have gone to the Crown.⁸⁴ But more often, it seems, a lord would claim the military service of his vassal. For instance, *c*. 1230 John of Scotland, earl of Huntingdon, son of Earl David, confirmed to Norman son of Malcolm son of Bertolf the whole feu created by his father Earl David for Norman's father Malcolm in the Garioch (Aberdeenshire) 'for the performance of the service of the feu of one knight to myself and my heirs'.⁸⁵ Some eighty or ninety years later, Christian de la Haye, lady of Parbroath in north Fife, granted an estate to her cousin John Ramsay for an annual rent of £6 and the incidents of ward and relief. John would perform the lord king's forinsec service and also the service of one knight to the earl of Fife on Christian de la Haye's behalf.⁸⁶

Fractional feus are highly characteristic of infeftments created by subject-superiors. In England such fractions have

---

⁸² *SHR* ii. 174–5 (with facsimile); see also *RRS* ii, no. 484.
⁸³ Compare the English Articles of the Barons, c.6 and Magna Carta (1215), c.15 (W. Stubbs, *Select Charters* (9th edn.), 286, 295).
⁸⁴ *CDS* i, no. 635.
⁸⁵ *Hist. MSS Comm.*, *4th Rep.*, App., 493; also *Panmure Reg.* ii. 203–4 (incomplete).
⁸⁶ NLS MS Adv. 34.6.24, pp. 409–10.

usually been explained in terms of the well-known practice of levying scutage. But there is no evidence for scutage in Scotland,[87] nor was any knight-service demanded from the Church. Scottish fractions must therefore be explained in some other way, either as vassals' share of a complete knight's service owed by the lord to the Crown, or as the result of partition among coheiresses and their descendants, or as a consequence of the sharp rise in the cost of a knight in the thirteenth century.

Before 1241, Gilbert Marshal earl of Pembroke, who held the lordship of Haddington in right of his wife Marjorie, the beautiful sister of Alexander II with whom Henry III was said to have fallen in love,[88] granted Garleton and Byres to David Lindsay of Barnweill for a half-knight's service.[89] Like Earl Gilbert, Philip de Moubray and his wife Galiena would certainly have owed knight-service to the Crown in round numbers. They are found infefting Hugh son of William (perhaps from the North Riding) in Kinmonth beside Moncreiffe for a quarter of a knight's service.[90] Earl Maoldomhnaich of Lennox granted 'Gartonvenach' as a marriage gift to Maurice son of Galbraith and his wife Catriona for the seventh of a knight's service.[91] William de Brus (before 1214) granted land at Pennersax to Ivo of Kirkpatrick for one-eighth,[92] his son Robert land near Lochmaben to Roger Crispin for one-twentieth,[93] Robert de Meyners (Menzies) granted Culdairs near Fortingall to the knight Matthew of Moncreiffe also for

---

[87] Barrow, *Kingdom*, 296, draws attention to a possibly unique instance of scutage being referred to in a charter issued by Walter de Windsor as lord of Clifton (in Morebattle), Roxburghshire (*Melrose Liber*, no. 116), which also mentions 'cornage'. I believe the explanation of this anomaly lies less in the practice of a clerk used to northern English terminology than in the probability that Walter's estate (like that of the Corbets, for which see Barrow, *Kingdom*, 34) lay on both sides of the Border, including land at Paston, Northumberland (above, p. 115, n. 150) and thus attracted Northumbrian terminology to it.

[88] Fraser, *Haddington*, ii. 225; *Comp. Pge.* X. 373 and nn. f and g; F. M. Powicke, *King Henry III and the Lord Edward* (Oxford, 1947), i. 159–60, ii. 768; Anderson, *Scottish Annals*, 343; *APS* i. 109 (quitclaim by Gilbert Marshal of the 'manor' of Jedburgh).

[89] Fraser, *Haddington*, ii. 225, no. 281.

[90] *Moncreiffs*, ii, App., no. I.

[91] *Lennox Cartularium*, 26–7. 'Cartonvenach' is presumably for *gortan* (or *gartan*) *mheadhonach*, 'middle field', but I have not been able to locate the place indicated.

[92] Fraser, *Annandale*, i. 2–3, no. 3.

[93] Ibid. 5, no. 7.

one-twentieth,[94] while Roger de Moubray, Philip's son, gave Echline in Dalmeny to Philip le Brun for only one-thirtieth, to be held as any knight holds of any baron.[95]

Fractions as small as one-twenty-fourth and one-thirty-second may be found in the Lennox,[96] where, characteristically perhaps for an intensely Gaelic area to which feudalism came late, landlords seem to have adopted the technicalities of the new system with almost too much enthusiasm. It would be unwise to dismiss the seemingly bewildering variety of fractions, halves, thirds, quarters, sevenths, eighths, tenths, twentieths, etc., as merely due to the lord's arbitrary whim, exercised in a period when knight-service possessed only fiscal or financial significance, and no longer referred to soldiering in the field. Certainly no such inference can be drawn from the fractions arising from partition. It is from this kind of fractionalization that we are able to deduce that Lauderdale was held originally for six knights' service and Cunningham—or at least the capital messuage of Cunningham—for two knights' service. For in 1296 the lady Helen la Zouche, a coheiress of the de Morvilles, was reported to have held one-third of the moiety of Lauder and Lauderdale for one knight's service and one-third of the moiety of Irvine for one-third of a knight.[97]

Bewildering as the variety of fractions may seem, a clear line of distinction was drawn between, on the one hand, whole-, half-, or (in the thirteenth century) quarter-knight's feus and, on the other, the lesser fractions such as sevenths, eighths, twentieths, etc. Above the line, all those tenants who held directly of the Crown and even some who held of subject-superiors, would normally expect to enjoy the baronial jurisdiction defined in the late Old English phrase 'sake, soke, toll, team and infangenthief', usually with the Latin addition *cum furca et fossa*, classically inverted in later medieval Scots as 'pit and gallows'. In other words, while knight-service by itself might be merely a matter of military and financial obligations, the possession of a whole or half knight's feu, or in the later

---

[94] *Moncreiffs*, ii, App., no. VIII (original charter *penes* Sir Iain Moncreiffe of that ilk, Easter Moncreiffe; photograph in I. Moncreiffe, *The Highland Clans* (1967), 234).
[95] NLS MS Ch. B 42.
[96] *Lennox Cartularium*, 27, 38–9.
[97] *CDS* ii, no. 824 (2), (6); also *Cal. Inqu.* iii, no. 363.

period a quarter-knight's feu, raised a man to a status of special importance within the realm and gave him a special relationship to the Crown. He held *in baroniam* or *in liberam baroniam*, 'in free barony', terms which though slow to establish themselves may be taken to represent a reality already acknowledged before the end of William the Lion's reign.

Record of early baronial courts in Scotland is pitifully meagre, but it would be wrong to regard them as unimportant before the fourteenth century. Consider the circumstances in which Patrick of Nawton surrendered his right in the land of Moncreiffe to David 'de Munehtes' about 1228 or 1229.[98] The deed was done in the graveyard of the parish kirk of Moncreiffe, or Dunbarney, on the day of peace (*ad diem pacis*), and yet at the same time in the court and presence of Patrick's and David's lord, Philip de Moubray. Among the seventeen persons named as attending this seigneurial court in addition to the lord himself were the king's chancellor, Master Matthew the Scot, the king's *judex* or hereditary judge (*breitheamh*), one of the king's clerks and the priors of Dunfermline and Cambuskenneth. The presence of such an array of notables points to a tribunal equal in status to that of the early courts convened by sheriffs. At other times, indeed, we can see a great lord apparently making use of this royal court of the sheriffdom, the later sheriff court, to transact essentially private legal business. For example, between 1196 and 1205 Philip de Valognes provided for his daughter Sybil, newly married to Robert de Stuteville, a dowry consisting of the Cumberland village of Torpenhow as Philip himself had best held it.[99] From the witness-list of Philip's charter, it looks as though his marriage gift, despite being in England and benefiting an English son-in-law, was made at a session of the sheriffdom court of Roxburgh, attended by the abbot of Jedburgh, the archdeacon of Glasgow and representatives or suitors of the baronies of Elliston, Hadden, Hawick, Hownam, Rule, Rutherford, and Wilton.[100]

---

[98] *Moncreiffs*, ii, App., no. II.
[99] *EYC* vi, 125, no. 54.
[100] Elliston represented by Robert de St. Michael (see *Dryburgh Liber*, no. 207), Hadden by Bernard of 'Hawedane', Hawick by Simon (Lovel?) of Hawick, Hownam (or perhaps Broxmouth) by Robert de Landeles, Rule by Alan of 'Ruele', Rutherford by Hugh of 'Ruwerfort', Wilton by John of Wilton.

The few examples of west-highland infeftments for military service which survive are bound to hold a special interest for us. This is not simply because of their rarity, although that poses the familiar problem of whether they are scarce because feudalism made little headway in the west or because historical accident has deprived us of documentary evidence for that region. Such documents as do survive, and other articulate linguistic evidence, give no countenance to any belief that feudalism advanced into the highlands in the manner of Original Sin raising its ugly head in the Garden of Eden. Place-names, for instance, suggest that proprietary feelings were, if anything, even more strongly developed in the west highlands than in other parts of the kingdom. We look in vain for primitive clan communism where the chief of the Lamonts of Cowal resided at Ardlamont,[101] the chief of MacLachlan sat at Castle Lachlan in Strathlachlan,[102] or Dugald MacSween, lord of Knapdale, was defended by the grimly forbidding fortification of Castle Sween on the shore of Loch Sween.[103] Castle Sween and Skipness, Dunchonnell and Inchchonnell, Dunstaffnage and Castle Tioram, Kisimul and Mingarry—all these remarkable stone fortresses of the west are agreed to belong to the thirteenth or early fourteenth centuries.[104] Even in ruin they are eloquent witnesses to a thoroughgoing, one might indeed say a harsh, form of lordship. The sentimental belief that Highland society was so pure that feudalism could only pollute it disregards the extent to which in the thirteenth century the whole of Scotland north of Forth and Clyde was still Celtic in low country and highlands alike. The companion belief in a conspiracy between monarchy and foreign feudalizing lords seriously underestimates both the strength of royal authority and the readiness of the native Highland nobility to adopt feudalism and adapt it to their needs.

---

[101] *OPS* ii, Pt. I, 51–3.
[102] Ibid. 75–6; *Glasgow St. Mary Liber*, 152–3.
[103] *OPS* ii, Pt. I, 40–2; W. D. H. Sellar, 'Family origins in Cowal and Knapdale', *Scottish Studies*, xv (1971), 21–37; S. Cruden, *The Scottish Castle*, 22–8.
[104] Ibid., chapter 2 *passim*. For Inchchonnell, see *RCAHMS Argyll*, ii, Lorn (1975), 223–31; for Dunchonnell see *Highland Papers*, i, 77; *OPS* ii, Pt. I, 277; *Chron. Bower*, i. 45 (I have also depended on an illustrated Lecture on Dunchonnell by Mr I. Fisher of the Royal Commission on Ancient and Historical Monuments).

Dugald MacSween himself provides a fairly early instance of adoption. In 1262 he granted to Walter Stewart earl of Menteith Skipness and other lands in Knapdale and Kintyre, together with an outlying estate in Cowal, to be held as Dugald had held them of the king 'as a free barony' (*in libera baronia*), for two-thirds of a knight's service in the king's army.[105] The implication of this charter, uniting scattered lands to form a feudal barony, for the reception of military feudalism in Argyll is clear. Even the uniquely early use of the term *in libera baronia* is instructive. It often happens that where innovation comes late it comes with special thoroughness and force. The men of Argyll seem to have taken the word 'baron' to their hearts, and it is in a highland charter that we find an even more exotic term such as *vavassaria*, presumably equivalent to the later Scots 'tenandry'.[106]

The earliest knight-service infeftment in the west highlands dates from 1240, when Alexander II, who was determined to impose royal authority on Argyll and died in the attempt, confirmed to Gillascop Mac Gilchrist much territory east of Loch Awe and about Loch Fyne for half a knight's service in the army and a full knight's service in aid.[107] Through an altogether unexpected line of inheritance, the king's original charter has been preserved among the Scrymgeour muniments.[108] We have no grounds for believing that as a feudal charter for Argyll in the mid-thirteenth century it was unique, or that between 1240 and 1262 no further feudalization took place in the west. Documentary evidence becomes adequate only in the reign of Robert I, but by then the barons of Argyll and the Isles appear to have taken for granted a military feudal relationship between themselves and the Crown, the

[105] NLS MS Adv. 29.4.2 (Hutton's Collections), II. 27. 'Glasrog' (probably Glassary) in Lorn was already a barony in 1297 (Stevenson, *Documents*, ii. 191).

[106] The 'barons of Argyll' appear in 1296 and 1308-9 (*Rot. Scot.* i. 32a; Barrow, *Bruce*, 254, 256), and note that Gilchrist MacNaughton of Argyll figures as a baron of the realm *c*. 1246 (*Inchaffray Chrs.*, no. 73). John earl of Atholl granted Alexander de Meyners Weem and Aberfeldy Beg 'as any *vavassurus* holds of any earl or baron in *vavassaria* in the realm of Scotland'; *Highland Papers*, iv. 192-3 and *SHS Misc.* iv. 324-5, no. 18 (=NSL Chr. 678). The word *vavassor* is used in charters of the knights Malcolm Murray and his lord Alexander Murray of Culbin, 1274 (relating to land in west Fife); *Dunfermline Reg.*, nos. 207, 209.

[107] *Highland Papers*, ii, 121-3.

[108] Ibid.

only peculiarity being that the service stipulated was more often a galley of so many oars than a mounted soldier.[109] By making infeftments for naval service (which, by the way, could still be described as 'in the army'),[110] Robert I was merely fitting an older obligation into the feudal framework. His predecessor Alexander III showed himself similarly adaptable when between 1262 and 1266 he put the native Lorne magnate Gilchrist Mac Naughton in charge of the king's castle and island of Fraoch Eilean at the north end of Loch Awe, recording the appointment by letters-patent.[111] This was not a permanent infeftment, nor was it the feudal obligation of castle-ward; but Gilchrist Mac Naughton regarded himself as a baron of the realm of Scotland, and after his death his widow Ethena possessed her terce, or third part, of his estates in Argyll 'by right and by the law of the land' (*de jure et [per] assisam terre*),[112] just as the widow of a feudal tenant-in-chief ought to have done. And it is probable that Sir Colin Campbell of Loch Awe, Mac Naughton's neighbour and fellow-baron, held much the same position, for he is described in 1291 as the king's bailie in the lands of Ardskeodnish.[113]

It is precisely at the point where we see the Crown and the great lords adapting the cut-and-dried, ready-to-wear feudalism imported in the twelfth century to the realities of thirteenth-century Scotland that we are able to see the Anglo-Norman Era in Scottish history reaching one of the limits of its penetration and influence. It nearly carried all before it, but not quite. A handful of documents from the thirteenth century—far more from the fourteenth—belong to a border zone where the newly-

[109] Barrow, *Bruce*, 405–7.
[110] e.g. in charters of Robert I (1323, *Hist. MSS Comm.*, *Mar and Kellie, Supplementary* (1930), 3; undated *RMS* i, App. I, no. 9) and also in a charter of Christian daughter of Alan Macruarie for Arthur son of Sir Arthur Campbell, knight, granting the lands of Moidart, Arisaig, Eigg, and Rum, to be held for the service of one twenty-oared ship 'in the common army of the lord king of Scotland' (*c.* 1320? Original *penes* the Royal Faculty of Procurators, Glasgow. I owe this reference to Professor A. A. M. Duncan). See also *OPS* ii, Pt. I, 103.
[111] SRO Reg. Ho. charters, no. 55 (printed *Highland Papers*, i. 107).
[112] Fraser, *Douglas*, iii. 6–7, no. 7 (1259). Cristinus is here a latinized form of Gillecrist. Fraser has misread the name of his father which is written Nauchtan. It is not clear whether Ethena, the name of Gillecrist's wife, is a latinized form of Bethoc, referred to as his wife *c.* 1246–7 (*Inchaffray Chrs.*, nos. 73, 74), or the name of an otherwise unrecorded second wife.
[113] *Rot. Scot.* i. 32a.

imported feudalism meets that older regime for which historians have no convenient name. Even as early as the 1170s William the Lion could confirm the lands of Cambo between St. Andrews and Crail to his mother's vassal Robert of Newham in feu and heritage 'for the service of one foot man in the king's army'.[114] In the opening decades of the thirteenth century, Alan lord of Galloway and constable of Scotland granted the estate of Fairlie in the parish of Largs to Alan de Ros, in feu and heritage, for habergeon service, paying the aids appropriate to one ploughgate of land and finding in what the donor called 'the expedition of our army' one young man with a habergeon.[115] About 1212, the last 'native' earl of Buchan, Fergus, issued a lengthy charter in strict feudal form for John son of Uhtred, exchanging for Slains and Cruden the lands of Fedderate in New Deer parish 'as any earl or lord in the Scottish realm may infeft any vassal'.[116] A large relief of £20 sterling was to be paid and thenceforward John was to perform the free service of one bowman and suit of court three times a year at the earl's headcourts held at Ellon. Almost exactly a century later the earl of Atholl granted to Sir Robert Menzies knight, 'his beloved and faithful confederate' (euphemisms for vassal are becoming ever more pretentious) the thanage of Crannach in Glen Lyon for the service of one bowman in the lord king's army and suit of court at the thrice yearly headcourts of the earldom of Atholl held at Logierait.[117] An inquest of 1304 shows that while the direct descendant of the thanes of Callendar by Falkirk held the old thanage as a knight's feu of the Crown he also held Kilsyth of the earl of Fife for the service of ten bowmen.[118] At some date in the last twenty years of the thirteenth century, John Lamont chief of the Lamonts, but himself the dependant of the hereditary Stewart of Scotland, granted to Sir Colin Campbell of Loch Awe two pennylands in Cowal in feu and heritage for suit of court at the donor's three headcourts, held perhaps at Ardlamont, and for providing at the musters of Argyll (*congregationibus Ergadie*), whenever

[114] *RRS* ii, no. 131.
[115] NLS MS 42676.
[116] *Aberdeen–Banff Collections*, 407–9.
[117] J. A. Robertson, *Comitatus de Atholia. The Earldom of Atholl: its boundaries stated, etc.* (printed for private circulation, 1860), 9–10.
[118] *CDS* ii, no. 1457.

Early Scottish Feudalism

required, two men with their victuals as long as the necessity lasts, 'as is the custom in that country' (*prout consuetum est in patria*).[119] Long before this, in the 1220s, the earl of Lennox, a province neighbouring Cowal and Argyll, granted land feudally to a number of free vassals on condition of rendering in the lord king's army two cheeses from every house in which cheese is made.[120] Footsoldiers and bowmen, and the cheeses which sustained them as they marched away to war, belonged to an order of society which existed in Scotland before the advent of feudalism and would still survive after its military impact had slackened and given way to lawyers and tax-collectors.[121]

In this chapter, I have argued for the *normality* of feudalism in thirteenth-century Scotland. The student of English or French feudalism, richly supplied with an abundance of Exchequer record, books of fees, inquisitions *post mortem*, *curia regis* rolls, the *Olim*, and a wealth of royal and private charters, may be altogether disconcerted to learn that so little documentation survives to help us to chart the course of royal government in Scotland before 1314. Most of what does survive consists of royal charters and brieves which have been haphazardly preserved in ecclesiastical cartularies and baronial charter chests. As for documents produced by the lieges, while we must be thankful that so much is extant we have to admit that its grand total is meagre compared with the material which survives for the study of feudalism in England or on the continent. Nevertheless, dismay and disappointment ought not to give way to despair. We should not be persuaded too readily

---

[119] *Lamont Papers*, 7–8, no. 10. It is not certain whether *patria* refers to Argyll (as supposed here) or to the Scottish kingdom as a whole.

[120] Barrow, *Kingdom*, 309.

[121] We may note here the grant (c. 1208) by David lord of Lyne, Peeblesshire to Simon son of Robert of the land of Scroggs (*Glasgow Reg.*, no. 85). Simon's rent was 12d. at Martinmas; he had to go on his own horse with his lord to perform the king's forinsec service, the lord furnishing all necessaries for man and mount as long as the service lasted, and even a remount if Simon's horse was lost on active service. Similarly, c. 1242–9, Henry Graham of Dalkeith granted Clifton in Midlothian to David Graham for the service of one bowman and as much *auxilium* in the king's army as pertained to two ploughgates in Lothian (*Hist. MSS Comm., 2nd Rep.*, App., 166); and in the later thirteenth century William Fraser lord of Drumelzier, Peeblesshire, granted a house to Bernard the shoemaker, on condition of paying such proportion of common aid in the king's army as the lord's husbandmen usually paid.

that Scotland was not a truly feudal kingdom, or only imperfectly feudalized. English historians, especially, are accustomed to a highly bureaucratic feudalism, and are apt to fall into the error of supposing that where there was no bureaucracy there can have been no feudalism. If our record, meagre though it be, nevertheless conveys a consistent impression for most of the country and for both royal and private transactions, that fact ought surely to carry more weight than the absence of some class of systematic feudal record.

In any event, it is not quite true to say that there was no bureaucracy in Scotland; there was merely a smaller bureaucracy. The Crown archives, now perished, included rolls of knights' feus and the original charters of feus which for one reason or another had been surrendered and had consequently escheated.[122] The Scots Crown, like the English, was jealous of its rights of wardship and marriage over tenants-in-chief and exacted reliefs from heirs to baronies. In 1196 Roland of Galloway, as husband of Helen de Morville, paid 700 merks as relief for the office of Constable and the wide lands held by Helen's brother William de Morville who had died without children.[123] When Henry Lovel of Castle Cary died in 1263, his son Richard Lovel paid 100 merks for the barony of Hawick.[124] In contrast with the long reign of Alexander III, the few years administration by the Guardians who ruled Scotland on behalf of the Maid of Norway from 1286 to 1291 happens to be represented by comparatively abundant surviving record.[125] One letter addressed by the Guardians to Edmund earl of Cornwall while he was Guardian of England during Edward I's absence in Gascony illustrates clearly enough how anxious the Scots Guardians were to protect the feudal rights of the Scottish crown and to preserve normal custom in the case of men and women who were feudatories in both kingdoms.

[122] *APS* i. 110, 118.
[123] *Chron. Fordun*, i. 278.
[124] *Exch. Rolls*, i. 28–9. The barony of Keith, East Lothian, was assessed in February 1312 as having a peace-time annual value of 100 merks (*CDS* iii, no. 245). Note also that in 1270 the earldom of Fife, during the minority of the heir, was assigned to support Alexander, prince of Scotland (*Chron. Bower*, ii. 113).
[125] G. G. Simpson, *Handlist of the Acts of Alexander III etc.*, 44–55; Stevenson, *Documents*, i. 1–374 *passim*; *CDS* ii, nos. 291–648 *passim*.

Whereas we firmly believe that the magnificent prince the lord Edward king of the English and you both wish that the usages and customs which have been in force between the kings and kingdoms of England and Scotland over a very long period should be maintained unbroken; and whereas it has been the custom between the two realms that whenever a woman holding land and tenements in both kingdoms is due to be married she will be allowed to marry with the permission of the ruler and king of that realm in which she is dwelling and may be found at the time she is due to be married; nevertheless, Sir Thomas de Normanville, knight, escheator of the king of England, has harassed Sir Andrew Murray and his wife Euphemia in their lands and chattels contrary to this usage and custom; we beg your excellency to allow Andrew and his wife to enjoy their possessions in peace, for which kindness we shall be especially grateful.[126]

After Edward I had taken over the government of Scotland in 1291 the English chancery began to keep *Rotuli Scotiae* for Scottish affairs.[127] Since these have been preserved, unlike the Scottish royal records, we find on them the information which is lacking for the reigns of Alexander II and his son. Thus we learn that in 1292 William Maule owed £122 10s relief for the knight-service barony of Panmure.[128] Simon Fraser made a bargain for the relief of his father's lands by paying 100 merks.[129] William of Hessewell owed 24 merks for relief but was pardoned because King Edward learned that he had performed praiseworthy service to Alexander III for many years.[130] Earl Patrick of Dunbar either owed a very heavy relief or else was shown extraordinary favour, for in 1293 he was excused payment of arrears of relief amounting to £200.[131] The Scotch Rolls are not the record of an English government suddenly imposed upon Scotland, but of an outside administration which had taken control of the apparatus of Scottish royal government. They afford glimpses of feudal lordship being exercised on behalf of the Scottish Crown. Thus, the bishop of Glasgow

---

[126] Stevenson, *Documents*, i. 26–7, no. 15; *CDS* ii, nos. 307, 376. The harassment was due to the English government's view that Euphemia widow of William Comyn should, as an English (as well as a Scots) tenant in chief, have sought the king's leave before marrying Sir Andrew Murray.
[127] The *Rotuli Scotiae* commence on 13 June 1291, immediately after Edward I had gained possession of the royal castles of Scotland, having persuaded the Guardians to indemnify the keepers of the castles in case they had surrendered them improperly; *Rot. Scot.* i. 1a.
[128] Ibid., 9b.
[129] Ibid.
[130] Ibid., 16a.
[131] Ibid., 18b.

is in trouble for beginning to build a castle of stone and lime at Carstairs without the king's licence;[132] John Wishart's status is in question because he had married Jean daughter of Nicholas of Plenderleith and, though some said that his father-in-law had held Plenderleith of the earl of Angus in socage, the earl himself claimed that it was held by knight-service and therefore subject to wardship;[133] Henry laird of Wiston has died, thus enabling the king of England to grant the wardship of his heirs and land to Walter Logan of Hartside;[134] King John Balliol has received an oath—improperly, or so King Edward alleged—from Isabel of Menteith widow of William Comyn of Kirkintilloch that she will not remarry without the king's consent;[135] Sir John of Callendar is given leave to arrange the marriage of David, son and heir of Sir William of Brechin, a tenant-in-chief;[136] Juliana MacDougall, married to Alexander MacDonald of Islay, has a lawsuit pending anent the third part of the isle of Lismore;[137] and King Edward himself has, as *superior dominus*, graciously confirmed John Balliol's infeftment of the Northumberland knight Sir John de Lisle in the Berwickshire estate of Whitsome, 'for the service of half the feu of one knight'.[138] Incidentally, King John's charter of Whitsome, with a fine seal—alas! carefully detached—is the Bodleian Library's only original Scottish royal charter dating from before the War of Independence.[139] In the foregoing survey of the evidence, unavoidably compressed though it has been, at least a prima-facie case should have been established for believing that Scotland became a feudal kingdom in the two centuries of the 'Anglo-Norman Era'.

---

[132] Ibid., 10a.
[133] Ibid., 10b.
[134] Ibid., 15b. Henry of Wiston is said to have held in chief 'of the royal dignity', an expression apparently used of the crown during an interregnum. See Simpson, *Handlist*, no. 347.
[135] *Rot. Scot.* i. 16a.
[136] Ibid., 21a-b.
[137] Ibid.
[138] Ibid., 22a-b.
[139] Bodleian Library, Charters, Northumberland, no. 4.

VI

The Other Side of the Coin

ADDRESSING the fathers of the Church assembled at the Council of Constance in March 1417, Thomas Polton (later to become in rapid succession bishop of Hereford, Chichester and Worcester[1]) inveighed against the spokesman of the 'Latin bloc' who had proposed that the Council should no longer recognize the English Nation as a constituent body within its membership.

> When [the French] [he said] go on to propose that the suffragan bishops of Scotland are not and have no wish to be in the English Nation . . . the answer is that they are undoubtedly and ought to be part of the English Nation, since they have no way of denying that Scotland is part of Britain, though not so large a part. The whole world knows that. Also they have the same language as the English. It is really remarkable that such educated men as [the French] would want to write that Wales, Ireland and even Scotland are not part of the English Nation simply because they do not do what the king of England tells them to do.[2]

Thomas Polton was neither the first nor by any means the last Englishman to identify Britain with England and to suppose that everyone whose mother tongue was English ought to acknowledge some kind of hegemony vested in the English Crown. Polton's ideas found their most powerful expression in the Brutus legend which had been developed as a weapon of propaganda on behalf of King Edward I and was still very much alive in Lancastrian and for that matter Tudor England.[3] In order to combat the Brutus legend the Scots propagandists of the later thirteenth century rediscovered the legend of

---

[1] *Handbook of British Chronology* (2nd edn., 1961), 217, 230, 261.
[2] Cited by C. R. Crowder, *Unity, Heresy and Reform, 1378–1460* (1977), 117 (see also pp. 108, 110), from the translation of L. R. Loomis, *The Council of Constance: the Unification of the Church* (ed. J. H. Mundy and K. M. Woody, New York, 1961), between pp. 335 and 339.
[3] T. D. Kendrick, *British Antiquity* (1950).

Pharaoh's daughter Scota, conveniently encapsulated in an easily-memorized jingle:

> A muliere Scota
> Vocitatur Scotia tota

'all Scotland takes its name from the woman Scota'.[4] Polton put his finger on the weakest part of the Scottish argument when he pointed out that the Scots spoke the same language as the English. It was no doubt primarily in this sense that Henry the Scot, long settled at Cork in 1297, described himself as *anglicus*.[5] In the third quarter of the fourteenth century John of Fordoun (a parish on the border between Lowlands and Highlands) wrote a description of his fellow-countrymen which tackles the linguistic and cultural question in a passage of the utmost importance.

> The customs and habits of the Scots [he wrote][6] differ according to the difference of language; for two languages are in use, the Scottish [what we should call Scottish Gaelic] and the Germanic[7] [that is, Middle English]. English is the speech of those living by the sea coast and in the Lowlands, while the people of Gaelic speech dwell in the Highlands and Outer Isles. The lowlanders are home-loving, civilised, trustworthy, tolerant and polite, decently clad, affable and pacific, pious in their worship of God, though always ready to resist an injury. The islanders and highlanders are a wild, untamed people, primitive and proud, given to plunder and the easy life, clever and quick to learn, handsome in appearance though slovenly of dress, consistently hostile and cruel towards the people and the speech of the English, even towards people of their own nation if their speech is different. Yet are they loyal to king and kingdom, and provided they be well governed they are obedient and ready enough to respect the laws.

Fordoun, in short, observed two cultures within a single nation.[8] Although he knew perfectly well that the 'Scottishness' of Scotland was not derived historically from the Anglian element, there was no doubt in his mind that the dominant

---

[4] *Chronicles of the Picts: Chronicles of the Scots*, ed. W. F. Skene (Rolls. Ser., Edinburgh, 1867), 242 (see also pp. 3, 109, 146). Pharaoh's daughter Scota appears in the *Historia Britonum* attributed to Nennius (*Lebor Bretnach*, ed. A. G. Van Hamel (Dublin, 1932), 25). The legend's full development may be seen in *Chron. Fordun*, i. 9–13 (third quarter of the fourteenth century); see also M. O. Anderson, *Kings and Kingship in Early Scotland* (1973), 243.

[5] *Calendar of the Justiciary Rolls of Ireland*, ed. J. Mills, i. 158.

[6] *Chron. Fordun*, i. 42.

[7] *Theuthonica*.

[8] On this in general, see R. Nicholson, *Scotland: The Later Middle Ages* (1974), 23–6, 274–80.

culture of the Scotland he knew was that of the English-speaking lowlands. As John Major put it a century and a half later, in his *History of Greater Britain*, when he practically reproduced Fordoun's earlier description, 'the political preponderance of the whole realm rests with the civilised (lowland) Scots, for they are better than the others, or at least less bad, at forming a polity'.[9] Fordoun's contemporary, Barbour, chose quite deliberately to write a popular history of Robert the Bruce and to write it, therefore, in English—a confident, vivid, racy, and still highly readable English which needs less translation than Chaucer to render it intelligible to the modern reader and which is eloquent proof of a prolonged and widespread growth of English speech among the inhabitants of Scotland.[10] A linguistic ambiguity was built into the fabric of the medieval Scottish nation. George Broun, who was bishop of Dunkeld at the turn of the fifteenth and sixteenth centuries, appointed Thomas Greig dean of Christianity in Atholl and Drumalban because of his knowledge of the Gaelic language, arranged for Franciscans and Dominicans well versed in Gaelic to preach at least once a year in the highland parts of his huge diocese, and even carved a new parish of Dowally out of Caputh so that Gaelic-speaking parishioners would be better provided for.[11] If the English delegation at Constance could argue that Scotland ought to be within the English sphere of influence because the Scots spoke English, Robert I could try to win allies among the native kings of Ireland by flattering them that their country was *Scotia Major*, his own no more than *Scotia Minor*, and that Scots and Irish shared a common tongue.[12]

What Edward I, and many English historians of a much later time, have found difficult to accept is that the Scots of the thirteenth century could feel themselves sufficiently distinct from the English not merely to count as a 'nation'—so much

---

[9] J. Major, *Historia Majoris Britanniae* (Edinburgh, 1740), 33–4 (in the edition and translation of A. Constable, SHS 1892, 49).
[10] T. F. Henderson, *Scottish Vernacular Literature* (3rd edn., Edinburgh, 1910), especially chapters I and III; F. Brie, *Die nationale Literatur Schottlands* (Halle, 1937), especially pp. 28–32; Barbour, *Bruce*, Appendices G and H.
[11] *Dunkeld Rentale*, 304, 312–13.
[12] R. Nicholson, 'A sequel to Edward Bruce's invasion of Ireland', *SHR* xlii (1963), 38–9; *Chron. Bower*, ii. 267 (Bk. XII, chap. xxxii).

might have been allowed them—but to wish to be politically independent of the kingdom of England. The last two generations of medieval scholars—and that, after all, means our greatest medievalists, with but one or two exceptions—have been so anxious to correct the false romantic nationalism of the nineteenth century that the very idea of nationalism in the middle ages has become one of our most rigidly-observed taboos. But surely we must take things as we find them. No doubt personal and feudal loyalty counted for much, no doubt men responded more fervently to the call of religious faith or to the sanctions of some lawful institution (especially if it were ancient) than to their country as such. Nevertheless, country had begun to make its appearance, and whenever it coincided with an ancient institution and was reinforced by a common language and culture, the resulting mixture became practically irresistible. National feeling ought not to strike us as an anachronism when a chronicler can write of 'general war between England and Scotland' (1296),[13] when burgesses of English nationality settled in Roxburgh can demand that burgesses of Scots nationality shall not be allowed to dwell with them (1305),[14] or when a Huntingdonshire jury can call Robert Bruce 'a traitor to England' (1319).[15] In 1299 the king of France praised the Scots for their loyalty to king and kingdom but also for defending their native land (*natalis patria*);[16] and in 1320 the Scots barons tried to gain Pope John's sympathy with their picture of 'this poor little Scotland, beyond which there is no dwelling place at all'.[17] The letter to the pope associated patriotism with traditional loyalty to king and kingdom in a masterly manner, but the document does not stand in isolation. Ten years earlier, three Scots knights, Sir Alexander Seton of Seton, Sir Thomas Hay of Lochwharret, and Sir Neil Campbell of Lochawe, had sworn a solemn oath to defend their king, Robert, and the liberty of his kingdom to the last of their breath.[18] Seton and Hay were descended from families settled in the twelfth century, one certainly, the other probably of

[13] BL MS Cott. Cleopatra D iii, fo. 49.
[14] F. W. Maitland, *Memoranda de Parliamento, 1305*, 192–3 (no. 319).
[15] *Cal. Inqu. p.m.* vi. 100 (*proditor Angl'*).
[16] *CDS* ii. 536.
[17] J. Fergusson, *The Declaration of Arbroath* (1970), 9.
[18] A. A. M. Duncan, *SHR* xlv (1966), 199; Barrow, *Bruce*, 332, Additional Note.

continental origin,[19] while Campbell represented an ancient native family of mixed Brittonic and Gaelic origin which may have moved from the Lennox into Argyll not long before it first emerges in record about 1260.[20] What united the three was not any particular ancestry so much as the fact that they were Scots lairds and lieges of King Robert I. But King Edward himself was surely just as aware of nationality as these knights, for how otherwise could he have issued a proclamation, perhaps in the aftermath of Falkirk, that all Englishmen must depart from Scotland?[21]

Much has been made of the lack of patriotism among the Scots nobility during the first War of Independence.[22] This has been attributed to their fear of losing English estates, and it has even been suggested that the war was essentially an affair of the common people under Wallace, who first of all discovered and then exploited democratic nationalism.[23] There is perhaps something typically English in the assumption that Scottish nobles would always put their English estates before those in Scotland. There seems to be the further implication that while an English patriotism at this date was only to be expected, a Scottish patriotism was out of the question—and, in fact, proved not to exist by the readiness with which Scotland was, as Trevelyan put it, 'deserted by her nobles'.[24]

Why do we hear almost nothing of the Englishmen who, driven by whatever motive, threw in their lot with the Scots and defied the wrath of Edward I and Edward II? I am not thinking of such prominent English landowners as John Balliol or (after 1304) Robert Bruce, for they were in a special position. Nor do I have in mind those unfortunate folk on the Borders, the men of Gilsland, Tynedale, or Redesdale, who

---

[19] See A. Wagner, 'The origin of the Hays of Erroll', *Genealogists' Magazine* (1954–5). The origin of the family which adopted the surname Seton, apparently from Seton in East Lothian, is unknown, but the personal names used by its earliest members, Philip and Alexander, indicate continental or Anglo-Continental origin.

[20] W. D. H. Sellar, 'The earliest Campbells—Norman, Briton or Gael?', *Scottish Studies*, xvii (1973), 109–25.

[21] Above, p. 117, n. 159.

[22] e.g. Stevenson, *Documents*, i, pp. lii–liii; J. R. Green, *History of the English People*, i (1878), 344–5, 365–6; F. M. Powicke, *The Thirteenth Century* (1953), 686, 696.

[23] G. M. Trevelyan, *History of England* (3rd edn., 1945), 218–19.

[24] Ibid. 218.

when Bruce had gained the upper hand and the English king could no longer defend them were forced to change their allegiance merely to survive.[25] I refer rather to those English men and women of substance and position whose roots or at least possessions were in many cases well south of the Border and the threat of Scottish raids. At the very beginning of the war, Robert de Ros of Wark on Tweed was minded to hand his castle over to the Scots because he was in love with a Scotswoman.[26] Sir Henry Latham, a Lancashire knight of Old English descent whom Edward I had made sheriff of Aberdeen after Balliol's defeat, joined the Scots when they revolted in the spring of 1297.[27] By the following February he had forfeited his English lands.[28] Stephen Pessun, a Lincolnshire freeholder, was in France with Sir Thomas Randolph in 1296 and though he did homage for his Scottish lands he was reported two years later to be in the retinue of Bishop Lamberton of St. Andrews, Wallace's friend and supporter.[29] Alice Muncaster, heir of a Cumberland tenant in chief, could not receive the homage of her tenant Robert del Crokedayk in 1304 because she stayed in Scotland with the king's enemies.[30] Maud of Carrick, co-parcener of the barony of Levington in Cumberland and a Scot only by marriage, gave her allegiance to the Scottish Guardians until the earl of Carrick, Robert Bruce, submitted to King Edward early in 1302, when she got her English lands back.[31] The Yorkshire knight Sir Christopher Seton had an outstanding record as an adherent of Bruce until he was captured in Loch Doon Castle in 1306 and drawn and hanged at Dumfries.[32] Thomas Clennell, captured when Stirling Castle fell in 1304, and Sir William of Burradon who accompanied Bruce when he took to the heather in 1306, were both Northumbrians, from the 'ten touns of Coquetdale'.[33]

In 1296 the English sheriffs were commanded to arrest the persons and seize the lands and property of all those known to

[25] Barrow, *Bruce*, 336.
[26] *Chron. Guisborough*, 271–2.
[27] *Rot. Scot.* i. 42a.
[28] Stevenson, *Documents*, ii. 217; *CDS* ii, no. 972; *Cal. Fine Rolls*, i. 396.
[29] *CDS* ii, nos. 735, 1601, 1838; Stevenson, *Documents*, ii. 94–5.
[30] *Cal. Fine Rolls*, i. 488.
[31] *CDS* ii, nos. 1302, 1303.
[32] Barrow, *Bruce*, 395 (and elsewhere).
[33] *SHR* lv (1976), 161–2, 164–5.

be within their counties who owed allegiance to King John Balliol.³⁴ The sheriff of Yorkshire seems to have set about the task with exceptional energy and thoroughness. The men and women whose land he seized or about whom he obtained information were a mixed bunch, ranging from the king of Scots himself and Sir Geoffrey de Moubray the Justiciar of Lothian to Peter the Miller of East Ardsley. A number of them, perhaps the majority, posed no kind of threat to the English government and were doubtless able to make their peace. But a few persisted in being Scots rather than English, and it is by no means easy to guess what motives led some to take one decision and some another. Simon de Cresseville, for example, held property at Attercliffe near Sheffield. He was in the garrison which continued to defend Jedburgh Castle against King Edward in the autumn of 1298 long after Wallace's shattering defeat at Falkirk.³⁵ The family of Geoffrey de Fressheley ('of Farsley') had perhaps become so thoroughly Scottish since the 1240s that his adherence to the Guardians and forfeiture by the English king are hardly surprising.³⁶ More puzzling is the case of Walter son of Thomas of Barkston, who held a quarter-knight's fee of the archbishop of York.³⁷ Owing to his disappearance, his lands were seized by the sheriff and an inquest was held in December 1297. The jury told the escheator that Walter had been at the battle of Dunbar (27 April 1296) 'along with the Scots, supporting them and under arms as an enemy of king and kingdom'. Asked if Walter was now alive or dead the jury answered that they did not know. Then, apparently conscious that their reply was bald and unconvincing, the jurymen ventured upon corroborative detail which at least makes up in interest for what it may at the time have lacked in artistic verisimilitude. 'We know well that he was in the battle of Dunbar, and afterwards he adhered to the Scots and he never again returned to the fealty of the king of England. If he is still alive, he is in league with the Scots, and is entirely at one with them in their wickedness, and he strives

---

³⁴ *CDS* ii, no. 736.
³⁵ Ibid., p. 172; Stevenson, *Documents*, ii. 413–14.
³⁶ Above, p. 114.
³⁷ *Yorkshire Inquisitions*, iii (1902), 107–8; *CDS* ii, no. 1603 (see also nos. 1481, 1594).

and labours to the best of his ability towards an invasion of England, which may God forbid.'

Walter of Barkston had been an enemy of the king and kingdom of England but he had evidently fought for the king and kingdom of Scotland. Men and women whose ancestors would have fought hard and sacrificed much for their lord in the twelfth century were now ready, at the turn of the thirteenth and fourteenth centuries, to fight and suffer for a kingdom. Sir William Olifard (Oliphant) of Gask who defended Stirling Castle bravely against King Edward in 1304 refused to join the general Scottish submission of that year because he held his commission 'of the Lion', that is, of the Scottish crown.[38] It was for the freedom of the Scottish kingdom, as well as for King Robert, that Seton, Hay and Campbell vowed to fight to their last breath, and this did but echo the theme expressed by the magnates assembled for the St. Andrews parliament of March 1309, when they thanked Philip the Fair for helping to rebuild (*reformare*) the liberties and laws of the kingdom of Scotland.[39]

Those who have studied the history of England between the Norman Conquest and the reign of Edward I are not likely to ignore the growth during this period of the concept of the 'kingdom of England', *regnum Anglorum, regnum Anglie*, or to underestimate its power in securing the acceptance of a common political nationality. Perhaps we are in danger of taking this for granted, of assuming its development to have been inevitable. Yet it is surely remarkable when we bear in mind that England had been very thoroughly conquered by the Normans in the eleventh century and brought within a predominantly continental power complex during the sixty years from 1144 to 1204.[40] At the beginning of the twelfth century, *regnum*—kingdom or kingship—appears strongly subjective, closely akin to priesthood or episcopate, a special quality, as it were, which though having reference to some community of human beings was nevertheless profoundly personal. By the end of the thirteenth century *regnum* had undergone a shift of emphasis and become itself the community or even the

[38] *Scalacronica*, 127.
[39] *APS* i. 459.
[40] On this in general, see J. Le Patourel, *The Norman Empire* (Oxford, 1976).

territory over which the king reigned.⁴¹ In England, the very foreignness of royal dynasties and the ruling class may have accelerated the process, for the concept of *regnum Anglie* was all there was to bind monarchy, nobility and people together.

I suggest that Scotland underwent an analogous process during the two hundred years, 1097 to 1296, which in the first chapter I fixed upon as the 'Anglo-Norman Era'. Analogous, not identical; for the country was smaller and poorer than England, had fewer external connections, and retained its native dynasty and much of its native ruling class, albeit greatly affected and modified by foreign intermarriage, intrusion, and influence.

We do not find the expression 'kingdom of the Scots' or 'kingdom of Scotland' in a clearly territorial sense, referring to more than merely the original Scotia north of Forth and Clyde, before the reign of Malcolm IV (1153–65).⁴² His predecessor, David I, had indeed referred to 'my kingdom' in the concrete or objective sense towards the end of his reign,⁴³ but more characteristic of his time was the address of one of his earlier charters 'to all Scots and English resident throughout his realm in Scotia and Lothian'.⁴⁴ It was left to Robert bishop of St. Andrews, who died in 1159, to speak of the 'kingdom of the king of Scots' in a formal document⁴⁵ and to an unknown clerk of King Malcolm, writing about 1161, to use, as far as we know for the first time, the expression 'kingdom of Scotland' (*regnum Scotie*) in an unambiguously territorial context.⁴⁶

⁴¹ *Regnum* could already be used in the sense of community as early as 1215, as when in the Articles of the Barons, c. 48, King John was said to have granted liberties 'to be held to the kingdom' (*regno tenendas*). This wording was altered in the formal text of Magna Carta a few days later, presumably because the clerks found either the concept too novel or the phrasing too awkward (J. C. Holt, *Magna Carta* (1965), 311, 332).

⁴² The well-known charter of King Edgar for Durham (A. A. M. Duncan, 'The earliest Scottish charters', *SHR* xxxvii. 103–5) had the words *totam terram de Lodeneio et regnum Scotie*, where *regnum*, if it balances *terram*, ought to have a territorial sense (although in any case referring to Scotland north of Forth). But despite Professor Duncan's persuasive arguments (art. cit. 105–18) for the authenticity of this charter, I am not convinced that its text has not been tampered with. The presence of these words in particular may be one indication that the text is not wholly genuine.

⁴³ Lawrie, *Charters*, no. 266.
⁴⁴ Ibid., no. 65.
⁴⁵ Ibid., no. 268 (=*St. Andrews Liber*, 124).
⁴⁶ *RRS* i, no. 183.

In the last decade of the twelfth century the use of this convenient phrase grew rapidly. Robert de Quinci granted a feu in Lothian *c*. 1170, to be held 'as freely as any knight holds of a baron in the kingdom of the king of Scotland';[47] Walter del Bois, *c*. 1180, granted land in Annandale to Saint Cuthbert of Durham (whose shrine he visited with his wife and son) 'as freely as any alms may most freely be given to any saint by any of my peers within the *regio* of Scotland'[48]—the context making it clear that *regio* has the sense of 'kingdom' most familiar in the tag *cujus regio ejus religio*. Dundas west of Edinburgh was granted, *c*. 1190, 'as freely as any knight holds of any baron in the whole land of the king of Scotland'.[49] Between 1204 and 1228 Malcolm earl of Fife gave the church of North Berwick to the Cistercian nunnery there 'as any abbey may hold any alms in the land of the king of Scots of any earl or baron'.[50] These instances relate to property south of the Forth–Clyde line, outwith *Scotia* or Scotland proper. But by the early thirteenth century an earl of Lennox could settle a tocher or dowry on his sister to be held 'as freely as any tocher is most freely held of any earl or baron of the whole realm of Scotland'.[51]

From the last years of the twelfth century the phrase becomes such a commonplace that it is impossible to glance through any corpus of Scottish private charters without encountering it again and again, usually in the form 'within the kingdom of Scots' (or 'of Scotland').[52] I am not suggesting that more than

[47] SRO GD 241/254.
[48] Raine, *North Durham*, no. 166 (cp. *Coldstream Chartulary*, no. 24).
[49] *APS* i. 92.
[50] *North Berwick Carte*, no. 7.
[51] Fraser, *Lennox*, ii. 402 (no. 203).
[52] Four collections may be cited, almost at random, in illustration of this statement: *Coldstream Chartulary*, nos. 1, 2, 7, 9, 10, 13 ('as any widow in her viduity within the realm of Scotland may grant . . .'), 15–20, 24, 26, 30; *Kelso Liber*, nos. 74, 76, 88, 100, 118, 121–3, 129, 130, etc.; *Inchcolm Chrs.*, nos. 3, 7, 12, 13, 24, 28; *Paisley Reg.*, pp. 7, 15, 18, 19, 21, 22 (*bis*), 24, 71, 74, 122, etc. The geographical spread may also be illustrated by SRO Crown Office Writs, no. 4 ('as the canons of Jedburgh hold any alms in the realm of Scotland', relating to Sorbie in Castleton, Roxburghshire, late twelfth cent.), NLS MS Acc. 7079 ('as any abbey of the Cistercian order within the realm of Scotland most freely holds alms', relating to Fechil in Ellon, Aberdeenshire, early thirteenth cent.), *Munro Writs*, no. 1 ('as freely as any barony is held in the realm of Scotland north of the Mounth', relating to the Black Isle, Ross-shire, late thirteenth cent.), *Moray Reg.*, 465 ('as any tocher is most freely held in the whole realm of Scotland', relating to Blackford,

a tiny handful of individuals actually wrote the charters in which these phrases occur, nor that many more than a handful would even read them or hear them read aloud. What I would argue is that the use of this terminology is explicable only if the notion of the kingdom of Scotland had become firmly planted in men's minds. The expression was, in a sense, the prosaic lawyer's counterpart to that poetic personification of Scotland which we can already see in the 1190s, when an anonymous versifier, eulogizing the king's chancellor Hugh of Roxburgh, tells us that 'Scotland rejoices in his many virtues'.[53] A century later it can be seen more strikingly in the delightful wedding hymn composed for the marriage of Margaret of Scotland with King Eric of Norway in 1281:

> Ex te lux oritur
> O dulcis Scotia,
> Qua vere noscitur
> Fulgens Norwagia

'a light has arisen from thee, Sweet Scotia, in which we know that Norway will shine'.[54] Of course, terms such as Lothian, Galloway, or Scotia had been used in the past and would continue to be used, purely geographically, as well as lesser institutional terms such as the 'fief of Haddington'[55] or the 'earldom of Dunbar'.[56] But there was less ambiguity about the kingdom of Scotland, the territory which the king ruled, in which his writs and laws were current, from which he levied his taxes and services. It was, moreover, a unifying concept, not only geographically, bringing together east and west, Lowlands and Highlands, the country besouth and the country benorth the 'Scottish Sea', as the Firth of Forth was called; but also culturally and racially, for the sense of *regnum Scotie* was identical for the native population and the Anglo-Continental incomers alike. However untamed the Highlanders might be

---

Perthshire, mid-thirteenth cent.), *Coldstream Chartulary*, no. 2 ('as any alms are most freely held anywhere in the realm of Scotland', relating to Lennel, Berwickshire, early thirteenth cent.), and *Paisley Reg.*, 133 (relating to Argyll, 1270).

[53] *Dialogi Laurentii Dunelmensis Monachi*, ed. J. Raine (Surtees Soc., 1880), 87–8 (from the MS cited in the following note).

[54] Uppsala University Library, MS C233, fo. 50^v. (I am grateful to Dr Kenneth Elliot, of the Department of Music, University of Glasgow, for this reference).

[55] Fraser, *Haddington*, ii. 225 (no. 281). For 'the whole of Lothian' as late as the mid-thirteenth century see Raine, *North Durham*, no. 139.

[56] *Coldstream Chartulary*, nos. 22, 23, 34.

in Fordoun's view, they were, he believed, responsive to the idea of king and kingdom. This opinion is strikingly exemplified by the solemn agreement of 1354 between John MacDonald of Islay, lord of the Isles, and John MacDougall lord of Lorne, that neither would rise in war against the other save in the company of the king of Scotland;[57] or in an episode of 1429, when King James I confronted the rebellious Alexander lord of the Isles in Lochaber and two clans melted away from MacDonald's host on seeing the king's standard unfurled.[58]

My main purpose in this book has been to describe and evaluate the Anglo-Continental contribution to the medieval *regnum Scotie*. In concentrating upon that contribution I have inevitably emphasized its importance. In this last chapter my object is to redress the balance somewhat. The Scottish kingdom was not an artificial creation in the sense in which the Norman kingdom of Sicily or the Frankish kingdom of Jerusalem were artificial. It might even be argued that it was not quite as artificial as the kingdom of Edward I after the Statute of Rhuddlan (1284), especially if we include under Edward's crown (as we surely must) the kingdom, or land, of Ireland[59] along with the kingdom of England. By the twelfth century the roots of the Scottish kingdom were already deep—the Pictish and Cumbrian almost prehistorically deep, the Scottish and Anglian reaching down some six or seven hundred years, and even the Scandinavian elements having a history of three centuries and more.

To this mixture the Anglo-Continental incursion brought feudalism and human settlement of much of the land, yet it fell far short of obliterating many fundamental features of Scottish society. It accelerated the anglicization of the Lowlands and surely heightened thereby the contrast between Lowlands and Highlands. But it would be difficult to argue that it had much direct impact at the level of the peasantry. To the free-

[57] *Highland Papers*, i. 76–8.
[58] R. Nicholson, *Scotland: the later Middle Ages*, 315–16.
[59] So described, possibly for the first time in an official document of the English chancery, in King John's surrender of England and Ireland to the papal see in 1213 (Stubbs, *Select Charters*, 280). As a rule the thirteenth-century English chancery used the expression *terra Hibernie*, although *regnum* is occasionally found (Matthew Paris, *Chronica Majora*, ed. H. R. Luard (Rolls Ser., 1872–83), iv. 381).

holders at large it brought feudal ways of thought and feudal law, with the security of tenure which feudalism implied. Yet that did not prevent freeholders, or knights either for that matter, attaching themselves to the great men, for whose followings or 'meinies' a sudden flush of synonyms is evident at the close of the thirteenth century—*familia, comitiva, retentio*.[60] This fact must be borne in mind when we weigh the significance of Walter of Guisborough's comment that in 1297 Wallace was not only followed by the common people of the land as their leader and ruler but was also joined by all the retainers of the great lords.[61] The retainers' normal attitude is illustrated by the words of John of Rait, owner of that delightful hall-house south of Nairn recently restored by the late Earl Cawdor. When John of Rait granted land to Arbroath Abbey in 1348 he looked back some sixty years or more: 'I make this gift for the souls of Alexander Comyn and John Comyn earls of Buchan, whom I used to serve in my youth, and of Hugh umquhile earl of Ross of good memory, my lord.'[62] Earl Alexander had died, a very old man, in 1290, and Earl Hugh was slain at the battle of Halidon in 1333.

As for the all-important lairds' class, that could be said to have been the creation of the Anglo-Norman Era and its most enduring monument. Even this did not mean the end of thanes and thanages, although a substantial thane might become a laird holding by knight-service,[63] while the lesser thanes became mere fermors of royal demesne.[64] It was at the highest levels of society and in certain aspects of royal government that preservation and continuity were most sharply contrasted with English experience. The earldoms survived intact. Five of them, admittedly, were by 1286 in the hands of families of

[60] *Rot. Scot.* i. 32a, 33a–b.
[61] *Chron. Guisborough*, 299.
[62] BL MS Add. 33245, fos. 152ᵛ–153ʳ. This was evidently the father of John son of John of Rait to whom Thomas son of John gave property in the Seagait of Inverbervie *c.* 1350 (*SHS Misc.* v. 16–18, no. 10).
[63] Sir John of Callendar, heir of the thanes of Callendar, held by knight service before 1304 (*CDS* ii, no. 1457); more typically, an incoming knight stepped into the shoes of a former thane as did Humphrey son of Theobald de Addeville at Conveth in the Mearns (*RRS* ii. no. 345).
[64] *Moray Reg.*, 27 (no. 34); *Rot. Scot.* i. 17a (Malcolm of Frendraught fermor of the thanages of Boyne and 'Mumbre'); BL, Add. Chr. no. 66979 (fermor of the thanage of Tannadyce).

continental origin—Sutherland with the descendants of the Fleming Freskin,[65] Buchan with the Comyns,[66] Angus with the Umphravilles,[67] Menteith with the Stewarts,[68] and Carrick with the Bruces.[69] But the remainder, Caithness, Ross, Mar, Atholl, Strathearn, Lennox, Fife, and Dunbar, were still possessed by native comital dynasties. As we have seen, these dynasties intermarried freely with the families of foreign settlers and even with families furth of Scotland altogether. The native nobility was not untouched by external influence or experience. Though the custom of fosterage seems to have been confined to the west,[70] the practice whereby sons acted as hostages on behalf of their fathers must have had an educative, mind-broadening effect, and in addition to that there were the attractions of pilgrimage and crusade.

In 1139 King Stephen took hostage the sons of two Scottish earls whose names were so uncouth in the ears of the Hexham writer that he could only attempt their first syllables, 'Mac' and 'Mel'—most likely they were the earls of Atholl and Strathearn.[71] In 1174 Earl Duncan II of Fife, Earl Gillebrigde of Angus, and Ness of Leuchars handed over sons or nephews as hostages to Henry II,[72] and the earl of Strathearn surrendered his son to King John in 1213.[73] In 1270 Adam of Kilconquhar, a kinsman of the earls of Fife and in his wife's right earl of Carrick, died at Acre while on crusade.[74] That incomparable

---

[65] *Moray Reg.*, p. xxxix; *Scots Pge.* viii. 319–23.
[66] Ibid. ii. 252–3.
[67] Ibid. i. 167–8.
[68] Ibid. vi. 130–2.
[69] Ibid. ii. 426.
[70] Charters of Uhtred son of Fergus lord of Galloway were witnessed by Gillechatfar, Uhtred's foster-brother (*Holyrood Liber*, no. 23; see also *Ayr–Galloway Coll.*, iv (1884), facing p. 55; *CWAAS Trans.* (NS) xvii, 218–19); likewise a contemporary charter of Guthred king of Man was witnessed by his foster-brother Gillocrist (*St. Bees Reg.*, no. 43). For fosterage among the Bruce earls of Carrick see R. Nicholson, *Scotland: The Later Middle Ages*, 73. The heir of the O'Donnell had been fostered by a lord of the Isles (Macruarie?) before 1258 (Orpen, *Ireland* iii. 274). Fergus 'Fostresone' was an Ayrshire freeholder in 1296 (*CDS* ii. 199).
[71] *Chron. Stephen*, iii, 177–8 (=Cambridge, Corpus Christi Coll. MS 139, fo. 46), '& filium Mel'7 filium Mac , scilicet duorum comitum de Scottia'. Mel' was probably Malise earl of Strathearn (d. *c.* 1150?), Mac probably Madet earl of Atholl (*c.* 1136–1159).
[72] Stones, *Relations*, 6–7 (no. 1).
[73] *Rot. Litt. Claus.* i. 137.
[74] *Scots. Pge.* ii. 426.

The Other Side of the Coin

tourist Visitors' Book, the *Liber Vitae* of Durham Cathedral,[75] shows a steady stream of Scots notables paying their respects to Saint Cuthbert. Dugald son of Somerled of Argyll, with his sons Olaf, Duncan, and Ranald, visited Durham in 1175 when he came to York to swear fealty to Henry II along with the other Scots magnates, promising Saint Cuthbert 1 mark annually during his lifetime.[76] Earl Duncan II of Fife with his brother Adam and a few retainers is entered in the book,[77] and so is his kinsman Laurence of Abernethy with his wife Dervorguilla.[78] A double family party, showing a fascinating mixture of personal names, is provided by Earl Malcolm son of Madet of Atholl and his wife Hextilda daughter of Uhtred, previously married to Richard Comyn.[79] The Atholl family included Simon, Henry, Duncan, Bethoc, Christina, Margaret, Gille-Eithne,[80] and Constantine, and the Comyns William, Christian, Edna, and Ada.

It was not simply the native *families* which survived. The constitutional position of the earls was preserved and its practical consequences not greatly diminished. Apart from the special case of the Law of Clan Macduff, about which so little is known,[81] we find the earls carefully reserving their rights of *haute justice*, so that while thieves, for example, might be convicted in their tenants' courts they were hanged on the earls' gallows.[82] Their sergeants were still entitled to free billeting—what in England and on the Welsh Marches was called puture, and in Scotland conveth or sorn, whence the 'sorners' of ill

---

[75] *Liber Vitae Ecclesiae Dunelmensis*, ed. A. Hamilton Thompson (Surtees Soc. 1923) [='Facsimile']; also *Liber Vitae Ecclesiae Dunelmensis*, ed. J. Stevenson (Surtees Soc. 1841) [='Stevenson'].

[76] 'Facsimile', fo. 13v, 'Stevenson', pp. 4, 135 (see also Anderson, *Scottish Annals*, 264).

[77] 'Facsimile', fo. 36v, 'Stevenson', p. 37.

[78] 'Facsimile', fos. 61 and 71v, 'Stevenson', pp. 94 and 112.

[79] 'Facsimile', fo. 63, 'Stevenson', p. 100.

[80] Kelehathonin. For the name Gille-Eithne see Watson, *CPNS*, 381.

[81] J. Skene, *De verborum significatione* (1597), s.v. 'Clan-Makduf'. The conservatism of rural Fife in juridical matters is shown by a confirmation by James I (*RMS* ii, no. 187) of a fourteenth-century charter where powers of imprisonment and discovery are linked with the power of scrutiny called *ranscauth*. This must be the Gaelic verb *rannsaich*, 'search', 'scrutinize' (itself a loanword from Scandinavian *rannsaka*: A. MacBain, *Etymological Dictionary of the Gaelic Language* (1896), s.v.).

[82] Fraser, *Lennox*, ii, 401 (no. 202); *Lennox Cartulary*, 57. For the earl of Strathearn's powers of hanging see *Inchaffray Chrs.*, no. 25; Anderson, *Oliphants*, 2.

repute in the sixteenth and seventeenth centuries.[83] Wherever English law and the jury system did not prevail the earls' sergeands could bring unsupported accusations or *superdicta* on their own account.[84] The ancient judicial caste in Scotland, the *judices* or *breitheamhan*, as well as the lesser court officers, the mairs, although in some respects functioning on behalf of the Crown, seem often to be closely associated with the earls, an association facilitated by the fact that the *judices* were attached to the old provinces rather than to the newer sheriffdoms.[85]

The earls' tenacious conservatism is well illustrated in a charter of confirmation given to Sir John the knight of Luss on Loch Lomondside in 1308 by King Robert I.[86] This is the earliest charter known to survive from Robert I's chancery, and it confirms privileges bestowed on John of Luss, probably towards the close of the thirteenth century, by the king's stalwart friend and defender Malcolm earl of Lennox.

> Out of reverence for our patron saint, the most holy man the Blessed Kessog, [runs the earl's charter] and in his honour, we have conceded to our bachelor, Sir John of Luss, and his heirs, freedom from the prises, seizures and carting services which we have previously demanded from him; and we also concede that henceforth, within the marches of the lands of Luss, John and his heirs and their tenants shall not be vexed by the bailies or sergeands of the lord king's Justiciar, or by our bailies or sergeants, for the purpose of obtaining testimony. And lest the lord king's service should be seen to suffer in the matter of obtaining testimony through our own default we shall at all times be ready to be sufficient witness for the other men of our earldom.

The compulsory provision of testimony, usually known as 'bode and witnessman', formed part of a bundle of seemingly ancient law-enforcement measures which the Cheshire historian Ronald Stewart-Brown traced in twelfth- and thirteenth-century Lancashire, Durham, Westmorland, and Cumberland.[87] It need hardly be said that although Stewart-Brown's

---

[83] R. Stewart-Brown, *The Serjeants of the Peace in Medieval England and Wales* (Manchester, 1936), 6–7, 81–2; Fraser, *Lennox*, ii. 401, *conevetum servientum; Glasgow Reg.*, nos. 139, 141, *corredium ad opus servientum*. See *New English Dictionary*, s.vv. 'sorn', 'sorner'.

[84] W. C. Dickinson, 'Surdit de Sergaunt', *SHR* xxxix (1960), 170–5.

[85] Barrow, *Kingdom*, 69–80; Anderson, *Oliphants*, 2.

[86] Fraser, *Lennox*, ii. 407 (no. 210).

[87] Stewart-Brown, op. cit. 82–6.

treatment of his subject was exemplarily thorough he did not look north of the Border. The existence of 'witnessman' in the Lennox, historically part of the old kingdom of Cumbria, is well worth remarking, especially as in north-west England it was intimately associated with the system of serjeants of the peace for whom there is evidence from the Lennox also.[88] But what is surely most remarkable is the way in which a Scottish earl could at his own discretion exempt some of his vassals in perpetuity from the operations of the king's Justiciar and take it upon himself to make up any consequent deficiency in the administration of royal justice.

Above all, the earls retained their control of at least the mustering and recruitment of the 'common army' of Scotland, bowmen and spearmen, a function in which royal and comital rights and duties seem impenetrably intermingled. It is significant that this service, though frequently called 'common army'[89] (once 'common ware of Scotland'[90]) and sometimes simply 'army',[91] was more often known as 'Scottish army', *exercitus Scoticanus*,[92] or 'Scottish service', *servitium Scoticanum*.[93] As such it was contrasted with the *exercitus militaris*[94] or *liberum servitium*,[95] knightly army or free service. The word Scottish (*Scoticus, Scoticanus*) was employed in this period to distinguish anything recognized to belong to the older order before the advent of French and English speech and customs, and with

[88] Ibid. 133; G. W. S. Barrow, 'The pattern of lordship and feudal settlement in Cumbria', *Journal of Medieval History*, i (1975), 129–30.

[89] Lawrie, *Charters*, no. 221, seems to be the earliest surviving instance of the expression, which is found frequently in thirteenth-century charters.

[90] *Hist. MSS Comm., 11th Rep.*, App., pt. VI (1887), 209–10, service of one bowman in the 'common ware of Scotland' (X 1345). I have not seen the original document, but the word is presumably OE *waru*, 'defence'.

[91] *The Scottish Tradition*, ed. G.W.S. Barrow, 33 (no. 7); *Hist. MSS Comm., 2nd Rep.*, App., 166; *Hist. MSS Comm., Rep. on Various Collections*, v (Hay of Duns), no. 2.

[92] *Spalding Misc.* ii. 312–13 (no. 16); *Coupar Angus Chrs.* i, no. 60; Fraser, *Grandtully*, i. 125 (no. 69); Fraser, *Grant*, iii. 5 (no. 6): 'forinscecum servicium domini regis scoticanum'. For a selection of examples, see the essay by J. R. N. MacPhail in *Highland Papers*, ii, 227–45.

[93] SRO GD 82/6; Raine, *North Durham*, no. 144. For other examples, see Sheriff MacPhail's essay cited in the previous note.

[94] *Coupar Angus Chrs.* i, no. 60.

[95] *Moray Reg.*, no. 263; *Formulary E. Scottish letters and brieves, 1286–1424*, ed. A. A. M. Duncan (University of Glasgow, Department of Scottish History Occasional Papers, 1976), 41 (no. 89).

particular reference to the country north of Forth and Clyde. Thus we have mention of the 'Scottish language' (i.e. Middle Gaelic),[96] a 'Scottish road',[97] 'Scottish mills',[98] a 'Scottish *mela*' or measure of corn and cheese,[99] and a 'Scottish ploughgate' of land,[100] presumably paraphrasing the vernacular word davoch (Old Irish, *dabhach*).

'Scottish army', in short, was what was there already when the feudalizers came on the scene. This must surely have a bearing on the controversial question of whether English feudalism was native, i.e. Anglo-Scandinavian, or foreign, i.e. Norman, in origin. As anyone knows who has acted as examiner in medieval history in many British universities, there is no conflict so evergreen as this. Yet though it has rumbled on happily for a century and more, it provides what must be my most striking example of insularity. If the debate were to continue for another fifty years, I confidently predict that the partisans of neither side will have made comparative use of the Scottish material or availed themselves of anything in these chapters.

Stated briefly, the argument is this. If the feudalism which can be seen clearly enough in England under Henry I grew naturally and therefore gradually from the military and social arrangements which were in force in Anglo-Scandinavian England before its ruling class was overwhelmed by the invading Normans, we would not expect to find traces of any alternative system. This much is common ground between the exponents of continuity and of cataclysm and those who seek

---

[96] *St. Andrews Liber*, 113 (*antiquo Scotorum ydiomate*); *RRS* ii, no. 469 (*qui scottice Tolari nuncupatur*).

[97] BL MS Add. 33245, fo. 179ᵛ (relating to Kingoldrum, Angus).

[98] Ibid., 'old Scottish mill called Schanualy'. See also *Arbroath Liber*, 226 (no. 295), where note especially the contrast between 'Hachethunethouer (read *Hacheth methon*') which *anglice* is called 'Midefeld' and 'the marsh which *scotice* is called Moynebuch'. For two mills called Scotismilne (Scotismylne) in Aberdeenshire, seventeenth century, respectively on Donside and in Buchan, see *Retours, Aberdeen*, no. 213, *Kincardine*, no. 70.

[99] *Coupar Angus Chrs.* i, no. 21; SRO RH 6/16.

[100] *RRS* ii, no. 469. The probability that 'Scottish ploughgate' (*carucata Scotica*) was equivalent to the davoch familiar north of the Forth is increased by the fact that Pope Honorius III confirmed to Arbroath Abbey a 'davoch' of land at Kingledoors in Tweeddale (*Arbroath Liber*, i, no. 223). The word 'davoch' was not used in the country south of Forth, and its presence in this papal privilege must be due to drafting by a clerk familiar with Angus usage employing the word as equivalent to the 'ploughgate' (*carucata*) normal in Tweeddale.

to moderate between the two extremes. Thus, the late Hilary Richardson and Dr George Sayles have written: 'The stages by which the liability of land-owners to provide knights for the king's army, assessed on the basis of hidage, gave way to an arbitrary quota or *servitium debitum* are obscure . . . but we may say this, here and now, that it seems manifestly impossible that the two assessments should have existed simultaneously.'[101] Professor R. A. Brown, writing from the opposite standpoint, says that 'the exponents of Old English feudalism and, more precisely, the exponents of continuity in these matters, cannot really have their fyrd evolving painlessly into the Norman feudal host, without cataclysmic change, since both fyrd and host are found together after 1066.'[102] And Professor C. W. Hollister, who stands in the middle of the road, has similarly pointed out the 'if the select fyrd—the *territorial* fyrd—survived the Conquest as an entity, this very fact precludes a direct evolutionary connection between the five-hide service of the Anglo-Saxons and the feudal service of the Anglo-Normans.'[103] It does not affect my argument that Messrs Richardson and Sayles have cut the Gordian knot with astonishing boldness by denying that the fyrd ever existed either before or after the Conquest and by asserting that throughout England there was only one single evolving system of contractual military service, reinforced when necessary by the hiring of mercenaries.[104]

It would be quite unfair to chide Richardson (who was an Englishman) and Dr Sayles (who is a Scot) for not turning their gaze north of the Border, since none of the protagonists in what has been called 'the most important single question in English medieval history'[105] has ever thought of doing anything so absurd. Yet the clue which the Scottish evidence provides is simpler and easier to follow than those from the widely varying English sources, no doubt because the country remained more conservative and feudalism was comparatively late in making

---

[101] H. G. Richardson and G. O. Sayles, *The Governance of Mediaeval England* (Edinburgh, 1963), 54.
[102] R. A. Brown, *Origins of English Feudalism* (1973), 61.
[103] C. W. Hollister, *The Military Organization of Norman England* (Oxford, 1965), 217.
[104] Richardson and Sayles, *Governance of Mediaeval England*, 48–55, and generally chapters IV and V.
[105] Brown, *Origins of English Feudalism,* publishers' statement on reverse of cover.

its appearance. The similarities between the feudalism of later twelfth-century Scotland and of England between 1066 and 1166 are so close and numerous that no one who has studied the evidence could have any doubt of their general identity, even while allowing some important differences of detail. If, therefore, we accept the hypothesis of continuity for England before and after 1066 we are bound to conclude that what was brought to Scotland after 1097 and especially after 1124 was nothing else but Old English—or should we say, Anglo-Scandinavian—feudalism, as modified under the early Norman kings. Scots and English had lived as neighbours for centuries without the former being tempted to import or the latter to export a system which the twelfth-century Scottish kings apparently and suddenly found indispensable.

Should we feel disposed to argue that, since it is only from the twelfth century that we begin to have feudal documents for Scotland, we cannot assume that feudalism was then newly introduced, but that on the contrary honours and castles, knights and knights' fees and vassalic commendation might all have been found in the Scotland of Malcolm III (1058–93) or even of Malcolm Mac Kenneth (1005–34), we must nevertheless explain how it happens that in the twelfth and thirteenth centuries there is sufficient and unequivocal evidence for an obligation of military service alternative to knight-service, explicitly distinguished from knight-service, and, as if to resolve any lingering doubt we might entertain, pointedly called 'Scottish service' or 'Scottish army'. Of the very many documents which make the distinction plain I will cite four. At the beginning of the thirteenth century Adam son of Abraham gave as a marriage portion to David Ruffus of Forfar land in Little Lour and Kincriech, which David himself, before setting out for Jerusalem, granted to the Cistercians of Coupar Angus.[106] David was to pay an annual rent for the land of $2\frac{1}{2}$ merks and he was to perform the king's forinsec service due from one davoch in respect of Kincriech and from the tenth part of two davochs in respect of Little Lour. Many years later, Adam's son Henry of Nevay, confirming David's gift to Coupar Abbey, says that his father specially stipulated how

---

[106] *Coupar Angus Chrs.* i, nos. 10, ii (in the text of no. 11, p. 25, the words *iterum ierlin* are to be read *iturus Ierusalem*).

the lord king's forinsec service was to be performed whenever it might happen that the knightly army and the Scottish army should operate in the king's service together or separately.[107] Unhappily, the charter in which Adam of Lour specified these arrangements has not survived, but we are left in no doubt of the distinction between the two types of service. My second illustration is from a royal charter of infeftment of 1 August 1240,[108] a grant of Fincharn on Loch Awe to Gillascop Mac Gilchrist, for which the stipulated service was that of half a knight in the army, aids appropriate for the full service of one knight, and 'Scottish service, as performed by the king's barons and knights for their lands on the north side of the Scottish Sea'. Thirdly, we may note an agreement of 1287[109] between the knight Reginald Cheyne the younger of Duffus in Moray and William of Fedderate and his wife Christina, portioners (co-parceners) of the barony of Duffus. This agreement stipulates that William and his wife shall perform the third part of the free service of one knight for their share of the barony of Duffus and Strathbrock, that Reginald shall perform the required suit to the king's courts of justiciary and sheriffdom and that the portioners' vassals and tenants shall do Scottish service whenever it shall happen that this is demanded or provided. Finally, we have the evidence, necessarily less authoritative since it comes to us from a formulary of the late fifteenth century, of an undated brieve of summons for army service.[110] Context and contents alike make it very probable that this brieve belongs to the years 1286–91, most probably to 1286.[111] The brieve calls on all who owe military service to the 'royal dignity' of Scotland, whether free service or Scottish service, to be equipped and ready with forty days' victuals and to be on notice of a day and a night[112] to go wherever required

---

[107] Ibid., no. 60; 'qui specialem mentionem facit quomodo forinsecum seruicium domini regis facere debeant quando exercitum militarem et scoticanum communiter uel per se seruicio domini Regis laborare contigerit'.

[108] *Highland Papers*, ii. 121–3.

[109] *Moray Reg.*, no. 263.

[110] *Formulary E*, ed. Duncan, no. 89.

[111] Ibid., nos. 86–8, appear to belong to the period after Alexander III's death in 1286, and the rubric to no. 89 actually reads 'citacio exercitus post obitum regis'.

[112] For the notice of a day and a night see Stones, *Relations*, 262–3, referring to Robert Bruce's actions in March 1306.

for the defence of the realm and the royal dignity and their liberty.

To complete both sides of the equation, it only remains to point out that among English historians all parties are agreed that before 1066 what may be called the normal or typical military service was territorial, one warrior (without begging the question whether he was ceorl, sokeman, thegn, or knight) being required from so many fiscal or valuation units of land, five hides, six ploughgates, and so on.[113] But in Scotland also, 'Scottish army' north of Forth and the king's forinsec service, including 'army', south of Forth, were levied on a territorial basis,[114] implying an assessment of all districts at so many ploughgates, davochs, ounce or penny lands, or (uniquely in the Lennox) arachors. This appears to be precisely analogous to the territorial system agreed to have prevailed in the last years of the Old English state. In Scotland, from the reign of David I to the outbreak of war with England in 1296, there existed side by side knight-service and Scottish service, a cavalry force and a national infantry. If we are to place any credence in our surviving documents, this coexistence, far from seeming 'manifestly impossible', was manifestly the reality. In England, the evidence for feudalism is abundant and pervasive, while the evidence for an alternative system, though present, becomes hard to trace through the twelfth century.[115] In Scotland both kinds of evidence can be found, modest in quantity no doubt, but unimpeachable in quality. In seeking an event which will explain both the similarities and the contrasts, we do not need to look further than the Conquest of 1066.

One of the most perceptive analyses of the question of Anglo-Norman feudalism and its origins ever to be attempted was contributed to *Past and Present* in 1963 by John Prestwich.[116] In that paper, he quoted the opinions of two notable historians

---

[113] See, for the fullest review of the evidence, C. W. Hollister, *Anglo-Saxon Military Institutions on the eve of the Norman Conquest* (Oxford, 1962); Richardson and Sayles, *Governance of Mediaeval England*, chapter III.

[114] Barrow, *Kingdom*, 309; *RRS* ii. 54–7; *Scone Liber*, 42 (no. 67). For the country south of Forth see *Hist. MSS Comm.*, 2nd Rep., App., 166; *Kelso Liber*, 361 (no. 471); NLS Adv. MS 37.1.1–37.3.4, vol. V (Gartshore charter); *Hist. MSS Comm., Milne-Home* (1902), 224 (no. 496).

[115] Hollister, *Military Organization of Norman England*, 216–67, reviews much of the evidence; see also F. M. Stenton, *The First Century of English Feudalism*.

[116] J. O. Prestwich, 'Anglo-Norman feudalism and the problem of continuity', *Past and Present*, xxvi (1963), 39–57.

of England, both *émigrés* from eastern Europe, Paul Vinogradoff and Lewis Namier.[117] 'The system', Vinogradoff wrote, 'according to which the commonwealth carries on its armaments cannot but exercise a potent influence on the whole constitution of society—it may lead to social equality, or to the predominance of the armed few, to the endowment of soldiers with the land, or to the sway of a plutocracy supported by hired armies.' These words are echoed by Namier's remark apropos England in the age of the American Revolution: 'the social history of nations is largely moulded by the forms and development of their armed forces, the primary aim of national organization being common defence.'

Professor Brown has recently emphasized the fact that feudalism was an 'upper class affair',[118] by which he means that of the choices listed by Vinogradoff, feudalism led to the predominance of the armed few and the endowment of soldiers —relatively few but highly professional soldiers—with land. As feudalism developed, first of all in Francia and its neighbouring territories, but after 1066 in England, the specialist mounted warrior, the knight, became ever more sharply distinguished from the ordinary free peasant. Military skill and responsibility created a new aristocracy, so that, to adapt Brown's words, a new social ruling class of knights tended to monopolize not only military worth but also the concept of social and legal freedom, as the peasant's military importance waned and he himself sank towards servitude.[119]

England was a big enough country in terms of wealth and numbers of inhabitants to allow this to happen in the generations following the Conquest—the feudalization and therefore in some sense the liberation of a large segment of the population who ruled the land and fought its wars, accompanied by the villanization of a much more numerous class of agrarian breadwinners who did not rule and were not supposed to bear arms, indeed not officially allowed to bear arms till well into the thirteenth century.[120] But in Scotland this did not happen to anything like the same extent. Of course, the king and the

[117] Art. cit. 41.
[118] Brown, *Origins of English Feudalism*, 23, 27.
[119] Ibid. 44.
[120] Stubbs, *Select Charters*, 363 (for this document of 1242 see also F. M. Powicke, *EHR* lvii (1942), 469–73).

great magnates dominated the land and its people, as they were to do until the eighteenth century, but the majority of baronies were small, knighthood remained comparatively rare, and there seems to have been much less intensive villanization of the peasantry.[121] An unmistakable continuity runs through from David I's reign to the eve of Robert I's, in recorded provisions that Edmund son of Forn of Pinkie might decline to join the lord king's army 'unless that army be so universal that the men of Inveresk cannot stay at home, in which case he must send one man' (before 1153);[122] that the estate of Sir Nicholas Hay of Inchyra in the Carse of Gowrie (c. 1286) was free from army service 'unless there be a proclamation that every man should go forth to defend his head';[123] and that in Carrick in 1302 the tenants of Melrose Abbey need not perform army service 'unless the common army of the whole realm is raised for its defence, when all inhabitants are bound to serve'.[124] Of that army Matthew Paris wrote with evident admiration when, in 1244, it marched from Caddonfoot to Ponteland under the standard of King Alexander II.[125] And of that army Andrew Murray and William Wallace carefully styled themselves the leaders or generals, *duces exercitus Regni Scotie*, when they defeated the earl of Surrey at the Bridge of Stirling.[126] We shall never know what England would have been like had there been no Norman Conquest; but if, instead of being conquered by the Normans, England had merely been engulfed by continental influence, we might not make a bad guess about some of its characteristic features if we studied the ascertainable character of Scotland during the two centuries of the Anglo-Norman Era.

[121] This whole question still awaits an adequately detailed study, but there is an excellent general discussion in A. A. M. Duncan, *Scotland: The Making of the Kingdom*, chapters 13 and 14.
[122] *Dunfermline Reg.*, 191 (no. 301).
[123] Earl of Moray, Darnaway Castle, Gray of Kinfauns Muniments, bdle. 84, no. 2 (Box 5). Cf. *Kinloss Records*, 130.
[124] *Melrose Liber*, no. 351.
[125] Matthew Paris, *Chronica Majora*, iv. 380.
[126] *Documents illustrative of Sir William Wallace, his Life and Times*, ed. J. Stevenson (Maitland Club, 1841), 53, 159; cp. p. 161, 'ductor exercitus ejusdem', a style used by Wallace alone, after Andrew Murray's death. See, for this last document, the facsimile in Anderson, *Diplomata*, pl. XLIII, from which it is clear that Wallace's style was *ductor exercitus*, although both Anderson's printed transcription and the text in Stevenson, *Wallace Docs.*, 161, have *exercituum*.

APPENDIX A

1. *Brieve of King Malcolm IV commanding that the woods of Coldingham Priory shall be the preserve of the prior and monks, under penalty of £10, saving the needs of the king's castle of Berwick upon Tweed. The prior and monks are in addition to have rights of warren in these woods and throughout their lands, as bounded by the just and ancient marches indicated. Hunting and woodcutting are prohibited save by permission of the prior and monks.*

Eldbottle (1153 X 1162).

Malcolumbus Rex Scottorum,[a] Episcopis, Abbatibus, Prioribus, Comitibus, Justiciis, Baronibus, Vicecomitibus, Prepositis, Ministris et omnibus hominibus, Francis et Anglicis et Scottis, tam futuris quam presentibus, tocius terre sue, salutem. Sciatis quod volo et firmiter precipio quod nemora monachorum de Coldingham, videlicet Grenewde et totum nemus de Ristone et Brocholwde et Akesside, Harwde, Denewde et Swinewde et Churchedenwde et omnia nemora sint sub defensione prioris et custodia, necnon et monachorum de Coldingham, ne aliquis super x libras forisfacture quicquam in predictis nemoribus capiat nisi per ipsum priorem vel per monachos prenominati loci, si ipse presens non fuerit, exceptis tantummodo necessariis de castello meo de Berevic, que mihimetipso solummodo conveniunt. Et si clientes mei pro necessariis meis ad opus castelli mei de Berevic ad nemora predicta venerint per priorem vel per clientes suos que opus fuerint mihi et ubi ipse vel clientes sui monstraverint accipiant. Insuper addo et illis concedo quod predictus prior et monachi habeant warennam[b] in prenominatis nemoribus et per totam terram suam sicut extenduntur recte et antique divise, videlicet a Lambertona usque ad Bilie et usque Driefurd usque ad rivulum qui manat[c] in mare per Aldecambus pethe; ita quod nullus ibi aliquid capiat nec lingna nec bestiam aliquam silvestrem nisi per ipsos. Quod si aliqui ibi capiantur venando vel ligna secando, prior et monachi habeant quod super illos et cum illis invenerint, et ego forisfacturam prenominatam. Testibus G.[d] Episcopo Sancti Andree, Waltero Cancellario, Ricardo Capellano Regis, Ricardo Capellano Comitis, Waltero filio Alani, Thoma Lundon*iarum*,[e] Ricardo de Morvill, Johanne de Vall*ibus*, Galfrido de Cunning*burg*, Alano filio Dapiferi, Willelmo Clerico Comitis, Waltero Clerico Cancellarii. Apud Ellebotel.

Notes on Text: [a] *Punctuation editorial.*
                [b] *MS* Waremiam; *RRS* ii, *no. 46 has* Gwarrennam.
                [c] *MS* manet, *with note correcting to* manat.
                [d] *sic; read* R(oberto) *or* A(rnaldo).
                [e] *fo. 145^v.*

Heading: Charta Malcolumbi Regis super nemoribus.

Source: National Library of Scotland, MS Adv. 35.3.8, pt. 2, fo. 145.

Comment: The date lies between the king's accession and 1162, the latest year in which Walter de Bidun could have been royal chancellor. Unfortunately, the miscopying of the initial of the bishop of St. Andrews' name makes it impossible to say whether the first witness was Bishop Robert, who died in 1159, or Bishop Arnold, who held office from 13 November 1160 to 13 September 1162. If the 'earl' whose chaplain and clerk are witnesses was the king's brother William, the date-limits would be 1153 X 1157, but it is possible that the reference is to the king's father, Earl Henry, who died in 1152. Walter, the chancellor's clerk, witnessed King Malcolm's great charter for Kelso Abbey, 1159 (*RRS* i, no. 131).

This text was overlooked when *RRS* i and ii were edited. It forms part of a collection of copies of original Scottish charters at Durham transcribed for the eighteenth-century antiquary Walter Macfarlane of that ilk in 1744, when the original of this brieve, now missing, was evidently still extant in the Dean and Chapter muniments. The copyist may have omitted some words in the description of marches, between 'Driefurd' and 'usque ad rivulum' (see *RRS* ii, no. 46).

RRS i, no. 194 (1160 X 1162) was also dated at Eldbottle. For the witness John de Vaux and his connection with Eldbottle, see above, pp. 19–20.

2. *Charter of Gervase and Ralph Ridel, sons of G. Ridel, granting the church of Abbotsley, Huntingdonshire, to Jedburgh Abbey.*

(28 Oct. 1164 X 9 Dec. 1165).

Gervasius Ridel et Rad*ulfus* frater eius ambo filii G. Ridel,[a] omnibus fidelibus salutem. Sciatis dedisse nos ambos pari et assensu equali benivolentia Deo et ecclesie beate Marie de Jeddeworth' et abbati canonicisque in eadem ecclesia Deo servientibus sub regula beati Augustini pro anima patris nostri et pro animabus nostris et animabus parentum nostrorum ecclesiam[b] de Alboldesley, cum omnibus pertinenciis et rectitudinibus suis, tenen*dam* a predictis Dei et beate Marie servis atque possidendam[c] in eadem integritate atque plenitudine teniture et possessione in qua aliquis eandem ecclesiam integrius et plenius cum pertinentiis et possessionibus et rectitudinibus suis unquam tenuit et possesserit, et in eadem integritate atque plenitudine libertatis, quietis et honoris in qua supradicti canonici aliquam de aliis ecclesiis suis quocunque loco totius terre domini nostri Regis Scot' liberius, quiecius et honorabilius tenent et possident. T*estibus* Engelramo Episcopo Glasgu et aliis, etc.

Notes on text: [a] *Punctuation editorial.*
[b] *MS* eciam.
[c] *MS* possidentibus.

Appendix A

Source: Balliol College, Oxford, Abbotsley Deeds, E 7/1.

Comment: The source of this and no. 3 is a single membrane, on which a report of a lawsuit of 1256 has been written in a hand of about that date. The heading is 'Placita coram Rogero de Turkeby et sociis suis Justic*iariis* de Banco de termino Sancti Michaelis Anno *regni* Regis .H. filii Regis Johannis quadragesimo'. The date of no. 2 is determined by the witnessing of Ingram bishop of Glasgow (consecrated at Sens, 28 Oct. 1164) and the fact that it is confirmed by no. 3. Probably both charters were issued at or about the same time. Charters issued jointly by two or more brothers do not seem very common, and it may be that Gervase and Ralph Ridel were twins. Their father was perhaps Geoffrey Ridel, *alias* Basset, lord of Weldon, brother of Ralph Basset of Drayton, for whom see Farrer, *HKF* ii. 269–70, 316. It is known that Gervase Ridel became a canon of Jedburgh, but evidently after he had been married to a lady named Christian who held land at Mervinslaw south of Jedburgh (*RRS* ii, no. 62). The names Gervase and Geoffrey were used by later members of the Ridel family in Scotland (ibid., references in index). For a slightly earlier example of a charter issued jointly by two brothers, see *HMC Report on the MSS of the Marquess of Lothian at Blickling Hall* (1905), p. 10, relating to Norfolk.

3. *Charter of King Malcolm IV confirming the grant of Abbotsley church to Jedburgh Abbey made by the brothers Gervase and Ralph Ridel.*

(28 Oct. 1164 X 9 Dec. 1165).

Melculmus Rex Scottorum omnibus fidelibus suis de Honore de Huntyngdon tociusque terre sue,[a] clericis que laicis, salutem. Sciant presentes et posteri me concessisse et presenti carta mea confirmasse Deo et ecclesie Sancte Marie de Jeddeworth' et abbati et canonicis inibi Deo famulantibus donacionem ecclesie de Alboldesley quam Gervasius et Radulfus frater suus eis donaverunt. Volo ita et precipio ut predictus abbas et canonici ecclesiam prefatam habeant secundum donacionem que eis facta est, et teneant ita libere et quiete sicut aliqua ecclesia infra honorem[b] Hunt' liberius et quiecius tenetur et possidetur. T*estibus* E*ngelramo* Episcopo de Glascu et aliis etc.

Notes on text: [a] *Punctuation editorial.*
[b] *MS* honore.

Source: Balliol College, Oxford, Abbotsley Deeds, E 7/1.

Comment: For the date-limits see comment on no. 2. This charter was omitted from *RRS* i, through ignorance, and is not referred to in *RRS* ii, no. 62, William I's principal charter of confirmation for Jedburgh Abbey, which simply refers to the original grant by Gervase and Ralph Ridel.

APPENDIX B

Notes on some families of Anglo-Continental origin which settled permanently in Scotland between 1097 and 1296.

de ALNETO
(AUNAY, AUNOU)
(Modern form: none known)

In a lawsuit of 1200 Henry de Aunay based his claim to Maidford, Northants, on a grant which he alleged had been made at the period of the Norman Conquest of England to his great-great-great-grandfather, Pain de Aunay, by Hugh Burdet, ancestor of William Burdet who served King Malcolm IV as steward of the Honour of Huntingdon (Farrer, *HKF* ii. 330; *RRS* i. 101). A Henry Daunay (de Alneto), perhaps the same, was a tenant on the honour of Kendal under Gilbert son of Roger Fitz Reinfrid, successor of William II of Lancaster, at the end of the twelfth century (*Kendale Records*, 131, 397). It is not known whether Henry was related to persons of this surname in Scotland, who seem to begin with Ralph de Alneto (see below) and the Yorkshire tenant-in-chief Thomas de Alneto to whom King Alexander II granted the Dumfriesshire lands of Auchencrieff, Dargavel and 'Brunschaith' as a quarter-knight's fee in 1223, an estate subsequently granted to Melrose Abbey (*Melrose Liber*, nos. 205, 206). Thomas had died before 11 July 1244 (*Excerpta e rotulis finium*, i. 420), and his English lands were surveyed in response to a writ of 15 January 1246 (*Yorkshire Inquisitions*, i, no. IV). Thomas was evidently a landowner in Cumberland (*CDS* i, no. 1117). There is no evidence to connect him with Roger de Alneto (Auno) who witnessed documents issued by Roger de Quinci and his wife Helen daughter of Alan lord of Galloway (*Glasgow Reg.* i, nos. 167–9). An earlier Thomas de Alneto appears in Norman record of before 1189 in association with Ralph de Tancarville chamberlain of Normandy (*Chartes du prieuré de Longueville*, ed. Le Cacheux, no. 39), and a Ralph de Alneto witnessed *EYC* vi, no. 54 of *c.* 1190–1205, probably issued in Roxburghshire.

In Scotland the heir of Thomas de Alneto in 1244 was evidently John de Aunhou, who figures in record of that year among the supporters of Earl Patrick of Dunbar (*CDS* i, no. 2672, p. 552). In 1297 John de 'Ammou' (read Aunnou) was a tenant-in-chief in Scotland in whom King Edward I showed some interest (*Rot. Scot.*, i. 40b). It does not seem possible to identify the lands then held by this family.
Black, *Surnames*, s.v. AULNOY.
See below under Derman.

Appendix B

BAARD (BARD etc.)
(Modern form: BAIRD)

The earliest traces of this family are to be found in record relating to northeast Yorkshire, and especially to Loftus in the North Riding and Butterwick in the East Riding. An account of the Butterwick family is given in Clay and Greenway, *Early Yorkshire Families*, 11–13, without, however, any discussion of the link between Butterwick and Baard or the connection with Loftus.

A grant made, 1150–*c*. 1160, by William count of Aumale to his niece Euphemia, wife of Robert (II) de Brus, and the heirs of this marriage, was witnessed by Richard Baard (*EYC* iii, 69). Loftus was held successively by Richard Baard and his son Geoffrey. Between 1160 and 1175 Adam II de Brus, lord of Cleveland, confirmed gifts made by his vassals to Guisborough Priory, which included the grant by Richard Baard of the service of Robert of Butterwick in Loftus and other property. Further charters of Adam II in the period *c*. 1170–90 were witnessed by Geoffrey Baard (Baart or Bard), who also witnessed a Yorkshire charter of Earl Simon III de Senlis, 1156 X 74. William Baart or Bard appears in one charter of Adam II de Brus and in a contemporary deed of Peter Escarbot (for the foregoing see *EYC* ii. 14 and nos. 656, 659, 661–3, 666, 694, 759, 763 and, for Earl Simon's charter, no. 1186).

Bridlington Priory charters provide evidence of a twelfth-century Durand Bard of Butterwick whose son was William Bard (Lancaster, *Bridlington Abstracts*, 90–1), and also of a Richard Baart—presumably identical with or related to the Richard Baard referred to above—associated with Walter of Ghent, who died in 1139 (ibid. 100). In 1166 a Durand son of William of Butterwick held two knights' fees of William Fossard (*Early Yorkshire Families*, 12), and it is hard to believe that he was not related to Durand Bard of Butterwick. But we must note that a rather earlier contemporary of Durand son of William was Durand son of Geoffrey son of Durand I of Butterwick (ibid.). It is a further complication that in a charter of *c*. 1120–35 Durand I names his own sons and also, in distinction, the son of his wife, named Roger Baarth (*EYC* ii, no. 1071). A much later William Bard of Butterwick appears in 1285 (*Yorkshire Inquisitions*, ii. 36) and the surname undoubtedly survived into the fourteenth century.

In Scotland Richard Bard, with the consent of his lord Robert son of Waltheof (son of Baldwin) of Biggar, confirmed to Lesmahagow Priory the land of Little Kype, in Strathaven, Lanarkshire, as the priory had held it of his father Richard Bard. Although the charter recording this confirmation is undated it must belong to the early thirteenth century, and thus the donor's father Richard Bard might have been either of the same generation as Geoffrey Baard of Loftus, i.e. a younger brother, or less probably a son of Geoffrey and perhaps a brother of William (*Kelso Liber*, nos. 181, 182). Hugh son of Robert son of Waltheof of Biggar confirmed to Lesmahagow Priory the corn teinds of the land in Strathaven belonging to Richard 'de Baard' [*sic*]. The markedly Flemish character of the witnesses to Hugh's charter is worth noting in view of the association of the earliest recorded

Richard Baard with Walter of Ghent. The two Richards settled in Lanarkshire were ancestors of the family of Baird of Strathaven.
Black, *Surnames*, s.v. BAIRD, where the name is wrongly said to be of territorial origin and the reference to Henry 'de Barde' is a mistake for Henry 'de Brade', i.e. Braid near Edinburgh.

de BERCHELEI (BERKELEY etc.)
(Modern form: BARCLAY)

In 1086 the manor of Berkley near Frome in Somerset formed part of the extensive estates held in chief of the crown by Roger Arundel, the whole forming an honour whose caput was at Powerstock or Poorstock in Dorset (Sanders, *Baronies*, 72). Roger's tenant at Berkley was named Robert, possibly the Robert 'de Gatemore' who held Skilgate and Milton of Roger, and also the Robert, without surname, who held Cary Fitzpaine (in Charlton Mackrell) and Raddington in Somerset and also Blandford and Rollington near Corfe in Dorset of Roger Arundel (*VCH, Somerset*, i. 494–6; *Domesday Book*, i, fo. 82^v). Godfrey de Arundel, whose relationship, if any, to Roger Arundel is not known, witnessed a charter of Malcolm IV, 1162 X 1164 (*RRS* i, no. 256). Before the end of the reign (1165) the brothers Robert and Walter 'de Berkeley' appear in Scotland, probably at the king's court (ibid., 283, n. 1). This was some twenty-six years after a group of Devon and Somerset opponents of Stephen had sought refuge at the court of David I, among them Robert of Bampton (son of Walter of Douai) and Ralph Lovel II, lord of Castle Cary and perhaps grandson of Walter of Douai. Ralph Lovel's son Henry (see below under Lovel) witnessed a royal charter issued at the very end of Malcolm IV's reign (ibid., no. 265), by which date he was no doubt lord of Hawick.

Robert and Walter of Berkley, who probably took their surname from the Somerset Berkley, both acquired land in Scotland. Walter held a large estate in southern Kirkcudbrightshire, including the important lordship of Urr (Barrow, *Kingdom*, 296; *Holm Cultram Reg.*, 49; *Dumfriesshire Trans.* xxi. 14–20; xxix. 167 ff.). From Robert of London, by whom he is called 'kinsman' or 'cousin', Walter of Berkley obtained a ploughgate in St. Boswells and the land of Plenmeller in Northumberland (BL MS Loans 29/355). In Angus he got the thanage of Inverkeilor ('Redcastle'), and apparently in Aberdeenshire the land of Ardoyne in the Garioch (*RRS* ii, nos. 185, 344, 345). It is probable that Walter was the builder of the Mote of Urr and the earliest phase of Redcastle. Although Walter had a son named John (*Joa* . . .; see *Melrose Liber*, no. 97) his heirs were evidently his two daughters who divided his estates between them. One, named Agatha, married Humphrey son of Theobald de Addeville. Humphrey and his heirs took the surname 'de Berkeley'. The other daughter, whose name is unknown, married Enguerrand de Balliol, and their heirs, keeping the name Balliol, and lords of Tours-en-Vimeu, Picardy, inherited Redcastle and Urr (*Arbroath Liber*, no. 58; *Holyrood Liber*, nos. 70, 81; *Dumfriesshire Trans.*, xxi. 18–19). Robert of Berkley married a lady named Cecilia, apparently the

Appendix B

heiress of Maxton in Roxburghshire. Like Walter he left no surviving sons and his estates passed by marriage to the family of de Normanville of Stamfordham (*OPS* i. 297–9).

It seems impossible to place in any relationship with Robert and Walter of Berkley the only other person of this surname in early-twelfth-century Scottish record, the Richard 'de Barclay' ('de Berclay') who is said by T. Pont and G. Crawfurd to have been a witness to the foundation charter of Kilwinning Abbey. According to Pont (*Cuninghame topographized*, 57) this charter was given by Richard de Morville (therefore 1162 X 1190) and Richard de Berclay was styled 'dominus de Ardrossen' (a style which would be distinctly unusual, not to say inconceivable, in a charter of that date). According to Crawfurd (*History of the Shire of Renfrew* (1710), 88) the charter was given by Hugh de Morville (therefore X 1162) and the witness Richard de Barclay was ancestor of the Barclays of Ardrossan. Equally unknown is the relationship, if any, between Walter and Robert on the one hand and Roger of Berkley on the other, who appeared in a few late twelfth-century charters (*Melrose Liber*, no. 153; *Kelso Liber*, no. 248; *RRS* ii, no. 277; see Barrow, *Kingdom*, 123).
Black, *Surnames*, s.v. BARCLAY.

de BOSCO
(del BOIS, de BOIS, etc.)
(Modern forms: BOYCE, BOYES)

A family of this surname settled in Annandale as vassals of the Brus lords during the twelfth century, well-recorded members being Walter del Bois and his son Richard (Raine, *North Durham*, nos. 166, 167) and Humphrey de Bosco (*CDS* i, nos. 606–7, 700, 704, 707, 1682; *Arbroath Liber*, i, no. 37; Fraser, *Annandale*, 1–3, 5). For the suggestion that this family may have been identical with a family taking its name from Bosc-Bénard near Bourgthéroulde (arr. Pont-Audemer, dép. Eure), see above, pp. 94–6. In the obituary of Lisieux Cathedral the name of Walter of Bosc-Bénard is entered at 10 September, and he is stated to have given Lisieux property at Touville (Le Prévost, *Mémoires* . . . *de l'Eure*, iii. 303), presumably the same person who, with an heir named Richard, gave property at Touville or Thiouville to Longueville Priory (Le Cacheux, *Chartes de Longueville*, 89, no. 80). Part of Bosc-Bénard was called Bosc-Bénard-Commin, after the local proprietorial family of Commin whose name suggests possible relationship to the Anglo-Scottish family of Cumin or Comyn (see A. Young, *William Cumin: Border Politics and the Bishopric of Durham, 1141–1144* (University of York, Borthwick Papers no. 54, 1978), p. 5). It is also noteworthy that in this same part of Normandy is Saint-Aubin-Guichard where a Robert Guichart appears in thirteenth-century record (Le Prévost, *Mémoires* . . . *de l'Eure*, i. 217, 368 ff.), since a continental origin is extremely likely, and should be sought, for the Angus family of Wishart (Guiscard, Wiscard, etc.) who first appear in Scotland in the earlier thirteenth century, and used the personal name Robert. Presumably the king's scribe and chancellor

William del Bois was a member of the family settled in Dumfriesshire, but no relationship has been established.
Black, *Surnames*, s.v. BOYCE.

de BOIVILLE
(BOYVILLE etc.)
(Modern form: BOYLE)

The church of Biéville (canton Douvres, arr. Caen) was granted to the abbey of St. Stephen, Caen, by Ranulf vicomte of Bayeux, a gift confirmed by his descendant Hugh earl of Chester, 1077 X 1101 (Delisle–Berger, *Receuil*, i. 277, 578, the forms of the name being Boeuilla, Boiauilla). Ranulf le Meschin, cousin of Earl Hugh, was given the lordship of Carlisle by Henry I. He created the barony of Levington, now Kirklinton, to be held by Richard (more correctly, Richer) de Boyville (*Ancestor*, no. 3, p. 80; *Wetherhal Reg.*, 385). For the subsequent history of this family in Cumberland, see *St. Bees Reg.*, 30, 35, 106–7, 438–9; *Wetherhal Reg.*, 156, n. 7; Clay and Greenway, *Early Yorkshire Families*, 6–7. Richer's elder son and heir at Levington was Adam. A younger son Gilbert evidently took service with Malcolm IV, probably obtaining Kilbucho, Peeblesshire, to be held in chief, and certainly acquiring Tarbolton in Kyle, Ayrshire, to be held of the Steward, Walter son of Alan (*Melrose Liber*, no. 66; *Scottish Genealogist*, December 1978, p. 106). Gilbert and his descendants did not use the surname de Boiville, but in the thirteenth century a family with this name appear as tenants of the estate of Kelburne in Cunningham (*CDS* ii. 205, 210, 216; NLS Adamton Chrs., no. 9, and MS 42676). The head of the family of Boyle of Kelburne, Lord Boyle, was made earl of Glasgow in 1703.
Black, *Surnames*, s.v. BOYLE.

de CLERE
(Modern form: none known)

For the history and possessions of this family in England and their Norman origin, see Clay and Greenway, *Early Yorkshire Families*, 20–1; Loyd, *Origins*, 29. The name is from Clères, canton Clères, arr. Rouen. In Scotland Ralph de Clere, brother of Roger (III) de Clere, was in the service of Malcolm IV and William I and was given the estates of Mid Calder, Midlothian, and Cambusnethan, Lanarkshire. He succeeded his brother in his extensive English estates in Yorkshire and Sussex before 1185. The male line of the senior branch of the family ended in the later thirteenth century with Roger (IV) de Clere; Scottish record does not seem to have any reference to his daughter and heir Agatha or her husband William le Rus. For charters of Mid Calder and Cambusnethan issued by Ralph I and his son Ralph II (the latter with consent of Roger IV) see *Kelso Liber*, nos. 348, 272 respectively.

de COLVILLE
(COLLEVILLE, COLAVILLA, etc.)
(Modern form: COLVILLE)

The family of de Colville which settled in Scotland was dependent on, or at least associated with, the family of Percy, especially prominent in Yorkshire and Lincolnshire in the generations following the Norman Conquest of England (*EYC* ii. 35, 41, 280; xi. 12, 14, 186). The Percys came from Percy-en-Auge (canton Mézidon, arr. Lisieux, dép. Calvados), and it seems probable that the Colvilles derived their name from either Colleville-sur-Orne, north-east of Bayeux, or else from Colleville-sur-Mer, north-west of Bayeux. In England, both Percys and Colvilles were associated with the earls of Chester, hereditary *vicomtes* of Bayeux.

Malcolm IV granted an estate at Harrold, Bedfordshire, to Philip de Colville, who witnessed acts of that king and of William I (*RRS* i, nos. 118, 139, 174, 184, 190, 195, 198, 255, 258; ii, nos. 106, 126, 135, 144, spanning the years 1153 to 1174). This was no doubt the Philip de Colville who had held Drax castle in Yorkshire against King Stephen at harvest time 1154 (*Chron. Stephen*, i. 94; Henry of Huntingdon, *Historia*, 291) and witnessed a grant by Avice de Percy (née Paynel) to Drax Priory, 1147 X 53 (*EYC* vi, no. 48). In Scotland Philip de Colville was successor to Henry de Percy and his brother Geoffrey at Heiton, Roxburghshire (*Dryburgh Liber*, nos. 224–5; for the brothers Henry, Alan, and Geoffrey de Percy see *EYC* xi, 3). A charter of Malcolm IV issued at Les Andelys in Normandy in 1159 was witnessed by William de Colville (*RRS* i, no. 155). At the turn of the twelfth and thirteenth centuries Thomas de Colville 'surnamed the Scot' was a landowner in Galloway and constable of the royal castle of Dumfries (*St. Bees Reg.*, no. 60; *Melrose Liber*, nos. 192–5). The fact that Thomas granted land in Galloway to Vaudey Abbey (at Castle Bytham, Lincolnshire) shows that he was the Thomas de Colville who witnessed two deeds anent Bytham church and William de Colville lord of Bytham, c. 1226 (*RAL* iii, nos. 1019–20), while the fact that the grant was made for the souls of the kings David I, Malcolm IV, and William I connects Thomas with the earlier Colvilles in Scotland. A Philip de Colville, perhaps grandson of the Philip mentioned above, appears in the period 1204–11 (*RRS* ii, nos. 456, 496; *EYC* ii. 41; called brother of Thomas, ibid. xi. 303).

There were links between the Colvilles and Malherbes lords of Morham, East Lothian (*Newbattle Reg.*, nos. 99, 211–13), the latter probably being offshoots of the family of Malherbe which held land in Yorkshire and Lincolnshire.

Black, *Surnames*, s.v. COLVILLE.

DALLAS
(see RIPLEY)

DERMAN
(Modern form: none known)

The lands near Dumfries granted by Alexander II to Thomas de Alneto in 1223 (see above) had previously been held by William son of Derman and his son William. (BL Loans 29, Ancient Chrs., no. 4.) Charters anent Ravenglass, Cumberland, dating X 1240, were witnessed by William son of Derman, *alias* 'de Derman' (*St. Bees Reg.*, nos. 486, 489). This was probably the William son of Dermann who granted land to the parish church of St. Michael, Burgh by Sands, *c.* 1234; and contemporaneously there is mention of Adam son of Derman and Robert son of Derman (*Holm Cultram Reg.*, 8). Derman, presumably original ancestor of the family, witnessed a charter for Lanercost Priory by Ada daughter of William Engaine lord of Burgh by Sands (*Trans.Roy.Soc.Lit.*, 2nd ser. viii. ii. 11, and index).

William Derman and his wife Maud levied a fine at York in 1208 with Ralph Wacelin relating to Birdsall (*Yorkshire Fines*, i. 144–5), and William Dereman witnessed a charter of Hugh de Morville lord of Burgh by Sands before 1202 (*Wetherhal Reg.*, no. 102).

de ESSEBY
(Modern form: ASHBY?)

Although there is an Esbie in Dumfriesshire which may have given rise to a Scottish surname, the family dealt with here took its name from Castle Ashby, Northamptonshire. In the reign of Henry I William son of Clarembald, perhaps of Flemish origin, was tenant of 3¼ hides in Castle Ashby and Chadstone (Farrer, *HKF* ii. 334). Among William's descendants, probably, were David de Essebi recorded *c.* 1147, and David de Essebi, a knight of the king of Scotland (as lord of the Honour of Huntingdon?) to whom custody of Fotheringay Castle was committed by the English regency government in 1219 (ibid.). David was so characteristic a personal name in this family that the estate it held in Castle Ashby was known as Ashby David (Davit or Davy).

In the earlier thirteenth century Clarembald de Esseby leased to St. Cuthbert and St. Æbba and Coldingham Priory two fishings in the River Tweed at Fishwick, in Hutton, Berwickshire (one probably the fishing known as Abstel), in perpetual ferme for 8*s.* per annum. These fishings had been given to Clarebald by his lord Walter (II) Olifard (Raine, *North Durham*, nos. 158, 159).

If it was this Clarebald after whom the farm of Clarabad in Hutton was named (above, p. 35, n. 23), then Clermiston west of Edinburgh must have received its name from a different person, for the *firma Clerenbaud* (whence Clermiston) is found before 1186 (*RRS* ii, no. 199); but it is possible that only one individual was involved, an earlier Clarembald (de Esseby?)

intervening between William son of Clarembald and the thirteenth-century Clarebald.

William de Asseby and his son Peter held land at Lilliesleaf, Roxburghshire and 'Inglisberry' (now Grange Hall), Lanarkshire in the late twelfth century (*Dryburgh Liber*, nos. 221–3), but their relationship to the foregoing, if any, is unknown.

Black, *Surnames*, s.v. ASHBY.

de EU
(Ew, Ou, Ouh, etc.)
(Modern form: none known)

A family taking its surname from Eu on the north-east boundary of Normandy and having a close though unexplained connection with the Norman family of Vieuxpont (above, pp. 73, 94) is found in Scotland from the middle of the twelfth century. Hugh of Eu (de Auco) was present with David I at the siege of the castle of Norham on Tweed in June 1138 (Lawrie, *Charters*, no. 119). Roger de Ou granted to Kelso Abbey the church of his toun of Langton, Berwickshire, for the soul's weal of Earl Henry (i.e. Henry son of David I, d. 1152), by a charter issued in the time of G[amel] dean of Fogo, *c.* 1150–62, confirmed by William I *c.* 1165–6 (*Kelso Liber*, no. 138; *RRS* ii, no. 63). By 1178 Langton was in the possession of William de Vieuxpont (ibid., no. 182). Roger's charter was witnessed by, i.a., Henry Parson of Langton, Hugh de Ou, and Thomas de Ou.

Philip de Ew granted a toft and 2 acres of arable, with common pasture for two horses and seven oxen, in the feu which he held in Carriden, West Lothian (as tenant of de Vieuxpont? See *RRS* ii, nos. 5, 182), to Soutra Hospital, by a charter witnessed by, i.a., Duncan clerk of 'Balueard' [i.e. Balbardie in Bathgate] and Roger Ew (*Soutra Reg.*, no. 3). As is shown by the rubric to the cartulary copy of this charter, Philip's estate became known as 'Philpdawystoun', i.e. 'Philip de Eu's toun', now called Philpingstone (for other forms see A. Macdonald, *Place-Names of West Lothian*, 32; and see above, p. 38). Philip's daughter Eda married (possibly not as her first husband) Reginald 'of Carriden', and his charter granting to Culross Abbey (founded 1218) land of his wife's marriage portion in Carriden (one acre of meadow in exchange for a toft and a small garden) was witnessed by, i.a., Roger son of Philip de Eu, Duncan the clerk (see above) and Walter 'son of Eda'. Reginald's charter mentions the boundary between the land of Philip de Eu and that of Sir William de Vieuxpont (*Analecta Scotica*, 2nd ser., Edinburgh: T. G. Stevenson, 1837, pp. 14–15).

A mid-twelfth-century charter of the earliest William de Vieuxpont to appear in Scottish record (*Holyrood Liber*, no. 43), anent Ogilface in Torphichen, was witnessed by, i.a., Reginald 'of Ponthieu' (de Puntiu), Ponthieu being not far to the east of Eu, along with Richard de Vieuxpont, Roger Quirem, Roger 'of Carriden', and Godwin 'of Carriden'.

de FERSELEY
(FRESCHELE, FRESSELEY, etc.)
(Modern form: FRIZELL)

In 1249 Geoffrey de Ferseley, knight, had a charter from Alexander II allowing him to hold his land at Crail in free warren (BL Add. Chrs. 66570). The surname is from Farsley north of Pudsey, in the West Riding of Yorkshire, between Bradford and Leeds. The chief sources for the history of the family in Yorkshire are the *Calverley Charters*, the *Pontefract Chartulary*, the *Kirkstall Coucher Book*, and *Yorkshire Fines*. One of the earliest references is to Ralph of Farsley, *c.* 1150–60 (*EYC* vi, no. 69), but the favoured personal names were Simon and Geoffrey.

In Scottish sources references become increasingly plentiful after *c.* 1280 (e.g. *CDS* ii. 172 and nos. 508, 730, 1197, 1481, 1594; *St. Andrews Liber*, 284, 341–2, 385; *Cambuskenneth Reg.*, 6, 9, 10, 12–14, 18, 20; *Scone Liber*, no. 84; *Kelso Liber*, no. 198; *Lindores Liber*, no. 10; *Spalding Miscellany*, ii. 312; *Dunfermline Reg.*, nos. 176, 349; Fraser, *Wemyss*, ii, nos. 6, 163, 164). Perthshire and Fife were the areas in which the family held land in the early period.

Simon 'de Freschele' (*alias* 'de Fersle', 'de Fersele', etc.), who swore fealty to Edward I at the high altar of Lindores Abbey, 23 July 1291, probably belonged to the branch of this family holding Fargie in Arngask. E. L. G. Stones and G. G. Simpson, *Edward I and the Throne of Scotland, 1290–1296* (OUP for University of Glasgow, 1979), ii. 124, 368, mistakenly assign him to the Fraser family (see index s.v. Fraser).

Black, *Surnames*, s.v. FRESSELEY, is wrong to state that the surname has entirely disappeared; it is likely to be represented at least in some instances by the modern name Frizell (etc.), usually regarded only as a variant of Fraser.

de GURLE
(GURLAI, GURNAY, etc.)
(Modern form: GOURLAY)

The place of origin was probably continental, and if forms with an 'n' were at all common it would be tempting to suggest Gournai-en-Bray (arr. Neufchatel) in eastern Normandy. But apart from the late examples of Aleyn Gurnay of Roxburghshire in 1296 (*CDS* ii. 199) and (in English records relating to Scotland) Thomas de Gornay or Gurney and Hugh de Gurney (*CDS* ii, nos. 1004, 1637) such forms do not seem to occur, and there is consistent spelling with 'l'. It may be tentatively suggested that we have to do with Gourel, in the canton of Bacqueville and arrondissement of Dieppe. L. Goudallier, 'Écosse et Picardie (relations entre ces deux pays)', *Bulletin de la Société des Antiquaires de Picardie*, xxi (1904), 502, connects the Scottish Gourlays with 'les Gourlay, seigneurs de Monsures', but without locating 'Gourlay' (I owe this reference to Mr Geoffrey Stell). The earliest members of the family to appear in Scotland were associated with a branch of the house of Balliol, whose original home was at Tours-en-Vimeu in Picardy, close to the north-eastern border of Normandy (*Holyrood Liber*, no. 81), and members of the family used Christian names, e.g. Ingram (Enguerrand) and Hugh, characteristic of the Balliols. Enguerrand Gurlai and his brother Sir 'Yardus' witnessed a deed by Enguerrand (I) de Balliol anent churches in Galloway (*Holyrood Liber*, no. 70, *c*. 1230), and this was perhaps the Sir Enguerrand de Gurlay found in Angus 1246 X 69 (*Arbroath Liber*, i, Appendix, Cartae Originales, no. X). Henry 'de Gurley' was first witness to Enguerrand (I) de Balliol's confirmation of Inverkeilour church to Arbroath Abbey (*Arbroath Liber*, i, no. 58), and the second witness was Thomas 'de Wadrithurt', undoubtedly Vaudricourt, about half-way between Eu and Abbeville and some 20 km west of Bailleul-en-Vimeu. In 1245 Enguerrand Gurle witnessed a royal charter in the company of Henry de Balliol the chamberlain (*Cambuskenneth Reg.*, no. 171). Hugh and William Gurle, brothers, were removed from the king of Scotland's council in 1255 (Stones, *Relations*, no. 10). Henry de Gorlay is found in the company of Enguerrand (II) de Balliol lord of Redcastle in 1286 (*Arbroath Liber*, i. 333). Black, *Surnames*, s.vv. GOURLAY (where the early chronology is unreliable) and GURNAY, which Black took to be a distinct surname.

de HORSEY
(HORCY, HORSI, HORSIA, etc.)
(Modern form: none known)

The surname is derived from Horsey, 1½ miles north of Bridgwater, Somerset. For the family in that county and Dorset, which survived until well into the sixteenth century, see especially J. Batten in *Proceedings of the Somerset Arch. and Natural Hist. Soc.* xliii (1897), 84–93; J. Hutchins, *History of Dorset* (1774), ii. 458–9; W. Pole, *Collections towards a Description of the County of Devon* (ed. de la Pole, 1791), 210; *Stogursey Charters*, 22. The earliest recorded members of the family were Philip (*temp.* Henry II) and his sons Walter and William, and there is also reference to a Thomas de Horsey. Hugh de Horsea, who had a hand in the murder of Thomas Becket in 1170, may also have belonged to this family.

In Scotland, grants of land in Beith (including Threepwood), Ayrshire, to Kilwinning Abbey by Philip de Horssey are said by T. Pont to have been recorded in the lost Kilwinning cartulary, where Philip's wife was named as Dorothea de Morville daughter of Richard de Morville (d. 1189) and their son and heir was named Walter (*Cuninghame topographized*, 254–5).

The surname does not seem to have survived in Scotland.

de la LECQUERAYE
(Modern form: none known)

The surname is from the village of Saint-Jean-de-la-Lecqueraye (canton Saint-Georges-du-Vièvre, arr. Pont-Audemer, dép. Eure). Men of this surname called Richard and Robert occur in the Norman exchequer rolls of the late twelfth century (*Rot.Scacc.Norm.*, i. 248, ii. 329). In Scotland Roger and William de la Lecqueraye were associated with the de Vieuxpont family (above, p. 94, n. 6) at the turn of the twelfth and thirteenth centuries (*Kelso Liber*, nos. 139–41; *Holyrood Liber*, nos. 33, 41, 44; *Cambuskenneth Reg.*, no. 73).

Black, *Surnames*, s.v. LACRAIE. The surname does not seem to have survived in Scotland.

de LASCELLES
(LACELES, LASCELAS, etc.)
(Modern forms: LESSELLS, LESSELS)

It seems most likely that the earliest Lascelles in Scotland belonged to an Anglo-Norman family from Loucelles in Calvados which acquired land in Bedfordshire, Yorkshire, and Westmorland and, through an early connection with the baronial house of Beauchamp of Bedford, became associated with the de Morvilles. A characteristic personal name was Alan, but a wide range of personal names was employed and a Peter de Lascelas occurs in a de Morville context, 1162 X 67 (*CWAAS Trans.* ix. 253–9; see also Loyd, *Origins*, 55, s.v. LOCELS; *HMC 10th Rep.*, App., 320–1, 324).

Alan de Lascelles witnessed Lawrie, *Charters*, no. 244, an act of Henry son of David I anent Holm Cultram Abbey in Cumberland, 1136 X 1152. Alan de Lascelles witnessed the confirmation, by Bishop Richard of St. Andrews, of the earl of Fife's grant of Cupar parish church to St. Andrews Cathedral Priory, 1165 X 1172 (*St. Andrews Liber*, 137), and by that time he had no doubt acquired an estate in Scotland, perhaps in north-east Fife. This was presumably the Alan de Lascelles who, an elderly as well as a wealthy man, was captured at Alnwick with King William in 1174 (Lawrie, *Annals*, 176–7). His wife was Juliana de Somerville (see below under Somerville), and their son and heir, also Alan, married a lady named Amable (*St. Andrews Liber*, 260, dating 1199 X 1202). It would be natural to assume that the elder Alan had acquired the lordship of Forgan *alias* Naughton were it not for the fact that his son Alan expressly says that his grant of the parish church of Forgan was made with the consent and at the prompting of his wife (but the church might have formed part of her dower). The younger Alan's charter was witnessed by Duncan de Lascelles, probably Alan's brother, and also by Henry (read Hervey?) and Richard de Lascelles. For Duncan's career see above, pp. 115–6. The senior male line of the family ended before the middle of the thirteenth century, leaving an heiress Marjorie de Lascelles who married firstly, Peter de la Hay, and secondly Richard Murray of Culbin. These marriages seem to have led to a permanent division of the barony of Forgan or Naughton.

The surname survives plentifully in Fife.

Black, *Surnames*, s.v. LESSELS.

de LONDRES
(LONDONIIS, LONDONIARUM, etc.)
(Modern form: none known)

Richard Londoniarum witnessed a charter for Bruton Priory, Somerset, 1142 X 66 (*Bruton Cartulary*, no. 4), no doubt the Somerset landowner Richard de London who in 1166 held a half-knight's fee of William de Mohun and a whole fee of William de Courcy (*RBE* i. 225, 227), as well as a fractional fee in Devon (ibid. 253). London is the name of an ancient township in Old Cleeve on the north coast of Somerset, but the forms of the surname point to derivation from the city of London.

It has been suggested that Richard de London was a son of William son of Humphrey by Emma, heiress of William de Falaise and Geva (*Stogursey Charters*, 23), Emma having been married previously to William I de Courcy. Richard's wife was Maud de Ferrers (*Dryburgh Liber*, no. 53), and their daughter Isota, who took her mother's surname, was mother of Alexander, William and Maurice de London (*Stogursey Charters*, 23).

Richard de London evidently had a brother Thomas who entered the service of David I and appears occasionally as a witness to acts of that king and of Malcolm IV (Lawrie, *Charters*, nos. 90, 220; *RRS* i, nos. 132, 133, 174, 197). Thomas married (as her second husband) Margaret, an heiress in Roxburghshire previously married to Ralph Lovel II. Thomas had evidently acquired Lessudden (St. Boswells) whose parish church he endowed (*Dryburgh Liber*, no. 58), and since he left no children this estate passed to his nephew Robert de London, son of Richard de London and Maud de Ferrers (ibid., nos. 53, 54; note that Robert's grant to Dryburgh Abbey was for the souls of Thomas and Maurice de London, while in *Melrose Liber*, no. 88, Thomas is said to be Robert's uncle).

Robert de London married Isabel Visdelou, heiress of the small Honour of Visdelou (most of whose lands lay in Berkshire). He obviously spent much time in Scotland and incurred the forfeiture of his English estates in 1174 doubtless because he had remained loyal to William I during the great revolt of 1173-4 (Farrer, *HKF* i. 55, 134). He must of course be distinguished from his namesake Robert de London the younger, the most prominent and favoured of William I's bastards. Nevertheless, the identity of surname and the younger Robert's landholding in Lessudden show that the two men were in some degree related. It seems probable that the younger Robert's mother was either a daughter or a sister of Robert the elder. King William's chamberlain Walter of Berkley (see above, under Berkley) was a cousin (*cognatus*) of Robert de London the elder. John de London, who appears in royal charters in the 1170s and 1180s (*RRS* ii, references in index) was probably a younger brother of the elder Robert, while Richard de London, appearing 1198 X 1214 (*Kelso Liber*, no. 139) may have been the son of either Robert or John. The likelihood that Richard of London (de Londres), keeper of Cork on behalf of William Fitz Aldelin in 1177 (G. H. Orpen, *Ireland under the Normans*, ii. 38; Giraldus Cambrensis, *Expugnatio Hibernica*, ed. A. B. Scott and F. X. Martin (Dublin, 1978),

184-5), belonged to this family seems to be strengthened by the prominence in Ireland of Maurice of London in the late twelfth/early thirteenth century (Orpen, op. cit., iii. 71, 89; *Calendar of Documents relating to Ireland*, ed. H. S. Sweetman, i (1875), *passim*, references in Index). Another member of the family (a long-lived daughter of Richard I de London?) was Eschina de London who married (as her first husband) Walter son of Alan the first of the Stewarts (above, p. 65).
Black, *Surnames*, s.v. LUNDIN, is seriously misleading.

de LOPEN
(DOLEPENE, DOLOPEN, de OLEPENE, etc.)
(Modern form: none known)

In 1166 Henry de Lopena and John Belet held one knight's fee in Somerset of William de Mohun (*RBE* i. 227). Henry's surname was taken from Lopen in south Somerset, divided into Lopen Magna (said to have belonged to the family of Malet, J. Collinson, *History of Somerset*, iii. 122) and Lopen Parva *alias* Lopen Abbatis, which belonged to the order of the Temple and was dependent on the preceptory of Temple Combe. The Lovels apparently had some interest in Lopen Parva (ibid.).

In Scotland a relatively prominent role seems to have been played in the 1170s by Brother William de Olepene (Dolopene etc.), who was either a knight of the Hospital (*St. Andrews Liber*, 319 would suggest as much) or (in view of the Templars' interest in Lopen) a knight of the Temple (Lawrie, *Annals*, 126; *Kelso Liber*, no. 214; *RRS* ii, nos. 59, 60). For reasons stated above (pp. 103-4) it seems probable that members of this family settled permanently in Scotland.
Black, *Surnames*, s.v. DOLEPAIN.

LOVEL
(LUPELLUS, LUVEL)
(Modern form: LOVELL)

For the main line of the family see *Comp. Pge.* viii. 199-205, and Sanders, *Baronies*, 27-8. In 1086 Ralph Lovel I was a tenant in Somerset and Sussex of the count of Mortain and of Walter of Douai. His son was perhaps Baldwin, and his grandson was Ralph II, keeper of Castle Cary in 1138 on behalf of Robert of Bampton, son of Walter of Douai. Ralph II's wife was Margaret who was either the heiress or else the dowager of Hawick, Roxburghshire. Their eldest son was Henry Lovel I, a tenant in chief in Somerset in 1166. A younger son may have been the Robert Lovel who was a sub-tenant in 1166.

Henry Lovel I witnessed *RRS* i, no. 265 and ii. nos, 80, 116, 183 (spanning the period 1165-77), and to this period belongs his grant of two oxgangs at Branxholm, west of Hawick (*St. Andrews Liber*, 261). There is little reference to Lovels in Scottish record between then and the mid-thirteenth century, but a Somerset fine of 1219 involving Richard Lovel I

refers to Scottish estates (*Somerset Fines, Richard I–Edward I* (1892), 33–4) and Richard Lovel II's relief for Hawick appears on the *Exchequer Rolls* (i. 28–9). The simultaneous possession of Hawick and Castle Cary was maintained, or claimed, until well into the fourteenth century, posing severe problems of divided loyalty after the Anglo-Scottish wars began in 1296. Richard Lovel III, who died in 1351, married Muriel daughter of Sir John de Soules, Guardian of Scotland, 1301–3.
Black, *Surnames*, s.v. LOVELL.

MALTALENT
(MAUTALAND, MAUTALENT etc.)
(Modern form: MAITLAND)

The account in *Scots Pge.* v. 275 ff. may be briefly supplemented by pointing out (1) that a Robert Maltalent witnessed Yorkshire charters of Roger de Mowbray, 1138 X 45 (Greenway, *Mowbray Charters*, nos. 195, 363); (2) that the earliest recorded member of the family which in the thirteenth century acquired Thirlestane in the lordship of Lauderdale seems to have been William Maltal(en)t, who witnessed a charter for Lanercost Priory, Cumberland, by Hugh son of Simon de Morville, lord of Burgh by Sands (*Trans.Roy.Soc.Lit.*, 2nd ser. viii. 454 and index); and (3) that a Gilbert Maltalent witnessed a charter of Philip de Valognes anent Torpenhow, Cumberland, *c.* 1200 (*EYC* vi. 125), noteworthy since the earliest occurrence of Thomas Maitland, undoubtedly one of the family established in Scotland, is as a witness to another act of Philip de Valognes, 1213 X 1215 (*Panmure Reg.* ii. 125–6). Apparently of a younger generation than Thomas were William Matalent (Mautalent) and Richard Mautalent who founded the family of Maitland of Thirlestane by marrying Avicia, heir of the older native Northumbrian-family of lairds of Thirlestane traceable back to Winter who lived in the first half of the twelfth century.
Black, *Surnames*, s.v. MAITLAND.

de MOUBRAY
(Modern forms: MOWBRAY, MOUBRAY)

The Moubrays, lords of vast estates in Yorkshire and the north midlands of England, were among the relatively small number of great feudal families to be deeply implicated in the great revolt against Henry II in 1173–4. The first member of the family to settle permanently in Scotland was Philip, younger brother of William de Moubray (one of the Magna Carta barons), both being sons of Nigel de Moubray who died at Acre in Palestine in 1191. Robert de Moubray who was second witness to a charter (*Kelso Liber*, no. 305, 1190?) of William of Conisbrough, nephew of Geoffrey of Conisbrough (first feudal lord of Stapelgordon, Dumfriesshire) was probably Nigel's younger brother Robert who outlived him (Greenway, *Mowbray Charters*, p. xxix and elsewhere *passim*).

Philip de Moubray married a Scottish heiress, Galiena daughter of

Waltheof son of Cospatric, lord of Dalmeny, Inverkeithing, and Moncreiffe or Dunbarney (*Dunfermline Reg.*, nos. 165, 166, 211; *Moncreiffs*, ii, Appendix, no. I). Other members of the Moubray family, and persons whose names connect them with the Honour of Mowbray, appearing in Scotland associated with Philip de Moubray were the clerk Robert de Moubrai (ibid.), Henry 'de Houtorp' (ibid.), evidently from Howthorpe near Hovingham; Patrick 'de Nagtun' (ibid., no. II), evidently from Nawton east of Helmsley, and with a brother called Bernald 'de Grahm' (unlocated); and Oliver de Busci (*Arbroath Liber*, i, no. 119).

Philip de Moubray had sons named Roger (who succeeded him) and Nigel; there are several references to Roger in *CDS* i, but no. 1868, a grant of a weekly market in Hovingham, 1252, refers to his first cousin and namesake, head of the senior line of the family and lord of the Honour of Mowbray.

According to Alexander Nisbet (Nisbet, *Heraldry*, ii, Appendix, 21–2) the senior line of the ancient family of Moubray in Scotland ended with the death *c.* 1675 of Sir Robert Mowbray of Barnbougle, and the family was represented in the mid-eighteenth century by John Mowbray of Cockairnie and his brother Robert, the king's master-carpenter for North Britain. Black, *Surnames*, s.v. MOWBRAY.

de MONTE ALTO
(MOHAUD, MONTALT, MUHAUT, etc.)
(Modern form: MOWAT(T), MOUAT(T))

The surname is derived from the Norman name given to the place in Flintshire now called Mold. An important tenant and vassal of Hugh of Avranches, second post-Conquest earl of Chester, was Hugh son of Norman, who held, among many other estates, the manor of 'Biscopestreu' or Bistre, where a conspicuous Norman castle was built, called in French *le mont haut*, the high 'castle hill' or 'motte', now Mold. Hugh's descendants, hereditary stewards of the earldom of Chester, adopted this as their surname (*Cheshire Domesday*, 50, 241; Farrer, *HKF* ii, pp. vi, 110–12, 236–7).

The earliest members of the family to appear in Scotland were Alexander, a clergyman, and William (both associated with bishops of Brechin), and two brothers Robert and Michael, who seem to have been dependants of William Comyn earl of Buchan (see above, pp. 27–8, and nn. 134–5). Black, *Surnames*, s.v. MOUATT (where the reference to Robert de Monte Alto in the reign of David I should be disregarded).

de MULCASTER
(MOLECASTRE, MULCASTRE, MAUECESTRIA, etc.)
(Modern form: MUNCASTER)

The lands of Muncaster and Pennington in West Cumberland were held in the twelfth and thirteenth centuries by a family which seems to have been of native Cumbrian stock. Members of the family were slow to adopt any fixed surname, but by the thirteenth century both Muncaster and Pennington were used and it is impossible to be sure whether any principle underlay the choice of one place-name rather than the other. Commonly used Christian names were Alan, Benedict, Robert, and William. It is not known how the family acquired possession of the feu of Giffen (Giffin), *alias* Trearn, in Cunningham, Ayrshire, but it was probably through a marriage between a male member of the Muncaster/Pennington family and an heiress of the west-Norman family of de Néhou which held Giffen in the twelfth century. The link may go back to the twelfth century, for *c.* 1136–41 William I of Lancaster, connected with the de Morvilles later lords of Cunningham, was said to be lord of Muncaster over the Penningtons and under Robert de Romilly (Farrer, *Lancashire Pipe Rolls and Early Charters*, 305). In 1278 Alan of Pennington, father of William, claimed Giffen as his hereditary right from his ancestor Benedict of Pennington, and bargained to exchange his land in Cumberland for Giffen with Robert of Muncaster (who apparently had possession of Giffen at that time); one of the conditions being that his son William would marry Alice daughter of Benedict, said to be the heir (possible granddaughter?) of Robert of Muncaster (*CDS* ii, no. 133). Scottish record seems to know nothing of these members of the family, but Dryburgh Abbey charters show that a Walter of Muncaster was the successor at Giffen of Alexander de Néhou son of William de Néhou and his wife Syrit (*Dryburgh Liber*, 164–8). It seems improbable that Alan's son William married Alice daughter of Benedict of Muncaster, for in February 1304 she was said to be residing in Scotland with King Edward I's enemies (*Cal.Fine*, i. 488), while William of Pennington was in possession of Muncaster in 1301, his father having died in 1293 (*St. Bees Reg.*, 241). In view of the appearance of Walter of Muncaster as successor at Giffen of the de Néhous we should note that Sir Walter of Muncaster knight witnessed Cumberland deeds of *c.* 1285 (ibid., 564, 569); and in general on the family and its earliest known members see ibid., references in index s.vv. Mulcastre, Pennington.

The surname does not seem to have survived in Scotland.

de MULINAUS
(MULINEYS, MULINAS)
(Modern form: MOLYNEUX)

The presence in Scotland of at least one person named Vivian de Mulinaus, perhaps of two in successive generations, was evidently due to the link between the families of de Morville and Lancaster. A charter of William de Morville, son of Avicia de Lancaster, for Furness Abbey, 1189 X 96, was witnessed by Vivian de Mulinas (*CDS* i, no. 265). A charter of William II de Lancaster, brother of Avicia, in favour of Thomas son of Adam of Raiswaith concerning land in Winsterthwaites (lost, in Crook,Westmorland) was witnessed by the donor's brother Roger and William de Molineus (*HMC 10th Rep.*, pt. 4, App., p. 325; *Kendale Records*, i. 342). Conceivably 'William' is a misrendering of 'Vivian', but even if the name is correct the witness was probably related to the family associated with Sefton in south Lancashire from the twelfth century to the present (*Lancashire Inquests*, 12; *VCH, Lancs*. iii. 67 ff.; *Cockersand Chartulary*, ii, pt. II, 591, A.D. 1219). In Scotland, Vivian de Mulinaus usually appears in a Morville (or post-Morville) context, and he acquired land in Lauderdale from Alan of Galloway, afterwards exchanged for land at Saltoun (*Glasgow Reg*., no. 46; *Kelso Liber*, no. 246; *Soutra Reg*., nos. 12, 32). Once he appears associated with Enguerrand de Balliol in a Kirkcudbrightshire document (*Holyrood Liber*, no. 70), but in the company of knights of Cunningham.

In *VCH, Lancs*. iii. 67, n. 7, the name is said to be derived from Moulineaux (unlocated) in the department of Seine-Maritime, but the place-name is not uncommon and proof seems lacking. In Scotland the surname does not seem to have survived.

le NAIN
(NANUS, le NEYM, etc.)
(Modern form: NEAME?)

No continental place of origin has yet been discovered for the family settled in Scotland from the mid-twelfth century which used the surname Le Nain (Nanus, Nainus, Namus, le Naim, le Neym, etc., 'dwarf'), not listed in Black, *Surnames*. A Maurice Nanus witnessed an act by the bishop of Saint-Malo in 1182 (Delisle–Berger, *Recueil*, ii. 227). The family survived in Scotland until the late thirteenth century, but it is noteworthy that there seems to be no mention of the surname in the voluminous record generated by the first war of independence.

The first recorded member of the family in Scotland was Ralph (I) le Nain, who is found witnessing royal acts in the reigns of Malcolm IV and William I (*RRS* i and ii, refs. in indices), perhaps as late as *c*. 1180, although the witness of *RRS* ii, no. 222 might have been Ralph I's son Ralph II.

Ralph I certainly lived until 1175 for after the consecration of Jocelin as bishop of Glasgow he granted the chapel of Broughton, Peeblesshire (a dependency of Stobo), a half ploughgate of arable in Broughton, with the consent of his son and heir Richard (*Glasgow Reg*., no. 48). The estates held by the main line of the family, apparently from their earliest appearance in Scotland, were Broughton and Yetholm (or at least a part of Yetholm) in Roxburghshire. Although the account of Yetholm in *OPS* does not give any hint of partition, some early territorial division of the parish seems to be indicated, first, by the present topographical distinction between Kirk Yetholm and Town Yetholm, secondly, by the existence in 1298 of an ecclesiastical benefice of Parva Yetham (Stevenson, *Documents*, ii. 290) and by the 'manorial' place-name Yetham-Naym (and variants; see *CDS* iii. 67, 322, 374; *RMS* i, App. II, no. 292, n. 1). Significantly the 'manorial' name does not seem to be recorded until after the family of that surname had disappeared, but presumably the place-name was in popular use well before the fourteenth century. The tenurial link between Broughton and Yetholm survived as late as 1407 (*OPS* i. 201).

Appendix B

A further property of the family, probably held by Ralph II rather than his father, was Inverugie St. Fergus in Buchan, Aberdeenshire, the church of which (with the dependent chapel of Fetterangus) was given by Ralph II to Arbroath Abbey (*Arbroath Liber*, i. 6, 137, 139); it may be that Hangmans Hill close to the ruins of Inverugie Castle is the site of a motte-castle built by Ralph II le Nain (see *Aberdeen–Banff Illustrations*, ii. 397–8).

Documentary references to members of the Le Nain family, too numerous to be cited here, suggest the following descent:

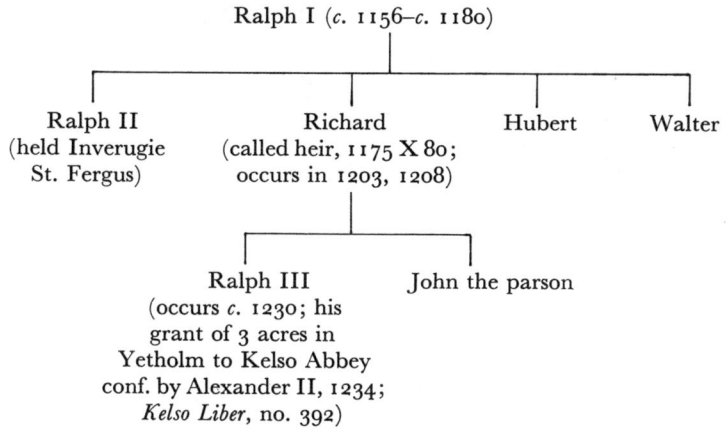

We may note that an early parson of Yetholm was Nicholas 'de Gleynwim' (i.e. Glenholm), for Glenholm is adjacent to Broughton (*OPS* i. 427). The surname does not appear to have survived in Scotland.

de NEHOU
(Modern form: none known)

For this family see above, p. 79, and n. 105, and also in this Appendix under de MULCASTER. The surname is from the commune of Néhou, at one time the *caput* of the Norman Honour of Vernon, in the arrondissement of Valognes and department of Manche. In Scotland, through dependence on the house of de Morville, William de Néhou acquired the estate of Giffen in Cunningham, Ayrshire. The surname survived in Scotland into the thirteenth century, but no form seems to have survived in modern times.

de PERCEHAY

A (Walter?) de Percehay witnessed a charter of Herbert son of Wimund of Etton (Yorks., E.R.), 1129 × 35, and a presumably later Walter de

Percehay appears in record relating to Birdsall in 1168, while a Walter de Percehay held half of Crambe, North Riding, of the fee of Paynel in 1219 (*EYC* ii. 44, 368, 395). In 1284 (at the time of Kirkby's Quest) Walter de Percehay held land of the fee of Lutterel at Ryton near Pickering in the North Riding (*Feudal Aids*, vi. 66, 68; see also R. H. Skaife, *Kirkby's Inquest for Yorkshire* (Surtees Soc., 1867), 434 (a Walter de Perscehay, £20 tenant in the Wapentake of Ryedale, 1255)). This last-named Walter would have been the Walter de Pershay who *c.* 1280, as son and heir of the lady Jean of Wilton, made a grant of land in Tarvit parish, Fife, confirming his gift a few years later as Sir Walter de Percehay knight (G. W. S. Barrow (ed.), *The Scottish Tradition* (1973), 35–7), the inference being that Walter's father had married one of the heiresses of the Roxburghshire barony of Wilton, whose lord in the earlier thirteenth century had acquired part of Tarvit. In September 1289 Sir Walter de Percehay was one of the band of men who ambushed and killed Duncan III, earl of Fife (one of the six Guardians of Scotland), at Pitpullox by Broomfield, west of Brechin. Sir Walter fled south with two esquires, but they were overtaken at Covington in Lanarkshire by Sir Andrew Murray of Petty, who had them executed on the spot (ibid. 37–8). It is possible that Philip de Perthay, a Lanarkshire landholder in 1296, belonged to this family (*CDS* ii. 213). For a later Sir Walter de Percehay, knight, in the North Riding see *Rot.Scot.* i. 528b, 574 (1338–9) and *Feudal Aids*, vi. 177 (1316).
Black, *Surnames*, s.v. PERTHAY.

PESSUN
(PESSHUN, PEYSSON, etc.)
(Modern form: none known)

In 1242–3 Ingram Pessun held one knight's fee in Barrowby, Lincolnshire, of Earl Richard (of Cornwall) as of the Honour of Eye, and William Pessun held a half fee in Keston, Kent, of William de Say (*Book of Fees*, 668, 675, 1034, 1085). By 1296 Ingram was dead and his widow Cecily had married Thomas de Quynquerstaynes. Ingram's heir was his grandson Stephen Pessun holding land in England and Scotland (*Cal.Fine*, i. 374, 405). It would appear that Stephen's mother had the same name as his grandmother, for Cecily mother of Stephen Pessun (who was deceased by 1305) is referred to in 1307 (ibid. 506, 555); unless this Stephen was Ingram's son and father of Ingram's grandson of that name.

In Scotland in 1296 Richard Pessun was a tenant of the bishop of St. Andrews in Stirlingshire (*CDS* ii. 205; *Rot.Scot.* i. 27a). William Pessun was a tenant at Tynninghame, an estate belonging to the see of St. Andrews (*CDS* ii. 201). In the same year, Stephen Pesson of Scotland, supporter of King John, had his Lincolnshire manor of Barrowby seized (ibid. ii. 171, 174); Stephen was in France with Sir Thomas Randolph the elder in 1296 (Stevenson, *Documents*, ii. 94–5), and with the bishop of St. Andrews (William Lamberton) in 1298. He was dead by 1304 and his widow Christian had married Ketell of Leitholm, Stephen's son William still

being a minor (*CDS* ii, no. 1838; for William in Edward II's peace in 1319, see ibid. iii, no. 678).
Black, *Surnames*, s.v. PESSUN.

REVEL
(RIVEL)
(Modern form: REVILL)

In 1166 Richard Revel (the elder) held a half knight's fee of Muchelney Abbey, Somerset, to be identified with Downhead in West Camel (*RBE* i. 224; *Muchelney Cartulary*, 111; *VCH, Somerset*, iii. 73). From Richard I Richard Revel received Langport and Curry (i.e. Curry Rivel), with the forest pertaining to Curry, for two knights' service (*Cartae Antiquae Rolls*, 11–20, ed. J. Conway Davies (Pipe Roll Soc., N.S. xxxiii. 1960), no. 513). From the same king he had a grant of socage in the royal manor of Somerton and a rent of £50 p.a. in Horncastle, Lincolnshire (ibid., no. 514; *RBE* ii. 796), and a meadow in Ilchester worth 2s. p.a. (*Book of Fees*, 78–9). In 1210–11 the abbot of Muchelney levied a fine with Richard Revel anent Downhead (*Somerset Fines*, 27). It was presumably this Richard who witnessed, with Henry Lovel II, lord of Castle Cary and Hawick, an acknowledgement made by Henry de Careville in the full county court of Somerset meeting at Ilchester (1209–11) in favour of Bruton Priory (*Bruton Cartulary*, no. 19b). With his son Richard, the elder Richard Revel was involved in a lawsuit in the county court of Somerset in 1204 (*Curia Regis Rolls*, iii. 129–30).

Richard the elder was dead by 27 June 1213 (*Muchelney Cartulary*, 63), and evidently died during the Interdict, for he could not be given Christian burial until 31 March 1215, at Muchelney Abbey (ibid. 31). His heir was his son Richard the younger, who confirmed a deed by his father for Muchelney in 1213 (ibid. 28).

Henry Revel was evidently a younger brother of Richard Revel the elder. He first appears in Scottish record in the 1170s, when King William gave him in marriage Margaret daughter of Orm lord of Abernethy, and with her granted to Henry an estate made up of the easternmost portions of the lordship of Abernethy, i.e. Corbie (now Birkhill), Coultra, Balmerino, etc. (*RRS* ii, nos. 147, 152; *St. Andrews Liber*, 271). Henry had a son named Alan (*RRS* ii, no. 330) who must have predeceased his father for Henry's heir in Scotland was his nephew Richard Revel the younger, to whom William I and Alexander II confirmed Coultra etc. (ibid., no. 573; *Balmerino Liber*, no. 3, Alexander II's charter dating X 1221). Richard the younger died c. 1222 (*Book of Fees*, i. 78), his heir by his wife Mabel Hunsworth (sister and heir of Walter of Ashley) being their daughter Sabina who married Henry de l'Orty (*Comp. Pge.* x. 181–2; *Somerset Fines*, 57). In Scotland, however, the heir of Richard the younger was his brother Adam 'of Stawell', whose surname was taken from the hamlet of Stawell 4½ miles north-east of Bridgwater (*St. Andrews Liber.* 271–2; *Balmerino Liber*, no. 1; *Somerset Fines*, 28; *Somerset Pleas*, no. 1288). Adam of Stawell sold his estates in Fife to the queen dowager of Scotland, Ermengarde, who was seeking land on which to found a Cistercian abbey (*Balmerino Liber*, nos. 1, 4). Black, *Surnames*, s.v. REUEL, is seriously misleading.

RIPLEY
(Modern form: none known)

This family (on the male side at least of native Northumbrian stock) took its surname from the village of Ripley on the River Nidd in the West Riding of Yorkshire, between Harrogate and Ripon. Information about the earliest generations of the family is given in *EYC* i. 403 ff.; and x. 63, 65, 97–9; W. T. Lancaster, *Early History of Ripley and the Ingilby Family* (1918).

A prominent member of the family at the turn of the twelfth and thirteenth centuries was Bernard 'the clerk' of Ripley. His brother Richard had sons named William and Bernard, both of whom seem to have settled in Scotland. To William King William I granted the estate of Dallas in Moray to hold by military service (SRO Reg. Ho. charters, no. 58), and he was progenitor of the ancient family of Dallas of that ilk (J. Dallas, *The History of the Family of Dallas and their Connections and Descendants from the Twelfth Century* (1921), esp. pp. 22–4). It seems equally probable that it was William of Ripley's brother Bernard of Ripley who obtained the hand of a Scottish heiress named Margaret and with her acquired the estate of Kirkandrews (in Borgue, Kirkcudbrightshire), from the mill of which they jointly granted a rent to St. Bees Priory (*St. Bees Reg.*, no. 67; *Wigtownshire Charters*, p. xxvi). If the Galloway branch of the family survived it must have adopted a different surname and the surname Ripley does not seem to have survived in Scotland.
Black, *Surnames*, s.v. RIPLEY.

de SANCTO MICHAELE
(de SEINT MICHEL)
(Modern form: none known)

Although a continental origin for this family may be regarded as certain, the actual place of origin and the circumstances in which the family came to Scotland are unknown. Moreover, it is difficult or impossible to connect the various persons of the surname in any clearcut relationship. The St. Michaels are probably to be related to the group of immigrants from Somerset, especially with the Lovels and perhaps also the Londons. In Scotland their estates seem to have been in Roxburghshire and Aberdeenshire.

The earliest known member of the family in Scotland was Walter of St. Michael who held land at Branxholm of Henry Lovel I lord of Hawick, half of which Henry gave to St. Andrews Cathedral Priory by a charter of c. 1160–70 which Walter witnessed (*St. Andrews Liber*, 261). Slightly later we have fuller record of William of St. Michael. He served with Robert 'de Huseville' (read 'de Boseville'?) as an envoy from King William I to the count of Flanders before the king of Scots decided to join the great revolt of 1173 (Lawrie, *Annals*, 130). He was given a toft in Montrose by King William (*RRS* ii, no. 577), subsequently given to Lindores Abbey by his son David (*Lindores Chartulary*, no. 38). He witnessed a charter of David, King William's brother, *c.* 1173 (*Kelso Liber*, no. 226), a charter of Peter of Graham, *c.* 1180 (*Newbattle Reg.*, no. 7), and a charter of Eschina widow of Walter the Stewart, dated 1186 (*Kelso Liber*, no. 146). At the turn of the twelfth and thirteenth centuries Robert of St. Michael witnessed a charter of Philip de Valognes which was probably issued in Roxburghshire (*EYC* vi, no. 54), and a surrender by his son Elmeras (?) suggests that they had property at Elliston in St. Boswells, Roxburghshire (*Dryburgh Liber*, no. 207).

Early in the thirteenth century, Roger of St. Michael gave land at Mundurno (in Old Machar, Aberdeenshire) to Arbroath Abbey (*Arbroath Liber*, nos. 81, 81 *bis*), a grant confirmed by his nephew John of St. Michael before 1239 (ibid., no. 82). It is not known whether this John is to be related to the sequence of Johns of St. Michael associated with Roxburghshire in the thirteenth century, beginning with John of St. Michael who with William of St. Michael witnessed a deed of Agnes widow of Laurence of Elliston in 1249 (*Melrose Liber*, no. 262). This John may be identified with the John who, with David of St. Michael, witnessed a charter issued by Richard Lovel I lord of Hawick (son of Henry I), who died in 1255 (*St. Andrews Liber*, 261–2). More problematical is the John son of John of St. Michael who in 1278 was accused with several other Scots of ill repute at Carlisle Assizes of the murder of Richard Bullock at 'Cambok' (Cambeckhill in Irthington, Cumberland), a crime said to have been instigated by Alan de Lascelles (*CDS* ii. 34). Sir John of St. Michael of Roxburghshire swore fealty to Edward I at Elgin on 28 July 1296 (ibid. ii, no. 796 and pp. 195, 211, 214), evidently laird of Heavyside in Morebattle, which he forfeited between 1298 and 1304 (ibid. iii, no. 258; see ibid. iv. 386).

Aberdeenshire St. Michaels appear in fourteenth-century record (*Arbroath Liber*, no. 231; *Aberdeen Reg.* i. 38, 185–6).
Black, *Surnames*, s.v. ST MICHAEL.

de SOMERVILLE
(SUM(M)ERVILL(-A, -E), etc.)
(Modern form: SOMERVILLE)

The printed accounts of the Scottish branch of the family are not satisfactory. According to Sir Richard Hardy, *A History of the Parish of Tatenhill* (1907), 35, 37, the Domesday ancestor of the Somervilles may have been Robert, tenant of Wichnor, Staffordshire, in 1086, while the earliest member of the family to appear with the surname in record was William, citing Dugdale, *Monasticon Anglicanum*, ii. 886. The reference should be to vol. I of the first edition, p. 886, and this is the document printed in Lawrie, *Charters*, no. 244, 1136×52. Hardy also states that the family home was near Évreux in Normandy (op. cit. 38, without evidence cited).

We are on reasonably secure ground if we start with Walter de Somerville, a tenant by knight-service in 1166 on the Stafford fee at Wichnor, Staffs. and on the Lacy fee at Seacroft, Birkby in Thorner, Barnbow and Wheatcroft in Barwick-in-Elmet, all east of Leeds (*EYC* iii. 306–9; *RBE* i. 423; W. E. Wightman, *The Lacy Family in England and Normandy*, 93, 100). Walter was amerced for concealment of duels in Skyrack wapentake in 1166 (*Pipe Roll 12 Henry II*, 47). He witnessed a charter of Malcolm IV at Carlisle, 1157–8 (*RRS* i, no. 139), and a charter issued by him for William de Rideware, witnessed by his wife Cecily and his sons Roger, Robert, and Alan, is printed by Hardy, op. cit. 40. We may note that Robert de Somerville, Walter's son, witnessed a charter of Duncan I earl of Fife, *c.* 1170, his name in a lengthy witness-list being placed next before that of William 'de Neuham' the Templar, who perhaps came from Temple Newsam close to the Somerville lands in the West Riding (*North Berwick Carte*, no. 3).

The William de Somerville who appears so frequently in Scottish record from *c.* 1124 to the 1160s was evidently a younger brother of Walter. He held some of the family's Yorkshire property, for his debt of 20 silver marks in 1158–60 is recorded on the Yorkshire Pipe Roll with the note 'but he resides (*manet*) in the land of the king of Scotland in Lothian' (*CDS* i, nos. 54, 66, 68). The estates which he was given in Scotland, presumably by David I, were Linton in Roxburghshire and Carnwath in Lanarkshire. A charter of 1161–2 by which he gave three acres in Linton to Glasgow Cathedral is printed in *Glasgow Reg.*, no. 16, while his quitclaim for Henry de Lacy (*c.* 1150–65) is printed in *EYC* iii, no. 1650. At the end of his life he may have entered a religious house, for *Glasgow Reg.*, no. 52 is a grant of Carnwath church to Glasgow Cathedral made originally to Bishop Ingram (1164–74) by William de Somerville on the advice of his father William. The donor, William II de Somerville, was doubtless the granter of six oxgangs in Barnbow to Robert de Lacy (*EYC* iii, no. 1651), who in a contemporary agreement with Kirkstall Abbey (ibid., no. 1652, *c.* 1185–93) refers to his uncle Walter (who was evidently dead by 1176).

William II de Somerville was succeeded (in Yorkshire as well as Scotland) by his son William III, who in 1226 confirmed a grant in Seacroft made by his father (*Yorkshire Fines, 1218–31*, 88) and was a benefactor of Kirkstall Abbey (*Kirkstall Coucher Book*, 127–8). It was evidently William III de Somerville who was present at the siege of Damietta in Egypt in 1218 in the company of John de Lacy constable of Chester (*Pontefract Chartulary*, i, no. 21). He died in 1242 and was buried at Melrose Abbey (*Chron. Melrose*, 90; *Excerpta e rotulis finium*, i. 401); being succeeded in Scotland by a line of de Somervilles (e.g. Fraser, *Douglas*, iii. 353; *Scots Pge* iii. 254; *Melrose Liber*, i. 239, 244–5; ii. 677; *Kelso Liber*, i. 143). In the West Riding the heir of William III was Walter de Tremblay (*Excerpta e rotulis finium*, i. 401; *Yorkshire Fines, 1232–46*, 128), and before 1264 he had acquired an estate in Kincardineshire (*Exchequer Rolls*, i. 13). The connection between Walter de Tremblay and the Somervilles is not known, but it looks as though there was a partition of the inheritance, and the Kincardineshire lands may perhaps have been given to Walter de Tremblay in compensation for his hereditary

claims to Linton and Carnwath. The conjunction of names may provide a clue to the place of origin of the Somervilles in Normandy, for north-west of Évreux (in the arrondissement of Neubourg) the two villages of Sémerville (Gravéron-Sémerville) and Le Tremblay (Le Tremblay-Omonville) are almost adjacent to each other. In this connection it may be worth noting that two charters of Amaury count of Évreux issued in the Holy Land (one of which must be dated 1188 because witnessed by the great Yorkshire magnate Roger de Moubray who died in that year, while the other cannot be later than 4 October 1189), were witnessed by Everard and Boschard de Tremblai (Le Prévost, *Mémoires* . . . *de l'Eure*, I, 133; Greenway, *Mowbray Charters*, p. xxxii).
Black, *Surnames*, s.v. SOMERVILLE.

de TREMBLAY
(TREMBLEY(E), TREMBLEE, etc.)
(Modern forms: TREMBLE, TRUMBLE, TURNBULL, etc.)

A well-known branch of the Scots family of Turnbull held the lands of Bedrule, Roxburghshire, in the later middle ages, and its most distinguished member, William Turnbull, who was bishop of Glasgow from 1447 to 1454 and founded the University of Glasgow in 1451, came from Bedrule. G. F. Black, *Surnames*, s.vv. TREMBLAY, TURNBULL, believed that there were two distinct surnames, the former giving rise to 'some or all of the Trimbills, Trombills, and Trumbles in Fife', the latter deriving from the OE personal name Trumbald. There is no evidence to confirm this and it is more likely that Trembles, Turnbulls, etc. all derived their surname from the Norman name de Tremblay. Since Walter was in later times a Turnbull personal name it is worth noting that the first de Tremblay in Scottish record was Walter, for whom see above under de Somerville.

Robert de Tremblee (Trembleye) was a landholder in Kincardineshire in the period 1296–1304 (*CDS* ii, nos. 730, 797, pp. 195, 209; Palgrave, *Docs. Hist. Scot.*, 182, 196). This Robert may have been the Robert (de) Tremblay who witnessed a charter of Sir Alexander Murray knight given at his full court at Newton, in Forgan, Fife, on 27 February 1282 (*St. Andrews Liber*, 341–2). This witness in any case would very probably have been the Robert de Trymblay who had held a ploughgate in Forgan subsequently surrendered by his daughter Cecily (*RMS* i, no. 186). Robert and John de Tremblay were jurors on an Angus inquest retoured to the king's chapel in 1322 (*RMS* i, App. I, no. 29).

The Tremblay presence in Forgan parish may have been connected with the twelfth-century marriage of Juliana de Somerville to Alan de Lascelles (*St. Andrews Liber*, 260).

Walter Turnbull had a charter from David II of the lands of Minto, Roxburghshire; presumably John Turnbull of Minto in the reign of Robert III was his successor (*RMS* i, no. 814 and App. II, no. 1034; see also *OPS* i. 322–3). John Turnbull (*alias* Trumble) had a charter of Hundleshope in Manor, Peeblesshire, from David II (*RMS* i, App. II, no. 917). Also in

David's reign Margaret Trymbille forfeited land at Eyemouth, Berwickshire (ibid., p. 90, no. 263).
Black, *Surnames*, s.vv. TREMBLAY, TURNBULL.

de VALLIBUS
(VALS, VAUS, VAUX, etc.)
(Modern forms: VANS, VAUX)

Acts of the Empress Maud, her son Henry of Anjou, and their supporter Baldwin de Reviers, mainly issued at or near Rouen, were witnessed by Hubert and Godard de Vaux (*Cal.Docs.France*, nos. 216, 593, 680, 681; see also no. 1276; *RRAN* iii, nos. 71, 72, 112, 116a, 580, 665, 711, 748, 824–5, 836, 909; see also nos. 130, 587, 666, 795). In the cartulary of Castle Acre Priory are copies of two charters (twelfth century?) anent a mill in Pentney, West Norfolk, the first by Robert de Vals, with mention of his brothers Ralph *pinguis*, Gilbert and Hubert, the second by William son of Robert (BL MS Harl. 2110, fo. 91).

The baronial fortunes and future of the family were laid in the late 1150s when Henry II gave Gilsland in north-east Cumberland to Hubert de Vaux to form a feudal lordship on the Border against Scotland, to be held by knight-service (resulting in the building of Brampton castle). In the reign of Malcolm IV and the early years of William I's reign Scottish royal charters were witnessed by John de Vaux (see Appendix A, no. 1; *RRS* i, nos. 205, 221, 222, 228, 230, 255; ii, nos. 44, 116, 179, 188, 204, 238, and see *St. Andrews Liber*, 334, A.D. 1178) who may be assumed to have been the first feudal lord of Dirleton or Gullane. Hubert I died *c.* 1164 and was succeeded by his son Robert I, founder of Lanercost Priory, who died without issue in 1195, being succeeded by his brother Ranulf (d. 1199), whose heir was his son Robert II de Vaux, a staunch supporter of King John. In Scotland John I was succeeded, *c.* 1180, by William I de Vaux, who was in turn succeeded by John II in the earlier thirteenth century.

The Hubert de Vaux who witnessed Uhtred lord of Galloway's grant to St. Peter's Hospital, York (*CDS* ii, no. 1606, p. 422) was Hubert I. The Hubert de Vaux who witnessed William I de Vaux's charter for Durham (Raine, *North Durham*, no. 172) would have been William's brother, Hubert son of John de Vaux, who witnessed two early Lanercost charters (*Trans.Roy.Soc.Lit.*, 2nd ser. viii. 456 and index). John de Vaux lord of Dirleton was prominent in the first wars of independence (*CDS* ii, *passim*, references in index).
Black, *Surnames*, s.v. VANS.

de VARENNE
(WARENNE, WARAND, etc.)
(Modern form: WARRAND)

In 1139 Earl Henry, son of David I, married Ada daughter of William II de Varenne, earl of Surrey (or Earl Warenne). Ada's brother Reginald de

Varenne witnessed Earl Henry's grant of five demesne manors of the Honour of Huntingdon to Eustace Fitz John, 1139 X 42 (*RRS* i, no. 11), and he also witnessed a brieve of Duncan earl of Fife (Duncan I, d. 1154, or Duncan II, 1154–1204?) exempting the monks of May from army service (*PSAS* lxxxvii. 54). Ada and Reginald were sister-in-law and brother-in-law of Ela, daughter of William Talvas count of Ponthieu and Ela, daughter of Eudes Borel duke of Burgundy (*Comp. Pge.* xi, 377, 379, xii, pt. I, 497). The name Ela was continued in the Varenne family in the person of Ela, daughter (born after 1164) of the countess Isabel and her second husband Hamelin Plantagenet bastard son of Count Geoffrey of Anjou (BL MS Harl. 2188, fo. 2). It seems probable that Ela, wife of Duncan II earl of Fife, was daughter of Reginald de Varenne, who was ancestor of the family of Warenne of Wormegay. It would be natural for Reginald to name one of his daughters Ela, especially if his sister-in-law, the Countess Ela, was a godmother (for the existence of Reginald's daughters, whose total number is not known, see *EYC* viii. 28). A charter of Reginald's son, William de Varenne, granting two virgates of arable at Brighton, Sussex, to Lewes Priory (where his father became a monk before his death in 1179) has as its last witness Duncan son of Duncan, probably the grantor's nephew (*Lewes Chartulary*, pt. I, 55).

In Scotland, a Reginald de Varenne (Warenna, Warennia) is found in the early thirteenth century as a landholder in Forgandenny, Kilgraston and Dron, south of Perth, in territory where the lords of Abernethy, close kin to the earls of Fife, had an hereditary interest (Fraser, *Douglas*, iii. 349–50, no. 281; *PSAS* lx. 72; *Lindores Chartulary*, nos. 70–3). He had brothers named Adam and Roger, nephews named Adam and David, and a grand-nephew named John (ibid.). Reginald married Orabilla, sister and heir of Hugh de Say (*Scone Liber*, 55), and appears prominently in record relating to the Perth district (ibid., 91). His charter for Laurence of Abernethy was witnessed by Malcolm earl of Fife and his sons seem to have been named Reginald and Malcolm, while contemporaneously there is record of the brothers Robert and David de Varenne ('de Warren') (Fraser, *Douglas*, iii. 349–50; *PSAS* lx. 72).
Black, *Surnames*, s.vv. WARRAND, WARREN.

WYRFAUK
(WIRFAUC, WIRFALD, WIRFAUD)
(Modern form: none known)

Charters of Adam II de Brus lord of Cleveland, dating between 1170 and 1190, were witnessed by William Wirfald. Half a ploughgate in Hinderwell was granted to Whitby Abbey by William Wirfauc, with the consent of his son William (*EYC* ii, nos. 663, 665, 906). The *Whitby Cartulary*, no. 100, provides evidence of a succession from William Wirfauc, *c.* 1139, to William Wirfauc, *c.* 1189, and then perhaps to Osbert Wirfauk in 1235 and William Wirfauc late in the reign of Henry III. *EYC* ii. 372 cites a lawsuit between William Wirfauk and Ingram de Munceaux anent land at Whitbystrand which Ingram had given to Meaux Abbey, and the editor dates this a few years after 1182. But an Ingram de Monceus witnessed, with Hugh de Beaumys, knight, a Brus deed of 1248 (*Lindores Chartulary*, no. 41) while Hugh de Beumes witnessed *Arbroath Liber*, no. 272, which refers to half a davoch in Laurencekirk, Mearns, formerly held by Hugh son of Waltheof (son of Baldwin 'the Fleming' of Biggar), given to Roger Wyrfauk. Possibly the lawsuit has been wrongly dated and should be attributed to the thirteenth century. The grant to Roger had been made by Richenda, daughter and heiress of Humphrey of Berkely (and ultimately heiress of Walter of Berkley), with consent of her husband Robert son of Warenbaud (Wernebald; evidently a descendant of the twelfth-century Flemish settler in Cunningham who held the feu of Kilmaurs); and Roger bestowed his land at Laurencekirk on St. Andrews Cathedral Priory; all this being completed by 1250 (*St. Andrews Liber*, 279–80, 285–7, 334–5).

Black, *Surnames*, s.v. WYRFAUT, who says that the name may be Flemish.

APPENDIX C

A select list of words and phrases in Middle English (including hybrids) occurring in Latin documents written in Scotland before c. 1250. Since the chief purpose of the list is to show the use of English becoming localized in non-English-speaking districts, the following have been omitted: all documents relating to burghs, and to the sheriffdoms of Berwick, Dumfries, Edinburgh, Haddington, Linlithgow, Peebles, Roxburgh, and Selkirk; and certain words and phrases whose use in formal documents had become almost universal before 1200, e.g. 'toft and croft', 'sake and soke, toll and team and infangenthief'. The majority of words and phrases in the list are component elements of place-names and/or topographical descriptions.

(1) From the records of Kelso Abbey, Roxburghshire (Order of Tiron)

Kelso Liber
nos. 102, 103, 109, 112 (various dates, 1147 × 1218, relating to Lesmahagow, Lanarkshire):
  birthinsake (birtinsake, birthnsake, byrinsake), 'jurisdiction in cases concerning goods not greater than what may be carried on a man's back'.
  blodewite (blodewyt, blodwit), 'fine for shedding blood'.
111, 115 (1160 × 1180, Lesmahagow):
  herieth, 'premium paid by heir in order to take up his inheritance'.
104, 109, 111, 112, 114, 115 (various dates, 1160 × 1218, Lesmahagow):
  merchet, merchet de filiabus, 'fine for leave to arrange a daughter's marriage'.
102, 103 (1147 × 60, 1208 × 18, Lesmahagow):
  smalbec, Smalbeg, 'narrow burn'.
103, 107 (as preceding):
  mossa, mos, 'peatmoss'.
107 (1147 × 1160, Lesmahagow and Douglas):
  crosseford, 'ford lying athwart' or 'ford marked by a cross'? (now Crossford).
  ford, 'ford'.
  thevisford, 'ford of the thief' (now Thievesford).
  longum fau, perhaps compare Scots *faugh*, 'ploughed, or fallow, ground' or 'furrow made in fallow' (see *Dictionary of the Older Scottish Tongue*, s.v. 'fauch'; A. H. Smith, *English Place-Name Elements* (1956), s.v. *falh*).

hirdelau, 'herd hill'.
110, 112 (1180 × 1203, Lesmahagow):
Haliwelburn, 'burn rising at the holy well'.
holmos super Naithan, 'meadows beside River Nethan'.
Kirkeburn, 'church burn'.
The use of Anglo-Scandinavian vocabulary, e.g. beck, holm, in Lesmahagow is noteworthy.
181 (c. 1200, Strathaven, Lanarkshire):
Haresawes, 'wooded country with hares' or 'woods on stony ground' (?) (now Hareshaw). (OE *hara*, 'hare', or *hær*, 'stony ground'?).
Bradewude, 'broad wood'.
194 (1240 × 1249, Lesmahagow):
petamore, 'peatmoss'.

(2) From the records of Paisley Abbey, Renfrewshire (Order of Cluny)

Paisley Reg.
pp.   5, 409, 441; see also *RRS* i, no. 184 (various dates 1159 × 1177, Dripps, Renfrewshire/Lanarkshire):
le Drep, Threp, 'debateable land', 'threipland'.
20, 112 (various dates, × 1177 and 1204 × 41, Renfrewshire):
mora, mores, 'moor(s)'.
21 (1204 × 41, Kyle, Ayrshire):
Selecrag, 'seal rock'.
Spetelcrag, 'hospital rock'.
48 (1230, Kyle, Ayrshire):
swineshales, 'swine meadows'.
213, 214, 216–17 (1224, 1228, River Leven near Dumbarton):
iar, yare, 'tidal fish-trap' (OE *gear*).

(3) From the records of Dunfermline Abbey, Fife (Order of S. Benedict)

Dunfermline Reg.
no.   168 (c. 1200, Aberdour, Fife):
terra que dicitur threpland, 'debateable land'.
192, 193 (1231, Dunfermline):
falumireside, falulecche, faluhil, 'yellowish-brown mireside/sluggish stream/hill,' respectively (OE *fealu*, ME *falu*, 'yellowish-brown').
198 (c. 1230, Masterton in Dunfermline):
redeforde, 'red ford' or 'ford with reeds'?
crocketlecche, 'crooked sluggish stream' (OE *læcc*, ME *leche*).
199 (c. 1240? Dunfermline):
villa Gospatric que nunc appellatur Kaldestanis, 'cold stones'.
201 (c. 1250? Luscar in Dunfermline):
milnetun, 'mill settlement'.

Appendix C

215; see also *Cambuskenneth Reg.*, no. 104 (1214–15, St. Ninians, Stirling):
fulelecches, fuleche, 'foul sluggish stream'.
216 (1220, Logie by Stirling):
Burgrevisflat, 'meadow of the burgh grieve or provost'.
Geffraisburne, 'Geoffrey's burn'.

(4) From the records of Arbroath Abbey, Angus (Order of Tiron)

Arbroath Liber, i
no.   144 (*c.* 1230? Maryton by Montrose):
pontem qui dicitur stanbrig, 'stone bridge'.
232 (mid-thirteenth century, Rescobie by Forfar):
fyschergate, 'fisherman's road'.
295 (1256, Kingoldrum, Angus):
hacheth methon' quod anglice dicitur midefeld, 'middle field' (the Gaelic form is for *achadh meadhonach* with the same meaning).

BL MS Add. 33245
fo.   179^v (1253, Kingoldrum):
le (ly) leche, 'sluggish stream'.
le gresiam stripe. The second element refers to a small stream (a characteristically Scottish usage: see *Scottish National Dictionary*, s.v. 'stripe, n^2'; Smith, *English Place-Name Elements*, s.v. 'strip'), the whole probably meaning 'oily or bituminous stream'.

(5) From the records of the Cathedral Church of the Holy Trinity, Elgin

Moray Reg.
nos.   21, 51 (*c.* 1230, Kirkhill near Beauly):
locus qui dicitur Wardelau Scotice Balabrach (Balcabrach), 'watching hill' (the Gaelic name is obscure, although its first element is *baile*, 'township', 'settlement'; perhaps the second element is *cabrach*, adjective from *cabar*, 'rafter', or *gabrach*, adjective from *gobhar*, 'goat'?).
29 (1226, Nairn):
Whytefeld, 'white field'.
40 (1238, near Nairn):
Leuedycothe, 'the lady's (or Our Lady's?) house or cottage'.
77 (1229, Forres):
Kyrkeburne, 'church burn'.
89 (1237, Urquhart near Elgin):
Sallelcot, 'sallow or willow house or cottage', or a miscopying of Saltercot, 'salters' cottage'?
99 (1248, Spynie near Elgin):
Saltecot, 'salt house or cottage'.

109 (1228, near the lower Spey?):
    Robenfeld, 'open ground with robins'?
119 (1187 × 1203, near Forres):
    le Logyndykis, second element 'walls' and/or 'ditches' (the rubric, which may be of later date than the text, has the name le Ermytdykys, 'hermit's walls').

(6) From miscellaneous sources, arranged roughly in geographical order

(a) North-east Scotland

NLS MS Acc. 7079 (printed *Aberdeen–Banff Illustrations*, ii, 427–8): (1219 × 1233, Ellon and Logie-Buchan, Aberdeenshire):
    le Bolghyl, perhaps a hybrid, with first element Gaelic *balg*, 'bag', second element OE *hyll*, 'hill'.
    le Byermos, 'peatmoss with byre'.
    Craucarn, hybrid of ME *crawe*, 'crow' and Gaelic *carn*, 'cairn', 'crows' cairn'.
    le gledcarn, first element gled, 'kite', 'kites' cairn' (*Dict. Older Scot. Tongue*, s.v. 'gled').
    Lamberhyll, 'lambs hill'.

Aberdeen–Banff Illustrations, ii. 426–7 (1219 × 33, Strathisla, Banffshire):
    mora mosse, 'moor with peatmoss'.
    Caetrin Stryp, for *stryp*, 'small stream', see above under (4).
    Staneycroft, 'stony croft'.
    Muirfurd, 'moor ford'.
    Stobstane, 'upright stone'.
    Urilhille, second element OE *hyll*, 'hill'.

BL Cott. Chr. xviii, 23 (1185 × 1219, Inverurie, Aberdeenshire):
    le Harlau, 'grey hill' or 'hill with stony ground'? (OE *haer*, 'stony ground').
    Rumfre, 'free to use a corn-mill whenever there is room in the hopper'.

BL MS Loans 29/355 (box of unnumbered documents) (*c.* 1200–10, Inverarity, Angus):
    blodwit, 'fine for shedding blood'.
    merchet, 'fine for leave to arrange a daughter's marriage'.
    unlah, 'wrongful acts falling short of felony', *anglicé* 'trespass'.

Panmure Reg. ii. 125 (*c.* 1190–1215, Panbride, Angus):
    Stinchende havene, 'stinking harbour'.

Lindores Chartulary, no. 40 (1237 × 48, Craigie near Dundee):
    Mylnetoun, 'mill settlement'.

(b) Central Scotland
SRO, J. M. Thomson photos, no. 6 (*c.* 1200, Cargill, Perthshire):
Withefeld, 'white field'.

SRO, Drummond Castle muniments, bdle. 1, no. 2 (*c.* 1210, Scone, Perthshire):
Radeforde, 'red ford' or 'ford with reeds'?

Lindores Chartulary, no. 2 (1198–9, Lindores, Fife):
insulam que vocatur Redinche, 'red island' or 'island with reeds'?
jhara, 'tidal fish-trap' (OE *gear*).

Inchaffray Charters, no. 56 (1226 × 34, Fowlis Wester, Perthshire):
fitheleresflat, 'fiddler's meadow' (*Dict. Older Scot. Tongue*, s.v. 'fidlar').

Ibid., no. 39 (1219, Strageath, Perthshire):
Ruuehalach, 'rough riverside meadow or haugh'.

Cambuskenneth Reg., no. 110 (1242, St. Ninians, Stirling):
Kirketoun, 'church settlement' (a partial translation of an earlier Eggles (etc.), Brittonic for 'church').

(c) South-west Scotland
Fraser, *Lennox*, ii, no. 2 (1177 × 1204, Neilston, Renfrewshire):
del West del Capilheuid, 'on the west of the valley head frequented by horses' (Gaelic, *capull*, 'horse', 'mare'; *Dict. Older Scot. Tongue*, s.v. 'capill').

Holyrood Liber, no. 70 (*c.* 1230, Kirkcudbrightshire):
a fonte qui dicitur tibereba et anglice cuwelle, 'cow well' (the Gaelic form being for *tiobar ba* (*bo*), with the same meaning).

Index

Places in France are located by department, indicated by number in bold type. The following are the departments involved:

14	Calvados	**59**	Nord
27	Eure	**61**	Orne
28	Eure-et-Loir	**62**	Pas-de-Calais
37	Indre-et-Loire	**76**	Seine-Maritime
50	Manche	**80**	Somme

Places in Great Britain are located by county as existing prior to the Local Government reforms of 1973–5. In the case of certain little-known places the name of the parish has been added. Abbreviations for counties are those used in M. Gelling, W. F. H. Nicolaisen, and M. Richards, *The Names of Towns and Cities in Britain* (1970), 30–1 (also listed in W. F. H. Nicolaisen, *Scottish Place-Names: their study and significance* (1976), xxvii–xxviii).

Patronymic names are indexed in the form 'A. son of B.', without cross-reference to 'B'. Surnames are indexed under the form most commonly used in the text.

Approximate dates are given in the form 'saec. xii, in., ex.', 'twelfth century, early, late'.

Abbotsley, HNT, 42 and n, 170–1
Abercarf, LAN, 40 and n, *see also* Wiston
Abercrombie by Torry, FIF, 85n
Aberdeen, sheriff of, 150
Aberdeenshire, 131
Aberfeldy Beg, PER, 138n
Aberlady, ELO, 33
Aberlosk, DMF, 49n
Abernethy, PER, 191; family of, 85; Hugh lord of, 132; Laurence lord of, 159, 197, his wife Dervorguilla, 159; Margaret daughter of Orm of, 104, 191
Abertarff, INV, 32
Abstel ('Saint Æbba's fishery'), BWK, 178
Acre, Palestine, 158

206 Index

Adam parson of Arran, 68n
Adam brother of Earl Duncan II of Fife, 159
Adam son of Abraham, lord of Lour, 164–5
Adam son of Derman, 178
Adam son of Edulf, 34
Adam son of Gilbert, lord of Hutton, 9n, 34
Adam son of Swain, 96nn
Addeville, Humphrey son of Theobald de, husband of Agatha of Berkeley, 103, 157n, 174
Adniston, ELO, 128
Affleck, LAN, 49n
Ailred abbot of Rievaulx, 14
Airdit, Easter, FIF, 104n
'Akesside', BWK, 169
Alan knight of the earl of Carrick, 124
Alan 'son of the earl' (Thomas of Galloway earl of Atholl), 3n
Alan son of Elsi, 129
Alan son of Flaald, 13, 14; his wife Avelina de Hesdin, 13, 14–15 and n, 68
Alan son of Roland (Lachlan) lord of Galloway, 45n, 47n, 79, 82n, 83n, 140, 188
Albright Hussy, SHR, 66
Aldborough, YON, 75n
'Aldecambus', BWK, 169
Alexander the knight (of Seton?), 126
Alexander I king of Scots (1107–24), 61
Alexander II king of Scots (1214–49), 4n (in error), 5, 63, 128, 131, 143, 168, 191
Alexander III king of Scots (1249–86), 30, 128, 142, 143
Alexander son of the earl of Fife, parson of Kinnoull, 87n
Allerston, Thorphin of, 31n
Alston, CMB, 76
Andrew, Saint, 10
Angus, 30, 61; Braes of, 128; earl of, 144; earldom of, 158

Annan, DMF, 49n
Annandale, 8, 12, 43, 47–9, 62, 94, 131, 154, 175
Annieston, LAN, 36, 37, 112
Anselm of 'Hwitheton' ('Wichetune'), same as Anselm of 'Hwichintona'?, 65n, 66n
Apdaine, see *apthenagium*
Appleby, WML, 73, 75
Apthenagium (apdaine), 11
Arbroath, ANG: abbey (O. Tir.), 77, 157, 162n, 189; Declaration of, 26
Archibald (Arkenbald), 37
Archibald bishop of Moray, 116
Archil, thegn, at Ripley, 113
Ardie Hill, in Balmerino, FIF, 104n
Ardlamont, ARG, 137
Ardoch, in Lesmahagow, LAN, 45n, 49n
Ardoyne, ABD, 174
Ardrossan, AYR, Barclay of, 175
Ardskeodnish, ARG, 139
Ardsley, near Barnsley, YOW, 10 and n
Argyll, 69, 128, 138, 140–1, 149; barons of, 138n; *patria* of, 141 and n
Arisaig, INV, 139n
Arkenbald, see Archibald
Arkleston, RNF, 39
Arnkell, 39
Arnold abbot of Kelso, 45n; see also Arnold bishop of St. Andrews
Arnold bishop of St. Andrews (1160–2), 93n, 170
Arran, Isle of, BTE, 17, 68
Articles of the Barons (1215), 133n, 153n
Arundel, SSX, earls of (Fitz Alan), 13
Arundel, Godfrey de (saec. xii), Roger (saec. xi), 174
Asa (Ace, Azo), 37
Asby, Great, WML, 31n
Ascoloc, Roland, 3n
Ashby (i.e. Castle Ashby, NTP), 41; Clarembald of, 41; David of, 178

Index

Ashley, Walter of, 191
Asseby, William de, his son, Peter, 179
Aston Abbots, SHR, 15n
Aston Somerville, GLO, 108
Athelgal(the)thywn (unidentified), 10 and n
Athelstaneford, ELO, 61, 127
Atholl: earldom of, 140, 158; David earl of, 140; Madet earl of, 158 and n; Malcolm earl of, his wife and family, 159
Aubigny, Maud d', countess of Strathearn, 89, 125
Aubigny, William II d', lord of Belvoir, 89
Aubigny, William III d', 89
Auchencrieff, DMF, 172
Auchterheadmuir, LAN, 45n
Auchtermuchty, FIF, 86
Auchtyfardle, LAN, 49n
Auldhame, ELO, 33
Aumâle, Agnes, daughter of (William) count of, 112; William count of, 173; his niece, Euphemia, see Brus
Aunay (Alneto, Alnou, etc.): family of, 172; Henry de, John de, Pain de, Ralph de, Roger de, 172; Thomas de, 131, 172
Avelina, see Alan son of Flaald
Avenel, Robert, 62; William, 123
Ayr, 46; castle, 46; sheriffdom, 65
Ayrshire, 6, 43, 46–7, 49
Ayton, David of, 88; William of, 88
Azay-le-Rideau, France 37, 42

Baard (Bard, Baird): family of, 67, 111 and n, 173–4; Durand I, 111n, 173, his son, Geoffrey, 111n, 173; Durand II, 111n, 173; Geoffrey, 111n, 173; Richard (in Yorkshire), 111n, 173–4; Richard (in Scotland, father and son), 111n, 173–4; Simon, his wife Isabel, 10
Baarth, Roger, 111n, 173
Bard, William, 111n, 173
Badenoch, INV, 11, 30
Bailleul-en-Vimeu, France **80,** 95n, 181; see also Balliol
Bainard, Agnes, lady of Burton Agnes, 112
Baird, Robert of Strathaven, 111; see also Baard
Balbirnie, in Markinch, FIF, 85
Balderston, WLO, 39
Baldred, 39
Baldric see Bodric
Baldwin, 37; the Fleming, lord of Biggar (saec. xii), 38; the Fleming, in Lincolnshire (saec. xi), 48n
Balfour of Denmilne, Sir James, 87
Balgonie, PER, 132
Ballindalloch, MOR, 86
Ballindean, FIF, 104n
Balliol (from Bailleul-en-Vimeu, q.v.): family of, 103, 107; Alexander de, lord of Cavers, 24; Bernard de, 95n; Dervorguilla de, lady of Galloway, 3 and n; Enguerrand I de, 103, 174, 181, 188; Enguerrand II de, 181; Eustace de, 3n, 11n; Henry de, lord of Cavers, 24, 181; Hugh de (also d'Eure q.v.), 3n, 11 and n; John de, lord of Barnard Castle (d. 1269), 2; John de, lord of Galloway, see John king of Scots; Walter de, 95n
Balmerino, FIF, 10, 104, 191; abbey (O. Cist.), 10, 105, 192
Bampton, DEV (Baentona, Paintona?): Robert of, 100–1, 174
Bandirran, FIF, 130
Banff, BNF, 128
Bangour, WLO, 85n, 86
Barbour, John, archdeacon of Aberdeen, 147
Barclay, Hugh, justiciar of Lothian, 119; see also Berkeley
Bardolf, Doun, 96n
Barkston, YOW, Walter son of Thomas of, 151–2
Barnack, Richard of, 122
Barnbow, YOW, 108, 194

Barnsley, YOW, 10, 11n
Barnwell, CAM, chronicler of, 84
Barrowby, LIN, 190
Basset (also Ridel), Geoffrey, Ralph, 171
Bayeux, France **14,** 71
Beath, FIF, 42n
Beaton, surname *see* Bethune
Beauchamp in Vouilly, canton Isigny, France **14,** 80 and n; family of, 71, 80; Beatrice de, 17, 71, 74–5; Hugh de, 17, 71, his son Robert, 71 and n; Miles de, Pain de Beauchamp, 71n
Beauly River, INV, 30
Beaumys, Sir Hugh de, 112n, 198
Becket, Saint Thomas archbishop of Canterbury (1162–70), 31n, 74–9
Bedford, assizes at, 10
Bedfordshire, 71, 98
Bedrule, ROX, *see* Rule
Beinn Macduibh, ABD and BNF, 86
Beith, AYR, 181
Bek, Anthony bishop of Durham (1284–1311), 8
Belet, John, 103; Ralph, 102
Bellême, house of, 13; Robert of, 18
Bellencombre, France **76,** 127 and n; William de, 88n
Benvie, ANG, 23
Berewald, 36
Berkeley (Berkley, afterwards Barclay): family of, 102–3, 174–5; Agatha of, 103, 174, her husband *see* Addeville; Alina of, 103; John (?) of, 174; Richard of, 175; Richenda of, 198; Robert of, 102–3, 174–5, his wife, Cecily, 174–5; Roger of, 175; Walter of, 24, 42n, 102–3, 174–5, 183
Berkley, SOM, 102, 174; Robert, Domesday tenant of (same as Robert 'de Gatemore'?), 174, *see also* Berkeley
Bernard the Shoemaker, 141n
Bernham, David of, bishop of St. Andrews (1240–53), 1, 2n; Robert of, Mayor of Berwick, 1, 2n;

William of (saec. xii), 2n; William of, Oxford student, 1–2
Bertram, Roger lord of Mitford, 74
Berwick upon Tweed, castle of, 169
Berwickshire, 9
Béthune, France **62,** 22; Robert de (Beaton), 23
Bidun, de: family of, of Lavendon, 98; Walter de, chancellor of Scotland, 169–70
Biéville-sur-Orne, France **14,** 80–1, 176; *see also* Boiville, Boyle
Biggar, LAN, 44; *see also* Baldwin, Waltheof
Billie, BWK, 169
Binham priory, NFK (O.S.B.), 4
Birgham, BWK, 33; Treaty of (1290), 118
Birkenside, BWK, 65
Birkhill (formerly Corbie), FIF, 104, 191
Bisset: family of, 32, 68; Thomas, 16, 68n; Walter, 16, 32n, 68n
Bitchfield, NTB, Denise of, 119
Blackford, PER, 154–5n
Black Isle, ROS, 154n
Blair, Alexander son of William of, 130
Blair of Adamton, Hugh (otherwise Hugh Franciscus), 81n
Blandford, DOR, 174
Bodric (Boderic), variant of Baldric? 36, 38
Bohun, Henry de, earl of Hereford, 124
Bois, del (de Bosc(h)o): family of, 94–6, 175–6; Humphrey, 175; Richard, 94, 175; Walter, 94, 154, 175; William, 7, 175; *see also* Bosc-Bénard
Boiville, de: family of, 81 and n, 176; Adam (son of Richer) de, 176; Godard de, 81n; Richer I de, 80 and n, 176; Richer II de *see also* Gilbert son of Richer
Bonds of manrent, 126
Borgue, KCB, 31, 73
Borrowdale, WML, 22

Borrowstoun (Bo'ness), WLO, 36, 40
Bosc-Bénard (Boscus Bernardi), France **27,** 95; Richard de, Walter de, 95, 175
Bosc-Bénard-Commin, France **27,** 175
Bosville, John de, 10; his daughter Amabilla, 11n
Botherickfield, in Houston, RNF, 38
Bothwell, LAN, 44
Bouttemont, in Ouilly-le-vicomte, France **14,** 94; William de (Butemund), 94
Boyle of Kelburn(e): family of, 81 and n, 176; Robert (saec. xiii), 81n
Boyne, BNF, thanage of, 157n
Bozeat, NTP, 17, 71
Bradford Mill, SHR, 66n
Bradpole, DPR, 78, 79n
Braid, Henry of, 121, 174
Braidwell, in Kettins, PER, 11
Braikie, ANG, 131
Branxholm, ROX, 101n, 184, 192
Brechin, ANG, 63 and n; lay abbots of, 131; David of, 144; Henry of, 63n; William of, 63n, 123, 144
Breton (Brett), le: family of, 72; Richard, 72n, 78
Bridlington, YOE, priory (O. Aug.), 173
Brighton, SSX, 88, 197
Briouze, family of, 99
Brittany, counts or dukes of *see* Conan
Briwerr, William, 78, 116
Brix, France **50,** 12, 70
'Brocholwde', BWK, 169
Brodick, Arran, BTE, castle of, 69 and n
Brompton, YON, 109
Brough under Stainmore, WML, 75
Broughton, PEB, 43, 188–9
Broughton, Dodin of, 34
Broun, George, bishop of Dunkeld, 147

Brown, Professor, R.A., 163, 167
Broy, family of, 99
Bruce *see* Brus, Robert I, king of Scots
Brun, le, Philip, 135
'Brunschaith', DMF, 172
Brus (also Bruce, q.v.; from Brix, q.v.): family of, 32, 48, 62, 94, 107, 111n, 175; Adam I de, 12; Adam II de, 111n, 112, 173; Agnes de, 36, 37, 112; Euphemia niece of Count William of Aumâle, 173; Robert I de, 12 and n, 18, 47, 62, 112; Robert II de, 12, 18, 133, 173; Robert III de, William de, 134
Bruton, SOM, priory (O. Aug.), 191
Brutus Legend, 145
Buchan, 43; earldom of, 158
Buittle, KCB, 3n
Bullock, Richard, 193
Burdet, Hugh, 172; William, 172
Burgundy, Ela of, 197
Burnham, BUC, 116
Burradon, Sir William of, 150
Buscy (Busci) de, family, Oliver de (saec. xii), 26n; Sir Oliver de (saec. xiii), 26n, 186; Ralph de, Robert de, 26n
Bute, Isle of, BTE, 68, 69
Butemund *see* Bouttemont
Butterwick, YOE, 111; Durand, son of William of, 173
Butterwick, YON, 111(?), 173; Robert of, 173
Byland abbey, YON (O. Sav., afterwards O. Cist.), 31n
Byres, in Athelstaneford, ELO, 134

Caddonfoot, SLK, 168
Cadzow, LAN (afterwards Hamilton), 44, 64
Caen, France **14,** 71; church of St. Stephen, 80
Cahagnes *see* Keynes
Caithness, 30; earldom of, 158
Calceby, Malger of, 122
Calder *see* Mid Calder, West Calder

Callendar, STL: thanes of, 140; Sir John of, 144, 157n
Calverley, YOW, 114; family of Scot of, 114
Cambeckhill, CUM, 193
Cambo, in Kingsbarns, FIF, 140
Cambridgeshire, 98
Cambuskenneth, STL: abbey (O. Aug.); prior of, 136
Cambusnethan, LAN, 110-11, 176; church of, 123
Camelon, Anselm of, 132
Campbell: family of, 70, 149; Arthur son of Sir Arthur, 139n; Sir Colin, of Loch Awe, 139, 140; Sir Neil, of Loch Awe, 148-9
Campeaux, France **14,** family of, 46
Canonbie, DMF, 43
Canongate, MLO, 43
Canterbury, KNT, 10; cathedral church of Christ, 14n, shrine of S. Thomas the Martyr at, 10; William of, 74
Caputh, PER, 147
Cardean, PER and ANG, 131
Careville, Henry de, 191
Carfrae, BWK, 129
Carmunnock, Henry of, son of Anselm, 65n
Carneille, la, France **61**: family of, of Great Stukeley, 99
Carnwath, LAN, 44, 107-8, 194-5
Carraw, NTB, 121n
Carrick, AYR, 30, 31, 46, 49, 119, 168; earldom of, 32, 158; earls of see Brus, Duncan, Kilconquhar, Neil; Maud of, 150
Carriden, WLO, 179; Godwin of, Reginald of, Roger of, 179
Carruthers, DMF, 94
Carslogie, FIF, 130 and n; family of, 130 and n
Carsphairn, KCB, 32n
Carstairs, LAN, 144
Cart, River, RNF, 67
Carvin, France **62,** 23n; Robert de, 23
Cary Fitzpaine, SOM, 174

Castle Acre, NFK: priory (O. Clun.), 14, 15 and n
Castle Ashby, NTP, 41, 178
Castle Bytham, LIN, 31 and n
Castle Cary, SOM, 100, 184-5
Castle Lachlan, ARG, 137
Castle Tioram, INV, 137
Castle Sween, ARG, 137
Castleton, ROX, 122
Causi (Chausi), William, clerk of, parson of Lessudden, 101n
Cavers, ROX, 95n; see also Balliol
Cawdor, Earl, 157
Ceres, FIF, Adam knight of, 89, 125
Cessnock, River, AYR, 6 and n
Champagne, 63; see also Theobald
Chaucer, Geoffrey, 147
Chesney (Quesnay): family of, Simon de, Sybil de, 15n
Chester, earldom of, 27; earls see Hugh, John of Scotland
Cheyne, Reginald, 165
Chocques (Cioches), Gunfrid de, 22n, 45n; Sigar de, 45n
'Churchedenwde', BWK, 169
Clackmannan, 128
Clan MacDuff, law of, 159
Clapham, YOW, 83; family of, 83; Alan of, Mark of, 83n; see also Clephane
Clarabad, in Hutton, BWK, 35 and n, 41, 178
Clare, Thomas de, 69
Clarebald (Clarembald), 36, 41 and n, 178; see also Esseby
Clay, Sir Charles, 88, 93, 106, 109-10
Cleish, FIF, 85n; castle, 87; Sir Gilbert the knight of, 87
Clennell, Thomas, 150
Clephane of Carslogie, family of, 83 and n, 130
Clere: family of, 42-3, 109-11, 176; Ralph I de, 42, 110, 123, 176; Ralph II de, 123, 176; Roger de (saec. xii), 110, 176; Roger de (saec. xiii), 110, 123, 176, his daughter Agatha, 110, 176

Clères, France **76,** 109, 176
Clermiston, MLO, 36, 178
Cleveland, YON, 12 and n, 48, 67, 111–12
Clifford, WML, lords of, 74
Clifton, MLO, 141n
Clifton, in Morebattle, ROX, 134n
Clifton Maubank, DOR, 78
Cliponville, France **76,** 95; Robert de (also de Chippenuill), 95 and n
Clyde, River, Firth of, 17, 65, 68, 69
Clydesdale, 43–5, 49, 128
Colbain, 39
Coldingham, BWK, priory(O.S.B.), 169, 178
Coldinghamshire, BWK, 34
Coleraine, Ulster, 69
Colleville-sur-Mer, France **14,** 177
Colleville-sur-Orne, France **14,** 177
Columbers, Philip de, 78n
Colville: family of, 31, 97n, 177; Ada de, 97n; Philip de (saec. xii), 97n, 177; Philip de (saec. xiii), 177; Thomas de 'the Scot', 31, 47, 177; William de (saec. xii), 177; William de (saec. xiii), 31n, 177
Colzie, FIF, 132–3
Commin, family of, at Bosc-Bénard, 175; *see also* Comyn
Comyn (Cumin) (same as Commin, q.v.?): family of, 28, 159; Alexander earl of Buchan, John earl of Buchan, 157; John lord of Badenoch, 121; Richard I, 62, 159; Richard II, 121n; William Cumin, chancellor of David I, 62; William Comyn earl of Buchan (1212–33), 27, 121n, 159, 186, his family, 159; William Comyn of Kilbride, 143; William Comyn of Kirkintilloch, his widow, Isabel, 144
Conan duke of Brittany (d. 1171), 62
Congleton, ELO: Walter (knight) of, 123
Conisbrough, YOW: Geoffrey of, 62, 169, 185; William of, 185
Constance, Council of, 145

Constance of Brittany, 8
Constantine (de Costentin), family of, 66
Conveth (now Laurencekirk), KCD, 103, 112n, 157n
Corbet, 95; family of, of Draughton, 98
Corbie *see* Birkhill
Cormac, 39
Cormiston, LAN, 39
Cornet (or Korneth), Milo, 34, 35, 41; Simon son of John, 35n
Cosmungho priest of Eddleston, his sons James, John and Matthew, 34
Cososuold son of Murin, 34
Cospatric, 34
Cospatric 'Romefare', 34
Cosyn, William, of Linthorpe, 116 and n
Cotentin, France **50,** 71
Coultra, FIF, 104, 191
Cound, SHR, 19
Coupar Angus, PER, 11; abbey (O. Cist.), 11, 164
Courrières, France **62,** 23n; Alan de, 23
Courcy, William I de, William II de, 183
Coventre (Coven Trees) in Forgandenny, PER, 131
Covington, LAN, 39, 190
Cowal, ARG, 68–70, 138, 140–1
Crail, FIF, 63, 114
Crailshire, FIF, 5n, 127
Crannach in Glen Lyon, PER, 140
Cranstoun Riddel, MLO, 42
Crawford (Lindsay), LAN, 123
Crawford, John, LAN, 36, 67
Crawford, Reginald, 67
Cresseville, Simon de, of Attercliffe, 116, 151
Crispin, Roger, 134
Cristinus *see* MacNaughton
Croc, Alan, 126; Robert, 36, 126n; Simon, 126
Crokedayk, Robert del, 150
Crookston, RNF, 36

Cruden, ABD, 140
Cuinchy, France **62**, 22; *see also* Quincy
Culdairs, in Fortingall, PER, 134
Culenes, Nicholas of, 121n
Culross, FIF, 85; abbey (O. Cist.), 85n; shire of, 85
Cumberland, 81, 116, 160, 176; Robert of (de Reigny?), 72n
Cumbraes, BTE, 68
Cumbria, 81, 84; kingdom of, 161; English, 34, 47, 72; Scottish, 9, 32, 34, 38
Cumin *see* Comyn
Cunningham, AYR, 46, 62, 72 and n, 131, 135; T. Pont's Survey of, 76
Cupar, FIF, 85 and n, 88; castle of, 85; church of, 182; shire of, 130; Peter constable of 85n
Curry Rivel, SOM, 104, 191

Dallas ('Dolaysmichel'), MOR, 113, 192; family of, 113 and n, 192
Dalmellington, AYR, 32 and n
Dalmeny, WLO, 25, 92
Dalton, YON, 26
Damietta, Egypt, siege of, 108, 194
Dardarach, in Lesmahagow, LAN, 45n, 49n
Dargavel, DMF, 172
David I king of Scots (1124–53), 18 and n, 19, 61, 64, 70, 72–3, 85, 91, 98–101, 107, 122, 127, 130, 153, 166, 168; before accession, 9, 17–18, 71, 98; Laws of, 118
David earl of Huntingdon (d. 1219), 19, 27, 63, 97, 103, 123, 193
David son of Earl Duncan II of Fife, 86
'day of peace' (*dies pacis*), 136
'Denewde', BWK, 169
Dennis, William, 105
Derman, 178; family of, 178
Derwentwater, Alan of, 83n
Devon, 70, 78, 100
Dillars, LAN, 49n
Dirleton, ELO, 20 and n, 21 and n, 196; castle, 21 and n

Dodin, 36, 96n
Dolepene, Dolepain, *see* Lopen
Domart-en-Ponthieu, France **80**, 95 and n; Enguerrand de (Dumard, Dunmar), 95 and n; Gerold de, 95n
Domart-sur-la-Luce, France **80**, 95 and n
Dorset, 70, 78, 100
Douai, Walter of, 78, 100; his son *see* Bampton
Douglas, LAN: Archibald son of William of, 130; David, 12; James, of Lothian, 111
Dowally, PER, 147
Downhead, SOM, 104, 191
Draffan, LAN, 45; James of *see* Loudoun
Drax, YOW, 31, 177
'Driefurd', BWK, 169
Dron, Wester, PER, 131, 197
Drumclog, LAN, 49n
Drumsleed, KCD, 66n
Dryburgh, BWK, 71; abbey (O. Prem.), 20n, 31, 75
Dryfesdale, DMF, 133
Duddingston, MLO, 36, 40, 96n, 98n
Duddingston, WLO, 36
Duffus, MOR, barony of, 165
Dugald son of Somerled, his sons, Olaf, Duncan, Ranald, 159
Dumfries, 31, 49n, 150
Dumfriesshire, 6
Dunbar, ELO: battle of (1296), 151; earldom of, 155, 158
Dunbarney *see* Moncreiffe
Duncan earl of Carrick, 47 and n, 68, 124; his son John, 124; *see also* Neil
Duncan I earl of Fife (d. 1154), 85–6, 197
Duncan II earl of Fife (1154–1204), 85–9, 158, 159, 194, 197
Duncan III earl of Fife (d. 1289), 87n, 130, 190
Duncan younger son of Earl Duncan II of Fife, 88 and n, 197

Duncan clerk of Balbardie, 179
Duncan, Professor A. A. M., 120
Dunchonnell, ARG, 137
Dundas, WLO, 25n, 92, 154; family of, 25 and n, 92; Elias of (saec. xiii), 25n; *see also* Elias son of Uhtred
Dundee, ANG, 63; Mr Ralph of, 69n
Dundonald, AYR, 46
Dunfermline, FIF: Gilbert of, 1; abbey (O.S.B.), 43, 89, 100; prior of, 136
Dunmar *see* Domart
Dunoon, ARG: castle of, 69; John constable of, 69n
Dunstaffnage, ARG, 137
Duredent, Robert, 95n
Durham, 170; cathedral church and priory (O.S.B.), 87n, 94, 122, 154, 159, 196; county of, 160; *Liber Vitae* of, 159

earls' ferry, between East Fife and East Lothian, 85
Eaton Constantine, SHR, 66
Echline, in Dalmeny, WLO, 135
Eddleston, PEB, 39, 72, 129; formerly Penteiacob, Gillemureston, 93 and n
Edgar king of Scots (1094(1097)–1107), 7, 12, 61, 153n
Edinburgh, Malcolm grandson of Serlo of, 14n
Edmund earl of Cornwall, 142
Edmund son of Forn, of Pinkie, 168
Edulf, 39
Edulf son of Uhtred, 93, 129
Edward I king of England (1272–1307), 5, 21, 104, 116–17, 119, 142, 143–4, 145, 147, 149–52, 180; his Ordinance for the Government of Scotland (1305), 118; his Scottish enemies, 10, 111
Edward II king of England (1307–27), 149, 191
Edward son of Peter, laird of Restalrig, 121

Eggard, 34
Eigg, Isle of, INV, 139n
Eilean Dearg, ARG, castle of, 69
Eldbotle in Dirleton, ELO, 20 and n, 21, 169–70; Island (Fidra), church of St. Nicholas on, 20n
Eilaf *see* Isleifr
Ela wife of Earl Duncan II of Fife (daughter of Reginald de Varenne?), 87–8, 197
Elias knight of Ranulf de Soules, 122
Elias son of Uhtred, 25n, 92
Elliston, ROX, 39, 193; barony of, 136; Agnes widow of Laurence of, 193
Elsi son of Winter, 129
Engaine: family of, in Cumberland and Somerset, 72, 98n; of Pytchley, 98; Ada, 72, 178; Geoffrey 'de Engene', 98n; Gilbert, 72n; William, 72n, 98n; William de, 98n
English, the, 6, 21–2, 145; language, 145–7; *see also* Middle English
Epaignes (Hispania), France **27**, 95; Walter de, 95 and n; Walter de, provost of Evreux, William de, 95
Eric king of Norway, 155
Ermengarde queen of Scots (1185–1234), 10, 63 and n, 191–2
Ernulf son of Swinton, 61, 122
Esbie, DMF, 178
Escarbot, Peter, 173
Esseby (i.e. Castle Ashby, NTP): Clarembald of, 41 and n, 178; David of (more than one), 178
Eu, France **76**, 179; family of, Hugh de, 179; Philip de, 36, 38, 179, his daughter Eda, 179; Roger de, Thomas de, 179
Euphemia, Scottish heiress, wife of (1) William Comyn, (2) Andrew Murray of Petty, 9–10, 143 and n
Eure, Hugh d' (of Iver, d'Euer; also Balliol, q.v.), lord of Kirkley, 11 and n
Evreux, Amaury count of, 109n, 195

Ewen (Eugenius) son of Duncan, lord of Argyll, 121n
Eyemouth, BWK, 196
Eynesbury, HNT, 99

Fairfax, William, 88
Fairlie, AYR, 140
Falaise, William de, his wife, Geva, 183
Falkirk, STL, 8, 21; battle of (1298), 149
Fantosme, Jordan, 84
Fargie, in Arngask, PER, 180
Farquhar, ancestor of Lamont family, 68n
Farrer, William, 106
Farsley, YOW, 4–5, 180; forms of name, 5n; family of, 5 and n, 112, 114, 180; Geoffrey of, Kt., 5n, 114, 180; Geoffrey of (in 1296), 5n, 114, 151; Philip of, 114; Ralph of, 180; Simon of, 114, 180
Faxton, NTP, 95n
Fechil, in Ellon, ABD, 154n
Fedderate, ABD, 140; William of, his wife, Christina, 165
Fenton, in Dirleton, ELO, 21 and n
Fergus earl of Buchan, 140
Fergus 'Fostresone', 158n
Ferrers, Isota de, Maud de, wife of Richard of London, 183
Ferselee see Farsley
Fetterangus, ABD, chapel of, 189
feudal law in England and Scotland, 120–1, 141–4
Fife, 5, 23, 30, 61, 92–3, 131; earldom of, 64, 84–90, 129–30, 158; earl of (unnamed), 133; earls of, 84–90, see also Duncan, Malcolm; Howe of, 85
Fincharn, ARG, 132, 165
FitzAlan of Oswestry, family of, 13; see also Stewart
Fitz Aldelin, William, 183
Fitz John, Eustace, 197
Fitz Norman, Hugh, 27, 186; his brother, Ralph, 27; see also Mowat

Fitz Reinfrid, Gilbert son of Roger, 172
Fitz Stephen, William, 77
Fitz Urse, Reginald, 72n, 78; Robert, 72n, 78–9
Fitz Walter, Robert (saec. xii), 15n, 24; his daughter Margaret, 15n; Robert (saec. xiii), 19n
Flanders, 6, 91
Flockhart, 41; see also Folcard, Folkard
Folcard (Fulcard), 36, 41, 67; see also Folkard
Foliot, family of, 18, 99
Folkard, Alexander, 67
Folkerton, LAN, 36, 41, 67
Fordoun, Mearns, 146; John (of), historian, 11, 146–7, 156
Forgan, FIF, 182, 195
Forgandenny, PER, 197
Formartine, ABD, 30
Forscote, William of, 102
Forthar, FIF, 130
Forveleth, daughter of Brice the *judex*, 131
Fossard, family of (in Yorkshire), 111n
Fossoway, KNR, 86
Fotheringay, NTP, 14, 178; see also Fotheringham
Fotheringham of Powrie, family of ('de Fotheringay'), 99
Fothrif (i.e. West Fife and Kinross-shire), 92–3
Fraoch Eilean, Loch Awe, ARG, 139
Fraser, family of, 32; Mr William bishop of St. Andrews, 3n; William, lord of Drumelzier, 141n; Simon, 143
Frendraught, ABD: Malcolm of, 157n; William of, 121n
Freshelee, Freshelegh, see Farsley
Freskin (Fresekin, Fretheskin), 37, 62; see also Murray
Frethebald, 37, 45n
Fretheskin, 37
Friselay see Farsley

Index

G. (error for Arnold or Robert), bishop of St. Andrews, 169–70
Galiena, daughter of Waltheof son of Cospatric, wife of Philip de Moubray, 25, 134, 185–6
Galloway, 30–1, 61, 127, 155; lordship of, 3n
Gamal, 34
Gamel dean of Fogo, 179
Garioch, ABD, 30, 63, 133
Garleton, ELO, 134
Gartonvenach, unidentified, in Lennox, 134 and n
Gatehouse of Fleet, KCB, 31
Gatemore, Robert de, 174; *see also* Berkley
Gerald, tenant of Illieston (same as Gerard?), 124
Gerard *see* Gerald
Gervase king's clerk, 7
Ghent, Walter of, 173–4
Giffard, family of, 43; Hugh, 43
Giffen (or Giffin) AYR, 9 and n, 79, 80n, 187, 189
Gifford, ELO, 43
Gilbert earl of Strathearn, 86, 89, 124–5, 158; his son Fergus, 125
Gilbert son of Fergus lord of Galloway, 31
Gilbert son of Richer (de Boiville?), 80, 176
Gillebrigde earl of Angus, 158
Gillechatfar foster-brother of Uhtred of Galloway, 158n
Gillemure, 39; *see also* Gilmor
'Gillemureston' (now Eddleston), PEB, 39
Gillequdberit ('Cuthbert's devotee'), 34n
Gillesbie, DMF, 48
Gillocrist foster-brother of king of Man, 158n
Gilmerton, DMF, 39
Gilmerton, ELO, 39
Gilmerton, FIF, 39
Gilmerton, MLO, 39
Gilmerton, PER, 39
Gilmor 'Hund', at Dawyck, 34

Gilsland, CUM, men of, 149
Gimmenbie, DMF, 48
Girig, 39
Glai, 126n
Glanvill, 75, 119
Glasgow, 33, 49; cathedral church of St. Mungo (Kentigern), 34, 49, 194; archdeacon of, 136
'Glasrog' ARG unidentified (Glassary?), castle of, 69, 138n
Glassary, ARG, 69
'Glemubsuirles' (lost), in Stobo, PEB (for Glenhope-swires?), 35n
Glendevon, PER, 86
Glenfarg, PER, 114
Glenholm, PEB, 189
Gocelyn, 36
'Gocelyneston' (lost), MLO, 36
Godard chaplain, 20n
Goldington, BDF, 75
Gourel, France **76,** 180
Gourlay (Gurle, Gurlai, etc.): family of, 180–1; Enguerrand (de), Henry, Hugh, William, Yardus, 181
Gournai-en-Bray, France **76,** 180
Gowrie, PER, 30, 61
Graham, David, 141n; Henry lord of Dalkeith, 141n; Peter, 193
Grahm, Bernald de, 186
Great Doddington, NTP, 97n, 122
Greenan, AYR, 46, 115
Greig, Thomas dean of Atholl and Drumalban, 147
Greigston, FIF, 39
'Grenewde', BWK, 169
Grimbald, family of, 18, 99
Grosseteste, Robert bishop of Lincoln (1235–53), 1
Guichart, Robert, 175; *see also* Wishart
Guisborough, YON, priory (O. Aug.), 173; Walter of, chronicler, 157
Gulden faber *see* Robert the goldsmith
Gullane, ELO, 20n, 196
Gunby, Simon of, 28

Gurnay (Gurney, Gornay), Aleyn, 180; Hugh, Thomas, 180; *see also* Gourlay
Guthred king of Man, 158n
Guthrie of that ilk, family of, 99

Hadden, ROX, barony of, 136; Bernard of, 136n
Haddington: fief of, 155; shire of, 127
Hague, La, France **50**, 79 and n; *see also* Haig
Haig of Bemersyde, family of, 79; Peter, 129
Halkerton, KCD, 116; family of, 116
Hall Teasses, FIF, 130
Hamelin (Plantagenet) earl Warenne, 197
Hamilton, LAN, *see* Cadzow
Hanle *see* Hedleia
Hardingstone, NTP, 73n
Harrold, BDF, 177
Hart, DRH, 8
Harterness, DRH, 8
Hartlepool, DRH, 94
Hartside, William of, 123
Harviestoun, CLA, 36, 41n
'Harwde', BWK, 169
Hassendean, ROX, 63, 65
Hastings, Edmund, 69n
Hastings, John, 69n
Haughmond abbey, SHR (O. Aug.), 15n, 66n
Hautôt l'Auvray, France **76**, 20n
Havering, Mr Richard de, 117n
Hawick, ROX, 101, 184; barony of, 136, 142, 184–5; Simon of, 136n
Hay (de la Haye), family of: Christian, lady of Parbroath, 133; Sir Nicholas, 87n, 168; Peter, 182; Thomas (of Lochwharret), 148–9; William I de, 122
Haya, Randulph de, in Yorkshire, 11n
Haye, la (-Bellefonds), France **50**, 122

Hector knight of the earl of Carrick, 124
Hedleia (Hanle, Heleia), Pain de, 23n, 37, 128
Heiton, ROX, 177
Hénin-Liétard, France **59**, 22
Henry I king of England (1100–35), 12n, 13, 18
Henry II king of England (1154–89), 6, 18, 20, 73, 75, 103, 158, 185, 196
Henry III king of England (1216–72), 134, 171
Henry abbot of Kelso, 41n
Henry earl of Atholl, 126
Henry of Scotland earl of Northumberland, 170, 196–7
Henry parson of Langton, 179
Henry the Scot, at Cork, 119, 146
Herbert steward of Beatrice de Beauchamp, 75
Herbert son of Wimund, 189
Herdmanston, ELO, 129
Heriot, MLO, 71
Hermand, MLO, 130
Hervey, 36
Hervey the marischal, lord of Keith, 42 and n
Hesdin, France **62**: Alexander of, 15; Ernulf of, 13; Reginald of, 15n; surname, 65
Hessewell, William of, 143
Hextilda daughter of Uhtred, countess of Atholl, 159
High Ercall, SHR, 66n
highlands of Scotland, 30, 68–70, 146–7, 156; west highlands, 137–9
Hillbeck, WML, 83; family of, 83 and n; Thomas of, William of (saec. xii), William of (saec. xiii), 83n
Hinderwell, YON, 112n
Holderness, YOE, William of, knight of the earl of Fife, 87, 125
Hollister, Professor C. W., 163
Holm Cultram, CUM, abbey (O. Cist.), 182
Holyrood abbey (O. Aug.), 43, 100

Hommet, du, family of, 24
Honorius III, Pope, 77, 162n
Horncastle, LIN, 191
Horsey, SOM, 78, 181; family of, 102, 181; Hugh of (Horsea), otherwise Mauclerc, 77, 79, 181; Philip of, 77-9, 83n, 181, his wife see Morville; Thomas of, 181; Walter of, 77-8, 181; William of, 181
Hosé (Hussy) family, 66
Hotoft (Hoto, Hotot) identified with Hautôt l'Auvray, q.v.? Reginald de, Robert de, Roger de, 20n
Houghton Conquest, BDF, 17, 71, 76n
Houston, ELO, 36
Houston, RNF, 9n, 36, 38, 40; see also Kilellan
Houston, WLO, 36
Howden, Roger of, chronicler, 31
Howgill Fells, WML, 73
Hownam, ROX, barony of, 136
Howthorpe, YON, 186; Henry of (Houtorp), 186
Hubchun, Alan, 123n
Hubeschaun, John de, 123
Hugh, 36, 38
Hugh bishop of Brechin (c. 1214-18), 27n
Hugh of Cyfeiliog earl of Chester, 27
Hugh earl of Ross (d. 1333), 157
Hugh son of Ingebald, 133
Hugh son of Norman, 27, 186
Hugh son of Reginald, 9n
Hugh son of Robert, 173
Hugh son of Waltheof lord of Biggar, 112, 198
Hugh son of William, in Kinmonth, 25n, 134
Hugh son of William in Yorkshire, 25n
Hunald (Hunaud), Robert, 66
Hundleshope, in Manor, PEB, 195
Hunsingore, YOW, 3n; Robert of, 3n; Mr Thomas of, 3 and n
Huntingdon, Honour of, 18, 93, 97-9, 105, 171, 197; earls of (Senlis), 18; (Scottish) see David, Henry, Malcolm, William
Huntingdonshire, jury of, 148
Huntingfield, Roger of, 19n
Huseville (error for Boseville?), Robert de, 192
Hutton in Dryfesdale, DMF, 9n
'Hwichintona', 'Hwitheton', see Anselm

Ilchester, SOM, 191
Illieston, WLO, 39
Inchchonnell, ARG, 137
Inchmahome, PER, 69n; priory (O. Aug.), 68
Inchyra, PER, John son of Duncan of, 87n
Inglis of Tarvit: family of, Richard, 130 and n
Inglisberry (now Grange Hall), LAN, 179
Inglistarvit (afterwards Scotstarvit), FIF, 130
Ingram (Engelram), bishop of Glasgow (1164-74), 170-1
Innerwick, ELO, 65
Innes, Fr. Thomas, 4n
Inverbervie, KCD, 157n
Inveresk, MLO, 168
Inverkeilor, ANG, 102, 174
Inverkeithing, FIF, 25
Inverlunan, ANG, 132
'inverse expectation', phenomenon of, 13
Inverugie, ABD, Castle and Hangman's Hill, 189; see also St. Fergus
Ireland, 30, 32n, 145, 147; kingdom of, 156; northern, 68; see also Ulster
Irish, 1
Irvine, AYR, 46, 49n, 72, 135; castle, 72
Isabel of Menteith, wife of William Comyn, 144
Islebeck, YON, 26; John son of Gilbert of, 26n, 116

Isleifr (Eilaf), 39
Iville, France **27,** 89; *see* Wyville

James I king of Scots (1406–37), 156, 159n
James the Great, Saint, 67
Jedburgh, ROX, 63, 119; castle of, 151; 'manor of', 134n; abbey (O. Aug.), 43, 101n, 122, 154n; abbot of, 136
Jerusalem, 164; kingdom of, 156
Joan of England, queen of Scots (d. 1237), 62–3
Jocelin bishop of Glasgow (1175–99), 77
John, 36, 67
John king of England (1199–1216), 19n, 23, 89, 116, 158
John king of Scots (1292–6; d. 1313), 3, 8, 26, 69, 128, 144, 149–52, 190
John abbot of Kelso (1160–80), 41
John constable of Dunoon, 69n
John earl of Atholl (d. 1306), 138n
John of Scotland ('the Scot'), earl of Huntingdon (d. 1237), 133
John XXII, Pope, 148
John son of Uhtred, 140
Johnstone, DMF, 36, 47
Joinville, Jean de, 8
Jolliffe, J. E. A., 24
Jordan son of Alan, 13, 14

Keith, ELO, barony of, 142n
Keith Marischal, ELO, 42
Kelso, ROX, abbey (O. Tir.), 45n, 77, 97n, 122–3, 170, 179, 189
Kempston, NFK, 15
Kendal, WML (Kentdale), 22, 73; honour of, 172
Ker, John, at Swinehope, 34
Keston, KNT, 190
Ketil(1), 38–9
Kettins, PER, 11
Kettleston, WLO, 38–9
Keynes (Cahagnes), family of, 99

Kilbucho, PEB, 176
Kilconquhar, Adam of, earl of Carrick (d. 1271), 158
Kilellan *see* Houston
Kilfinan, ARG, 68n
Kilgraston, PER, 197
Kilmarnock, AYR, 49
Kilmaron, FIF, 130
Kilmaurs, AYR, 198; church of, 72n
Kilmorie, ARG, 68n
Kilmun, ARG, 68n
Kilpeter, RNF, 40; *see also* Houston
Kilsyth, STL, 140
Kilwinning, AYR, 49; abbey of (O. Tir.), 76–7, 79, 175
Kimmerghame, BWK, 33
Kinbuck, PER: Joachim knight of, Richard knight of, 125
Kincriech, ANG, 164
Kingarth (Kengaif), BTE, 68n
Kinghorn, FIF, 63
Kingledoors, PEB, 162n
Kingoldrum, ANG, 162n
Kingston in Dirleton, ELO, 21 and n
Kinmonth in Moncreiffe, PER, 25n
Kinnerley, Stephen of, 66
Kinnoull, PER, 86–7 and nn
Kintyre, ARG, 69, 138
Kipling, Rudyard, 19
Kippax, YOW, 47n
Kirkanders (lost), KCB, 114, 192
Kir(k)by, Kir(k)ton, names in Yorkshire, 106
Kirkcudbright, 31
Kirkleatham, YON, 94; *see* Lithum
Kirklinton, CUM, *see* Levington
Kirkpatrick, Ivo of, 134
Kirkstall, YOW, abbey (O. Cist.), 194
Kirkurd, PEB, 15n
Kirk Yetholm, ROX, 33, 188–9
Kisimul, Barra, INV, 137
Knapdale, ARG, 68, 138
Knaresborough, YOW, 73
Kyle, AYR, 46, 65; King's Kyle (South Kyle), 31; Kyle Stewart (North Kyle), 62, 65, 72n

Index

Lachlan (*alias* Roland) son of Uhtred lord of Galloway, 17 and n, 79n, 142
Lacy, family of (Hereford branch), 47 and n; (Pontefract branch), 47n; honour of, 46, 108; Henry de, 108n, 194; Hugh de earl of Ulster, 47; John de, 108, 194; Robert de, 194
Lamberton (Lambertona), BWK, 169; Mr William bishop of St. Andrews (1298–1328), 150
Lambin, 36, 44
Lambin, Asa, 45 and n; his son *see* Loudoun
Lamington, LAN, 36, 45
Lammermuir, BWK and ELO, 122
Lamont family, 68 and n, 137; Angus son of Duncan, 68n; John, 140; Lauman son of Malcolm, Malcolm, 68n
Lanark, 33, 44, 49n; castle, 44
Lanarkshire, 67n, 104
Lancashire, 160
Lancaster, honour of, 82
Lancaster, family of, 187; Avicia of, daughter of William I, 73, 187; William I of, 73, 187; William II of, 22, 172, 187
Landeles, Robert de, 136n
Lanercost, CUM, priory of (O. Aug.), 20–1, 185; chronicle of, 21
Langford Budevile, SOM, 105
Langport, SOM, 104, 191
Langton, BWK, 179
languages, mixture of, in Cumbria, 34–5
Lanquetôt, France **76**, 123n; Richard de, 123
Largs, AYR, 77
Lascelles, from Loucelles, France **14**: family of, 115–16, 182; Alan I de, 115, 182, his wife *see* Somerville; Alan II de, 115, 182, his wife Amable, 182; Alan de (in Cumberland), 193; Duncan de, 115–16, 182, his wife *see* Windsor; Henry (error for Hervey?) de,

Marjorie de, Peter de, Richard de, 182
Latham, Sir Henry de, 150
Lauder, BWK, castle, 72
Lauderdale, BWK, 62, 71–2, 77, 129, 135, 188
Laurence (son of Orm) lord of Abernethy, 131
Laurencekirk, KCD, 112n, 198; *see also* Conveth
Lecqueraye, la (St Jean de), France **27**, 94 and n, 181–2; Richard de, Robert de, 94n, 182; Roger de, W(illiam) de, 94 and n, 182
Legerwood, BWK, 65
Leitholm, BWK (Letham), Ketell of, 190
Lennard, Reginald, 13
Lennox, 128, 131, 135, 141, 149, 166; earldom of, 158, 160–1; earls of, 126, 141, 154; *see also* Maoldomhnaich, Malcolm
Lennel, BWK, 155n
Lens, France **62**, 23n; Hugh de, 23
Le Patourel, Professor John, 12, 15–16
Leppeine *see* Lopen
Lesmahagow, LAN, 49; priory (O. Tir.), 173
Lessudden *see* St. Boswells
Lethington (now Lennoxlove), ELO, 88n
Leuchars, FIF, 19n
Leving, 36
Levington (now Kirklinton), CUM, 150, 176
Lewes, SSX, priory (O. Clun.), 197
Lhanbride, MOR, 132
libera baronia, 136, 138
Liddesdale, ROX, church of St. Martin of, *see* Castleton
Lilliesleaf, ROX, 61, 179
Lincoln, Richard of, 7; *see also* Richard bishop of Moray
Lindores, FIF, 63; abbey (O. Tir.), 63n, 180, 193
Lindsay (i.e. of Lindsey): family of, 18, 41, 98; David II of, lord of

Crawford, 123; David, of Barnweill, 134; Walter of (saec. xii), William of (saec. xii), 62
Linton, ROX, 107, 194–5
Linton in Spofforth, YOW, 88–9; Richard son of Andrew of, 88, 130; *see also* Inglis
Lisle, John de, 144
Lismore, Isle of, ARG, 144
Lithulf, 74
Lithum, Robert of, 94
Little, A. G., 21
Little Kype, in Strathaven, LAN, 173
Little Lour, ANG, 164
Liulf, 38–9
Liulf son of Eάgi, 34; his five sons, Cospatric, Eggard, Gamal, Macbeth, Reginald, 34
Liulf son of Liulf, his son William, 65n
Livingston, WLO, 36, 130
Loccard, 36, 48; (Lockhart), family of, 46; Malcolm, 46n; Simon (saec. xii), 46; Simon (saec. xiv), 67; Stephen (Steven), 46
Lochaber, INV, 156
Loch Awe, ARG, 138
Loch Doon, AYR, 150
Loch Fyne, ARG, 138
Lochkindelo (now New Abbey), KCB, 93
Lochmaben, DMF, 134
Lochore, FIF: family of, 92–3 and n; Constantine of, 93n
Loch Sween, ARG, 137
Lockerbie, DMF, 36, 40, 47
Loftus, YON, 111 and n, 112, 173
Löfvenberg, Professor M. T., 5
Logan, John, 45n; Walter, of Hartside, 144
Logierait, PER, 140
London (Londoniis, Londres, Lundoniarum), 183; family of, 14, 101–3, 183–4; Alexander of, 183; Eschina of, wife of Walter I Stewart, 14, 65, 184, 193; John of, 183; Maurice of, 183–4;

Richard of (saec. xii), 101, 103, 183, his wife *see* Ferrers; Richard of (saec. xiii), 183; Robert of, nephew of Thomas, 101–2, 104, 174, 183, his wife Isabel, 101, 183; Robert of, bastard son of King William I, 63–4, 102, 183; Thomas of, 101 and n, 104, 169, 183, his wife Margaret, 101, 183; William of, 183; '——' of, mistress of King William I?, 101–2, 183
London, in Old Cleeve, SOM, 183
Londoniis, de, *see* London
Londres *see* London
Long Buckby, NTP, 22
Longforgan, PER, 63
Longueville-la-Gifart, France **76**, 43
Longueville, France **76,** priory of Saint Faith (O. Clun.), 95
Lopen, SOM, 103, 184; family of (Dolepene, Dolepain, de Holepen, etc.), 103–4, 184; Gilbert of (saec. xiii in.), 103; Gilbert of (saec. xiii ex.), 104; Henry of, William of (brother), 103, 184
Lothian, 32, 38, 49, 131, 154, 155; East Lothian, 6, 85–6; Midlothian, 2; West Lothian, 6, 63
Loucelles, France **14,** *see* Lascelles
Loudoun, AYR, 45, 129; A. son of James of, Adam of, Sir Andrew of, 45n; James of (also James of Draffan, James son of Lambin), 45 and n, 129
Louis VII king of France (1137–80), 8
Louis IX king of France (1226–70), 8
Lour, ANG, 132
Louvetôt, France **76,** 125n; family of (later Loutit), 124–5 and n; Nigel de (saec. xii), Nigel de (saec. xiii), Richard de, lord of Hallam (d. 1171), 125n; Roger de, 124–5; William de, 124n
Lovel: family of, 101–3, 184–5; Henry (saec. xii), 101, 174, 184, 192; Henry (saec. xiii), 142, 191;

Index

Ralph II, 100–1, 174, 183–5; Richard I, 184, 193; Richard II, 142–85; Richard III, his wife Muriel de Soules, 185; Robert brother of Henry, 101, 184
Lowthorpe, YOE, Ranulf son of Walter of, 116
Loyd, Lewis, 93
Lundoniarum *see* London
Luss, DNB, 160; Sir John knight of, 160
Lyleston, BWK, 38–9
Lyne, PEB, David lord of, 141n

Macbeth, 34
MacCulloch, Thomas, 3n
Maccus, 38–9
MacDonald: Alexander, lord of Islay, 119, 144; John, lord of Islay, 156
MacDougall: John, lord of Lorne, 156; Juliana, 144
Macfarlane of that ilk, Walter, 170
MacGilchrist, Gillascop (Gillespie), 132, 138, 165
MacLachlan, family of, 137
MacLeod, Gillandres, 131
MacNaughton, Gilchrist (Cristinus), 138n, 139; his wife Bethoc, 139n; his wife Ethena, 139 and n
MacRuarie, Christian daughter of Alan, 139n
MacSween, Dugald lord of Knapdale, 68, 137–8
MacWilliam, Donald, 86
Maelcarf, 39
Magna Carta (1215), 133n, 153n
Maidford, NTP, 172
Maitland (Maltalent, Mautalent, etc.): family of, 32, 81–2, 129, 185; Gilbert, 82n, 185; Richard, 32n, 81n, 185; Robert, 185; Thomas, 82n, 185; William I, 82, 185; William II, 81n, 185; William III, 81n
Major, John, 147
Makerston, ROX, 39

Malchael, Ralph, 71n
Malcolm II MacKenneth king of Scots (1005–34), 164
Malcolm III 'Canmore' king of Scots (1057–93), 9, 164
Malcolm IV king of Scots (1153–65), 19–20, 31, 64, 65n, 67, 70, 97–8, 102, 107, 108n, 110, 122, 153, 169–71, 174, 177, 183, 194
Malcolm I earl of Fife (1204–28), 85n, 86, 88–9, 129–30, 154, 197
Malcolm earl of Lennox, 160–1
Malcolm son of Bertolf, 133
Malger, 36, 122
Malherbe: family of, 96–7 and n, 177; John, Maud, 96n; *see also* Morham
Malise earl of Strathearn, 158 and n
Malleville-sur-le-Bec, France **27**, 96; *see also* Melville
Malmesbury, William of, 2
Malvoisin, William, chancellor of Scotland, bishop of St. Andrews (1202–38), 7
Mandeville, Geoffrey de, earl of Essex, 24
Mangerton, ROX, 36, 122n
Manhood, SSX, 19, 67; End, chapel at, 19n
'manorial' place-names, 41–3
Maoldomhnaich earl of Lennox, 126, 134
Mar, 11; earldom of, 158
Marchamley, SHR, 66
Margaret of Scotland, queen of Norway, 155
Margaret (Saint) queen of Scots wife of Malcolm III, 9
Margaret queen of Scots (the 'Maid of Norway'), 142
Margaret of Scotland duchess of Brittany, 62–3
Margaret of Scotland daughter of William I, 63
Margaret (Marjorie) of Scotland daughter of William I, wife of Gilbert Marshal earl of Pembroke, 134

Marshal, Gilbert, earl of Pembroke, 134
Mr Matthew the Scot chancellor of the king, 136
Mauclerc, Hugh otherwise of Horsea, 77; *see also* Horsey
Maud (Matilda), Empress, daughter of Henry I of England, 20 and n, 196
Maud daughter of Earl Gilbert of Strathearn, wife of Earl Malcolm I of Fife, 89
Maulds Meaburn, WML, 73
Maule: Harry, of Kellie, titular earl of Panmure, 4 and n; William, lord of Panmure, 143
Maurice son of Galbraith, his wife Catriona, 134
Mautaland, Mautalent, *see* Maitland
Maxton, ROX, 38–9; Cecile of, 103
Maxwell, ROX, 39
May, Isle of, FIF, priory (O. Clun.), 197
Maybole, AYR, 6 and n
Mearns, KCD, 30, 61
Mearns, RNF, 65, 72n
Melrose, ROX, 33; abbey (O. Cist.), 2n, 32, 108, 119, 122, 124, 131, 168, 172, 194; chronicle of, 2; Peter of, 2n; Old Melrose, 71
Melville, MLO, 36, 40; family of, 96–7; Geoffrey I de, 36, 40, 96; Geoffrey II de, 96n; Geoffrey de (Malevilla) in Normandy, 96; Gregory de Melville, Maud de Melville (née Malherbe), Richard de Melville, 96n; *see also* Malleville
Menteith, PER, earldom of, 158
Merlay, Roger de, lord of Morpeth, his daughter Ada, 88
Merse, 6, 32; *see also* Berwickshire
Mervinslaw, ROX, 171
Meschin, Ranulf, vicomte of Bayeux, William lord of Coupland, 80
Meyners (Menzies): Alexander de, 138n; Robert de, 134, 140
Mid Calder, MLO (Calder Clere), 42, 110–11, 176

Middle English, 199–203
Mihhyn 'Brunberd', at 'Corrukes', 34
Milburga, Saint, 67
Miles, Milo, 36
Milton, SOM, 174
Mingarry, ARG, 137
Minto, ROX, 195
Mirren (Mirinus), Saint, 67
Mohun, William de, 101, 103, 183
Moidart, INV, 139n
Mold, FLI (formerly Bistre), 27, 186; *see also* Mowat
Molyneux of Sefton: family of, 82 and n; Richard, Simon, 82n; *see also* Moulineaux
Monceaux, Ingram de, 112n, 198
Moncreiffe, PER (parochially also Dunbarney), 132, 136, 186; family of, 25 and n; David of, 25n; Matthew of, 26n, 132, 134
Monkland, LAN, 43
Monkton, AYR, 43
Monkton, MLO, 43
Montacute (SOM) (Montagu): Drogo de (saec. xi), Drogo de, younger (saec. xii), 100n; Robert de, 100 and n; William son of Robert de, 100n
Montebourg, France **50,** abbey (O.S.B.), 71n
Montgomery, Wales, 40; family of, in Scotland, 40n; John laird of Eaglesham, 67; Robert of, 66, 67
Montgommery, France **14,** 40n
Montrose, ANG, 193
Moray, 61, 128; Braes of, 128; Laich of, 30
Morham, ELO, 96n; family of (also Malherbe, q.v.), 96–7, 177
Morice, 36
Morriston, BWK, 36
Mortain, France **50,** church of Our Lady, 96n
Morton, DMF, 115
Morton, MLO, 63
Morville, France **50,** 70; family of, constables of Scotland, 62, 64, 70–84, 98, 187–8; Ada de, 74;

Dorothea de, wife of Philip de Horsey (q.v.), 77, 79, 181; Helen de, 17, 76, 83n, 142; Herbert de, 78; Hugh I de (d. 1162), 31 and n, 71–5, 84, 175; Hugh II de, 18 and n, 31 and n, 72n, 73–5; Hugh de, son of Simon, lord of Burgh by Sands, 81–2, 178, 185; Malcolm de, 74; Maud de, 73, 75, *see also* Vieuxpont; Richard de (saec. xii in.), 71n; Richard de (saec. xii med.) 17, 72–7, 79, 83, 93, 129, 169, 175, 181; Simon de, lord of Burgh by Sands, 72, 74; William de, 79, 83n, 129, 142, 187
Motherwell, LAN, 45n
Moubray (Mowbray): family of, 25–6, 107, 185–6, of Barnbougle, 26, 186; Honour of (in England), 25n, 26n, 186; Sir Geoffrey de, 151; Nigel I de, 25; Nigel II de, 25, 185; Nigel de (saec. xiii), 25n, 26; Philip de, 19, 24–6, 29, 134, 136, 185–6, his wife *see* Galiena; Sir Philip de (saec. xiv), 26; Robert de (saec. xii), 185; Robert de clerk, 186; Roger de (saec. xii), 25 and n, 109n, 185, 195; Roger de, in Yorkshire (saec. xiii), 26n, 186; Roger de (saec. xiv), 26; Roger son of Philip de, 25n, 132, 135, 186; William de, 185; *see also* Mowbray
Moulineaux, France **76**, 82n, 188
Moulineaux, Vivian des, 82 and n, 187–8; *see also* Molyneux
Moulineaux, William (error for Vivian?) des, 187–8
Mow (Molle), ROX, 65 and n; Henry of (son of Anselm?), 65n
Mowat (de Monte Alto, of Mold): family of, 27, 186; Alexander, 27 and n, 186; David, 28n; Michael, 28, 186; Ralph II, Robert II, 27; Robert Mowat in Scotland, 19, 26–8, 29, 186; Roger I, 27 and n; Roger II, 28n; William, 27, 186; Mowat of Blair, 28n

Mowbray, John, of Cockairnie, his brother Robert, 186
Mowbray, Sir Robert, of Barnbougle, 186; *see also* Moubray
Muchelney, SOM, abbey (O.S.B.), 191
Much Wenlock, SHR, priory of (O. Clun.), 67
Mumbre, BNF, thanage of, 157n
Muncaster, CUM, 187 family of, 9n, 186–7; Alice, 9, 150, 187; Benedict, 187; Robert, 9, 187; Walter, 80n, 187; Sir Walter, 187; *see also* Pennington
Mundurno, in Old Machar, ABD, 193
Munehtes, David de, 136
Munster, north (Thomond), 69
Murdac, family of, at Palgrave, NFK, 15; Eve ('Morthach'), 15n; Walter, 15 and n; William (also 'of Palgrave'?), 15n
Murdieston (Murdostoun), LAN, 39
Muredach, 39
Murray (de Moravia, of Moray): family of, 62; Mr Andrew, bishop of Moray, 28; Sir Andrew, lord of Petty, 143, 190, his wife, 143; *see also* Euphemia
Murray, Alexander, 138n, 195
Murray, Andrew (d. 1297), 8n, 168
Murray, Austin, 67n
Murray, Malcolm, 132, 138n
Murray, Richard, of Culbin, 182
Murray, William, 132
Muschamp(s), family of: Reginald de, 18n; Thomas de, 18 and n
Myles in Tranent, ELO, 35, 41

Nagtun *see* Nawton
Nain, le (Nanus, Neym): family of, 43, 95, 188–9; Hubert, John, 189; Maurice, Ralph I, Ralph II, 188; Richard, 188–9
Namier, Sir Lewis, 166–7
Naughton, FIF, 182
Naval Service, 138–9
Navar, ANG, 131

Nawton (Nagtun), YON, 186; Patrick of, 25n, 136, 186
Néhou, France **50**, 79 and n; church of St. Mary in the castle of, 71n; family of, 79 and n, 187, 189–90; Alexander de, Richard de, 79n; William de, 79n, 189, his wife Syrit, 80n
Neil (Nigel), 36
Neil earl of Carrick, 124
Neilston, RNF, 36
Nenthorn, BWK, 71
Nes (Ness) son of William, lord of Leuchars, 23, 158; his sons Constantine and Patrick, 23
Ness, Great and Little, SHR, 66
Neuham, William de, Templar, 194
Nevay, ANG, 132; Henry of, 132, 164–5
New Abbey, KCB, formerly Lochkindelo, 93
Newbattle abbey, MLO (O. Cist.), 43
Newham, Robert of, 140
Newton in Hawick, ROX (Chamberlain Newton), 42n, 102 and n
Newton, NFK, 15
Newton Dun, BWK, 71
Newton Reigny, CUM, 42n
Newtyle, ANG, 63
Nicholas parson of Glenholm, 189
Nisbet, ROX, 122; Archil grieve of, Hethna of, 122
Nithsdale, DMF and KCB, 128
Noble, Ralph, 96n
Norham on Tweed, NTB, 179
Norman son of Malcolm son of Bertolf, 133
Norman Conquest of England, 6, 168, 172
Normandy, 6, 91, 94–7
Normans in Yorkshire, 106
Normanville, family of, 103; Sir Thomas de, 143
Northampton, NTP, 91, 98
North Berwick, ELO, priory of (O. Cist.), 154
North Stoke, SSX, 19

Northumberland, 49, 116; Assizes, 119
Northumbria: English, 107; Scottish, 33, 65, 107

O'Donnell king of Tirconaill, 158n
Offord, HNT, 17
Ogilface, WLO, 179
Oldhamstocks, ELO, 33, 38n
Olifard (Oliphant): family of, 18, 41, 44–5, 98; David, Roger (saec. xi), 45n; Walter II, 132, 178; Sir William (saec. xiv), 152
Orabilis daughter of Nes son of William, 22–3
Orby, LIN: family of, 28; Simon of, in Moray, 28; Simon of, in Newton Solney, 28n
Orchies, France **59**, 23n; Roger de, 23
Orm, 39
Ormiston, ELO, 39
Ormiston, FIF, 39
Orty, de l' (de Lorty), Henry, 104–5, 191
Outerside, in Roberton, ROX, 101n
Ovington, YON, 16
Oxford, university, 1–3; Balliol College, 2, 3 and n; Burnell's Inn (London College), 2 and n
Oxton, BWK, 82

Pagan (Pain), 36, 37
Painell, FULK, 78
Paisley, RNF, 33, 49 and n; abbey (O. Clun.), 43, 49, 67
Palgrave, NFK, 15 and n, 65n; Robert of, 15n; Roger of, 15; William of (also Murdac, q.v. ?), 15n; surname, 65
Panmure, ANG, 23; barony of, 143; earl of *see* Maule
Paris, Matthew, historian, 168
Paston, NTB, 134n
Patrick II earl of Dunbar, 172
Patrick IV earl of Dunbar, 143
Paul, Sir James Balfour, 3, 4 and n

Index 225

Pearsby, DMF, 36, 37, 47
Peebles, 33
Peeblesshire, 9
Penneld, RNF, 9n
Pennersaughs, DMF (formerly Pennersax), 9n, 47n, 134
Pennington, CUM, 186; family of, 9n, 83n, 186–7; Alan of, 9, 187; Benedict of, William of, 187; *see also* Muncaster
Penrith, CUM, 22
Penston, ELO (Painston etc.), 36, 37, 128
Percehay (Perthay, Pershay, etc.): family of, 189–90; Philip de (?), 190; Walter de (saec. xii), 189; Walter de (saec. xiii in.), Sir Walter de (saec. xiii), Sir Walter de (saec. xiv), 190
Perceton, AYR, 36, 37
Percy-en-Auge, France **14**, 177; family of, Alan de, 97n, 177; Avice de, 177; Geoffrey de, Henry de, 97n, 177
Perth, Duncan of, 121n
Perthshire, 5
Pessun: family of, 190–1; Ingram, his wife Cecily, Richard, 190; Stephen, 150, 190, his wife Christian, 190; William (in Kent), William (at Tynninghame), 190; William (saec. xiv), 191
Peter (Piers), 36
Peter the constable of Cupar, 85n
Peter the Miller, of E. Ardsley, 151
Peverel, William, of Dover, 66n
Philip, 36
Philip II Augustus, king of France (1180–1223), 95
Philip IV le Bel, king of France (1285–1314), 148, 152
Philpingston(e), WLO, 36, 38, 179
Philpstoun, WLO, 36
Picardy, 6
pit and gallows (*furca et fossa*), 135–6
Pitcombe, SOM, Roger of, 101n
Pitpullox, ANG, 190
Pittengardner, 66n

Plenderleith, ROX, Jean daughter of Nicholas of, 144
Plenmeller, NTB, 102, 174
Plent(r)idoc, otherwise Baltrudoc (now Temple), MLO, 43
Plompton (Plumpton) in Spofforth, YOW, 88 and n; Nigel of, 88 and n
Pollok, RNF, 49n; Peter son of Fulbert of, his daughter, Muriel, 15n
Polton, Thomas (afterwards bishop of Hereford, Chichester, and Worcester), 145–6
Pont, Revd Timothy, 76–7
Ponteland, NTB, 168
Ponthieu, Ela de, 88n, 197; Roger de, 179
Poole, Dr A. L., 74
Portbury, SOM, 78
Powerstock, DOR, 174
Prestwich, John, 166
Prestwick, AYR, 6 and n

Queensferry, FIF and WLO, 25
Queschutbrit, Gillemihhel, at Traquair, 34
Quincy (Cuinchy, q.v.): family of, 22 and n, 23; Robert de, 19, 22–3, 28, 29, 35, 128, his wife *see* Orabilis, 154; Roger de, earl of Winchester, 23, 35n, 172, his wife, Helen of Galloway, 172; Saher I de, 22; Saher II de, 99; Saher III de, earl of Winchester, 19n, 35
Quirem, Roger, 179
Quynquerstaynes, Thomas de, 190

Race (Razo), 37
Raddington, SOM, 174
Rait, NAI, hall house of, 157; John of, 157, his son John, 157n
Raiville, Miles (also Milo?) de, 87 and n, 125
Ralph (Raoul, Radulf), 36, 37
Ralph bishop of Brechin (1198–1212), 27
Ralston, RNF, 36, 37

Ramsay: family of, 99; John, 133; Nes of, Nes son of Nes, 130 and n; Mr Peter of, bishop of Aberdeen (1247–56), 1
Randolph: family of, 115; Sir Thomas the elder, 150, 190
ranscauth (right of scrutiny), in Fife, 159n
Redcastle, in Inverkeilor, ANG, 103
Redesdale, NTB, men of, 149
Redgorton, PER, 86
Redvers (Reviers): family of, 70–1 and n; Baldwin de, 20, 71n
Reginald, 34
regnum Anglie, regnum Scotie, concept of, 152–5
Reigny: family of, 72n; Maurice de, 102; *see also* Cumberland, Robert of
Renfrew, 33, 49n, 62, 65, 67, 72n
Renfrewshire, 65
Revel: family of, 104–5, 191–2; Adam 'of Stawell', 10, 104–5, 191; Alan, 104, 191; Henry, 10, 104–5, 191; Richard I, 104–5, 191; Richard II, 10, 104–5, 191, his wife Mabel, his daughter Sabina, 104, 191; *see also* Orty
Reviers *see* Redvers
Rhuddlan, Statute of (1284), 156
'Ricardestun' lost, in Rhynd, PER, 36, 41n, 48n
Riccarton, AYR, 36, 48n, 67
Riccarton, ROX, 36, 48n
Riccarton, WLO, 36, 48n
Richard, 36
Richard I king of England (1189–99), 104
Richard (of Lincoln), bishop of Moray (1187–1203), 86
Richard chaplain of King Malcolm IV, 169
Richard chaplain of the earl, 169–70
Richard earl of Cornwall, 190
Richard son of Baldwin, 71n
Richard son of Lugan (Luguen), his brother Geoffrey, 125
Richard son of Solph (Folchard?), 41n
Richard son of Truite, 93
Richardson, H. G., 163
Rickerby, DMF, 48
Riddell *see* Ryedale
Ridel: family of, 42, 98; G. (Geoffrey?), 170–1; Gervase, 170–1, his wife Christian, 171; Hugh, 42; Ralph, 170–1
Rideware, William de, 194
Rievaulx, YON: abbey (O. Cist.), abbots of *see* Ailred
Ringwood, in Teviothead, ROX, 23–4
Ripley, YOW, 112–13; family of, 112–14, 192; Adam of, 113n; Bernard of (clerk), 113 and n, 192; Bernard of (saec. xiii), 113–14, 192, his wife, Margaret, 114, 192; Norman of, 113n; Richard of, 113, 192; Uhtred of, Waltheof of, 113n; William, son of Richard of, 113, 192; *see also* Dallas
'Ristone', BWK, 169
Ritchie, R. L. Graeme, 98
'Roberdesbi' (lost), DMF, 36, 41, 47
Robert, 36
Robert of Roberton, LAN (saec. xii), 45n
Robert of Roberton, LAN (saec. xiii), 45n
Robert of Roberton, ROX? 101
Robert I king of Scots (1306–29), 26, 66, 138, 147, 148, 149–50, 160, 168; as earl of Carrick, 150; *see also* Brus
Robert II king of Scots (1371–90), formerly Robert seventh Stewart of Scotland, 64
Robert bishop of St. Andrews (1127–39), 153
Robert earl of Strathearn, 125
Robert Curthose son of William I, duke of Normandy, 18
Robert the goldsmith ('Gulden faber'), 96n
Robert son of Derman, 178

Robert son of Wernebald, his son Robert, 72n, 198
Roberton, LAN, 36; Henry of, 45n; Robert of, 123; William of, 45n
Roberton, ROX, 36
Roberton of Earnock, family, 45n
Roger, clerk of Robert of London, 102
Roger son of Glai, 126
Roland lord of Galloway *see* Lachlan
Rollington, DOR, 174
Romilly, Robert de, 187
Ros (later Ross): family of, in Cunningham, 80; Alan de, 140; Godfrey de, 129; *see also* Rots
Ros, Robert de (of Helmsley and Wark), 150
Ross, 30; earldom, 158
Ross, in Cadzow, LAN, 45n
Rothes, MOR, 15n
Rothesay, BTE, castle of, 69
Rots, near Bayeux, France **14,** 80; *see also* Ros
Rouen, France **76,** 20
Round, J. H., 4 and n
Roxburgh, ROX: burgesses of, 148; castle, 107; sheriff court of, 136
Roxburgh, Hugh of, chancellor of Scotland (d. 1199), 155
Roxburghshire, 9
Ruffus, David, 164
Rula Herevei, now Abbotrule, ROX, 36
Rule, ROX (Bedrule?), barony of, 136, 195; Alan of, 136n
Rum, Isle of, INV, 139n
Rumgally, FIF, 10
Rus, William le, 176
Rutherford, ROX, barony of, 136; Hugh of, 136n
Ryedale, YON: family of, in Scotland (later Riddell), 116; Walter of, 61, 116

St. Albans, HRT: Richard of, Walter of, 7

St. Andrews, FIF: Cathedral church and priory (O. Aug.), 10, 85, 101n, 182, 192, 198; parliament of (1309), 152
Saint-Aubin-Guichard, France **27,** 175
St. Bees, CUM, priory (O.S.B.), 192
St. Boswells, formerly Lessudden, ROX, 63, 64, 101–2, 174, 183
St.-Clair-sur-l'Elle, France **50,** 80 and n; *see also* Sinclair
St. Cyrus (Eglesgirig), KCD, 63 and n
St. Fergus, ABD (formerly Inverugie St. Fergus), 43, 189
St. Hilaire, Emma de, 73n, 76n; *see also* Vieuxpont
St. Martin by Bellencombre, France **76,** 127; Adulf de, 74; Alexander de, 61, 89, 127; Henry de, 9n; Ralph son of Gilbert de, parson of Bolton, 127n
St. Martin-d'Aubigny, France **50,** 25
St. Michael: family of, 192–3; David of, Elmeras of, John of, John son of John of, Sir John of, lord of Heavyside, 193; Robert of, 136n, 193; Roger of, 193; Walter of, 192; William of (saec. xii), 192–3; William of (saec. xiii), 193
Saltoun, ELO, 71, 82, 188
Sampford Brett, SOM, 72
Sans Manche, Hugh, 115
Say, Hugh de, 197; Orabilla de, wife of Reginald de Varenne, 197; William de, 190
Sayles, Professor George, 163
Scalebroc *see* Skelbrooke
Scandinavian elements in place-names, 47–8
Schanualy (now Shannally in Lintrathen), ANG, 162n
Scholes, YOW, 47n
Scot, Michael, of Rumgally, 10
Scot, Michael, of Balwearie, 10
Scot of Scotstarvit, Sir John, 130; *see also* Calverley, Henry

Scota daughter of Pharaoh, legend of, 145–6
Scotismilne, ABD (two), 162n
Scottish army, service, etc., 161–2, 164–6, 168
Scoular, James, 128
Scroggs, in Lyne, PEB, 141n
Seacroft, YOW, 108, 194
Selkirkshire, 9
Sémerville (now Graveron-Sémerville), France **27**, 109 and n, 195
Senlis, family of, 99; Maud de, wife of Saher I de Quincy, 22; Maud de, wife of William d'Aubigny; also wife of Richard de Louvetôt, 89, 125n; Simon I de, earl of Northampton, 45n; Simon III de, earl of Northampton, 173
Seton (de Setona): family of, 148–9; Alexander of (saec. xiii), 126n; Sir Alexander of (saec. xiv), 148
Seton, Sir Christopher, of Yorkshire, 150
Shap Fell, WML, 73
Shap Summit, WML, 22
Ship service, 138–9
Shropshire, 91
Sibbald, 36, 48; family of, of Kair, 124; *see also* Sybald
Sibbaldbie, DMF, 36
Sicklinghall, YOW, 88n; Silvester son of William of, 88; William son of Robert of, 88n
Simon (Simund), 36
Simon brother of Walter and William sons of Alan, 'of Norfolk', 13–14, 15 and n
Simon son of Bertolf, his son Simon, 126
Simon son of Robert, 141n
Simpson, Dr Grant, 128
Sinclair: family of, 80 and n; Alan I, de, Alan II de, 80n; Henry de 80n, 129
Sinnington, YON, 110
Skelbrooke (Scalebroc), YOW, 46; Butlers of, 46; Roger of, 46, 47 and n, 115, 124; William of, 47n

Skilgate, SOM, 174
Skipness, ARG, 137, 138
Slains, ABD, 140
Smardale, WML, 83; family of, 83 and n; Adam of, Simon of, 83n
Smith, A. H. (Hugh), 4, 5
Snell, John, of Colmonell, 3
Somerset, 70, 78, 93, 97, 100–5
Somerton, SOM, 191
Somerville (from Soumerville, now Sémerville, q.v.?): family of, 44, 108–9, 193–5; Alan de, 194; Juliana de, wife of Alan de Lascelles, 182, 195; Robert de (saec. xi?), 193; Robert de (saec. xii), Roger de, 194; Walter de, 108n, 194, his wife, Cecily, 194; William I de, 62, 107–8, 193–4; William II de, 107n, 194; William III de (d. 1242), 108 and n, 109, 194; *see also* Tremblay
Sorbie, in Castleton, ROX, 154n
Sorrowless, William, 41
Sorrowlessfield, in Melrose, ROX, 41
Soules, de: family of, butlers of Scotland, 62, 98; Muriel, daughter of John de, 185; Ranulf I de, 62, 122
Soulles, France **50**, 122
Soumerville *see* Sémerville, Somerville
Spey, River, 30
Sporle, NFK, 15, 65n
Stawell, SOM, 191
Stein, Professor Peter, 119–20
Stenton, ELO, 38, 65
Stephen (Steven), 37
Stephen king of England (1135–54), 18, 158, 177
Stephen son of Richard, 129
Stevenson, ELO, 37
Stevenson, Joseph, 21, 24
Stevenston, AYR, 37
Stewart (Senescallus): family of, 13–14, 62, 64–70, 122–3, 126; Alan (1177–1204), 14 and n, 68, 122, 169, his daughter Avelina,

68; Alexander 'of Dundonald' (1241–83), 68; James (1283–1309), 69–70; John, of Jedburgh (d. 1298), 69; Robert, 72n, *see also* King Robert II; Walter I (*c.* 1136–1177), 9n, 13–14, 15 and n, 19, 62, 64–8, 84, 169, 176, his wife *see* London; Walter II (1204–41), 14 and n, 69n, 122–3; Walter ('Ballach') earl of Menteith, 68–9, 138; *see also* Jordan, Simon brother of Walter, William son of Alan
Stewart of Scotland, office of, 14, 64–5
Stewart-Brown, R., 160–1
Stirling: castle, 152; bridge, battle of (1297), 168
Stirlingshire, 128
Stobo, PEB, 34
Stockton, WAR, 108
Stratha'an (Strathavon), BNF, 86
Strathardle, PER, 30
Strathaven, LAN, 67, 111, 173–4
Strathbogie, ABD, 86
Strathbraan, PER, 85
Strathbrock, WLO, barony of, 165
Strathearn, PER, 30, 124–5; earldom of, 158, 159n; earls of *see* Gilbert, Malise, Robert
Stratherrick, INV, 32 and n
Strathgryfe, RNF, 62, 65, 72n
Strathlachlan, ARG, 137
Strathleven, FIF, 85
Strathmore, PER and ANG, 64, 131
Strath Tay, PER, 30
Stretton, RUT, 99
Stuart, Dr John, 4
Stuteville: Robert de, 136; William de, 18n
Sutherland, 30; earldom of, 158
Sveinn (Swain, Swein), 39
Swaffham, NFK, 65n; Richard of, William of, 65n
Swanston, MLO, 39
'Swinewde', BWK, 169
Swinton, BWK, 61, 122; Alan, grandson of Cospatric of, 133

Sybald, knight of Mearns, 124; *see also* Sibbald
Symington, AYR, 36, 67
Symington, LAN, 36

Taillebois, Ivo, 71
'Talahret' (lost), RNF, 49n
Tancard (Thancard), the Fleming, 37, 45–6, 111; his son Thomas, 45n
Tannadyce, ANG, thanage of, 157n
Tarbolton, AYR, 176
Tarvit, FIF, 190; *see also* Inglistarvit
Teasses, FIF, 130
Temple, MLO (formerly Plentridoc), 43
Temple Newsam, YOW, 194
Temple, order of, *see* Lopen, Stretton, Temple, Temple Newsam
Teviotdale, ROX, 6, 32
thane, thanage, 11
Thankerton, by Bothwell, LAN, 37, 45 and n
Thankerton (Upper Clydesdale), LAN, 37, 45–6
Thennes, France **80**, 97 and n; Saer de, 97 and n
Theobald, 37
Theobald count of Champagne and Brie, 63
Thirkleby ('Turkeby'), Roger of, justice, 171
Thirlestane, BWK, 82, 129, 185; Alan of, 14n, 129; Avicia of, 185; Thomas of, 32; Winter of, 185; *see also* Maitland
Thomas son of Adam of Raiswaith, 187
Thomas son of Thancard, his sister Beatrice, 45n
Thor, 39
Thorner, YOW, 108, 194
Threepwood, in Beith, AYR, 181
Thurston, ELO, 39
Torpenhow, CUM, 136, 185
Tosny, family of, 109–10
Tours-en-Vimeu, France **80**, 174, 181

Touville, France **27**, 95, 175
Town Yetholm, ROX, 43, 188
Trailtrow, DMF, 49n
Tranent, ELO, 22, 33
Trano, Gioffredo di, 120
Trearn, in Beith, AYR, 187; *see also* Giffen
Tremblay, le (now Le Tremblay-Omonville), France **27**, 109 and n, 195; family of, 108–9, 195–6; Boschard de, 109n, 195; Cecily de, 195; Everard de, 109n, 195; John de, Robert de (saec. xiii), Robert de (saec. xiv), 195; Walter de (Trembleye), 108–9, 194–5; *see also* Somerville, Turnbull
Trevelyan, G. M., 149
Treverlen, MLO, 40; *see also* Duddingston
Troquhain, AYR, 49n
Trynedin, Laurence son of Henry, 119
Turkeby, *see* Thirkleby
Turnberry, AYR, band of (1286), 69
Turnbull: family of, 195–6; John, 195; Margaret, 196; Walter, William bishop of Glasgow (1447–54), 195; *see also* Tremblay
Tweeddale, 6, 32, 49, 162n
Tynedale, NTB and CUM, men of, 149
Tynninghame, ELO, 33, 38n

Uhtred son of Fergus, lord of Galloway, 31, 93, 158n, 196
Uhtred son of Halden, lord of Catterlen, 115
Uhtred son of Liulf, 65; his son Adam, 65n
Uhtred son of Osulf, his sons Ralph and Thomas, 24
Ulkelestun, unidentified, ELO, 128
Umfraville, Odinel de, 18
Urr, KCB, 174
Uthrogle, FIF, 130

Vallance, surname (from Valognes, q.v.), 24
Valognes, France **50**, 70; family of, 4; Honour of, 24; Philip de, 19, 23–4, 29, 82n, 102, 185, his daughter Sybil, 136; William de, his daughter Lora, 24
Vans *see* Vaux
Varenne, France **76**: family of (Warenne, Warrand, Warren, etc.), 24, 43, 87–9, 196–7, of Wormegay, 87, 197; Ada de, wife of Henry of Scotland, mother of Malcolm IV and William I (d. 1178), 62, 87, 88n, 89, 97, 127; David de, 197; Isabel de, 88n, 197; Malcolm de, 197; Reginald de (saec. xii), 87–8, 197, his son William, 88, 197; Reginald de, Perthshire landowner (saec. xiii), 88, 131, 197, his brothers Adam and Roger, his grand-nephew John, his nephews Adam and David, his son Reginald, 197; Robert de, 197; William II (earl) de, 196; William III (earl) de, 88n
Vaudey abbey, LIN (O. Cist.), 32, 177
Vaudricourt, France **80**, 181; *see* Wadrithurt
Vaux (de Vallibus, de Vals, Vans): family of, 20, 196; Gilbert de, 196; Godard de, Hubert I de, lord of Gilsland, 20, 196; Hubert II de, 21n, 196; John I de, 19–20, 21n, 29, 169–70, 196; John II de, 20 and n, 21, 196; John (III?) de, Ralph (Ranulf?) de, 196; Robert I de, 18, 20, 21 and n, 196; Robert II de, 196; William de, 20n, 21, 196; William son of Robert de, 196
Vermelles, Philip de, 23
Vernon, France **27**, Honour of, 79 and n, 189
Vesci, Eustace de, lord of Alnwick, 19n

Vieuxpont-en-Auge, France **14**, 75, 94; family of, 73–4, 94, 179, 182; Ivo de, lord of Alston, 19n, 76; Richard de, 179; Robert de, 18, 76; William (I?) de, 73n; William (II?) de, husband of Maud de Morville, 73, 94; William de, stepson of Maud de Morville, 76; William de, name of three sons of William de Vieuxpont by Emma de St. Hilaire, 73n; William (III?) de, 179

Vincent, J. A. C., 4

Vinogradoff, Sir Paul, 166–7

Visdelou: Honour of, 101 and n, 183; Isabel, 183

Wadrithurt (Vaudricourt), Thomas de, 103n, 181

Wake, Baldwin, 19n

Wales, 145; Anglo-Norman conquest of, 30; Marches of, 65, 159

Walkelyn the brewer, 7n

Wallace (Walensis, le Walais, le Waleys): family of, 66 and n; Adam, Alan, Henry, Richard, Stephen, 66; William, 8 and n, 66 and n, 149, 157, 168 and n

Walter clerk of the chancellor, 169–70

Walter (Olifard, q.v.?) in Lilford, NTP, 45n

Walter son of Alan *see* Stewart

Walter son of Eda, 179

Walter son of Geoffrey, 102

Waltheof son of Baldwin, lord of Biggar, 111, 173

Waltheof son of Cospatric, lord of Dalmeny, 25 and n

Wardon abbey, BDF (O. Cist.), 75

Warmanbie, DMF, 37, 47

Warnebald (Werenbald), 37

Warwick, in Wetheral, CUM, 83n

Warwick, family of, in Cunningham, 83–4; Richard of, Thomas of, in Cumberland (not related?), 83n

Warrickhill in Dreghorn, AYR, 83n

Warrix, in Dreghorn, AYR, 83n

Warwyk, Richard de (saec. xiii), 84n

Wassand, YOE, Ralph of, 94

Weem, PER, 138n

Weremund, 37, 48

Wessex, 17, 97, 100–6

West Calder, MLO (Calder Comitis, Earl's Calder), 85, 130; church of, 89

Westmorland, 73, 75, 160

Whisby Graffoe, LIN, 48n

Whissendine, RUT, 17

Whitby, YON, abbey (O.S.B.), 97n, 112 and n

'Whiteshopessuirles' (lost), in Stobo, PEB, 35n

Whitsome, BWK, 144

Whittingeham, ELO, 33, 38n

Whitton, ROX, 61

Whitwell, RUT, 17

Wice (Wizo), 37, 48n

'Wichetune' ('Hwitheton') *see* Anselm

Wichnor, STF, 108, 194

Wihomarc, steward of Earl Alan of Richmond, 113

'Willambi' (lost), DMF, 37, 41, 47

William, 37

William I king of England (1066–87), 22

William II Rufus, king of England (1087–1100), 71

William I 'the Lion' king of Scots (1165–1214), 4n, 19, 63, 64, 77, 84, 85, 90, 103–4, 113, 115–16, 126, 128, 136, 140, 171, 182, 183, 191–2

William brother of King Henry II, 96n

William clerk of the earl, 169

William 'Longespee' earl of Salisbury, 19n

William son of Alan ('Fitzalan'), 13, 14, 15 and n

William son of Clarembald, 178–9

William son of Derman, his son William, his wife Maud, 178

William son of Humphrey, his wife Emma, 183

Williton, SOM, 78
Wilton, ROX: barony of, 136, 190; Jean of, 190; John of, 136n
Windsor, BRK, 116; Council of (1072), 2; family of, 116 and n; Christian of, 116; Walter of, 116n, 134n
Wingate, origin of surname, 20n
Winsterthwaites, in Crook, WML, 187
Wishart (Guiscard, Wiscard, etc.): family of, 175; from Saint-Aubin-Guichard? 175; John, 144; Mr Robert bishop of Glasgow (1273–1316), 143–4; Mr William bishop of St. Andrews (1273–9), 3n
Wiston, 37, 40; Sir Henry of, 67n, 144; Walter of, 67 and n
Wiston, PEM, 48n
witnessman (testimony), 160–1
Wodehouse, Robert, escheator, 117n
Worcester, Thomas of, 123
Wormistone, in Crail, FIF, 41n
Wrington, SOM, 101n

Wyrfalc (Wyrfald, Wirfauk, etc.): family of, 112 and n, 197–8; Osbert, 197; Roger, 112, 198; William, his son William, 112n, 197; William Wirfauk (saec. xiii), 112n, 197
Wyseby, DMF, 37, 48
Wyville (Guidvilla), de: family of, 89; William de, 87, 89

Yester, ELO, 43; *see also* Gifford
Yetholm, ROX: Kirk, 33, 188–9; Town, 43, 188
Yetholm-Neym (obsolete), ROX, 43, 188
York, 159; archbishop of, 151; St. Peter's hospital, 31n, 196
Yorkshire, 88–9, 93, 97, 106–17; sheriff of, 10, 150–1; West Riding of, 4
Yorkshiremen, Society of, in London, 115
Ysenda (Iseult), countess of Strathearn, 125

Zouche, la, Helen, 135